William Arthur

The Pope, the Kings and the People

A history of the movement to make the pope governor of the world by a universal

reconstruction of society from the issue of the Syllabus to the close of the Vatican Council

William Arthur

The Pope, the Kings and the People
*A history of the movement to make the pope governor of the world by a universal
reconstruction of society from the issue of the Syllabus to the close of the Vatican Council*

ISBN/EAN: 9783743407770

Manufactured in Europe, USA, Canada, Australia, Japa

Cover: Foto ©ninafisch / pixelio.de

Manufactured and distributed by brebook publishing software (www.brebook.com)

William Arthur

The Pope, the Kings and the People

THE POPE
THE KINGS AND THE · PEOPLE

A HISTORY OF THE MOVEMENT TO MAKE

THE POPE GOVERNOR OF THE WORLD

BY A UNIVERSAL

RECONSTRUCTION OF SOCIETY

FROM THE ISSUE OF THE SYLLABUS TO THE CLOSE OF THE VATICAN COUNCIL.

By WILLIAM ARTHUR

'Take thou the tiara adorned with the triple crown, and know that thou art the Father of princes and of kings, and art the Governor of the world.'
Coronation Service of the Pontiffs

VOL. I.

WILLIAM MULLAN & SON
34 PATERNOSTER ROW LONDON
4 DONEGAL PLACE BELFAST

1877

Printed by Hazell, Watson, and Viney, London and Aylesbury.

PREFACE.

THE sources of the information contained in this work are, 1. Official documents; 2. Histories having the sanction of the Pope or of bishops ; 3. Scholastic works of the present pontificate, and of recognised authority; 4. Periodicals and journals, avowed organs of the Vatican or of its policy, with books and pamphlets by bishops and other Ultramontane writers; 5. The writings of Liberal Catholics.

Of the official documents the greater part have been officially published. The list of authorities, and the references in each particular case, will sufficiently indicate where these are to be found. Besides these, the *Documenta ad Illustrandum* of Professor Friedrich are a store of documents of special value, both in themselves and as throwing light upon those officially published. They came into his hands as an official theologian at the Vatican Council, and he published them on his own responsibility. The *Sammlung* of Friedberg is a vast store, combining the documents of the Vatican with those of Courts, public bodies, and important individuals.

The official history of Cecconi, now Archbishop of Florence, though professedly that of the Vatican Council, is really occupied with the secret history of the five years preceding the

Council. That very curious narrative throws a light back on the foregoing years, and a light forward upon the Council, by aid of which many things otherwise indistinct become well defined. I have waited in hope that a second volume would appear, but in vain. The eight superb folios of Victor Frond come out with an assurance, under the Pope's own hand, of being preserved by due oversight from error, and with a guarantee of divine patronage. They contain a life of the Pope, biographical notices of the Cardinals and prelates, a full account of ceremonies, authentic portraits of men and vestments, with pictures of 'functions,' and so contribute to enable one to set events in their frames, and to invest them with their colours. Except military annals, perhaps, no history ever had more colour than this portion of Papal history, and perhaps in no history whatever has the action been more deeply affected by the scenery. The *Civiltá Cattolica* fulfils the invaluable office of a serial history, in the pages of which official documents and the chronicle of events illustrate one another, and at the same time discussions often prepare the way both for documents and for events, and always follow and elucidate any that are of consequence. The same office is in a less degree also fulfilled by the *Stimmen aus Maria Laach.*

To appreciate the height of authority on which the *Civiltá* stands, the reader should bear in mind the fact that in 1866,[1] after it had already for sixteen years been recognised as the organ, at one and the same time, of the Pope himself and of the Company of Jesus to which its editors belonged, his Holiness in a brief and by a declared exercise of apostolic authority, formally erected *in perpetuity* the Jesuit Fathers who composed the editorial staff into a *College of Writers,*

[1] See *Civiltá*, Serie VI., vol. vi. pp. 5-15.

which college should be under the General of the Society of Jesus, but, it is added, so 'as to Us and to Our successors shall seem most expedient.' In this brief the Pontiff recorded, as to the past, the 'exceeding gladness of soul' he had felt in witnessing the labour, erudition, zeal, and talent with which the *Civiltà* had 'manfully protected and defended the supreme dignity, authority, power, and rights' of the Apostolic See, and had 'set forth and propagated the *true doctrine.*' He also recorded the fact that all this had day by day more and more merited the 'goodwill, esteem, and praise,' not only of the hierarchy, but of men of the greatest eminence, and of all the good. This, coming at a time when the expositions of the Encyclical and Syllabus given by the *Civiltà* had awakened among Liberal Catholics serious opposition and even alarm, was decisive as to what was, at Rome, held to be the *true doctrine,* and as to who were held to be its real teachers. As to the future, the Pontiff, adopting the well known motto of the Company of Jesus, decreed that, *for the greater glory of God,* the writers should, as we have said, constitute *in perpetuity a college* possessing peculiar rights and privileges. As if formally to claim some share of this glory, the Jesuit editors of the *Stimmen aus Maria Laach,* when in 1869 commencing a new series, notified on their title-page the fact that they availed themselves of the labours of the *Civiltà,*—a liberty which no Jesuit durst have taken without the highest sanction.

All the numbers of the *Civiltà* and of the *Stimmen* being under my hand, they have yielded a steady light by which to examine opinions relating to the movement of 'reconstruction,' whether those opinions were hostile or sympathetic. The Italian journal, the *Unità Cattolica,* and the French one, the *Univers,* written with a consciousness of the highest favour on the one hand and of an overwhelming influence among the clergy on the other, comment upon the operative clauses of official documents—generally intelligible only to the initiated—in forms more popular than those of the two great magazines. But it is only by the still clearer comment of daily narratives and polemics that the elucidation becomes complete.

The Roman work of the Marchese Francesco Vitelleschi (Pomponio Leto) has now appeared in English—*Eight Months at Rome* (Murray). This is welcome, as enabling one to refer the English reader to his pages, of which even Ultramontanes in Rome do not impugn the accuracy. *Quirinus* is also happily in English. Professor Friedrich's *Tagebuch* ought to be, but is not. Those and smaller works by Liberal Catholics, compared with the sparkling volumes of M. Louis Veuillot and the Ultramontane serials and pamphlets, and with the Old Catholic writers in the *Rheinischer Merkur,* the *Literaturblatt* of Bonn, the *Stimmen aus der Katholischen Kirche,* and so forth, slowly bring home to our English understanding the strange principles and wonderful projects which at first we either fail to apprehend, or else imagine that they cannot be seriously entertained.

On those principles and projects four distinct controversies have shed a steadily increasing light—the controversy on, 1. The Syllabus; 2. The Vatican Council; 3. The Old Catholic Movement; 4. The Falk Laws. The last two do not come within the scope of this work, but very much of the light by which we gradually come to understand the preceding stages of the movement, is due to the keen discussions to which these two controversies have given rise.

Having subscribed for the *Civiltá Cattolica* for years before the Syllabus appeared, I was not wholly unprepared for the controversy which followed. The *Civiltá* also enabled me to see how Liberal Catholics connected the Vatican Council with a movement in the past, dating from the Pope's restoration, and with a plan of vast changes for the future. While the hopes of the Ultramontanes seemed visionary, and the fears of the Liberal Catholics seemed exaggerated, it did nevertheless appear possible that great events might come out of a deliberate attempt, made by a large and organised force, to reconstruct the world. Soon after the close of the Franco-German war, a visit to Paris, Munich, Vienna, Berlin, Brussels, and other centres, supplied me with much material, casting light on the enterprise in which the Vatican Council was the legislative episode, and from which the Old Catholic movement was the recoil.

It was while engaged in studying such material that I threw off the translation of the discussion held in Rome on the question whether St. Peter had ever visited that city. Soon after broke out the controversy on the Falk Laws. Six weeks spent in a German country town, reading journals and pamphlets, and also in collecting, added to my light, and to the means of getting further light. In the course of the time employed upon the study of growing material was thrown off the review of the Pope's Speeches, under the title of *The Modern Jove.*

Though conscious that I had not yet the groundwork for a well connected account of the whole movement, I began to write, not with any intention of publishing for a long time, should I live, but under the feeling that, should I be called away, it would be right to leave behind me information which had not been gained without cost and labour. After a while appeared the official history of Cecconi. His authentic if incomplete disclosure of the secret proceedings of five years was a stem for many hitherto perplexing branches. A plan now began to shape itself, and I commenced to recast all I had done. Shortly afterwards came out the great work of Theiner, the *Acta Genuina* of the Council of Trent. This settled many points keenly debated between Catholic and Liberal Catholic, affecting the rights of kings, of bishops, of the divinity schools, of the lower clergy, of the laity, and affecting the relations of all these to the Pontiff.

While I was working with these additional helps appeared Mr. Gladstone's *Expostulation*. The great amount of knowledge it betrayed contrasted with one's previous idea of the state of information on the subject among our public men. The controversy which followed might have brought some temptation to haste, had it not also brought proof that it was even more necessary than I had supposed to beware of assuming that phrases, modes of conception, and projects, well understood in Italy or Germany, were at all understood here. Some of those who reviewed Mr. Gladstone took for strange what in all countries in the south or centre of Europe would have been taken as familiar, and for doubtful what in Rome or Munich was as clear as day. Accredited terms and phrases were treated as inventions; by some as inventions of genius, by others of animosity. It was often more than hinted that principles and designs habitually proclaimed at the Vatican were ascribed to priests only by opponents. Not unfrequently a gentleman would seem to think it more generous to attribute his Protestant ideas to Ultramontanes, than to take it for granted that they preferred their own. It was incredible how political questions pregnant with future controversies, perhaps with future wars, were evaded as theology !

The replies to Mr. Gladstone placed the ignorance of the English public on the subject in a different but a very impressive light. It is often said abroad, by those who know us, that no nation in Europe is so liable as we are to treat gravely statements from priests or their advocates which any reasonable amount of information would render entertaining. The reviews of these replies showed a growing sense of the interests involved, but intensified one's feeling that the elements of clear understanding were wanting. Men did not know the terms, the facts, the publications, or the political doctrines of the movements under discussion. Had what has been written in our best journals during the last twenty years from Italy, or even during the last five from Rome and Berlin, been well read, it would have led to study, and in that case Dr. Newman and others would not have had so cheap a laugh at our ignorance of what is meant because of our false interpretation of what is said. While this controversy proceeded, a stay of nearly three months in Rome, employed in seeking material and information, added considerably to my stores, which were further increased by two subsequent visits to Munich and one to Bonn.

I have often been reminded of an incident which occurred in Rome. One of our celebrated scholars, hearing what I was engaged in, exclaimed ' Oh, Theology! ' Of course, he was fresh from home. Not many minutes before, a resident diplomatist, in whose house this took place, having heard me say ' I began the study of this subject as a religious question, *but*—' smiled and said, ' Yes, *but*—you find it is all politics, and the further you get into it the more purely political will you find it.'

The controversy which had sprung up at home showed that a book written as this one had been begun would be frequently misunderstood. In that controversy it was often taken for granted that when an Ultramontane disclaims Temporal Power, he disclaims power over temporal things ; and that when he writes Spiritual Power, he means only power over spiritual things; that when he writes Religious Liberty, he means freedom for every one to worship God according to his conscience ; that when he writes the Divine Law, he means only the Ten Commandments and the precepts of the Gospel ; that when he writes the Kingdom of God, he means righteousness and peace and joy in the Holy Ghost ; and that when he writes the Word of God, he simply means the Bible. One reasoning with false interpretations like these in his mind must reason in such a fog as Dr. Newman, in his letter to the Duke of Norfolk, cleverly depicts. Ambiguity similar to that now indicated prevails over the whole field of phraseology—theological, political, and educational. English Ultramontanes are doubtless in part responsible for these misapprehensions, but only in part. If their writings are *studied*, they will be seen to use such terms differently from their fellow-countrymen. But certainly the Papal press of Rome, and even that of France, is not in any degree responsible for our illusions, but has, on the contrary, left us without excuse.

The consequence of all this is that in this book, where a mere allusion would have been made, a fact is now often related ; where the sense of some particular utterance would have been condensed, that utterance is verbally recited ; and where one sentence would have been culled out, more are given. Very often, where a statement of the principles of the Papal movement would have been accompanied only by a reference to a contemporary authority, that authority is made to speak for himself, and occasionally at some length. Terms and phrases, which might have been left to the chance of being understood, are either coupled with narratives or discussions, to bring out their sense, or else they are explained. When I do give explanations, let me not be trusted, but watched. Much will be found of the language both of Catholics and of Liberal Catholics, and with it the reader can confront my strange-looking explanations. In the end he will be able to do what, thank God, every Englishman is inclined to do—form an opinion for himself as to the real sense in which the speakers employed their own words.

It need not be said that this change of method rendered necessary a larger book than was at first planned. It was also unfavourable to the flow and unity of the narrative. Perhaps it compensated for that disadvantage by more fully showing the grounds on which statements are made, and by bringing the reader frequently, almost continuously, into communication with Italian, Frenchman, or German, each expressing his own views, whether those of statesman or priest, of journalist or magistrate, of Catholic or of Liberal Catholic.

My thanks are due to many' who have forwarded my researches. The kindness of Count Cadorna, then Italian Minister at our Court, procured for me valuable facilities in Rome. My true gratitude was deserved by the distinguished Minister of Education, Signor Bonghi, especially for his personal introduction of me to the great library of the Collegio Romano, not then open to the public. Our own Ambassador, Sir Augustus Paget, and the German Ambassador, Baron Keudell, both rendered me real service, with all possible courtesy. The Marchese Francesco Nobili-Vitelleschi, himself author of a history on which I must often draw, took pains to procure for me valuable material. Among many benefits received from our own countrymen, I must specify that derived from the vast information on all Italian matters possessed by Mr. Montgomery Stuart, and also that arising from the constant kindness of the Rev. H. J. Piggott. Those two gentlemen have kindly read on the spot certain sheets containing local observations. Two

German scholars were constant and practical friends, Dr. Benrath and Dr. Richter. Other gentlemen who, by literary or official position, were able to give information, uniformly showed the greatest readiness in doing so.

The difficulty of procuring in Rome pamphlets and other minor helps surprised me, though somewhat prepared for such results by experiments made under the old *régime.* The great libraries of the Collegio Romano and the Casanatense contained, one might say, nothing published during the Vatican Council, or respecting it. I cannot, however, mention these establishments without recording my thanks to Signor Castellani, of the Collegio Romano, for his very great personal attention.

In Munich the National Library, with its clear catalogue and good collection, contrasted with the great libraries of Rome. The kindness of Dr. Döllinger was great and eminently practical. He had kept all pamphlets, bearing on the subject, which had come into his hands. He not only gave me free access to this collection, but, where he had duplicates, presented me with them. Dr. Reusch, Professor of the University of Bonn, with a collection at least equal, though without duplicates, gave me similar facilities. The lists thus procured, and the energy of the German booksellers, enabled me to get almost everything contained in either collection, including Italian and Latin publications which I had in vain sought in Italy, and even French ones which I could not find in Paris. Many an obscure pamphlet or fugitive article has laid me under real debt to the author, and that not unfrequently, by illustrating the true meaning of terms on which—fancying it was charitable—I had long tried to put a false English sense.

The weakness of my own eyesight has increased the obligation which, in any case, I should have felt to my two valued friends

Dr. Moulton and Dr. H. W. Williams, who have kindly read the proofs. Dr. Moulton also compared the translation of the speech of Darboy with the original, and suggested improvements. Dr. Karl Benrath, of Bonn, whose long residence in Rome and whose study of the subject lent to his judgment a special value, has laid me under great obligation by examining every sheet as it passed through the press.

The very frequent translations rendered necessary by the plan of letting men speak for themselves are as close as I knew how to make them. Most of those from the Latin have been revised by my neighbour, Mr. Henry Jefferson; those from the German by Fräulein Weinhagen; many of those from the French by the Rev. C. A. Chastel de Boinville; and most of those from the Italian by Signor Schiapparelli. To each of these am I indebted for hints and amendments. Even where marks of quotation are not used, and yet I profess to give the sense of some utterance, those who can go to the originals will find that the language, though condensed, is preserved, and, in any important matter, closely rendered.

Reversing the ordinary practice as to quotations, where the italics were in the original, I generally mention that it was so. It would have been tedious to say that they were my own in every case where they seemed necessary to direct attention to a phrase or a term having a meaning different from ours, or to one the full significance of which might easily escape notice.

Nothing but a conviction that the movement here traced is of an importance for which ordinary terms are not an adequate expression would have justified me, in my own view, in giving to the study of it years of a life now far advanced. If the authors of the movement are not deceived, the generations that will come up after I am no more will witness a struggle on the widest scale, and of very long duration, during which will disappear all that to us is known as modern liberties, all that to Rome is known as the Modern State, and at the close of which the ecclesiastical power will stand alone, presiding over the destinies of a reconstituted world. Not at all believing in the possibility of this issue, I do not disbelieve in the possibility of the struggle. To avert any such repetition of past horrors, to turn the war into a war of thought, a war with the sword of the writer and of the orator, instead of that of the zouave and the dragoon, is an object in attempting to serve which, however humbly, a good man might be content to die. Had I at any time during my preparations seen the same work undertaken by some one whose position or whose name would have commanded a degree of attention to which I have no claim, gladly should I have buried the fruit of my labour. Such as that fruit is, I now submit it to the public, in humble hope that the very absence of titles to consideration by which a work on the subject should have been recommended, will turn to a plea for more indulgence in weighing the only claims I have to put forth, those of hard work and honest intention.

May He who has given to our nation the blessings of free prayer, free preaching, free writing, free speech, and free assembly, with their wholesome fruit of equal laws, tempered power, and moderated liberty, grant that this humble labour may · in some measure contribute to make those inestimable boons dearer than ever to the hearts of our people, and that it may contribute also to place them in a position more readily to foil every endeavour to snatch those boons or to steal them away from us and from mankind!

CLAPHAM COMMON, 1877.

POSTSCRIPT TO THE PREFACE.

June 6th, 1877.

ON CARDINAL MANNING'S 'TRUE STORY OF THE VATICAN COUNCIL.'

HAD not the time occupied in bringing out this work far exceeded my expectations, it would have appeared as early as the first portion of Cardinal Manning's 'True Story of the Vatican Council,' in the pages of the *Nineteenth Century*. As it is, I have been able to read the fourth paper, in which the Cardinal concludes his narrative of the Council itself, though he intimates an intention of hereafter adding comments on extraneous matters. I cannot but feel that, in more respects than one, the appearance of the *True Story* immediately before that of this book is an advantage. The general reader is thus supplied with means of checking many of my statements, and of estimating the value of my authorities. Although this advantage is limited to such ground as is common to the 'True Story' and to my history, that ground is a portion of sufficient importance to afford some criterion for judging of the whole. One of my fears, arising from the way in which, both in recent controversies and in former ones, authorities have been dealt with before the English public, was that we might find it soberly intimated that Cecconi was not a writer of high credit, that the *Civiltà Cattolica* was a private magazine, that the *Acta Genuina* of Theiner was a publication brought out in an obscure place, and so on through the list. Now, however, the reliance placed by Cardinal Manning on authorities which supply essential features of my narrative, and the importance unwillingly assigned by him to others frequently cited by me, will act as a restraint on those who might have made light of them.

Another considerable advantage is this. It almost seemed as if it would prejudice Englishmen against a writer to state what from time to time it was needful to intimate—how histories issued from official or semi-official sources systematically withheld information on the points of chief importance. Such points, so far as the Council was concerned, were the actual differences of opinion between prelate and prelate, the tenor of the debates, the arguments employed on one side or the other, the written memoranda of bishops on the questions disputed, their printed pamphlets, their speeches, their truly important petitions, recording complaints against the Rules of Procedure imposed upon them, and against the disabilities under which the Pope had placed them. Those petitions recorded, further, their personal disbelief in the new dogma, with the fact that they had always taught in opposition to it, and that they anticipated from its adoption grave perils of collision between Church and State. Other matters kept out of view comprised interesting facts credibly alleged and circumstantially detailed relating to personal acts of the Pope, to proceedings of the Curia and of the Presidents of the Council. Still more interesting, and of graver import, were the reasons assigned by Ministers of State and others, for regarding with more than ordinary jealousy the projected changes in the Papal system. It seemed even more invidious to note the practice of adopting, in order to cover all these suppressions of facts, and of alleged facts, an air of giving information by entering into details of ceremonies, enlarging on unimportant matters, telling, as if it was of great moment, how many meetings of this sort were held, how many of that, how many spoke, at what time this Decree was proposed, and how many votes were taken on another, without in all this allowing a word to transpire of what was said or thought. I am now relieved of all fear about those features of my narrative. Any one who has a relish for the curiosities of literature may match, and perhaps overmatch, what I have told of French priests and Italian Jesuits, by what an Englishman has done.

I had never, however, to accuse the Italian Jesuits of keeping out of sight the political, or, as they generally say, the social aspects of the movement, and of covering them up in theological disquisitions. They did, indeed, use wondrous theological phrases with political meanings, but any one who studied their writings soon penetrated that veil. They also invariably used theology as the motive power of all their politics. But from 1850, when the movement which has characterised the present pontificate began, to 1870, when it reached its legislative climax, they set forth prominently as their object the reconstruction of society, on the model of what, in their own dialect, they call the Christian civilisation. They loudly proclaimed, as the elements of that Christian civilisation, the revocation of constitutions, the abolition of modern liberties, especially those of the press and of worship, with the subjection to canon law of civil law, and, above all, the subjection to the jurisdiction of the Pope of all nations and their rulers, whatever the title of those rulers might be. They justly conceived the ills they had to repair, as, having begun with the bad teaching of John Wyclif, in which his doctrine of 'dominion' was the head and front of all his offending, and of that of every succeeding age. As he had striven for the emancipation of kings from the Pope, of legislatures from the ecclesiastical powers, and of the individual from the priest, so did they set themselves to bring back again the dominion of the priest over the individual, the dominion of the ecclesiastical authorities over lawgivers, and above all, the dominion of the Pope over kings. Of this the reader will meet with evidence from their own lips, at almost every stage of our narrative. Those Italian Jesuits did not expound the Syllabus, according to the new and *naïve* notion of Cardinal Manning, as a code containing very little to which 'any sincere believer in Christian revelation would, if he understood the Syllabus, object. The Italian Jesuits, ay, and even the German ones, on the contrary, made a boast of its diametrical opposition to every form of Liberalism, and in particular to Liberal Catholicism, of its efficacy as an instrument for overturning the Modern State, and of its solidity as the foundation-stone on which was to be reared the fabric of reconstructed society. In all their writings society was taken as meaning, not families, nor Churches, but nations, and each one of the nations was to form a province within a Church ruling over it and over all other nations in every one of their laws and public institutions.

In speaking of the idea that all believers in revelation would accept nearly all of the Syllabus, I have assumed that Cardinal Manning, writing for an English audience, uses the term 'Christian revelation' in the English and not in the Papal sense. To a sincere believer in Christian revelation in the Papal sense, the Syllabus, if not in form, yet in substance, is an infallible and 'irreformable' portion of that revelation. And so it would very simply come to pass that a sincere believer in Christian revelation would admit, not merely most of it, but all of it so far as it contains any teaching. And to such a believer the kingdoms of the world will never become the kingdom of God, and of His Christ, but by ceasing to be kingdoms at all in any independent and proper sense, and by merging into provinces under the Priest and King, or, as in phrases still more mystic they style him, the Shepherd-King of the Vatican.

Now a *True Story* of the Vatican Council, in which, to the apprehension of an ordinary reader, all these topics are kept out of view, though to an adept they are not wholly kept out, seems to me to be constructed as if a *True Story* of the controversy on free trade said much about principles of political economy, but covered up all allusion to the corn laws under recondite phrases not plain either to millowner or landowner, unless one who was specially trained. Or, to take a more recent case, it seems like a *True Story* of the civil war in the United States which should largely dwell upon State rights, forgetting all about slavery, or speaking of it only in an esoteric dialect.

The *True Story* affords us some foretaste of what history is to be after dogma has completed the conquest over it which has been promised. Had my narrative been written after its appearance, the topics totally ignored, and those virtually ignored, in the *True Story*, might easily have been thrown into stronger relief. As it is, however, the succession of events necessarily brings them again and again into view, and perhaps the effect of the outline may be rendered more distinct to the English reader through the contrast with the *True Story*.

Of the prelates on this side of the Alps, Cardinal Manning was not the one from whom we should have expected that in an account of the five years preceding the Vatican Council, with a brief retrospect of the whole of the present pontificate, and a history of the Council itself, scarcely one clear utterance should be made as to the bearing of the movement on those governments, liberties, and institutions which to the Vatican are very evil and to us are very dear. It was not so in 1867 and 1869. In

both of those years the Cardinal indicated the political relations of the movement in words of warning which, if only
echoes of those of the Jesuits in Rome, were perhaps more
intelligible and vehement than those of any other prelate on
this side of the Alps.

Statements of mine will frequently be found to conflict with
statements made in the *True Story.* In most of those cases—I
hope in all—the materials from known sources furnished to the
general reader will suffice for a not unsatisfactory comparison,
while the authorities indicated will enable the scholar to form a
judgment. In very many of these cases statements of Cardinal
Manning, made in previous works and virtually amounting to
the same as the most material of those made in the *True Story,*
will be found side by side with the statements of other authorities, with official documents, or with facts no longer disputable.
Of these statements, one to which the Cardinal seems to attach
much importance is his assertion that none of the prelates, or
at most a number under five, disbelieved or denied the dogma
of Papal infallibility, and that all their objections turned on
questions of prudence. This is not a slip, nor a hasty assertion,
and it is very far from being peculiar to Cardinal Manning. It
is now the harmonious refrain of all that hierarchy of strange
witnesses of which he has made himself a part. The point is
one on which illustrations will occur again and again, in events,
in words, and in those documents which, in spite of all precautions, have been gained to publicity.

Notwithstanding the method adopted in the *True Story,* the
fact crops out at every turn that the modern strife of the Papacy
is not to make men and women, as such, godly and peaceable,
but to bring kings as kings, and legislatures as legislatures, and
nations as nations, into subjection to the Pope. It crops out

sufficiently, at least, to be obvious to all who know the difference, in the Cardinal's phraseology, between the two sets of terms employed to indicate those two distinct objects. For instance, what an excellent description of that *Catholic Civilisation* which, in the great contest of the Vatican, is ever signalised as the goal, does the Cardinal give when, picturing the ' public life and laws and living organisation of Christendom ' in the times when all these, according to his ideas, were ' Christian,' he says, '*Princes and legislatures and society* professed the Catholic faith, and were *subject to the head* of the Catholic Church.' Cardinal Manning does not here use the word ' society' in the domestic but in the political sense. He means, not families or social parties, but nations—as the Jesuit writers almost always do. Any one may, therefore, possess himself of a key to the true meaning of many pious phrases which occur in the following pages, if he will first of all clearly realise in his own thoughts just what it would involve for England and for us were the conditions stated by the Cardinal fulfilled by our princes, our legislature, and our ' society.' One seeking to do this must realise the fact that the prince and the legislature not as individuals, and the ' society' not in its separate members, but the prince as a prince, the legislature as a legislature, and the nation as a society, shall *profess the Catholic faith*. Ordinary Englishmen do not realise all that is meant by that formula. But beyond that, the prince as a prince, the legislature as a legislature, the nation as a society, are not only to believe in the Pope, but to be *subject to him*. What fulness of meaning that formula possesses will gradually open up to the reader as the narrative unfolds. He will often hear ecclesiastical politicians of the school to which Cardinal Manning belongs, talking in their native dialect, not modulating their voice to win the ear of Protestants. This national *profession of the faith*, and this subjection of kings, law-givers, and nations to the Pope, constitute in one word the *Civiltá Cattolica* (the Catholic civilisation); or, in plain English, the Catholic civil system ; or, in other terms, the true Catholic constitution, the reign of Christ over the world, to establish which in all nations the Vatican is to move heaven and earth.

In his first paper Cardinal Manning seeks to impress us with the belief that the raising of Papal infallibility to the rank of a dogma was not a chief object of the Pontiff, much less his only one, in convoking the Vatican Council. On that point the narrative will often incidentally present the expressions of prelates, official writers, and others, so that the reader will be able to form an opinion of his own. In his second paper the Cardinal shows that throughout the whole of the present pontificate the dogma has been kept in view as an essential object. Of that position illustrations will frequently occur. In the second paper, also, the Cardinal repeats his old allegation that it was Janus who invented ' the fable of an acclamation.' The course of the tale will tell whether it was or was not Janus who originated the talk of a design to get up an acclamation, and whether that talk was or was not a fable.

The Cardinal, while attempting to justify, though for the most part keeping out of sight, the disabilities imposed upon the bishops by the Pope, disabilities of which they loudly complained, glances at one out of many of the real ones. He says that the Commission which was empowered to say whether any proposal emanating from a bishop was worthy to be recommended to the Pope for consideration, without which recommendation it could not come before the Council, was ' a representative commission.' The fact is that it was a selection of prelates made by the Pope, who excluded from it all who

had avowed themselves opponents of his infallibility, and included in it creatures of his own, who had nothing of the bishop
but the orders and the pay which the favour of the Court had
given to them.

The Cardinal, after ample time for correction, repeats his old
declaration that in the Vatican Council 'the liberty of speech
was as perfectly secured as in our Parliament.' That assertion
has the merit of being free from all ambiguity, and moreover
is one on which plain men can judge. As I have told the story,
the readers will over and over again meet with facts, equally
free from ambiguity and equally patent to plain men, which will
show whether the assertion is true or not.

On the great question of secrecy the Cardinal risks a statement which exceeds what Italian Jesuits, if writing for a
periodical of the rank of the *Nineteenth Century,* would be
likely to hazard. He says: 'At the beginning of the Council
of Trent this precaution (of secrecy) was omitted ; wherefore,
on the 17th of February, 1562, the legates were compelled to
impose the secret upon the bishops.' The Cardinal would seem
to imagine that there was at least a substantial agreement, if
not an actual identity, between the acts by which silence was
enjoined, and also between the extent of the silence demanded
in Trent and at the Vatican ; and that indeed from the 17th of
February, 1562, forwards, the Council of Trent was laid under
a bond something like that by which the Vatican Council was
from the beginning fettered. Was it so ? Was there a substantial agreement in the two acts by which silence was enjoined ?
Was there a substantial agreement in the extent of silence
imposed ? Was there at Trent a formal decree ? Was there
an oath imposed on the officers ? Was there an exclusion of
the theologians from debates, and of the public from the debates

of the theologians? Was there any vow required, any threat held out? And does even Cardinal Manning fancy that there was at Trent a new mortal sin made on purpose for the benefit of the bishops? Of all this there was nothing. The act of the legates was simply what it is described as having been by Massarellus, the Secretary of the Council, who says: 'The Fathers were admonished not to divulge things proposed for examination, and in particular Decrees, before they were published in open session.'[1] That Massarellus, when he wrote *admonished*, meant exactly what he wrote, is proved by the terms of the 'admonition,' which he immediately subjoins, and of which we give the original below. In this the legates do not 'impose,' do not 'decree,' nay, they do not even 'enjoin' secrecy: they only 'admonish and exhort.'

The Cardinal is apparently also under an impression that the extent of silence imposed in the two cases was at least sub-

---

[1] Theiner, *Acta Genuina*, i., 686. *Admonitio ad Patres ne evulgent Decreta et alia quæ examinanda proponuntur, antequam finientur.* Rm̄i patres. Sciunt Dominationes vestræ quam indignum sit quamque indecens, ut decreta et alia, quæ patribus examinanda proponuntur, antequam firmentur, et in publica sessione edantur, evulgentur, et extra hanc civitatem ad extraneos mittantur. Quo fit, ut alias sæpe vidimus, ut decreta ipsa sub ea qua dici forma primum concepta, et (ut ita dicam) informia, pro decretis firmis, et a s. Synodo approbatis disseminentur. Quare illm̄i dn̄i legati et presidentes admonent, atque etiam hortantur dominationes vestras, ut pro honore et existimatione hujus sacri Concilii, et ad obviandum scandalis, quæ oriri possent, tam decretum, quod modo a me lectum fuit, quam cetera decreta, et alia quæcunque, quæ in futurum examinanda vobis proponentur, non evulgent, neque eorum exemplum alicui extra gremium Concilii exhibeant, neve extra civitatem ad aliquos transmittant. Idque ne a suis familiaribus fiat, severissime prohibeant. Quod ut commodius fiat, dominationes vestræ cum miserint ad me pro exemplis presentis decreti, simul mihi per cedulam eorum manu subscriptam significent nomen ejus, cui voluerint, quod tam hoc exemplum, quam alia, quæ suo tempore proponentur, exhibeantur. Hæc pro nunc visa sunt expedire. Si quæ alia commodior via alicui ex patribus occurrerit, ut ea, quæ proponuntur, secreto retineantur, de ea poterit illm̄os dn̄os legatos privatim admonere.

stantially the same. Was that so? Did the legates censure the admission of laymen to hear the theologians argue? Did they censure the permission given to theologians who were not bishops even by the fiction of a see *in partibus,* to dispute in presence of the Council? Did they censure any remarks made out of doors on speeches, opinions, or projects? Did they censure anything but the one indiscretion of circulating proposed Decrees, or other things proposed, while yet the formulæ were, ' so to speak, unshaped,' but were in their inchoate condition made public as if they had been passed? Did the legates suggest that the duty of secrecy extended further than that of not publishing such tentative formulæ, of not sending them out of the city, and of forbidding persons attached to the households of bishops to commit those indiscretions? At Trent there were faults and causes of complaint in no small number. But what Cardinal Manning calls ' the secret ' which would shut up every mouth as to all subjects proposed, as to all opinions expressed, as to all speeches made, as to all designs mooted,—' the secret ' which forbad men to print their own speeches, to read the official reports taken of them, to read those of their brother bishops, and other extravagances besides, of which the *True Story* has not one syllable to tell,—that ' secret,' or any such, is not hinted at in the admonition of the legates at Trent. The extent of silence imposed at the Vatican would seem to have been as original as the mortal sin there invented.

Still further, the Cardinal would appear to be under an impression that the reason why at Trent certain inconvenient publications occurred was because that, at the outset, the strict precautions had been there omitted which at the Vatican were not only taken in time, but, with manifold forethought, were, before the time, as our story will tell, tied and bound by edict and by oath. As to disclosures, however, that occurred at the Vatican, which most Romans would tell any Englishman, except a priest or a convert, would be certain to occur, namely, that the 'pontifical secret' would be dealt in as a thing to be sold. Did the precautions omitted at Trent, but adopted at the Vatican, prevent so much from transpiring as compelled the Pope to loose from the bond four selected prelates, including the eminent author of the *True Story*, in order that they might disabuse the outside world ? Did it prevent the famous canons which opened the eyes even of Austrian and French statesmen from making a quick passage to Augsburg and to Printing House Square?—of which canons, by the way, as of most essential matters, the *True Story* tells not a word.

It would be very tempting to select for remark other assertions of the Cardinal, but this may suffice to do all that I here wish to do; that is, to set the reader upon intelligently watching and sifting statements of my own ; for what is to be desired on this subject is that the public shall cease to be easily contented with what is said on one side or the other. My statements, like those of others, are sure to contain a fair proportion of mistakes, but when all these are winnowed away, there will remain a considerable peck of corn.

Not content with formally vouching, in his title, for his own truthfulness, the Cardinal formally impeaches that of others. Both of these proceedings would be perfectly natural in a priest in Rome, and especially in one attached to the Jesuit school. If such proceedings are to be introduced among us, we may hope that so long, at least, as England is not ruled by priests, the language employed will be tempered to suit our Protestant atmosphere in some such degree as that in which the Cardinal has tempered his own, and that we shall not have it flung about red hot from the hearth, as is the wont in Rome and in other places where bishops and editors emulate the masters.   Had I foreseen the cautious beginning of such habits that was so soon to be made by high authority, certainly I should not have so far yielded to the repugnance one feels to put specimens of priestly imputations into our language,—a language which had for ages, up to the date of the *Tracts for the Times,* been steadily acquiring an antipathy to all the arts of untruthfulness, and consequently to all the forms in which other languages habitually insinuate or openly allege it.   But I cannot regret that my story purposely excludes full specimens, and only by force of frequent necessity admits morsels, of the style in which in Rome every shade of untruthfulness, from suppression and equivocation to the worst kinds of perjury and forgery, is on the one hand charged upon heretics, on Liberal Catholics, on statesmen, and is on the other hand in return, and with extreme good will, charged upon bishops, cardinals, and popes.

The veracity of Pomponio Leto—that is, as all Italy knows, of the Marchese Francesco Vitelleschi, brother of the late Cardinal Vitelleschi—is openly impugned by Cardinal Manning. We already know, on more points than one, the opinion of Vitelleschi as to the eminent author of the *True Story;* and retaliation would have been natural had it only been fair. If Vitelleschi wrote English, and if he cared to compare his truthfulness with that of such a competitor, it would be interesting to hear him fairly fight out the question, Which of us two has, to the best of his power, tried just to tell what he knew, inventing nothing and concealing nothing ? it does not seem at all certain that the Englishman would bear away from the Italian the palm of straightforwardness.   The Cardinal is evidently not aware that certain alleged particulars of the famous Strossmayer scene, which he ascribes to Pomponio Leto, are not in his description of it either in the Italian or in the English version. From where the Cardinal gets them I do not know. But his picture of Schwarzenberg 'carried fainting from the *ambo* to his seat,' his idea that Pomponio professes on that day to have been outside the Council door and to have seen 'the servants rushing,' and his other idea that at the fourth session Pomponio professes to have been inside and consequently forgot that many of those who were outside could see through the great door which was wide open, are all alike. He certainly did not get any of them from Vitelleschi. As it is after stating these errors, that his Eminence cries, 'Such melodramatic and mendacious stuff!' we must imagine how Vitelleschi will smile at this new display of certain qualities which did not escape his keen eye.

Professor Friedrich is slightingly spoken of by the Cardinal. Here again retaliation, if fair, would have been natural; for Cardinal Manning has already felt the steel of Friedrich. Judging from my own impression that under the slashes of Friedrich what the Cardinal had employed as if he took it for argument appeared perfectly helpless, I should expect that if the learned professor should think it worth while to try his strength on the sort of history, theology, and logic which the Cardinal thinks may pass in England, they would in his hands, at almost every debatable point, fly to pieces. As to veracity, however, Friedrich has already, on that score, as our story will show, crossed swords with more bishops than one; and whether on that or other matters, certainly he is not the man to turn his back on Cardinal Manning, whose measure he has long ago taken, as, even under the eyes of the Papal police, he did not fear to show.

Cardinal Manning occupies pages with imputations, and with quotations which he apparently thinks warrant the imputations. Does he, or do the witnesses he calls, disprove any of the specific facts alleged? Yes, he does disprove one. Vitelleschi, in describing the great session of the Council, said that Cardinal Corsi and other discontented Cardinals pulled down their red hats over their eyes. Now, Cardinal Manning properly says that on that occasion they had no hats of any colour, meaning that they wore the mitre. Therefore a real blot is hit. And it is curious how exactly this is the same kind of blot as the Jesuits of the *Civiltà* were able to hit in the early part of Vitelleschi's book, when, like the *True Story*, it first appeared in a periodical. They clearly convicted the author, then unknown even to them, of saying that in certain solemnities the robes were red, whereas in fact they were white. We must, however, do the Roman Jesuits the justice to say that from this tremendous error they did not attempt to prove that the writer was given to ' mendacious stuff,' though they did argue that he was wanting in reflection.

But it is a well-known fact that grave matters—very grave matters—were with sufficient particularity alleged against the Pope, against the Presidents, against the Rules of Procedure, against the authorised press, against the favourites of the Court among the bishops, against the secret way in which ' the Council was made beforehand,' and above all against the political designs which were entertained ; and, one must ask, with what single fact of all these is any manly attempt made to grapple by the Cardinal, or by the bishops whom he cites in his support ? Besides these facts, of which some were amusing, some absurd, some discreditable, there were others which for all good men except Papists, in the proper sense, were seriously alarming,

and these were alleged by Catholic and Liberal Catholic, by
men in opposition and by men in all places of authority up
to the highest,—by Vitelleschi, by Friedrich, by Veuillot, by
Guérin, by Frond and his contributors, by *Ce Qui se Passe
au Concile*, by Hefele, by Kenrick, by Darboy, by Rauscher,
by Place, by Dupanloup, by the hundred and thirty bishops
who signed the protest against even discussing infallibility, by
the groups of bishops who signed that against the Rules of
Procedure, by those who signed the solemn one against the new
Rules, by those who petitioned for the A B C of deliberative
freedom, by the scores who signed the historical petition of
April 10th, 1870, by those who protested against the unfair and
arbitrary attempt of the 5th of July, and by those fifty-five who,
the day before the final session, placed in the hands of the Pope
their protest, saying that if they voted in the public session
they could only repeat, and that with stronger reasons, their
previous vote,—that is, of *Non placet;* a protest of which
Cardinal Manning has taken a strangely inaccurate and misleading view. Such facts were alleged by *La Liberté du Concile*,
by *La Dernière Heure du Concile*, by Mamiani, by Bonghi, by
Beust, by Daru, by Arnim, by Acton, by Montalembert, by
Döllinger; and still more by the *Civiltá Cattolica*, the *Stimmen
aus Maria Laach*, the *Univers*, the *Monde*, and the *Unitá
Cattolica;* and most of all were they embodied in the words
and official manifestoes of Pope Pius IX. What one of these
alarming or discreditable or equivocal facts is disposed of by
the passages which Cardinal Manning in his need has cited?
He cites Hefele to prove that people who were outside of the
Council told falsehoods as to what passed inside. But with the
wonted sequence of his logic, what he proves out of the mouth
of Hefele is that people who were inside of the Council sold the

secret, though in doing so they incurred the pains of mortal sin. The proof is quite as apposite as many of those relied upon by Cardinal Manning, and it is no wonder that such a habit of reasoning should have landed him where he is. He cites of all men Ketteler. Now supposing that Ketteler was the person to invalidate serious testimony, what particular fact is disproved by the passage cited? The only one it affects to touch is the question as to whether, in substance, the anti-infallibilist doctrine of Döllinger was not also that of the majority of the German bishops. That question is not faced in front. Ketteler only raises a side issue. He denies that on some certain occasion, certain bishops had in a certain way made a statement to that effect. Cardinal Manning has not lived so long in Rome, and learned so much there, without knowing something of the value of such contradictions. But if he means—as, however reluctantly, one must take him to mean—to use Ketteler to prove to Englishmen that the majority of the German bishops were not, before July 1870, opposed to that as a doctrine which is now a dogma of their creed, then let Ketteler by all means stand on one side, but pamphlets, memoranda, speeches, petitions, votes, protests stand on the other. Ketteler is cited against Döllinger, and agreeably to the all but infallible felicity of the Cardinal's logic, about the most definite thing Ketteler says against the Provost is that *Janus,* for falsification of history, can hardly be compared to anything but the Provincial Letters of Pascal. Had the Cardinal cited the whole body of the German bishops, he might, indeed, with English Catholics have gained some show of authority; but how would it have been with the fellow-countrymen of those prelates? or with any who, like their fellow-countrymen, had, in the two Fulda manifestoes of 1869 and 1870, and in other words and deeds of those mitred diplomatists—

words and deeds which cannot be erased—learned at what rate to prize statements signed by their episcopal crosses? There are in Europe few bodies of functionaries who stood in sorer need than did these German bishops of something to rehabilitate the credit of their Yea and Nay; not that even yet it seems to have fallen quite so low as that of their superiors of the Curia; at least, not quite so low in matters of purely personal reputation, when no official obligation exists to make a public impression which is contrary to the facts, and when dissimulation, if practised, arises from a habit partly professional, partly personal, and one sometimes indulged in as an exercise of cleverness. Cardinals hardly do prudently to raise on English soil questions about truthfulness; for the English public will not much longer be content to take information at haphazard or at second-hand, but will go to the fountains, and learn about things in Rome as things in Rome in reality have been.

LIST OF WORKS QUOTED OR REFERRED TO AS AUTHORITIES.

The titles and editions being here given, the references in each particular instance will be no longer than is sufficient to identify the work.
Some works cited only once are not here entered, their titles being given at full in the body of the book. The few English writers quoted are not inserted here.

Acta et Decreta Sacrosancti Œcumenici Concilii Vaticani. Romæ Impensis Paulini Lazzarini Typographi Concilii Vaticani: 1872.

Acta et Decreta Sacrosancti et Œcumenici Concilii Vaticani cum permissione Superiorum. *Friburgi Brisgoviæ :* Herder, 1871.· Contains the Encyclical and Syllabus of December 8th, 1864, and some other useful documents not published in the Roman edition; but does not contain its brief historical notes of the public sessions.

Acta Genuina SS. Œcumenici Concilii Tridentini, nunc primum integra edita ab Augustino Theiner. *Zagrabiæ Croatiæ:* 2 vols., small folio, 1874. Always referred to as *Theiner.*

Acta Sanctæ Sedis in Compendium Opportune Redacta. Romæ S. C. De Propaganda Fide. A volume has appeared annually since 1865.

Actes et Histoire du Concile Œcumenique de Rome, 1869. Publiés sous la direction de Victor Frond. Paris: Abel Pilou. 8 vols., large folio, with numerous illustrations. A brief of the Pope warrants to the Editor the 'counsel and approbation of the Holy Apostolical See;' and also gives him the Apostolic Benediction 'as a guarantee of the divine patronage.' The references are always to *Frond.*

Acton, Lord—Zur Geschichte des Vaticanischen Conciles. München: 1871.— Sendschreiben an einen Deutschen Bischof des Vaticanischen Concils. Nördlingen : September, 1870.

Annuario Pontificio, 1870. Roma Tipografia della Rev. Cam. Apostolica.

Bibliothèque Universelle et Revue Suisse. Lausanne. Montalembert's L'Espagne et la Liberté is contained in Nos. 217-221, from January to May, 1876.

Ce Qui se Passe au Concile. Paris : 1870. Condemned by the Council.

Cecconi, Eugenio (now Archbishop of Florence)—Storia del Concilio Vaticano scritta sui documenti originali. Parte prima Antecedenti del Concilio. Vol. I. Roma: A Spese di Paulini Lazzarini, *Tipografo del Concilio Vaticano*, 1873. The official history of the secret proceedings of five years.

Civiltà Cattolica (*La*), Anno Vigesimottavo. Serie X., vol. i. Quaderno, 641. Firenze: 3 Marzo, 1877. This is the title of the latest number. It has appeared fortnightly since the year 1850. It is quoted as *Civiltà* (*e.g.*) X., i., 5—the first numeral noting the series, the second the volume, the third the page.

Concile du Vatican, le, et le Mouvement Anti-infaillibiliste en Allemagne. 2 vols., octavo. Brussels: 1871.

Concile Œcuménique, le. Par Mgr. l'Evêque de Grenoble. Paris: 1869.

Dernière Heure du Concile. München: 1870. Condemned by the Council; said by Quirinus to be by a member of the Council, possessing 'almost unique opportunities.'

Desanctis, L.—Roma Papale descritta in una serie di Lettere. Firenze: 1871.— Il Papa, osservazioni Dottrinali e Storiche. Firenze: 1864.

Deschamps, Archbishop of Malins (now Cardinal).—Réponse à Mgr. l'Evêque D'Orléans. Paris: 1870.

Documenta. *See* Friedrich.

Documenti (i) Citati nel Syllabus edito per ordine del Sommo Pontifice Pio Papa IX., Preceduti da Analoghe Avvertenze. Firenze: 1865. Like the French *Recueil*, contains the documents cited in the Syllabus, but with Italian notes, and without any translation.

Döllinger, D.—Erwägungen für die Bischöfe des Concilium's über die Frage der päpstlichen Unfehlbarkeit. München: October, 1869.—Die neue Geschäftsordnung des Concils und ihre theologische Bedeutung. Augsburg: 1870.—Erklärung an den Erzbischof von München-Freising. München: 1871.

Dupanloup—Lettre de Mgr., L'Evêque D'Orléans au clergé de son Diocése relativement a la définition de l'infaillibilité au prochain Concile. Paris: 1869. The original is reprinted with the English version of Vitelleschi, Eight Months at Rome.—Réponse de Mgr. L'Evêque D'Orléans à Mgr. Deschamps. Paris: Duniol, 1870.—Réponse de Mgr. L'Evêque D'Orléans à Mgr. Spalding, Archevêque de Baltimore, accompagne d'une lettre de plusieurs Archevêques et Evêques Américain à Mgr. l'Evêque d'Orléans. Naples: 1870.

Fessler, Dr. Joseph, Bishop of St. Pölten—Das letzte und das nächste allgemeine Concil. Freiburg-in-Brisgau: 1869.

Friedberg, Dr. Emil, Professor, Leipsic—Sammlung der Aktenstücke zum ersten Vaticanischen Concil. Tübingen: 1872. Always quoted as *Friedberg*.

Friedrich, Dr. J., Professor, Munich—Tagebuch während des Vaticanischen Concils geführt. Zweite vermehrte Auflage. Nördlingen: 1873.—Documenta ad Illustrandum Concilium Vaticanum, anni 1870. Both the first and second Abtheilung are of Nördlingen, 1871. Quoted as *Documenta*.— Der Mechanismus der Vaticanischen Religion. Bonn: 1876.

Fromman, Theodor—Geschichte und Kritik des Vaticanischen Concils. Gotha: 1872. A Protestant writer, therefore scarcely ever cited. •

Frond, Victor—Actes et Histoire, etc. 8 vols.. fol. *See* 'Actes,' etc.

Gury, P. Joanne Petro—Compendium Theologiæ Moralis, S. I. editio in Germania Quarta. Ratisbon: 1868.—Casus Conscientiæ in Præcipuas Quæstiones Theologiæ Moralis editio in Germania prima. Ratisbon: 1865.

Guérin, Mgr., Paul Chamberlain to Pius IX. —Concile Œcuménique du Vatican son Histoire ses décisions en Latin et en Francais. Professes to give all the documents, but gives only a portion even of those officially published. Bar-le-Duc: 1871. 2nd ed.

Gregorovius, Ferdinand.—*Geschichte der Stadt Rom im Mittelalter vom V. bis zum XVI., Jahrhundert.* Zweite Auflage: 1869. 8 vols. octavo.

Hefele, Carolus Josephus Episcopus Rottenburgensis—Causa Honorii Papæ. Neapoli: 1870.

Hergenröther, Dr. Joseph, Professor, Würzburg—Katholische Kirche und Christlicher Staat in ihrer geschichtlichen Entwickelung und in Beziehung auf die Fragen der Gegenwart. Freiburg-in-Brisgau: 1873.—Kritik der v. Döllingerschen Erklärung vom 28 Marz d. I. Freiburg-in-Brisgau: 1871.

Holtgreven, Anton, Königl. Preuss. Kreisrichter—Das Verhältniss Zwischen Staat und Kirche. Berlin: 1875.

Kenrick, Archbishop of St. Louis in America—Concio Petri Ricardi Kenrick, Archiepiscopi S. Ludovici in Statibus Fœderatis Americæ Septentrionalis in Concilio Vaticano Habenda at non Habita. Neapoli: 1870. This invaluable pamphlet is reprinted with Friedrich's *Documenta*, and is always cited as there found, the pamphlet itself being within the reach of but very few.

Ketteler, von, Wilhelm Emmanuel Freiherr, Bishop of Mainz—Das Allgemeine Concil und seine Bedeutung für unsere Zeit. Mainz: 1869.—Die Unwahrheiten der Römischen Briefe vom Concil in der Allgemeinen Zeitung. Mainz: 1870. Several other pamphlets by Bishop von Ketteler not referred to are of value.

Langen, Dr. Joseph, Professor, Bonn—Das Vaticanische Dogma in seinem Verhältniss zum Neuen Testament, etc. Bonn: 1873.

Liverani, Monsignor Francesco, Prelato Domestico e Protonotorio della Santa Sede.—Il Papato, L'Impero e Il Regno D'Italia. Firenze: 1861.

Maret, Mgr. H. L. C., Bishop of Sura, Dean of the Theological Faculty of Paris—Le Concile Général et la Paix Religieuse. 2 vols., octavo. Paris: 1869.

Martin, Conrad, Bishop of Paderborn.—*Omnium Concilii Vaticani Quæ ad doctrinam et Disciplinam pertinent Documentorum Collectio.* Paderbornæ: 1873. A very incomplete collection, but very useful.—*Katechismus des Römisch-Katolischen Kirchenrechts.* Zweite Auflage: 1874.

Menzel, Professor—Ueber das Subject der Kirchlichen Unfehlbarkeit (als Manuscript gedruckt). Braunsberg: 1870.

Menzel, Wolfgang—Geschichte der neuesten Jesuitenumtriebe in Deutschland. Stuttgart: 1873.—Die Wichtigsten Weltbegebenheiten vom Prager Frieden bis zum Kriege mit Frankreich (1866-1870). 2 vols. Stuttgart: 1871.

Michaud, L'Abbé—De la Falsification des Catéchismes Francais. Paris, 1872. Many other works of Michaud, not cited, are of great value.

Michelis, Dr. F., Professor, Braunsberg.—*Kurze Geschichte des Vaticanischen Concils.* Constanz: 1875.—*Der Neue Fuldaer Hirtenbrief in seinem Verhältniss zur Wahrheit.* Braunsberg: 1870.—*Der häretische Charakter der Infallibilitätslehre. Eine Katholische Antwort auf die Römische Excommunication,* 1872.

Observationes Quædam de Infallibilitatis Ecclesiæ Subjecto. Vindobonæ: 1870. Cardinal Rauscher (*see* Friedberg, 111). Also published in Naples, without name of printer or publisher.

Phillips, George—Kirchenrecht. 7 vols., octavo. Regensburg: 1855-72.

Pope Pius IX.—Discorsi del Sommo Pontefice Pius IX. Pronunziati in Vaticano ai fedeli di Roma e dell' Orbe; raccolti e pubblicati dal P. Don Pasquale de Franciscis. Roma: 1872; and the second volume, 1873. It is to be regretted that these curious and instructive volumes are not translated into English.

Recueil des Allocutions Consistoriales Encycliques et Autres Lettres Apostolique des Souverains Pontifs Clement XII., Benoit XIV., Pie VI., Pie VII., Léon XII., Grégoire XVI., et Pie IX., citées dans l'Encyclique et le Syllabus du 8 Décembre, 1864. Octavo, p. 580. Paris: 1865. Every document cited in the Syllabus is given at full, with a French translation.

Reform der Römischen Kirche an Haupt und Gliedern. Leipsig: 1869.

Reinkens, Dr. Joseph Hubert, Bishop—Revolution und Kirche Beantwortung einer Tagesfrage mit Rücksight auf die gegenwärtige Tendenz und Praxis der Römischen Curie. Bonn: 1876.—Ueber päpstliche Unfehlbarkeit. München: 1870.

Rheinischer Merkur. Erscheint jeden Samstag, Köln. A weekly journal, organ of the old Catholics. Now published in Munich as the *Deutscher Merkur.*

Sambin, Le R. P. de la Compagnie de Jesus—Histoire du Concile Œcumenique et Général du Vatican. Lyon: 1871.

Schrader, P. Clemens, S. I.—Pius IX. als Papst und als Kœnig. Wien: 1865.—Der Papst und die Modernen Ideen. Wien: 1865.

Sepp, Professor Abgeordneter—Deutschland und der Vatikan. München: 1872.

Soglia—Septimii M. Vecchiotti, Institutiones Canonicæ ex operibus Joannis Card. Soglia excerptæ et ad usum seminariorum accommodatæ. Editio decimasexta ad meliorem formam redacta et additamentis locupleta. In 3 vols., octavo. Turin: 1875. Sold at Milan, Venice, Naples, and Romæ apud Tipographiam de Propaganda Fide.

Stimmen aus der Katholischen Kirche München. A series of pamphlets containing writings of Döllinger, Friedrich, Huber, Schmitz, Reinkens, Liano, and others—of great value.

Stimmen aus Maria Laach, Katholische Blätter—Freiburg-in-Brisgau. The first number appeared in 1865, after the publication of the Syllabus; the Neue Folge, commenced in 1869, has on the title 'Unter Benützung Römischer Mittheilungen und der Arbeiten der Civiltá.'

Summi Pontificis Infallibilitate Personali (de). Naples: 1870. Friedberg (p. 111) says that this tract was distributed by Cardinal Prince Schwarzenberg, but written by the Cistercian Franz Salesius Mayer.

Tarquini, Camillo E., Societate Jesu (Cardinal)—Juris Ecclesiastici Publici Institutiones. Editio quarta. Roma S. C. de Propaganda Fide. 1875.

Theologisches Literaturblatt. Erscheint alle 14 Toge. Bonn, herausgegeben von Prof. Dr. F. H. Reusch. A fortnightly publication, of great value to all who wish to understand the literature of the modern phases of Romanism, and also of the old Catholic movement.

Unitá Cattolica, edited by Don Margotti, appears daily in Turin. Holds in Italy a position similar to that of the *Univers* in France.

Univers, edited by M. Louis Veuillot, appears daily, Paris. Veuillot is a layman.

Veuillot, Louis—Rome pendant le Concile. 2 vols., octavo. Paris: 1872. Contains important matter dating from 1867.

Vitelleschi, Marchese Francesco—Otto Mesi a Roma durante il Concilio Vaticano per Pomponio Leto. Firenze: 1873. An English translation has now appeared entitled *Eight Months at Rome*, by Pomponio Leto. Always referred to as *Vitelleschi*. The real authorship of the work is no secret in Rome, nor is it treated as such.

CONTENTS.

BOOK I.

FROM THE ISSUE OF THE SYLLABUS TO ITS SOLEMN CONFIRMATION, DECEMBER 1864 TO JUNE 1867.

CHAPTER VII.

CHAPTER VIII.

CHAPTER IX.

CHAPTER X.

CHAPTER XI.

CHAPTER XII.

CHAPTER XIII.

BOOK II.

FROM THE FIRST PUBLIC INTIMATION OF A COUNCIL TO THE EVE OF THE
OPENING, JUNE 1867 TO DECEMBER 1869.

CHAPTER I.

xl

Contents.

BOOK I.

CHAPTER I.

The First Secret Command to commence Preparations for a General Council, December 6th, 1864—Meeting of Congregation—All but Cardinals sent out —Secret Order—Events of the 8th—Solemn Anniversary—A historical *coup de soleil.*

ON the 6th of December, 1864, Pope Pius IX. held in the Vatican a memorable meeting of the Congregation of Rites. That body consists of some eighteen or twenty cardinals, with a few prelates and a number of consulters. It holds a prominent place among the congregations, or boards as they would be called at our Court, which, taken collectively, may be said to constitute the Roman Curia. It determines not only questions touching the canonisation of saints, and the patron saints of towns and countries, but also questions touching relics, rubrics, and the title of sacred images to worship. The all-important matters of robes, adornments, and precedence, are said by different authorities to be regulated by it, and by the smaller Congregation of Ceremonies. The pontifical masters of the ceremonies have a seat at both boards.

The day in question fell within three months after the signing of the convention of September, by which the new kingdom of Italy had succeeded in binding Napoleon III. to withdraw his troops from the Papal States, at the close of 1866. It was, therefore, at a moment when thoughts were forcibly directed to the contingencies which might arise to the Papacy should it be left alone with Italians. It was, moreover, only two days before the occurrence of an incident which has already grown into an event, and was designed to mark a new era in society at large. To that era the proceedings of the six years which we are about to trace were to form the introductory stage, up to a grand inauguration both legislative and ceremonial.

We have no information as to the business for which the meeting we speak of had been convened. It was, however, opened as usual by the reading of a prayer. After the prayer, the Pontiff commanded all who were not members of the Sacred College to withdraw, and leave him alone with the Cardinals. The excluded dignitaries interchanged conjectures as to what might be the cause of this unusual proceeding, and hoped that on their readmission they should be informed. But the Pope did not condescend to their curiosity; they found that the Congregation only went on with the regular business, and when events cleared up the doubt it proved that not one of them had guessed the truth.

In the short but eventful interval, Pius IX. had formally communicated to the Cardinals his own persuasion, long cherished, and now quickened to the point of irrepressible action, that the remedy for the evils of the time would be found only in a General Council. He commanded them to study the expediency of convoking one, and to send to him in writing their opinions upon that question.

The above incident is the first related in the sumptuous volume of Cecconi, written by command of the Pope, who, after it appeared, conferred on the author the archbishopric of Florence. That volume exclusively narrates the secret proceedings of the five years which intervened between this meeting and the opening of the Vatican Council. But, while telling us what took place on the 6th of December, the Court historian passes in dead silence over the eighth. On that day, however, the Vatican launched manifestoes which had been for years in preparation, and which have been mentioned every day since. These summed up all the past policy of Pius IX., and formed a basis for the future government of the world. They furnished to the Vatican Council, still five years distant, the kernel of its decrees, both those passed and those only presented. They are, in fact, printed with the Freiburg edition of its *Acta* as preparatory documents.

December is to Pius IX., as it is to the Bonapartes, a month of solemn anniversaries. On the eighth of that month, ten years previously to the time of which we are writing, surrounded by two hundred bishops, he proclaimed the immaculate conception of the Virgin Mary as a doctrine of the Church. In his own imagination, this act formed an epoch of glory, to the lustre of which three distinct triumphs contributed. In the first place, a darling bye-belief was lifted from the humble posture of pious opinion, to that of a dogma binding on all, who must admit changes into their creed with every change of Rome. In the second place, a new and mighty advance in the power of the Papacy was achieved, for a formal addition to the creed was made without the sanction of a General Council. Those bishops who attended manifestly acted, not as members of a co-ordinate branch of a legislature, but as councillors of an autocrat. The absent were placed under the necessity of accepting the *fait accompli*, or of attempting to undo it in the face of the Pontiff, the Curia, and the majority of the prelates. ' Gallicanism,' said the *Civiltá Cattolica*, ' was, in fact, bruised under the heel of the Immaculate, when Pius IX., by his own authority, laid down the definition.' [1] Thirdly, an impression of the personal inspiration of Pius IX. was conveyed, with embellishments, so as to prepare the way for the recognition of his infallibility.

When he was in the act of proclaiming the new dogma, the beams of the sun streamed gloriously upon him; the fact being that his throne was so fixed that this must take place if the sun shone at the time. Nevertheless, the visible rays were hailed as evidence of the light which makes manifest things not seen.

[1] Serie VII., viii., p. 668.

The Pope sought, in the great fresco of Podesti, to popularise and perpetuate his own conception of this event, which is called, in French guide-books to the Vatican, the *coup de soleil historique.* That picture, filling an entire side of a chamber, near to the renowned frescoes of Raffaele, represents the Virgin looking down from celestial glory upon Pius IX., and, by the hand of an angel, who holds a cross, pouring a stream of supernal light on his enraptured eye. Hence may the faithful gather that this is the light by which he reveals the truth to men.

CHAPTER II.

The Encyclical *Quanta Cura*, December 8th, 1864.—Causes of Ruin of Modern Society: rejection of the 'force' of the Church—Religious Equality—Pretensions of Civil Law and of Parents to Control Education—Laws of Mortmain—Remedies—Restoration of the Authority of the Church—Connecting Links between Encyclical and Syllabus—Retrospect of Evidences that all Society was in Ruins—The Movement for Reconstruction.

THE tenth anniversary of the auspicious day of 'The Immaculate' being now at hand, Pius IX. had, as we have seen, chosen its fore-eve for setting in motion the preparations for his General Council. He reserved for the day itself the great deed of publishing the Encyclical *Quanta Cura* and its accompanying Syllabus of Errors. It is said that the inception of those documents dates back to a point not very long subsequent to the proclamation of the Immaculate Conception, and that the first Special Congregation named to prepare them spent more than five years without agreeing, after which it was dissolved by his Holiness, and a second named, which completed the task.

The key-note of the Encyclical is that of an alarm, in the martial sense; not a panic cry, accompanied by a throwing away of arms, but a note of danger, with a call to take them up.

The cause assigned for alarm is the ruinous condition of

society—that word being used in its political, not its domestic sense. The very bases of society were shaken by evil principles, which had spread on all sides and raised a 'horrible tempest.' Before proceeding to the errors to be now condemned, the Pontiff is careful to connect with them those other 'principal errors of our sad times' which he had already condemned in previous encyclicals, allocutions, and letters apostolic. He thus lays the logical foundation for the collection of them in the Syllabus. He first reminds the bishops how he had stirred them up to war against these errors, and how he had also commanded the children of the Church to abhor and shun them. Secondly, he enumerates certain additional errors, condemns them in turn, and commands his sons to shun them likewise. Condemnations pronounced in this formal manner are judicial and sovereign. The Pontiff does not speak as a mere teacher, but as the supreme tribunal of the Church. The judgments pronounced are not for the guidance of individuals merely, but are a rule for every officer of the Church. Every such sentence fixes the state of the law.

After many generalities, the first token of ruin in modern society particularised is the design manifested to check and set aside the salutary *force*[1] which ought always to be exercised by the Church, not only over individuals, but also over nations, both 'peoples' and sovereigns. The second token of ruin is the prevalence of the error that the State may treat various religions on a footing of equality,—the error that liberty of worship is in fact a personal right of every man, and that the citizen is entitled to make a free profession of his belief, orally or by the press, without fear of either civil or ecclesiastical power. This is condemned as being the 'liberty of damnation.' The next token of ruin is hostility to the religious orders, which were established by their founders only by the inspiration of God.

---

[1] The word is *vis*, which both the *Civiltà Cattolica* and the French *Recueil* translate by 'force.' But not so the German *Stimmen aus Maria Laach*, which makes it 'influence'—*einfluss* (Heft i., p. 10). Such a difference in versions meant for Germans, Englishmen, and Americans is not rare.

Another token of ruin is the belief that all the rights of parents over their children arise out of civil law, especially the claim to control their education. The Pope would seem to think that this notion is the ground for denying the right of priests to take the control of education out of the hand of parents, or the ground for claiming the protection of civil law for the natural and Scriptural right of the parent against the alleged right of the priest. Such denial of the right of the priest is dilated upon as a further token of ruin. The existence of laws of mortmain is an additional token. After these civil and ecclesiastical matters, one theological point is adduced, with formal yet fervent language, as if it were some new plague, broken out in our own times—the denial of the divinity of our blessed Lord. This seems to be the only question in theology proper directly raised in the document. The errors now signalized are all condemned, and formally added to those previously condemned.

Just as the Emperor Nicholas of Russia, before undertaking the campaign that led to the Crimean war, found his sick man and pointed out his symptoms, so had Pius IX. done. In the former case, the sick man was only one wide-spread but despotic empire. In the latter, it included everything that could be called, in the dialect of the Vatican, the Modern State.

Proceeding from his enumeration of the evils which mark the ruin of contemporary society to the remedies by which it is to be repaired, his Holiness once more wraps up much of what he may mean in generalities. When he does come to particulars, the hierarchy are directed to teach that kingdoms rest on the foundations of the faith; that kingly power is bestowed, not only for the government of the world, but still more for the protection of the Church ; that nothing can be more glorious for rulers than to permit the Catholic Church to govern according to her own laws (*i.e.*, canon law), not allowing any one to impede her free action, and not setting the regal will above that of the priests of Christ. Here is touched the great question in government. The Modern State had not only emancipated the throne from the supreme tribunal of the Church, that is, the Pope, but it had also emancipated the civil courts from the external tribunal of the Church, that is, the ecclesiastical court. The latter as well as the former evil must be redressed. To such prescriptions for the healing of society is added a proclamation of indulgences, and then follows an exhortation to pray both to God and to the Blessed Virgin, ' who has destroyed all heresies throughout the world,'—whatever that may mean in history, theology, or rhetoric. ' She is gentle and full of mercy; . . . . and standing at the right hand of her only Son, our Lord Jesus Christ, as queen, in gilded clothing, surrounded with variety, there is nothing which she cannot obtain from Him.'

This curious document was a necessary introduction to the Syllabus. The external connecting link between the two was formed by a covering letter of Cardinal Antonelli conveying Syllabus to the hierarchy by direct command of the Pope, ' that they might have all the errors and the pernicious doctrines which have been condemned by him under their eyes.' [1] The internal link lay in the title of the Syllabus, which recited the language of the Encyclical referring to the antecedent judgments of the Pontiff. It is not a syllabus of errors *in general*, nor of errors merely disapproved and abhorred by Pius IX. in particular, nor of errors rebuked and denounced by him only in sermons, speeches, or briefs; but a syllabus of *The Principal Errors of our Times, set forth by him in Consistorial Allocutions, Encyclicals, and other Letters Apostolic.*

Before proceeding to consider the Syllabus as the new foundation laid for the reconstruction of society after its ruin, we may for a moment glance at the facts which might seem to prove to observers, looking from the Vatican, that it had been reduced to a ruinous condition.

Coming to the throne in 1846, Pius IX. inherited the sovereignty of States which had long been in a condition of

---

[1] *Recueil,* end of preface.

chronic disaffection. The state of things is described as follows by Monsignor Liverani, a learned but seemingly disappointed prelate, who wrote hoping to redeem the glory of the Papacy by the re-establishment of a Holy Roman Empire with an Italian head, after the example of that interval between the line of Charlemagne and that of Otho, when Guido of Spoleto, his brilliant son Lambert, and Berengarius wore the imperial title. 'The people,' says Liverani, 'have spoken for forty years, groaning, agitating, shaking off the yoke by frequent revolutions, accompanied by crimes and continuous misfortunes, by slaughters, wars, bombardments, banishments, and desolations.'[1]

Nevertheless, prelates from the north, coming to pay their homage to the new Pontiff, on reaching the last spurs of the Alps, might embrace in the glance of their mind all thence to Ætna, and say, Happy land! the throne of his Holiness in the centre, the faithful Bourbon on the south, the Hapsburg on the north, with Tuscany under a branch of the Hapsburgs, and Piedmont under the House of Savoy,—what a spectacle of Catholic power! Holy land! not a heretic temple; not one teacher but in communion with Peter: blessed scene of Catholic unity!

A poor representative of the oft-extirpated Waldenses might say in silence—for such words durst not then disturb the Catholic unity of Italian air—You forget a few teachers in the valleys behind you, who never left the word of God to turn lords either of the earth or of the faith. Before you there is not a pulpit with the Bible, nor a man who ever drinks the cup of Christ, excepting priests alone; not a temple with God's commandments on its walls, but many a decalogue altered by the authority of a man who, making the law of God reformable, claims that his own shall be irreformable!

Beyond the limits of the Pope's temporal dominions soon arose commotions which spread over the principal seats of his spiritual power. In Switzerland the Jesuits provoked the war

[1] *Il Papato*, etc., p. 188.

of the Sonderbund, and were foiled. Beyond the Atlantic a considerable portion of Mexico passed into the hands of the Protestant United States. Portugal was plagued with revolt. A famine thinned and dispersed the Roman Catholic population of Ireland. France drove away her good king. The Emperor of Austria was compelled to abdicate, and the empire was not saved from dismemberment without aid from Russia. The King of Bavaria also had to lay down his crown. The sovereigns of Tuscany and Naples were compelled to fly; as was, alas! the Pontiff himself. Spain and her Queen were seldom heard of, except for an insurrection or a scandal. Only two Roman Catholic countries were thriving—Belgium, with a Protestant king, and a constitution which the Church had solemnly and vehemently condemned; and Piedmont, which, worse than Hannibal, had opened the passes of the Alps to religious liberty.

This was the first sweep of the hurricane. During its prevalence, those portions of the world which lay without the Papal circle enjoyed as much rest as was to be looked for beside such troubled waters. Both schismatical Russia and heretical England were stable and expanding. Prussia was for a time seriously disturbed, but, nevertheless, was manifestly advancing to the first place in Germany. Holland, Denmark, and Sweden held on their way; and the United States were growing apace.

From his exile the Pope called on the Catholic powers for armed aid. Austria crushed and held the Emilia. Spain took Fuimicino and the cities on the Tyrrhenian shore. Naples conquered Frosinone and the south up to Palestrina, but was driven back at Velletri by Garibaldi. Finally, France declared herself ready to terminate the war; and, after failing for weeks before the slight defences of Rome, ultimately took the city.[1]

[1] The Pope, in the Allocution of April 20th, 1849, says that Spain first stirred up the other Catholic nations to form a league among themselves for his restoration (*Recueil*, p. 228). His description of the Holy City during his absence was, 'a thicket of roaring beasts'—*silvam frementium bestiarum* (Id., 224). His description of himself at the same time was, 'being counted worthy to suffer shame for the name of Jesus, and being made in some measure conformable to His passion' (Id., p. 234).

Indebted for a welcome restoration to the unwelcome hand of a Bonaparte, Pius IX., on re-entering his States, found himself permanently dependent for possession of the capital on the sword of France, and for that of the provinces on the sword of Austria. Under their protection he enjoyed some years of struggling sovereignty. This could hardly be called a restoration of the temporal power, for a power is not really restored till it can again stand alone. Instead of being an opponent of the Jesuits, a Liberal, and a Reformer, as he had been, the Pope was now transformed into a violent reactionary, and had fallen entirely under the influence of the Jesuits. His admirers proudly point to his acts from that time forward as evidence that they have been uniformly aimed at one end. That end, viewed on its negative side, they call combating the Revolution, and, viewed on its positive side, the reconstruction of society. In the introduction to his Speeches, his peculiar mission is said to be that of reconstruction. This reconstruction was to begin with the restoration of ideas, and was to proceed to the restoration of facts.

It is this movement that we are about to trace. First, we shall take a brief retrospect from the time of its inception at Gaeta up to the appearance of the Syllabus, which, as the ostensible ground-plan of a cosmopolitan code, was meant to be the charter of reconstruction. We shall then, from that stage onward, as far as our materials enable us, detail the progressive steps of the movement up to the end of the Vatican Council, which was meant to complete the constituent arrangements of the new theocratic monarchy. We shall see unfolding a movement for dominion as distinctive as was that of Leo III. when he linked the fortunes of the Papacy to those of a new Western Empire; as distinctive as was the movement of Hildebrand when from political dependence he lifted up the Papacy to unheard of domination; as distinctive as was the movement of the Popes after the Reformation, when through war and the Inquisition they restored in several countries of Europe their spiritual ascendancy. We shall witness the rise of a curious and powerful literature—scholastic, serial, and popular—which has steadily swollen in volume, and now acts with ever accelerating force on the religious antipathies of many nations, pointing to future wars on a scale unheard of, fixing the aim of those wars, and hinting at the disappearance of all existing institutions but the Church. We shall see a well-sustained endeavour, in the name of freedom of instruction, to take all schools and universities out of the hands of parents and of States, and to put them into the hands of priests. We shall see such rights in matters ecclesiastical as in the Church of Rome had still survived to the laity, the priests, and the bishops, gradually suppressed in action till the way was prepared for their abolition in law. We shall see the subordination of the civil law to the canon law, and the subjection of the civil magistrate to the 'ecclesiastical magistrate' insisted upon as the essence of social order. We shall see all the inherited rights of kings and rulers, within their own dominions, to put limits upon the action of the Pope of Rome, first impugned, then contested, then defied, and finally, as far as the Church could do it, legislated out of existence. We shall see all kings and rulers challenged to accept the Pontiff as their head, and even as their judge in all matters involving moral responsibility. We shall find it taught and taught again that all Catholic countries have two rulers—the universal and the national one, the universal one superior, the national one subordinate; and that every citizen of those countries is more the subject of the Pope than of his prince. We shall see the relation between the civil and the ecclesiastical authorities as existing within the Papal States solemnly and repeatedly declared to be the normal relation of those two orders of authority, and to be the only example of their proper relative position extant in all the earth. We shall see the Papal States earnestly held up as the model for the new theocracy in the entire world.

Further, we shall see, for five successive years, secret proceedings of the Court of Rome sufficiently laid open by official divulgence to enable us to note the slow, sure steps devised for depriving kings of all their rights in self-defence against the Pope; for depriving bishops of all their powers of checking or restraining the Pope; for depriving theologians of any voice in the councils of the Church; and for depriving the parochial clergy of their individual and collective franchises. We shall see great pomps and ceremonies, long prepared, employed with dexterous adaptation and astuteness almost beyond belief, to cover over and to carry the adoption of measures of organic change, while attention was diverted from constitutional questions to external display. We shall at almost every turn hear modern laws and constitutions—liberty of worship, liberty of the press, liberty of meeting, with representative legislatures and responsible governments—denounced as the curse of mankind in all the varying accents of a strange dialect, or a dialect happily strange to us. We shall witness the preaching of a new crusade, on a cosmopolitan scale, with considerable art, making the bearing of arms for St. Peter to appear, pre-eminently, the life of the Cross, and dying in arms for St. Peter to appear as the martyr's end, the fairest of deaths, and the most enviable. We shall see how the most jealous and obstinate oligarchy in the world were led on from step to step of subjugation till they were made the instruments of reducing their collective body, when in Council assembled, from a co-ordinate branch of a legislature to a mere privy council to the Bishop of Rome, and of reducing the members of their body, when dispersed, from the position of real diocesan bishops to that of prefects of the Bishop of Rome.

Still further, we shall see evolved under our eyes the process by which opinions are elevated into doctrines, and doctrines are erected into irreformable dogma. We shall see how the bishops, while dispersed, were induced, in order to facilitate the making of a new dogma, to discredit their acknowledged standard of belief, tradition, substituting for it the general consent of the Church; and how, when the passing of the dogma was secured, the assembled bishops were induced to disavow the consent of the Church as unnecessary. We shall see ecclesiastical magnates prostrate and petitioning the Bishop of Rome for the elementary liberties of a legislature, and petitioning in vain. We shall see how such magnates in secret petitions represented the principles about to be erected into dogma as contrary to their traditional belief and constant teaching, as fraught with peril to the State, and as certain to bring discredit on the loyalty of any sincere believer in such dogma ; and how the same magnates afterwards in public documents affirmed the opposite in all these respects. We shall see how renowned champions of the Papacy complained late in life that they had been used for its glory and deceived as to its principles ; how others, aware of the tendency of those principles, endeavoured to check it ; how light and information came out of conflict ; and how some submitted, while others maintained their convictions. We shall see how, while all the sovereigns who had been threatened with revolution if they did not submit to the Pope, sat securely on their thrones (excepting only the one who held him up), the Pope himself fell and cried for aid to the kings. Finally, we shall see set in motion an immense apparatus of means for effecting, in a course of ages, the complete social, political, and ecclesiastical reconstruction of all society, which reconstruction will culminate only when the spiritual and the temporal powers meeting as in an apex in the Vicar of Christ, he shall be by all men regarded as not only High Priest, but as King of kings and Lord of lords ; when, all authority and dominion, all principality and power, being put under him, there shall in the whole earth exist only, as we should express it, one master and all men slaves, or, as he would express it, one fold and one shepherd.[1]

---

[1] The question whether Pius IX. was or was not a Freemason is of no interest whatever, yet it has been matter of considerable dispute in Italy. It was so well denied by the Court organs that it ought to have been settled. But, unhappily, in Italy denials from that quarter often pass for corroborations. So it was in this case, until in February, 1876, the *Capitale,* of Rome, published the certificate of his admission into the Order, with all marks and tokens of authenticity. so far as the uninitiated can judge. The *Nuova Firenze* then published a letter to a Lodge, signed by Count L. R. W., and with marks to identify the Lodge, saying that he demurred to their judgment on Brother Mastai, and relating how,

CHAPTER III.

Foundation of a Literature of Reconstruction, Serial and Scholastic—The *Civiltà Cattolica* : its Views on Education and on Church and State—Tarquini's Political Principles of Pope and King—Measures Preparatory to the Syllabus.

WITH the year 1850 was commenced a magazine, at the instance of the Jesuits, and under their direction, bearing the title Catholic Civilisation (*Civiltà Cattolica*), in opposition to modern civilisation. We may here say that the daily organ of the same complexion bears the title of Catholic Unity (*Unità Cattolica*), in opposition to Italian unity. Above one hundred volumes of the *Civiltà* have been published ; and it must ever be named in connection with Pius IX., as the intimate organ of his policy, and the most complete store of his published records. Perhaps its place in the history of literature is unique. Considering the number of books, serials, and journals, in different languages, of which it is the inspiring force, and considering the modifications it has already succeeded in bringing about in the ideas and even in the organisation of the whole Catholic society, they can scarcely be charged with vain boasting who call it the most influential organ in the world. The Jesuit Fathers forming its editorial staff reside close to the Pope's palace, and work under his immediate direction. Dr. Friedrich, during the Vatican Council, told some bishops that if they would understand the Council, they must study it with the *Civiltà* in their hands. For our part, before reading that re-mark we had applied the same principle to the entire movement.

The leading idea of the *Civiltà* is expressed, says the article

on a certain occasion, after, as a diplomatist, transacting business with Pius IX., he had a private interview, and told his Holiness that he must tell him that Pius IX., in anathematising all Freemasons, had perjured himself, and anathe-matised Cav R.·. + ·. Masti-Ferretti among the rest. The Pope told him that he was still a Freemason, but that he took the Jesuits in. The editor says that he took the Count in, and so say other editors who reprint the document. This controversy is principally curious as showing how the Italian mind is saturated with a belief in the deceitfulness of all who surround the Papal throne.

on the programme, in its title. *Catholic Civilisation* is flag, device, and profession of faith.[1] The substance is civilisation, the quality Catholic. Civilisation is not polish, but organisation in community, under rule. Civilisation, after the Catholic ideal, had continued steadily to grow up to the fifteenth century, but was broken in the sixteenth by Lutheranism ; was again enfeebled in the seventeenth by Jansenism ; yet again was it undermined in the eighteenth by Voltairianism, and now in the nineteenth it is lacerated by Socialism. The evil has actually entered Italy, and even heterodoxy itself threatens to invade the Peninsula. Heresy is, in fact, likely to become connected with that aspiration after national unity by which the people are misled. *Almost everything having been overhauled in a heterodox spirit, almost everything must be reconstituted from the foundation.*[2] These words express the mission of the new periodical, and of the restored Papacy. They are the original announcement of a policy ever since pursued without flagging.

To reconstitute society according to the Catholic ideal is the single object set forth. Designs such as religious men would expect to find on the lips of a Christian bishop, or in the front of a bishop's magazine, were out of the question. Exposition of Scripture—Biblical studies, how to convert sinners from the error of their ways—not these things. We have talk of revolutions, monarchies, republics, authority and anarchy, interspersed with snarls at heresy and heretics.

' On the brink of social dissolution,' the one necessity felt, pressed, reiterated, is that of re-establishing on the Catholic ideal the notion of civilisation,—that is of the civil system ; and of leading back the movement of civilisation to that Catholic ideal from which it had been departing for three centuries.[3] ' Perhaps some years, it may be some lustres, will pass ere it is seen what a large and variegated web may be woven on these threads (Catholic civilisation), simple as they seem at first sight.'[4]

---

[1] *Civiltà*, vol. i., p. 13.   [2] Ibid., p. 15.   [3] Ibid., p. 13.   [4] Ibid., p. 13.

The essential point in this fabric is 'the idea of authority.' The question relates not to the form of governments as between monarchy and republic. *The authority must be legitimate, and the operation just.*[1]   But the idea of authority cannot be restored except by quickening it, and reinforcing it by the Catholic conception.   When the divine authority was shaken, men would no longer hear of the human (*i.e.,* when the Papacy was rejected, civil government fell into contempt).   The Catholic ideal is idly reproached with absolutism.   But, among Catholics, pure monarchy, if not limited by certain conventional checks, is tempered by a higher law, not abstract, but practical, active, and operative.   Absolutism in the sense of despotism is the creation of Protestantism and Voltairianism, and if it may sit on the throne of a king, it is more frequently found in constitutional chambers or democratic assemblies.[2]   Therefore the one sufficing remedy is the restoration in ruler and subject of the notion of authority according to the Catholic ideal.   For this the new organ calls for *a salutary conspiracy, a holy crusade;*[3] two phrases that mean all that has since taken place, and all that has yet to come.

We need hardly say that the centre of the Catholic ideal of the civil system is the Papacy ; and the centre of the Papacy is the notion that the Pope represents God upon earth.   Among Christians, all authority flows from the Pope, as among men all authority flows from God.   Authority coming from below is never legitimate.   Authority seems to be always considered as coming from below, when it is given by the heads of all the houses in a nation acting in a peaceful and deliberate manner through chosen representatives, and making ONE the depositary of the collective authority of all the heads of houses in so far as it touches the duties and the interests common to them all.   The constitutional monarch who in this manner becomes the Great Father, uniting in himself the executive authority of all the fathers of the land, and there-

---

[1] *Civiltá*, vol. i., p. 19.   [2] Ibid., pp. 20, 21.   [3] Ibid., p. 14.

fore becomes the head of the only true paternal government, is, in the *Civiltà* and its manifold echoes, constantly represented as a poor slave. The reason of this is that in legislation he admits the collective authority of the fathers of the land as a co-ordinate authority with his own. He is also represented as a ridiculous puppet, because in executive action his ministers are responsible to the collective fathers of the land. This authority, which in the common affairs of a community is the most clearly divine one we know of, is constantly treated as from below. It would be hard to express in English the hatred and contempt for constitutional monarchy and responsible ministers which are ever flowing from the fountains of the Vatican.

It would seem that authority may be recognised as being from above if it emanates from a decision taken, not by a vote which declares the majority of opinion, but by a fight which declares the majority of force. The Papacy has in all ages recognised and blessed the authority of the conqueror if he has only taken the right side ; whether, as in the case of Pepin, it was the minister supplanting his sovereign, or, as in many cases, it was the German crushing the Italian, or, as in the case of Robert Guiscard, it was the Norman subjugating both. We cannot, however, understand modern writing except on the principle that even authority once so blessed must, in order to retain its legitimacy, be used to withhold the franchise from all heads of families, denying to them any collective voice in their common affairs, and asserting that the joint authority of all fathers is no authority at all ; that the ruler, be he king, president, or prince bishop, is not only the depositary, but the fountain of authority; not only the Great Father, but the Sole Father, and that all the rest are children. The reader will, as we proceed, have ample opportunity of comparing these hints with original utterances.

The very first article of the *Civiltà*, after that upon the programme, is on education : 'the question which holds all the future destinies of the European nations struggling within its ballot-boxes.' With this appreciation of its theme, it takes ground which has since become familiar to Europe, and enunciates principles which have now frequently been reproduced in our own discussions; so that a slight sketch of its reasoning will not be without interest to English readers. The interest is increased by the fact that its aims have steadily gained ground in France. In England, some of them, if not recognised as principles, have been, to a considerable extent, practically embodied, as undetected principles are apt to be.

Beginning with the theme of Freedom of Instruction, it denounces the tyranny and monopoly of the University of France. Had not the spirit of Catholicism, it says, broken the chain, it would soon have become unlawful for one man to tell another the right road, unless he had a Bachelor's degree, for doing so was a sort of instruction. The line properly limiting freedom of instruction it finds in the line which divides the truth from falsehood. The private lie is condemned by the private conscience, the social lie by social law, and the public one by public law. The lie in instruction is the most hurtful of all lies. They who demand liberty of instruction do so in order to teach the truth. But in excluding the teaching of lies, it may be even ' necessary to protect children betrayed by the barbarous apathy of their parents.'

The writer then asks, But who is to determine what is the lie? Governments? ' Until a government can show itself infallible, it must renounce all pretensions to regulate instruction and opinion.' A government might say, I do not indeed pretend to be infallible as to the truth, but I aim at the *good* of the subject. But gain acquired at the cost of accepting falsehood robs man of the sublimest good, the truth, to which no material good can be compared. Moreover, is it true that the public good is advanced by a lie? ' You must either admit that the government is infallible, or forbid it to mix itself up with education, *so far as it relates to truth and falsehood.*' The pretension on its part to do so is tyrannical, because interference here is trespassing on the sanctuary, where the truth alone bears rule.

The position that it belongs to a government to fix the limits of freedom of opinion is denounced as having originated in the Reformation, as being Protestant, and, further, as being destitute of foundation. The Church is the moderator of instruction, precisely because she is the infallible moderator of opinions in all that relates to the moral order. Consequently there is in existence a competent, effectual, and revered tribunal. Then follow taunts at journals which complain of communal authorities for giving up their educational rights to the clergy. These are succeeded by jeers at such statesmen as doubt if the liberty of communal authorities extends so far as to give them the right of surrendering their liberty.

The objection is then faced, that liberty may be as justly claimed by the non-Catholic as by the Catholic. Of course, replies the *Civiltà*, the only case in which that question can become a practical one for Catholics is where they form the majority. Is it to be supposed that a majority shall be bound, for the sake of a minority, ' to pass a law opening all the pits of hell for its fellow-citizens? . . . . With Catholics the liberty of dissidents cannot be a natural right.' The dissident, when in a minority, cannot 'justly pretend that his right to publish his opinions should menace the most vital interests of a whole nation, much less offend them with impunity.'

The position taken by statesmen, that the Church is not infallible in politics and economy, and that therefore these subjects must be under the control of the State, is first laughed at. It reminds the writer of a musketeer who should say to his general, 'I see that your artillery is of no avail against these Alps; let us open upon them with our rifles.' After this comes the principle. The assertion that politics and economy ought to be under the control of the State rests on one or other of three errors : (1) Politics and economy do not belong to the moral sciences ; or, (2) The moral sciences are not subject to moral laws ; or, (3) The Church is not the authentic exponent of moral law. The first of these errors is refuted by every university in Europe, in all of which politics and economy are classed among the moral sciences. The second is a contradiction in terms. The third is a heresy in every Catholic ear.

It will help to a clear understanding of many expressions which must occur hereafter, if the reader, at this stage, will set before his mind's eye the scope of the three principles here asserted. Phillips, a modern lay doctor, quoted by the humblest polemic and the mighty *Civiltá*, in his seven volumes on ecclesiastical law (*Kirchenrecht*), discusses the relations of Church and State at great length. He shows that the Church is supreme and the State subordinate, in all things that come under the *divine laws*. Holtgreven, a Catholic judge, and an opponent of the Falk laws, explains this clearly : ' To the divine laws, in this sense, belong, not only the ten commandments, but also the canons of the Church, as the Council of Trent shows. The things subject to the divine laws include all such worldly things as are *connected with* morality.' [1]

This much is conceded by the *Civiltá*, that, if danger to the public interests should arise from false teaching of any *material* science, the government may interfere, as it would in a case of adulteration of food. The Church is not infallible in material instruction. *But as to the universal principles of law*, where experiments are not sensible, and demonstration comes only after lustres, perhaps after centuries,—here it is that *governments are impotent* with their intellect, by no means that of wizards; here it is that Catholic society derives inestimable benefit from the infallibility of the Church, which declares the truth, and that in the end cannot fail to be great gain. Had Catholic governments given due reverence to this teaching, instead of giving genuflexions and Jewish bows, European society would not to-day have been beating backward and forward between the daggers of the secret societies and the bayonets of the communists.

We may, perhaps, remark that the parts of Europe most

[1] *Holtgreven*, p. 9.

driven about between bayonets and daggers, at the time when the reverend father wrote, were those in which the experiment of taking principles of law from the infallible Church had been more or less tried for centuries. Those parts of Europe which have since been so driven about are those in which the experiment has been persisted in for the five lustres which have since then elapsed. The article, it will be seen, claims the right to take the teaching of the child out of the hand of the parent, and that of the subject out of the hand of the State.[1] The latter may mix itself up in the matter as to material things, not as to moral. Royal supremacy, in university, college, seminary, or primary school, must not be allowed. It has the twofold evil of setting the authority and responsibility of the parent for his child above that of the priest, and of setting the local authority of the national ruler above the all-embracing authority of the universal one. The State is not only welcome to appear in school, but ought to appear in its subordinate capacity, finding money, secular status, and instruction in *material* things. But in all that part of schooling which may be called education in the higher sense, of a father, a Christian, or a king, the State is not to have a word to say.

It would seem difficult to ask a community to do an action involving a more serious disregard of moral considerations than to find money and power for schools and colleges, and not have a word to say as to the principles taught in them. We are far from ascribing such a disregard of moral considerations to a devout Ultramontane. On the contrary, he is persuaded that the State, in committing its money and authority to the Church, takes not only the highest human guarantee, but a truly divine one, for the protection of every moral interest. The motto of the article is a sentence intimating that, all over Europe, the question of the future must be the establishment of universities canonically instituted.[2]

In order to the *restoration of ideas* now undertaken, as pre-

---

[1] *Civiltà*, vol. i., pp. 25-51.   [2] Ibid.

paring the way for the *restoration of facts*, it was a practical necessity to establish an invariable association between the two ideas of the only Judge of true and false, the only Arbiter of right and wrong, and the one holy Roman Church. This association could not be established so well by any arrangement as by making each school an arena on which every day the authority of both the parent and the State should be—not pranced upon, not even trampled upon, but serenely and devoutly walked over, by what M. Veuillot calls the crushing sandals of the monk.

Another article in the first volume of the *Civiltà* gives such expression to the principles which underlie the whole struggle ever since conducted, that some account of it will do more to put the reader in possession of certain of those principles than formal explanations. It is on the central question of the relations of Church and State; or, as the *Civiltà* puts it, of the separation of Church and State—a phrase which, like almost every other, has a different meaning in its pages from what it has with us. The following headings give an idea of the drift of the article: ' 6. The nation is a part of the Church.' ' 7. The part ought to be subordinate to the whole.' ' 8. Because the Church has authority.' ' 9. The authority of jurisdiction.'[1]

I believe in the holy Catholic Church, in the Apostles' Creed, is thus interpreted : ' I believe that every Catholic individual and *nation* forms a part of the Catholic society, and that only by virtue of its being a part does it partake of the benefit of the whole, through being subordinated to the laws of the whole.' The writer proceeds : 'Now comes the difficulty. Ought the part to be subordinate to the whole? Here the question changes its aspect, and the axiom becomes a problem. But how? Is it possible to doubt that the part is to be subordinate to the whole? the leg to the man, the chemical forces to the vital

[1] Vol. i., p. 647.

ones? to doubt that the present perishable life should give way to the future and immortal?'[1]

On the point of jurisdiction, the writer first unearths 'the serpent,' which is the notion that the Church may judge about sins, virtues, doctrines, rites, and such-like, but must not touch temporal jurisdiction. This serpent he proceeds to kill. First, he solemnly appeals to the faith of the reader. 'Do you believe that the Church is infallible in dogmatic Bulls, at least, unless they are formally rejected by the episcopate?' After this, he resorts to pleasantry: 'Come close to me, and I will tell it in your ear. The Bull of John XXII. condemned John Gianduno and Marsilius of Padua as heretics, because they denied to the Church the right of punishing by corporal pains, and it declared that she could inflict pains even unto death.[2] But I tell you this in secret, solely that you may know what is the doctrine of the Catholic Church, which you profess—doctrine put in practice through very many centuries, down to the last Council (Trent), which fulminated I know not how many penalties, and material ones, even against counts, marquises, princes, and emperors. Woe to us if they should hear us!' Thus jauntily did those who had only just been reinstated by foreign arms treat the neo-Catholic doctrine, or, as it has since been called, the Liberal Catholic one. 'I tell you plainly,' adds the writer, 'that if the Church cannot rule her sons, even in material things, the

[1] Princes are the sons of the Church, armed with the sword for her protection; but not the fathers of the Church. Hence, in ecclesiastical affairs they have no laws to give, but have humbly to expect them from the Church. They have to hear and to believe. They have to obey, and by means of their authority *to make others obey.* Protectors of ecclesiastical liberty, they may not curtail it, else their protection becomes a yoke.—*Phillips*, ii , 561.

[2] Cardinal Tarquini (*Institutiones*, p. 35, ed. 4th), whom Cardinal Manning. in his reply to Mr. Gladstone (p. 94), names as teaching differently on such points, from the earlier Jesuits, Bellarmine and Suarez, quotes this case, saying that the Bull in question 'more particularly attributes to the Church that which is the special property of a perfect society, the power of coercion, even to the use of material force; but Marsilius, who denied this. was on that account condemned as a heretic.' His words are, ' *Quod maxime proprium est societatis perfectæ, jus potestatis coactivæ etiam quoad inferendam vim materialem; Marsilius autem, qui hæc ipsa negabat damnatur eam ob rem ut hæreticus.*'

Church is lost; at least, the Catholic Church. She might survive as that invisible Church which was discovered by Luther among the ruins of the middle ages, and, reconstructed as the *amphitherium* and *palæotherium*, were discovered in the geological strata, and reconstructed by Cuvier.'

Referring to a debate in Turin, the writer continues :—' Considering the great good which Catholic unity would be to the human race ; considering also that any such social unity is impossible without some sacrifice of liberty by the associated parts ; considering further that among nations this sacrifice of liberty consists precisely in subordinating the diversities of legislation in particular States to the laws of *the universal ruler,* Advocate Garbarini had the courage to say that it is the part of the State to subordinate itself to the Church.' Proceeding to show that in Paganism religion was a means to the welfare of the social fabric, and that in Christianity the social fabric is a means to religion, which alone secures the glory of God, the writer thus urges his point : ' Thus, courteous reader, will you clearly see the essential correlation between the religious idea and the political one. And hence will you perceive that it would be impossible, and absurd, for Pagan society not to form a religion for the good of the State, and that it would be the same for the Catholic society not to subordinate the State to the good of religion.'

Addressing kings, the writer solemnly counsels them to bring forth all their codes, and pass them under a careful examination. But the light by which such examination is to be conducted must be that ' of pure Catholicism, to which all other legislation must be subordinated. Restore every article of your code, according to the articles of your creed, not only in what relates to the duties of subjects, but also in what would seem to diminish the rights of rulers. And that the Catholic influence, which modifies codes, may shine in all its fulness, *let it not be ministers or legists, but bishops and the Pontiff, who shall minutely search into your legislation for every anti-Catholic element.*' It is added that it was in this manner that the reforms then taking place in Austria had been inaugurated, and that if they were only carried on until administration, politics, civil life, judicature, and all the departments breathed true Catholic air, the torrent of universal rebellion would be stayed . . . . 'Let the State know that if the priest is the subject of the State, the State is the subject of the Church.'

The theocratic Papal polity might have been almost intentionally framed to contrast with the first principles of the Mosaic theocratic polity. The latter, put in one word, seems to be this: God as the general Father is the great right-holder, and He identifies the rights of every creature with His own, identifying at the same time their welfare with His own glory. Therefore He leaves no creature to the care of a Vicar, no province to any departmental divinity. Every act done for the benefit of our fellow-creatures He reckons as a tribute to Himself. Every infringement of their rights He treats as an offence against Himself. Every man was taught to see, not an abstract principle, but a great Father standing beside the gleaning widow, the supperless hireling, the pauper forced to pawn, and having no second coat,—was taught to hear this common Father saying for these to happier neighbours, 'I am the Lord.' Every man tempted to lie, cheat, steal, oppress, seduce, or strike, saw the same great Father rising up *against* him, and saying, 'I am the Lord.' Every man was taught to hear the voice of the Creator calling to all men, and saying, 'Come, do this man good, and I will bless you for it ;' and to hear the same voice whispering within himself, and saying, 'Go, and do good to one of the least of these little ones, and I will bless thee for it.'

It was of the essence of this theocracy that all who held authority did so by and under a written law in the vulgar tongue. Of this law every father in his own house was made the guardian, and in it he was the responsible instructor of his children. Every prophet professing that he bore a fresh message was to be brought to the test of this written law. Those who ·

were to apply the test were the men of the whole community. Every one who claimed to bear a special commission was bound first to conform to the law, and secondly, to show signs of special divine power. It was a theocracy of direct divine government, not of government by a Vicar; a theocracy of written law, not of arbitrary will styling itself authority; a theocracy of private judgment, not of a veda shut up from the low caste, to be read and interpreted only by the twice-born Brahman. Finally, it was a theocracy in which whatever came from God became its own witness by benefits to God's children not to be mistaken, and obvious to all.

The style of thought which separates what promotes the glory of God from what promotes the welfare of man has no affinity with this system, but flies in the teeth of the Old Testament. It moreover defrauds man of the test which God has given to him for proving all institutions, doctrines, governments, that come in His name. Whatever is found to blight the offspring of God, whether in the individual or the community, bears the mark of being itself unblessed. Whatever has God's blessing in it will leave tokens of His blessing after it. The Father-King who reigned over the old Israel never left child of His to a Vicar—nay, not even for punishment. Woe to him that smote without express command! And of all offences, the one He repelled with the greatest loathing was that of putting forward religion in lieu of righteousness, and making holy office a cloak to dignify unholy acts. Hands that heaped His altars with honours, to cover wrong to His offspring, were of all hands unholiest to Him.

These principles Christ did not annul, but illuminate and perfect—'fulfil.' The godliness that is not profitable for this life is none of His, any more than is that which seeks here its end, its glory, or its gain. He took care that no Church should ever be in a position both to take charge of temporal interests and to decline any judgment of 'the laity.' He laid down a criterion expressly on purpose to enable not only laymen, but common men—fishermen, carpenters, money-changers, centurions, tax-gatherers—to test the pretensions of all who should speak in His name, and to judge whether they were worthy or not to be entrusted with their eternal concerns : ' If therefore ye have not been faithful in the unrighteous mammon, who will commit unto your trust the true riches ? ' A Church taking temporal interests in hand appeals to this test of the temporal mammon, and to that test must she go. The religion of the Bible, Old Testament and New, is pre-eminently a religion of the individual conscience, and therefore of the private judgment. But a natural corollary of a God who governs through a Vicar is that of a conscience kept by another. The doctrine that God governs through a Vicar sets a man between us and our Maker ; the doctrine that our conscience is to be kept by another sets a man between us and our own souls. No longer the object of God's direct government, no longer accountable guardians of our own conscience, the sinews of individual character are cut, and the march of the nation must be less steady,—in time must slacken and even halt.

The statement made in the *Civiltà* as to the guidance under which the reactionary policy in Austria was devised, gives light upon the duties then engrossing nuncios and confessors at the various Courts where Papal influence was powerful. All that appeared to the world was, that at every one of those Courts a cold current of reaction set in and ran strong. The Jesuits took it for a tide, and the bark of St. Peter was to sail cheerily over all the shoals. But the Liberal Catholics were proportionably disquieted as to the prospects of the Church. The first days of Pius IX. had fired them with hope that Rome might yet be fit to face three things of which she was shy—the Bible, History, and Freedom. But the advent of the Jesuits to power caused serious forebodings, which soon began to be realised. To quote the memorable words of Montalembert, ' Who could have thought that the clergy, after crying out for liberty in Belgium, would turn round as they did in 1852, till we found them beating down all our liberties and privileges—in fact, all our ideas—as held in times preceding Napoleon III. ?'[1]

We now find that at the time when the Pontiff was using his clergy to help kings in taking away constitutional rights from their subjects, he was himself preparing to take from the kings what they indeed looked upon as rights, but what he regarded in the light of constitutional concessions, infringing the higher rights of their divinely appointed suzerain. When the Italian government took possession of the *Collegio Romano*, it was found that the Jesuits had left in the great library of the establishment little belonging to the present pontificate. One pamphlet is of some significance. A manuscript note on the title-page proudly tells how his Holiness wished to have it circulated as widely as possible. It also adds that on February 1st, 1853, when the fathers of the *Collegio Romano* stood before his Holiness, he singled out the author, Father Camillo Tarquini, in presence of the other Jesuits and of the Court, and addressed him thus: 'Father Tarquini, I am delighted; bravo! well done! I confirm it, and confirm it with all my heart.'[2] This was an early foretoken of the purple in which Tarquini died. He is the writer to whom Cardinal Manning appeals, as softening the doctrine of Bellarmine and Suarez to a temper fitter for our times. The pamphlet signalised by this display of favour aims at proving the wickedness of kings in subjecting the bulls, briefs, or any acts whatever of the Pope, to a *placet, exequatur*, or other form of royal assent, before recognising them as having the force of law in their States. This is one form of the error of regalism. The tract is published in a Latin version,

[1] Letter quoted in *Unità Cattolica*, March 10th, 1870. *Friedbergh* p. 120.

[2] *Del Regio Placet :* Dissertazione del P. Camillo Tarquini, D.C.D.G. . . . Estratto dagli Annali delle Scienze Religiose, Roma, 1852. Tipografia della Rev. Cam. Apostolica.

The note in manuscript on the title-page is as follows: 'S. S. Pio IX. Volle che presente dissertazione si diffondesse quanto più si potea; e nel dì, 1 Febbrajo, 1853, veduto l'autore dissegli alla presenza della sua corte e degli altri Padri del Collegio Romano. P. Tarquini me rallegro, bravo, bene. Confermo, e confermo di tutta volontà.'

with the *Institutiones* of Tarquini. The aims of the writer have been steadily pursued till, in the third chapter of the Vatican Constitution upon the Church, his end was gained, as far as it could be gained by the action of the Church alone.

Father Tarquini contends that fourteen hundred years of Church history had passed before the so-called kingly right of *placet* took its rise. Certain prelates, indeed, had exercised some such right in their dioceses. The claim on the part of kings to do so is traced to *an association of ideas.* Apparently, he means that, seeing bishops have something to say to laws which were to come into force in their dioceses, the kings took it into their heads that they also should have something to say to such laws as were to come into force in their dominions.

The power of the Pontiff, argues Father Tarquini, is this— What he binds on earth is bound in heaven. But if the king, stepping in, says, To bind implies the force of law, and your acts shall not acquire the force of law without my *placet,* how then? Why, the Pontiff becomes the one really bound. The king refuses to allow the pontifical judgments to take effect of themselves. It is not with him 'said on earth and done in heaven.' His *placet* must intervene.

It is competent, indeed, he admits to the Pontiff, to *grant* a right of *placet;* but such a right, founded on the grace of a Pope, cannot be confounded with one inherent in the crown. We quote the following in full:—' You say that the *placet* is a real right, demanded by justice, and essential to political government. The Church condemns it by a series of judgments, perhaps without parallel in her history, extending from her foundation down to Pius IX. She expressly defines it, with Leo X., Clement VII., Clement XI., and Benedict XIV., as opposed to all justice, as indecent, absurd, rash, scandalous, as insufferable depravity, and worthy of eternal pain. Therefore she punishes it with the greatest of penalties, the anathema.

' In this matter there is no middle course. You must either

lay aside the mask of Catholicism, which no longer becomes you, and boldly avow that the Church has defined good as evil, justice as injustice, an inherent right of the crown as an absurdity and a wrong, done and so in a judgment perpetuated from her foundation to our own day; or you must, on the other hand, confess that you are in an error not to be tolerated.'

Thus it seems that what with a Christian minister would only be a claim to announce the belief and the moral precepts which he found in the Holy Scriptures, becomes with the Roman Pontiff a claim to put his decree on any matter which he deems conducive to the good of ' the Church ' into the form of law, and to set it up without, or in spite of, but anyhow above, the national law, be it republican, royal, or imperial. This boundless pretension—for boundless it is—will often be found gently expressed as the right of the Pontiff *to communicate with the faithful.*

The writer then asks what, from his point of view, would seem to be a natural question. Would kings like the Pope to demand that his *placet* should be required before their laws came into force ?[1] He replies that some of them have so far unlearned ' Christian doctrine as to say that, in case the Pope did so, he would usurp sovereign rights in their States.' But such a proposition is heretical, pronounced to be so by the Holy Office in 1654, with the approbation of Innocent X.[2] By virtue of this, even our children know that the Church presided over and governed by the Vicar of Christ is a kingdom which has the ends of the earth for its bounds. Therefore it belongs to the Vicar of Christ to make laws in all parts of the world for her welfare and for her government.'

---

[1] ' It would be very natural that the Church which makes laws from God Himself should demand of the State that it should make no law for her subjects to which she had not previously given her approbation.'—*Phillips,* ii., 577.

[2] ' In 1644, the Holy Office, in a decree approved by Innocent X., condemned as schismatical and heretical the proposition which asserts that, when the Pontiffs promulge their decrees in places subject to the dominion of other temporal princes, they promulge laws in territories that are not theirs.'—*Civiltá,* Serie VII., vol. vi., p. 292. Tarquini says 1654 (*Inst.,* p. 159), the *Civiltá* 1644.

Father Tarquini then makes a pathetic appeal to princes against persecuting 'your mother' by preventive regulations, which take away her rights and liberties. It is unheard of tyranny! ay, as much as that tyranny would be unheard of which should condemn a private person to perpetual imprisonment, lest he should turn homicide. Furthermore, the claim set up by the State implies that temporal good is more precious than eternal. If this be so, the communists are right.[1]

Drawing towards his conclusion, our author says :—

'The royal *placet* was really a constitution imposed upon the Church by sovereigns. Things found their level, so constitutions are now imposed upon the sovereigns by the people. The pretext for the *placet* was that of having a guarantee for the rights of the crown against the Church. The pretext for the constitution is that of having a guarantee for the rights of the people against the crown. The kings cared not when they saw the spouse of Christ made sorrowful. And Christ turned His face away from the kings when He saw them, in their turn, put to sorrow and used despitefully. [Alluding to the dethronements of 1848, etc.] But not wholly did He turn it away. A touching spectacle was then displayed. The Church, which had been humbled and afflicted by the sovereigns, ran to their defence. She prayed, wept, struggled to avert the storm. And the storm has seemed to calm down. Will the world profit by such lessons? God grant that the religious movement which at the present time we have seen manifesting itself in so many august minds may not be cut short by the flattery of courtiers, whose designs lead to nothing but the ruin of kings, ministers, and nations.'

Here the 'august minds' are evidently the same as those who, in the pages of the *Civiltà*, were called '' the heads of Catholic States.' The *Civiltà* warned them to beware of legists and ministers—Tarquini to beware of courtiers. Liberal Catholics trembled for the consequences to Church and State of Jesuit Court confessors and far-aiming but short-seeing plans. They

---

[1] 'It is impossible that such a power should lie in the right of the State as such ; ... God would in that case have connected with the temporal power in the kingdoms of men an authority capable of destroying the effective action of His own kingdom, which is endued by Himself with the utmost fulness of power. In strong contrast to this, the Church brings with her to kings the *placet* of the Most High King of kings, who has given her the might and the power of legislation.'—*Phillips*, ii., 501.

knew that the devout Jesuit calls upon all to regard the
Papal government as the model for the whole world ; and that
if statesmen and jurists could be replaced by Jesuits at the
various Courts, a combination of plan and an unity of action
might be secured everywhere for a great movement to establish the dominion of Christ in a higher degree than the
Thirty Years' War did in Austria and Bohemia.

The argument that kings have no choice but between Papal
supremacy and communism is as fresh to-day as if it had not
been well worn twenty-five years ago.   The notion often uttered
in France, Italy, Austria, and Germany, that communist centres
are kept up by Jesuit arts and Jesuit subsidies, may be entirely
groundless.   The fact that such a belief is frequently expressed
by Roman Catholics, and hardly ever by Protestants, is a proof
—certainly not that the assertion is true, but—that the political
play of the Society of Jesus is extensively suspected of being
foul, by those who belong to the Church which the Society
rules.   The twin argument, that there is no alternative but to
be either an Ultramontane or a heretic, has at last been driven
home and clinched.

The view taken of constitutions by Father Tarquini, that they
are contracts imposed by those under authority upon those in
authority, carries with it two corollaries,—that constitutions
were submitted to only from want of power to resist, and that
therefore they may be lawfully recalled when the ruler once
more becomes a really free agent.

But there is a point illustrated in this pamphlet, which seems
to enter into the English head more slowly than any other.
We mean the conscientious view of a true Ultramontane as to
what constitutes religious liberty, or violates it.   Englishmen
sometimes not only transfer their own views on this subject to
Ultramontanes, but betray the feeling that they are generous in
doing so.   It is never generous, or even just, to ascribe views
to a man which he religiously condemns.   If the Englishman
will clearly set before his mind the first postulate of the Ultra-

montane, that God has appointed a vicar upon earth, to whom He has committed all power, surely he will see that religious liberty must principally consist in the freedom of that vicar to do all which he conceives it to be in his province to do, and in the freedom of those who receive his commands to carry them out, exactly according to his intentions. If any king or nation limits his freedom to act and command, 'the Pope becomes the one really bound.' The Englishman may say that, on this principle, no guarantee is left for any liberty but that of the Pontiff, or of those who represent authority derived from him. But that is precisely what the Ultramontane does not believe.

On the contrary, he holds that the highest guarantee for all legitimate liberty lies in the complete freedom of the Pontiff. No liberty can be legitimate that consists in exemption, or assumed exemption, from divine authority. And further, the authority of the Vicar of God, being exercised under unfailing guidance, is not liable to commit violations of any right. The Ultramontane is a partisan of religious liberty as warmly and as conscientiously as the Englishman. But they differ totally as to the meaning of the terms. The Englishman does not know how the words used at the Pope's coronation penetrate the heart of a full believer. But the Liberal Catholic in Rome does. It is the Marchese Francesco Nobili Vitelleschi who reminds us of them. And, on the other hand, Professor Massi, in his Life of Pius IX., takes care not to pass them by: '*Know that thou art the father of princes and of kings, and art the governor of the world.*'[1] It is not likely that many would, on paper, still interpret this as meaning father of believers and ruler of the Church. But it is time that men began, even in thinking, to attach a serious and definite sense to terms chosen with prodigious deliberation to express what is claimed, without offending susceptibilities more than is unavoidable.[2]

---

[1] *Frond*, vol. i., p. 16 ; and *Vitelleschi.*

[2] Father Schrader says : 'The Allocution of December 15th, 1856, contains not merely the condemnation of FREEDOM OF WORSHIP, but also the condemnation of unrestricted FREEDOM OF THOUGHT, FREEDOM OF SPEECH, and FREE-

We thus see begun the movement for the restoration of ideas, as preparatory to the restoration of facts. In literature this movement commands the two departments, the scholastic and the popular. In the one, Tarquini represents the Jesuits as leading the colleges and the schools ; in the other, the *Civiltà* represents them as leading the reviews, magazines, journals, and popular books. But, concurrently with this literary restoration of ideas, it was necessary that a mightier propaganda by measures should proceed. Of these, some were to be procured, and some were to be taken. The confessors and nuncios were charged with the measures to be procured ; those to be taken were the direct task of the Curia. Each new measure must have the double value of impelling the movement of ideas, and of clearing the way for more considerable facts. Ranke has traced the course of the 'ecclesiastical restoration,' which was rendered necessary by the damage inflicted on Rome by the Reformation, without being careful to mark the principles or to track the processes by which 'restoration' was effected in Bohemia, Austria, Spain, Italy, and France. That restoration, however, had been real and momentous. A second restoration had taken place after the wreck of the French Revolution, when the Papacy had been smitten by its own sons. It was the pride of the clergy to cite the fact that the rulers of England and Prussia had co-operated in that restoration, as proof that the Papal throne was even in Protestant eyes the central point of order. Now a third restoration was to be effected,—one which would do all that had been left undone by the other two. The Pope's throne was not only to be reared up again in Rome, but was to be gradually

DOM OF THE PRESS.' The small capitals are Schrader's. (*Der Papst und die modernen Ideen*, Heft ii., p. 35.)

Speaking on the twenty-second proposition of the Syllabus, Schrader says : 'We speak without fear of contradiction when we say that the rightful freedom of science—namely, the freedom of seeking the truth and following the truth— has no greater friend or protector than the Pope ; but that the *modern idea* of freedom of science is utterly condemned by the Holy See, because it claims, not only freedom for the truth, but also for error, ay, as the above-quoted brief has it, " shamelessly commends errors as progress " ' (p. 42).

elevated to a spiritual supremacy equal to the highest claimed in former Bulls, and to a temporal supremacy as complete as when Hildebrand triumphed at Canossa.

The first of these restorations had been fought out with the weapons of the Inquisition and the war-plots of the Jesuits. The second had been fought out with the weapons of the Liberal Catholics, borrowed from the Reformation and the Modern State. When the Jesuits had pushed, not too far, but untimely far, they were for the day disowned; not, however, as inimical to the Church, but as hateful to the nations, and as, therefore, lowering the credit of the Church with the outside world. Now had come the moment when the Liberal Catholics, having done their work, were in turn to be disowned; but on other grounds. They were to be cast out as children of the world, infected with principles subversive of the 'kingdom of God,' of that polity in which the priest of God is the king of men, and the affairs of an erring race are unerringly guided by consecrated hands.

CHAPTER IV.

Measures preparatory to the Syllabus.—Changes in Italy since 1846—Progress of Adverse Events—A Commination of Liberties—A Second Assembly of Bishops without Parliamentary Functions—The Curse on Italy—Origin of the phrase 'A Free Church in a Free State'—Projected Universal Monarchy.

BEING notoriously deficient in theological training, Pius IX. was not unnaturally seized with a desire to reduce the rebel nations by raising contested doctrines to the rank of dogmas. When the reactionary movement in politics had attained its full momentum, he called an assembly of bishops, whose splendour, surrounding his throne, might restore to it some of the departed *prestige*. At the same time, summoning the bishops for consultation and for ceremonial purposes, but not at all for parliamentary ones, would be a secure step of progress in the absorption of the power of the collective episcopate into the Papacy. In the midst of two hundred prelates, as we have already seen, he proclaimed the Immaculate Conception, in 1854. As a display of absolute authority in the highest realm, that of dogma, this act did more to advance the proper ideas than an immensity of writing. We have already quoted the assertion that it crushed Gallicanism. But ideas were only stepping-stones to facts. Professor Michelis asserts that even during the gathering of 1854 an attempt was made in some large assembly of bishops to induce them to proclaim Papal infallibility as a Catholic dogma.[1]

The prelates, who, on their way to Rome in 1846, had looked with joy on the spectacle of unity, now found that spectacle slightly blemished. One heretic temple stood in Turin—a proof that after all the extirpations of the Waldenses, a root had still lurked in the ground. This temple had no images, and had the Bible in mother-tongue. It bore outside, in words that any cowherd might read, if he could read at all, a verse of Jeremiah : 'Stand ye in the ways and see, and ask for the old paths, where is the good way, and walk therein, and ye shall find rest for your souls.' And this was not only suffered, but done by the House of Savoy!

As the prelates went south, whispers might reach some of them that in Tuscany the police, now and then, discovered secret bands of Bible-readers, somewhat as in old times the Lollards were unearthed in England. The historical name of Guicciardini was implicated in the offence, and a number of vulgar people. Even at Rome, Luigi Desanctis, parish priest of St. Maria Maddalena, had abandoned as fair prospects as erudition, character, and favour could well give to an ecclesiastic. He had quietly withstood flattering and influential efforts to bring him back. First he had sheltered under the British flag; but, finding that the flag of Savoy really shed upon Italian soil the all but inconceivable right of freedom to worship God, he

[1] *Kurze Geschichte des Vaticanischen Concils,* p. 9.

had taken refuge under it. He was now devoting his clear, keen, learned pen to teaching Italy the religion of Christ as he found it in the New Testament. Even in writing for Italians he found it needful to say that it was only by living in Rome, and by knowing Pope, Cardinals, and Curia, that they could come to a clear understanding of the religion of the city. The great cause of this difficulty he found in the three separate circles ot doctrine in which that religion was wont to be taught, which he called (1) the official, (2) the theological, (3) the real.[1] The official doctrine was that for use with heretics, the doctrine presented by Bossuet and Wiseman ; the theological doctrine was for use with men of culture ; the real doctrine was for practical use among the people. The eloquent Barnabite, Gavazzi, was now thundering against the Papacy. Nay, even the threshold of the Inquisition had been crossed by the ·force of Protestant unity. A priest, avowing heresy, who once had held good preferment, had been seized after the French took the city. At the urgent instance of the Evangelical Alliance, General Baraguay d'Hilliers put on such hard pressure that even in sacred Rome a renegade priest walked out of the palace of the Holy Office a ransomed man.

The confidence that the Virgin would reward her new exaltation by corresponding exaltation of him who had procured it, was often expressed in language picturesque and ardent. But scarcely had the incense of the fresh offering cleared away when premonitory symptoms appeared of the storm rising again. Meantime, many Catholics became anxious when they found the Pope's favourite organ treating even such writers as Bellarmine, Suarez, and St. Thomas Aquinas, as too much inclined to Liberalism. Liverani, in referring to articles of this kind, says that Bellarmine had been 'the author of the Night of St. Bartholomew,' and he thinks that Italian Catholics in the nineteenth century might be allowed to be Liberals up to the standard of Bellarmine and Suarez.

[1] *Roma Papale,* p. 7.

In 1855, Piedmont, sending a force to the Crimea, took her place beside France and England. The next year, at the Congress of Paris, Cavour lifted up his voice among the representatives of Europe, and protested against foreign occupation in Italy. Mexico abolished the external tribunal of the Church, the ecclesiastical court; abolished tithes, offered protection to all of either sex who might choose to forsake their convents, and declared its resolution not to submit its acts to the supreme authority of the Apostolic See. Other nations of South America met the aggressive ecclesiastical movement by asserting the supremacy of civil law, even in matters directly ecclesiastical.[1] Three years later, the same hand which upheld the Pope in Rome took Lombardy from Austria, and gave it to Piedmont, in exchange for Savoy and Nice. Tuscany, Parma, and Modena banished their dukes; the Romagna cast off the Papal yoke; and all these, uniting themselves to Piedmont, formed the kingdom of Italy.

These events were met, on the part of the Vatican, by more stringent denunciations of modern liberties. In the *Civiltá* these were inveighed against under the name of the principles of 1789. Liverani says (p. 160) that the *Civiltá*, in a Catechism of Liberty, hardly left a man the use of air and water. The article so alluded to gives what the writer of it calls a Litany, which ought to be repeated with the refrain, Good Lord, deliver us.[2]

'Liberty of conscience is a perverse opinion diffused by fraudulent endeavours of infidels.

'It is a corrupt fountain, a folly, a poisonous error.

'It is an injury to the Church and the State, vaunted with shameless impudence as becoming to religion.

'It is the liberty of error and the death of the soul.

'It is the abyss, the smoke whereof darkens the sun, and the locusts out of which lay waste the earth.

'The liberty of the press is an evil liberty, never sufficiently execrated or abhorred.

[1] *Allocution of Dec. 15th*, 1856. *Receuil*, p. 382.
[2] *Civiltá*, Serie IV., vol. iv., p. 430.

'It is an extravagance of doctrines, and a portentous monstrosity of errors, at which we are horrified."

To give one specimen in the catechetical form :—

'What think you of those who dare to invoke and to promote this liberty of error?

'Ah, painful thought! That is effrontery, an insulting frowardness, a thing not to be named ; .it is the commission on set purpose of mortal sin, it is the gulping down of poison in hope of an antidote. It is a doctrine false, presumptuous, opposed to the watchful solicitude of the Holy See, outrageous to that See, and fertile in the worst evils for the Christian people.'

It would be incorrect to suppose that these principles exclude all possibility of toleration in fact, though not by right. Toleration may be allowed, but never on principle; never but as the means of avoiding a greater evil. If more harm to the cause of *religion* would result, in any given country, from intolerance, than from toleration, the latter becomes lawful to the prince of the country. Otherwise it cannot be so. Even this qualified admission of a mere *de facto* toleration of heretics was not left uncontested. Priests of the Appolonare in Rome about this time, publicly maintained the thesis that 'it will never be possible to imagine reasons which should induce a Catholic prince to grant liberty of worship to heretics.' They maintained other theses, to the effect that unlimited freedom of worship, and civil rights, granted to heretics, laid the prince open to suspicion of heresy, apostasy, or atheism.[1] This doctrine, cries Liverani, would require the Catholic king of Saxony, with two millions of Protestant subjects, and fifty thousand Catholics, to exterminate the former by means of the latter. It is, he says, putting this alternative—the creed or the stake. Yet this debate was held in presence of the Pope's vicar, Cardinal Patrizi, and was noticed with commendation by the *Civiltá*.

Montalembert proposed that the voting in the Romagna on the question of annexation to Italy should take place under

[1] *Liverani*, p. 163.

the eye of French troops. Liverani, a native of the Romagna, prelate as he was, replied, 'If the French army left, without being replaced by a strong force to guard the lives of the clergy, at the end of a week all the priests and friars would be exterminated, so wild and savage is the public indignation against the government of these last years' (p. 46).

On the 26th of March, 1860, in the famous and terrible Letters Apostolic *Cum Catholica*, all the actors and abettors of the territorial changes were placed under the greater excommunication. The Pope[1] expressly decreed that no hand but his own, or that of his successors, should have the power of releasing any one of the countless offenders from the ban, except in the article of death. He proceeds on what seems the fair principle that the dominion of the Pontiff, though in its own nature temporal, takes on a spiritual character because of its spiritual design, as giving to the Head of the whole Church a position independent of any one nation. Therefore, robbing him of it becomes a spiritual offence. If he is the representative of God upon earth, it is hard to see how rebellion against him can fail of being a spiritual offence. If he is not the representative of God upon earth, he has altogether misconceived his own position, and, like any other ruler, may be judged by his merits, not by his pretensions.

Before the publication of the Pope's Speeches we were exposed to manifold interpretations of the spiritual import of this anathema. It was even possible that we might find letters in the *Times* assuring us that the Church never curses. But on the 23rd of June, 1871, Pius IX. uttered language which put his view of the spiritual import of his own action beyond cavil. He had the words afterwards reprinted, with the explanation that the allusion to Peter referred to the death of Ananias and Sapphira. 'True,' said the Pontiff, 'I cannot, like St. Peter, hurl certain thunders which turn bodies to ashes ; nevertheless, I can hurl thunders which turn souls to

[1] *Receuil*, p. 400.

ashes. And I have done it by excommunicating all those who perpetrated the sacrilegious spoliation, or had a hand in it.'[1]

But if to the spiritual eye of Pio Nono his curse had strewn Italy with the ashes of millions of blasted souls, his Bulls were, in a temporal point of view, as powerless as his dogmas. In the autumn of 1860, the Pontiff saw Umbria and the Marches wrested from him by the new kingdom, to which also the whole of the Neapolitan territory was added by Garibaldi. After this, Europe grew impatient of the French occupation of Italy, and that last stay of his temporal power became painfully insecure.

The Parliament in Turin proclaimed that Rome was the capital of Italy; and now we have to note the birth of one of those phrases which, becoming watchwords, grow into appreciable forces in history. Cavour, in a speech, alluding to Montalembert, said great authorities had shown that liberty might turn to the profit even of the Church. Montalembert addressed to him a reply, in October 1860, in which he made use of the words, 'A free Church in a free State.' Five months later, when the Turin Parliament set up the claim to Rome, Cavour used the same phrase. Montalembert, with literary jealousy, publicly claimed it: 'You have done me the unexpected honour of using the formula I employed in writing to you a few months ago.' And, doubly to secure his patent right, as late as August 1863, in a Catholic Congress at Malines, he declared that it was by the example of Belgium that he had been taught a formula that had now become famous, 'which has been stolen from us by a great offender.' He printed his address under the title, 'A Free Church in a Free State.'[2]

The French father of the phrase lived to write what showed that he had employed it without having defined its terms in

---

[1] *Discorsi*, vol. i., p. 158.

[2] See the whole narrative in *Unità Cattolica*, March 17th, 1870. Also Mrs. Oliphant's Life of Montalembert.

his own mind. Had its Italian foster-father, who repeated it in death, lived to govern with it, he would have learned, in the school of action, to select some one of the many interpretations which it invites, or else to discard it as a formula, applicable, indeed, to a Church proper, and a State proper, but incapable of application to a mixed institution like Romanism, which, however much of a Church, is still more of a State.

The loss of Rome, to which political symptoms now pointed as impending, was a calamity to be warded off by all the weapons of the Papacy, sacred and profane. A great assembly of prelates was projected, to surpass in splendour even that of 1854. It was to be equally well guarded against any parliamentary character. In June 1862 three hundred bishops from all parts of the world were actually collected around their chief. The prelates, in coming up to the city of their solemnities, had changes to bewail. Could this be the Italy which in 1846 offered such a spectacle of Catholic power, such a scene of Catholic unity? The frontiers of the Papal territories had fallen in. No faithful Bourbon in Naples now! The Bible Society dared to put up its name close by the palace of him whom the voice which some of the bishops called the voice of God among men had described, not in a passing speech, but in a consistorial allocution, as 'that king who, intent upon promoting the true and solid happiness of his people, shines with such religion and piety, that he might be taken as an example by his subjects.' There were no Protestants now in Tuscan prisons; they had emerged into odious little conventicles! Piedmont had relentlessly protected religious liberty, in the heretical sense—that sense which violates Catholic unity by allowing men to worship God otherwise than under the direction of the Pope. What was most inscrutable of all, Providence had seemed to favour Piedmont. The flag which they saw in 1854, waving with the cross of Savoy in Italian sunlight over a temple of heretics, now waved over the tomb of Ambrose and of Hildebrand; ay, over the holy city of Loretto. No Hapsburg now in Florence. And that faithful Francis Joseph, whose pious intentions to do away with restrictions long imposed by his house on the liberty of the Church, were announced by the Pope with much feeling, in the same consistory where he put a wreath round the brow of Ferdinand of Naples; Francis Joseph, whom the *Civiltà* had set forth as the example of a monarch revising his code, not by the counsel of jurists or statesmen, but by that of priests; even he could no more guard Catholic unity around the Cathedral of Milan. Shops under its shadow were vending heretical books, not to speak of Bibles.[1] Thousands of the Italian clergy had declared for a surrender of the temporal power and a reform of the Church.

The ceremonies during this assembly displayed a gorgeous pomp, which even Rome, accustomed since the days of the Emperors to government by spectacle, was fain to recognise as an effort, and a success in its kind, worthy of the historical stake in dispute. The ostensible object was the canonisation of certain Japanese martyrs; but the real anxiety of the moment was so absorbing that the new constellation in the heavens seemed to rise only to rule and decide questions pending as to boundary lines on the earth.

In these turbulent and pitiless times, said the Pope, when the Church is pierced with so many wounds; when her rights, liberties, and doctrines are so miserably violated, especially in Italy, 'we urgently desire to have new patrons in the presence of God,' by whose prevailing prayers the Church, buffeted with such a horrible tempest, as well as civil society, may obtain

---

[1] The allocution referred to, *Quibus Quantisque* of April 20th, 1849, was delivered only ten days before Ferdinand invaded the Roman States to restore Pius IX. (*Recueil*, p. 228). Perhaps not many in England are aware that under Ferdinand it was a punishable offence to read Dante. A professor himself a priest, in speaking to me of this fact, added that students were often registered with the police as hatters, painters, or anything to conceal the fact that they were students, that line of life not being viewed with favour by the police.

the much-longed-for repose.[1]　The aid of the new patrons was that to which faith and hope pathetically turned, in the concluding prayer put up on Whit-Sunday by the Pontiff: 'Regard Thy Church, now afflicted with such calamities: take not away Thy mercy from us; but for the sake of these Thy saints, and through their merits, cause Thy Church,' etc., etc.[2]

Besides the influence to be exerted by the exalted Japanese on behalf of the temporal sovereignty, valuable results might attend a solemn declaration from the episcopate of the whole world.　This would at all events silence priests who had dared to think amiss, and would affect not only the calculations of statesmen, but also the complexion of public opinion.　The faith of Romanists in a display is, to all who have been trained not to take an impression for a reason, absolutely incomprehensible. Lamartine, in relating the perplexities of Mirabeau when the gusts of the Revolution had begun to appal even him, exactly pictures what is the outcome of their sensuous training.　'He would save the monarchy by a royal proclamation and a ceremony to make the king popular.'

A declaration was made by the assembled bishops with all possible gravity and force.　Its purport was suggested with not less gravity and force by the Pope himself in his allocution *Maxima Quidem*, addressed to the congregated hierarchy on the 9th of June.　The language chosen by Pope and prelates was the strongest to be found.　They were not content with pledging themselves to the temporal dominion as a good, useful, helpful, or urgently desirable thing.　Staking the future for the present, as well as the spiritual for the temporal, they declared that it was 'necessary' in order to the exercise of the full pontifical authority over the whole Church.　If this is so, there has been no proper exercise of authority over the whole Church since

[1] Schrader, *Pius IX., als Papst und als König*, p. 21. Iccirco summopere optamus novos apud Deum habere patronos, qui in tanto rerum discrimine validissimis suis precibus impetrent ut, tam horribili discussa malorum procella optatissimam Catholica Ecclesia et Civilis Societas assequatur pacem.

[2] *Papst und König*, p. 23.

1870, nor can there be any till the Pope again finds some few hundred thousand of Italians calling him king. If it is not so, the collective hierarchy, and the Pope with them, erred in setting forth a doctrine, touching the Head of the Church, for the guidance of all mankind. The Pope himself not only said that the temporal power was necessary, but that it had been given by a matchless counsel of Providence. The reason he gives for its necessity is the stock one, that the Pope may not be a dependent of any prince, as if he had not been the helpless dependent of Napoleon III. The bishops, forgetting both this dependence and the sanguinary measures by which the temporal power was upheld, actually used such words as ' noble, tranquil, and genial liberty.'[1]

Besides their testimony to the necessity of the temporal power, the bishops put on record words well adapted to prepare the way for the dogma of Papal infallibility—words often afterwards recalled to those of them who opposed that dogma in 1870. ' Thou art to us the teacher of sound doctrine, thou the centre of unity, thou the quenchless light of the nations, set up by divine wisdom. Thou art the rock, and the foundation of the Church herself, against which the gates of hell shall not prevail. When thou speakest, we hear Peter; when thou dost decree, we yield obedience to Christ.'[2]

But the new saints of 1862 did not turn the tide any more than the ' Immaculate' of 1854 had done. Italy held together, though Cavour was gone. The effort of the two Catholic emperors to secure Mexico for the Church, by placing a monarch of approved principles on the throne, ended in a

---

[1] *Civiltá Cattolica*, Serie V., vol. ii., p. 721. Their words are : ' In nobili, tranquilla, et alma libertate catholicam fidem tueri,' etc.

Monsignor Nardi proudly referred Mamiani, in the summer of 1869, to the folio volumes in which 835 bishops had inscribed their adhesion to the necessity of the temporal power. (*Stimmen, Neue Folge*, v., p. 153.)

[2] *Civiltá*, Serie V., vol. ii., pp. 719, 723. ' Tu populis lumen indeficiens. . . . Tu Petra es, et ipsius ecclesiæ fundamentum . . . . Te loquente, Petrum audimus, Te decernente, Christo obtemperamus.' The text even of the Vulgate is changed in the words, Tu Petra es.

tragic failure.   The grief felt everywhere at the fate of Maximilian of Hapsburg was intensified for Pius IX., because, as it
is expressed by Professor Massi, the promises made to the Pope
by Maximilian, when he came to Rome before taking the reins
of empire, 'were to remain void.'[1]   Finally, in 1864, the Convention of September brought home to the Pope the fact that,
unless the Virgin should work a miracle for him, he was to
be abandoned by the foreign auxiliaries whose presence he
hated, but the terror of whom was the only shade in which he
could rest.   Perhaps he remembered how soon after the foreign
Emperor had held the Pope's bridle, the Italian Lambert called
him ' My Lord,' as he would have done to any other baron,
and drove him to hard straits.

It was in this position of affairs that the seers of the Vatican
beheld all human institutions as if reduced by a cataclysm to a
dark and roaring chaos.   And on their principles chaos it was.
Not only had kings and lawgivers withdrawn themselves from
under the authority of the supreme tribunal, not only had
civil courts been withdrawn from under the authority of the
external tribunal, but almost all governments had ceased to
enforce by law the attendance of their subjects on the internal tribunal of the Church which they thus degraded to
the level of a voluntary confessional.   In each of the three
circles of all-embracing authority, therefore, order was now
disrupted, and chaos had broken in.   The seer could see
but one remedy.   Society must be RECONSTRUCTED, and that
upon the basis of one world-wide. monarchy.   This monarchy
must rest on divine authority, and consequently must have
power to define the limits, to balance the claims, and to control the exercise of all power civil and ecclesiastical.   The
susceptible Pius IX. was by these seers represented, to himself
and to his admirers, as specially raised up to carry out the
mission of such a reconstruction.   Not to speak of the many
utterances of these views in his accredited organs of the press,

[1] *Life of Pius IX.* Frond, vol. i., p. 102.

the preface to the first volume of his own speeches says:—
' The work of the great Pontiff is to settle anew and reconstitute the close union between civil and religious society. He
will replace the social constitution on its divine bases, over-
turned by the revolution. . . . . He will redress social revolution by social reconstruction.' [1]

It is but slowly that minds accustomed to judge by ordinary
standards learn to attach a precise meaning to such expressions
as the above, in the language of the Vatican. Even after
having learned how definite is the meaning, we do not soon
begin to associate ideas of deliberate plan and serious expectation with what would seem to be only dreams of the cloister.
We therefore give a few clear sentences from *Il Genio
Cattolico*, a publication praised by the authoritative *Unità
Cattolica*. [2] It describes the true ideal of the Papacy as being
' an immense variety of languages, traditions, legislations,
letters, commerce, institutions, and alliances, under the moral
and pacific empire of a single Father, who, with the sceptre of
the word, upholds the equilibrium of the world. The Papacy is
not, as German jurists call it, a State within the State, but is a
cosmopolitan authority, the moderator of all States, the supreme
and universal standard of law and justice. It is a world-wide
monarchy, from which all other monarchies that would call
themselves Christian derive *life, order, and equilibrium.*'

Coupling this distinct conception of the appointed place of
the Papacy in the human commonwealth with the equally distinct
conviction that modern society is in ruins, the writer proceeds :
' What is the remedy ? The recognition of a common father,
who shall teach subjects to obey as sons, and sovereigns to
rule as fathers ; a *supreme judge, to declare and give sanctions to
the rights* of the one and the other. Without this, how can the
want of balance in the conflicting forces be redressed ?'

[1] *Discorsi*, vol. i., p. 23.
[2] Il Genio Cattolico Periodico Religioso—Scientifico, Litterario, Politico di
Reggio Nell' Emilia, 1873.

The ambiguity which might be found here by the uninitiated is not designed by the writer. To him such terms as ' teach ' and 'sceptre of the word' do not convey the idea of employing only moral force. Indeed, the expression ' the power of the word' of any supreme judge would not convey that idea. On the contrary, our author quotes the proposal of Campanella, that a senate should sit in Rome, consisting of representatives of all Catholic princes, with the Pope as head. This senate should decide all international questions of State, should compose differences between Catholic princes, and should determine upon ' war against infidels and heretics.' All would be compelled to take arms against any one who should resist its decisions. ' In such a senate consists the unity and safety of Christianity, and the glory of the Papacy, as well as the security of all the princes, who would not be disturbed by Catholics while making war on infidels, and thus Christian enterprises would have a happy issue; but otherwise the princes run manifest risk of losing what they now possess.'

With views thus radical and all-comprehending did the Court of Pius IX. proceed to build up, after a very ancient ideal, an empire over all peoples, nations, and languages, the test of which should be acceptance of the religious symbol set up by the autocrat. In the projected reconstruction the *ultimate end*, the restoration of facts, would always include these cardinal points. Every man and every woman in Christendom, and, by a due extension of 'the kingdom of God,' every man and every woman living, must be bound by law to appear, at the least annually, in the internal tribunal of the Church, the confessional. In order to this, every civil magistrate must be set in obvious and in practical subordination to the ecclesiastical magistrate or bishop, by the subjection of the civil court to the external tribunal of the Church, the ecclesiastical court. In order to this, every king or lawgiver must be set also in obvious and in practical subordination to the supreme tribunal of the Church, the Pope, by a restored state of international law, giving to the

Pontiff, or, to speak accurately, recognising in the Pontiff what God had given to him, full power to deliver sentence as supreme judge upon the rights of all kings, and upon the merits of every law.

We, for the sake of clearness, say three tribunals, though technically they are only two, the Pope being in both supreme. Whether the subject enters by the *foro externo* or by the *foro interno*, by the ecclesiastical court or by the confessional, both in the ultimate instance conduct him to the one bar, that of the Judge of judges. The supreme tribunal is he, in all causes not purely material, in all causes whereinto enters any moral or religious consideration. Protestants would seem generally to imagine that the ecclesiastical court is a higher tribunal than the confessional. Not so. When a conflict arises between the sentence of the external tribunal and that of the internal, the suitor at the bar of God's kingdom is bound by the judgment of the internal tribunal! [1]

In Carleton's *Traits and Stories of the Irish Peasantry*, where the only symbol of any tribunal is a rickety chair, standing on an earthen floor full of holes, the priest of God has no sooner put on robe and stole than 'the tribunal' is as truly constituted as when in the palace of Charles V. sat Domenico Soto with the imperial penitent kneeling before him, and said, 'So far you

---

[1] This is briefly and well put in the *Acta Sanctæ Sedis* (V., 146), where an article of the *Times* on the bull of convocation of the Vatican Council is belaboured through twelve pages of double-column Latin. That journal had the audacity to set up conscience against Pope, and to name Luther. 'What do you understand by conscience? for it is solemnly held by Catholics that we may not and cannot act contrary to conscience. Indeed, we confess that, in point of fact, we may be bound to act even against the sentence pronounced by an ecclesiastical authority, seeing that the external tribunal, as we say, does not always concur with the internal tribunal, and whenever the internal tribunal is in opposition to the external tribunal, we are bound to follow the internal. On this point consult our Catholic authors when they treat of moral theology. Immo fatemur, posse in re facti contingere, ut agere teneamur contra ipsam latam auctoritatis ecclesiasticæ sententiam ; quandoquidem forum externum, ut loqui solemus, non semper cohæret cum foro interno : et quoties forum internum in oppositione sit cum foro externo, primum sequi tenemur. De qua re consulendi sunt auctores nostri Catholici de morali theologia agentes.'

have confessed the sins of Charles, now confess those of the Emperor.' In that tribunal has the peasant bride to learn, and has the Queen to learn, that not the husband is the head of the woman, but the priest of God. In that tribunal has the shoeless Connaught child and has the imperial prince to learn that not the parents are the head of the children, but the priest of God. In that tribunal has the debtor and has the creditor, the executor and the legatee to learn that not the law of the civil bench obliges, but the law pronounced by the priest of God. In that tribunal have all these to learn that not even the law which falls from the ecclesiastical judge in the external tribunal is to be taken, but that which in the internal tribunal, in holy secrecy, between the conscience alone and the judge alone, falls with full force of binding and of loosing from the lips of the priest of God. So, proceeding outward but, in this step, not upward, in the other, the external tribunal, has every citizen to learn, and every public servant, that not the magistrate is the head of the town, and not the chief magistrate is the head of the city, but that the bishop is head of both one and the other, for he is the head of the priests of God. Finally, proceeding upward—and here it may be either in the holy secrecy of the inward or in the qualified and potential publicity of the outward tribunal—at the supreme bar have the princes, the governors and captains, the judges, the treasurers, the counsellors, the sheriffs, and all the rulers of the provinces, to learn that not the president, not the grand duke, not the king, not the emperor, is the head of the nation, but the thrice-crowned King of kings, the Great High Priest of God.

This kingdom, it is held, with some stretching of the facts, did in the Ages of Faith prevail, and it is to be restored.

The restoration of facts, could not be effected without a foregoing restoration of the idea of Hildebrand. Constantine had founded a State Church. Leo III., with Charlemagne, had founded what Mr. Bryce accurately describes as a Catholic State, with the Pope as spiritual and the Emperor as temporal head. Cardinal Manning points out that in this Mr. Bryce makes the Holy Roman Empire a two-headed monster.[1] Nevertheless Mr. Bryce gives the true human history, though doubtless Cardinal Manning, following Boniface VIII., gives the correct Papal doctrine. According to that doctrine, the dualism of a double-headed State amounted to a sort of Manicheism. History, which is guilty of tainting many with one heresy or another, must bear the fault of Mr. Bryce's Manicheism. But Hildebrand would abolish all dualism. The whole world must have one head. No matter what the number of kings to whom he may be lord paramount, they must hold the sword under his sword, the sceptre under his crosier. Constantine's idea of a State Church had its merit of unity, but it was unity by perversion of rights. The true idea was that of a Church State, embracing the whole world, and placing all mankind as one fold under one shepherd. This true idea was to be restored.

We shall, in its place, be taught how we err in calling power over temporal affairs temporal power. More accurately does Cardinal Manning speak of 'the supreme judicial power of the Church in temporal things.'[2] He speaks of the time when 'the civil society of man became subject to the spiritual direction of the Church,' speaks of the State as having become 'subject to the divine law, of which the Roman Pontiff was the supreme expositor and executive.'[3] He speaks of 'the indirect spiritual power of the Church over the temporal State,'[4] thus showing the error of the notion that spiritual power means only power over spiritual affairs. He speaks of 'the Christian jurisprudence in which the Roman Pontiff was recognised as the Supreme Judge of Princes and People, with a twofold coercion, spiritual by his own authority, and temporal by the secular arm.'[5]

The turn of phraseology in the last sentence is probably not undesigned. Had it been employed by a Protestant, Ultramontanes, *if writing in Italy*, would have cried out, Ignorance and

[1] *Vatican Decrees*, p. 67.   [2] Ibid., p. 82.   [3] Ibid., 83.   [4] Ibid.   [5] Ibid., 84.

inaccuracy! Does the Cardinal mean that the authority whereby
the Pope through the secular arm applies temporal coercion is
not his own authority? No, assuredly. Yet he leaves us in a
position to slip into some such idea. In such coercion as that
of which he speaks it is not that the secular power acts of its
own authority, but that it acts with its own arm, but with the
Pope's authority. The interesting doctrine of the Brahman as
sprung from the Creator's head, and the King-caste as sprung
from His arm, reappears in the Papal system, in which the
priest anointed on the head and the prince anointed on the arm
symbolize respectively the authority that gives law and the
force that carries it out. But Cardinal Manning's definition of
Christian jurisprudence as that wherein the Pope is recognised
as Supreme Judge of Prince and People is not only strict
but it also explains a whole set of terms,—*Christian* government, *Christian* law, *Christian* order, *Christian* civilisation, and
so forth.

'In the Pontiff meet, as in an apex,' says the *Civiltá*, incidentally, in
arguing that the Pope cannot be the subject of the king, 'both the powers
(temporal and spiritual), and that because he is the Vicar of Christ, who
is not only the eternal Priest, but is also King of kings and Lord of
lords. . . . This manifestly springs out of the idea of a sole supreme head
in ordering the social life of men. Not otherwise can be rightly understood the order of the world, the wisdom of the divine plan, or the
concord and unity of movement in human life. If then the Pontiff, in
consequence of his high dignity, is at the summit of both the powers, how
can he, without a contradiction of ideas, be conceived of as a subject of
one of them? (VIII., i., 664) . . . What is the reason of the immunity
which in a State is enjoyed by the ministers of a foreign Court? It is
simply that they publicly represent an independent sovereign or people.
This being so, what must be said of him who is not merely in some sense
or other the representative, but is in strict propriety of language the
Vicar of Christ, a sovereign, not only independent of every terrestrial
sovereignty, but having over each and all of them a veritable dominion?
. . . Certainly, if we do not mean to say that the prince, though he may
be a Catholic, does not belong to the fold of Christ, we must admit that
in the words, "Feed my sheep," spoken to Peter, is included authority
even over him, *in all his deeds wherein he acts morally*, which assuredly
are those wherein he exercises his political power. With regard to these,

moreover, the Pope has power to bind and to loose, in other words, to command and prohibit' (p. 600).

' The Pontiff is by God set in an absolute manner at the summit of all sovereignty as such. Whatsoever thou shalt bind on earth shall be bound in heaven, and whatsoever thou shalt loose on earth shall be loosed in heaven. These words admit of no exceptions whatever, and express a jurisdiction universal and absolute. It comprehends everything, *quod-cumque*' (p. 658).

It was obvious that to effect in Europe such a restoration as these claims implied, a lengthened preparation of ideas must go before the restoration of facts ; and that restoration of ideas it was which we now see undertaken.

In the process of restoration, the first step was to settle for ever the relative standing of Church and State, or, in esoteric language, of the Christian society and civil society. In determining their respective positions, all depended on a clear conception of the principle that the Church constitutes a *perfect society*. The full scope of this formula we shall not here attempt to unfold, but the reader will do well to keep its terms in view. The fact that the ends of this perfect society are eternal, and that those of civil society are temporal, is in itself sufficient proof of the higher rank of the former. As the priest is the head of the perfect society, framed for eternal ends, and guided by laws immediately inspired from heaven, while the prince is only head of the civil society, framed for temporal ends, and guided by laws evolved by human counsel, the priest is manifestly above the prince.[1] And as the Church of Rome is the mother and mistress of all Churches, and the Roman Pontiff is

---

[1] Phillips proves—1. That the State cannot be above the Church; 2. They cannot be equal—that ' a glance at the distinction between spiritual and temporal power shows the impossibility of equality. The Church is the kingdom of Christ, founded immediately by God, all-comprehending, resting upon unalterable laws, and having for its end eternal salvation; but States are separate and single human kingdoms, existing for the end of earthly welfare. How can the kingdom founded by man be co-ordinate [he means equal] with the divine one; that which is limited by time and space with the all-comprehending one; laws daily changing with the eternal ones; the end of earthly welfare with that of blessedness in glory with Christ ? Yes, even if in opposition to the truth it were assumed that every human authority had its power immediately from God, even then the spiritual power should rank high above the temporal, on account

the source of all priestly authority, in him meet all the powers belonging to the representative of God upon earth, all powers necessary to control the laws, the literature, and institutions of any civil society, whether it be a nation, an association, or a family.

Monsignor Liverani says (p. 158), 'The perfect society, according to the *Civiltá Cattolica,* extends from Aquapendente to Terracina (*i.e.,* over the States of the Church); the imperfect extends over Europe, Asia, Africa, and America, which form the exception.' This may not be very unfair in a practical sense. But the Jesuit doctrine is, in theory, more guarded. The State also is acknowledged to be a perfect society *in its order ;* but as the order is inferior, it cannot be supreme, or equal, but must be subordinate. Having now glanced at some preparatory steps, we are ready to consider the *Magna Charta of Reconstruction.*

CHAPTER V.

The Syllabus of Errors, December 8th, 1864—Character of the Propositions condemned—Disabilities of the State—Powers of the Church.

TO ordinary readers the Syllabus would rather appear to be a destructive instrument than a constructive one. Its authorised expounders, however, with remarkable unanimity, treat it

of its catholicity, on account of its eternal laws, and especially on account of its end.'—*Phillips,* ii., 617.

¹ Since Jesus of Nazareth, . . . the anointing of princes is changed from the head to the *arm;* but the sacramental anointing is still maintained upon the *head* of the bishop, because he, in his episcopal office, represents the person of the Head. There is, however, a distinction between the anointing of the bishop and of the prince, because the head of the bishop is anointed with the ointment, but the arm of the prince is rubbed with oil, that it may be shown what a difference exists between the authority of the bishop and the power of the prince.'—*Phillips,* ii., 621,—quoting Bennetti's *Priv. S. Petri Vindiciæ.*

'Now, here are two things to be noted. First, that the emperor holds an office of human creation,—the Pontiff an office of divine creation. Secondly, that the office of divine creation is for a higher end than the office which is of human origin.'—*Cardinal Manning,* ' *Vatican Decrees,*' p. 68.

as the foundation for the enduring fabric of reconstructed society. Its form accounts for the first impression on the part of the outside world. It is a series of *condemned* propositions, drawn from official and authoritative utterances of Pius IX.—a syllabus or collection of errors, condemned in judgments pronounced by him as supreme judge of Christendom. These, taken collectively, form a politico-ecclesiastical system. The propositions expressed in the Syllabus, however, are not those which the Pontiff affirms, but those which he reprobates. This form is natural to the habit of appealing more to antipathies than to attachments. But it obscures the meaning if it does not hide it from untrained readers. Such find, for instance, proposition 42, 'In case of a conflict between the two powers (civil and ecclesiastical), the civil law prevails,' and think it mild, forgetting that it is the proposition anathematised, and that the one approved is the counter-proposition, namely, 'In case of a conflict between the laws of the two powers, the civil law does not prevail.' Even this is not all that is meant, but, 'the ecclesiastical law does prevail.'

The eighty propositions range over most subjects. As all stand under the head of *condemned errors*, each proposition is, logically, to be read with the prefix, 'We reprove and condemn the following proposition.' Some of these sentences express the beliefs of infidels, and some those of all Christians but Romanists ; some the crudest notions of socialists, and some the fundamental principles of free States, or the maxims of all thriving communities; some the crotchets of obscure theorists in philosophy and ethics, and some the postulates of all free science. These heterogeneous beliefs and disbeliefs are strung together and delivered over, before the universe, to eternal anathema.

Passing from abstract to concrete, embodiments of evil are condemned, whether the body is a Church, a Bible Society, a Freemasons' lodge, a pack of communists, or even such clandestine gangs as were known in Christendom only to the territory of the Pope and his favourite Italian princes.

Perhaps the eventual importance of this manifesto was, at the time, exaggerated at the Vatican, and is exaggerated even yet. The Pope still calls it 'the only anchor of salvation,'—of course meaning for society, not for the soul. In the introduction to his Speeches it is called, with much expansion, 'The *Magna Charta* of Social Reconstruction.' Even in November 1876 the voice of the Vatican in the *Civiltá Cattolica* calls it 'The Code of Christian Civilisation.'[1] 'In this century,' says the *Genio Cattolico*, already quoted, 'rises up the sublime and gigantic figure of Pius IX., another Hildebrand. He is charged by divine Providence with the erection in our day of a new edifice upon the *débris* of the religious and political revolution, as in former times Gregory VII. was commissioned to reconstruct a similar edifice upon the scattered remains of tyranny. Gregory had his Dicta; Pius IX. has his Syllabus.'

If there is exaggeration here, it lies in the calculation of effects, not in the estimate of intentions. The Syllabus was no less than a deliberate and resolute attempt to change the face of the nations by setting up a single central authority, on which all other authority should depend.   The two acknowledged models of Pius IX. are, first, Hildebrand, the model of polity, as the assailant of Constantine's ideal of a State Church, and the founder of the counter ideal of the whole world as one Church State ; and, secondly, Ghislieri, or Pius V., the model of personal action, as the inquisitor Pope saint.

The *Civiltá Cattolica* has never ceased to glorify the Syllabus. A periodical, expressly devoted to expounding and commending it to the Germans, and making it the basis of a new social condition in that country, was commenced at a Jesuit monastery near Bonn, under the title of *Stimmen aus Maria Laach*. Catholic journals spoke of the universal scope and pregnant consequences of the Syllabus in terms at which men of the world were more inclined to smile than to take warning. The views taken of the document by learned Catholics not of the Ultra-

[1] P. 456.

montane school are briefly put by Michelis : 'Constitutional freedom, equality before the law, liberty of the press, all the foundations of modern civilisation, were all at once pronounced to be hostile to the Catholic faith.'[1]   Hints were not wanting that it might introduce a conflict which would rage through centuries, and perhaps leave nothing standing but the Church. Still, for the time, politicians were rather annoyed than alarmed, and perhaps no Protestant statesman thought the matter serious enough to feel even annoyance.

Protestant statesmen were still somewhat in the state of mind expressed by Ranke : 'What is there that can now make the history of the Papacy interesting and important to us ? Not its peculiar relation to us, which can no longer affect us in any material point ; nor the anxiety or dread which it can inspire. The times in which we had anything to fear are over; we are conscious of our perfect security. The Papacy can inspire us with no other interest than what arises from its historical development and its former influence.' This prognostic, the shortsightedness of which the Germans have been painfully taught, obviously sprang out of a confusion of ideas, expressed immediately afterwards, where Ranke identifies changing professions and claims diplomatically presented with fixed maxims, with objects and claims founded on cherished dogma, and felt to be inalienable. As to the Papacy, Ranke says, 'Complete metamorphoses have taken place in its maxims, objects, and claims.'[2]

In contrast with the indifference founded on this supposed change was the view of the *Civiltá* in surveying the events of 1864. The year had been, according to it, one marked by that silent preparation of ideas which brings around great

---

[1] *Kurze Geschichte*, p. 10. It will be seen that here, as in the *Civiltá*, the meaning of civilisation is concrete, the civil system.

[2] *History of Popes*, Engl. tran., 2nd ed., p. 19. The learned author, forty years after he wrote the above, in publishing his sixth edition, referring to these words, says that they expressed the view of the epoch, 'but I cannot conceal from myself that a new epoch of the Papacy has commenced.'

events. To the unobserving this preparation was unseen; but the process was going on and the issue certain. Casting a glance around the world, the *Civiltà* showed that everywhere what it calls the revolution, what we call representative government, was becoming ruinous, and the old Catholic ideal of government regaining its place in the mind of the thoughtful. In Belgium, it had come to that pass that an important paper declared that the tyranny of a majority was worse than that of an autocrat. By a manifest Providence, that immense Babylon, the United States, founded on the principles of the revolution, was broken up and undone. The new Mexican empire had all the more promise of stability, as it would retain, at least in part, Catholic principles.

This historical article proceeded to say that the greatest merit of the past year lay

'In the highly important pontifical documents with which it had been so solemnly closed. The Encyclical of his Holiness Pius IX. of December 8th, and the Syllabus accompanying it, speak clearly enough of themselves, and need not our comments. Those exceedingly grave utterances of pontifical wisdom and fortitude are already perused in every tongue spoken by Catholics, that is, by the civilised world. Nor do Catholics alone read them; even Liberals do so too. And already we begin to hear a distant echo of the fear and wrath felt by the Liberals. They, who themselves change moment by moment, cannot understand that the Church should never change, in her principles or in her doctrine. They, who would conciliate everything—and, when they can do no more, conciliate fact with law—by the stupid word *fait accompli,* cannot be at peace, because the Church will not be reconciled to impiety and absurdity. They do not believe with divine faith in the potency of the pontifical word; but they do believe by an instinct of terror, as the devils also believe and tremble. Hence the stream of filth now vainly flowing against those documents from the Italian and foreign journals. The Liberals tremble at this warning, and cannot restrain their vexation, because so many hypocritical efforts to mask their Liberalism under Catholicism are at last brought to nought. They are now compelled to lay aside the mask more and more. No longer can they deceive the simple. They must now declare themselves open enemies of the Church and of her definitions. Liberalism is now condemned in all its newest and most current formulæ. He that has ears to hear let him hear, and he that does not hear must blame himself, and not the Church, which, like a tender mother (without condemning either the constitutions or the constitutionalists), puts her sons on their guard against the poisonous Liberal doctrines. Thus, with this new, clear monition, she proclaims to the world the absolute incompatibility of Christ and Belial, of the Gospel and the world, of sound principles and those which are called modern civilisation, but in fact are nothing but masonic civilisation. This new, clear monition closes the past year, and if it is heard and received, as assuredly it will be, by all the faithful, as everything which comes from the common mother, the Church, is always received, it will open up in the new year more and yet more joyful hope of the restoration of sound ideas, the sure presage and infallible forerunner of the *restoration of facts.*"[1]

Father Schrader was one of the many Jesuits who had in recent years been sent from Rome into Germany, to carry the newest forms of the Court theology into the schools. He had been a member of the Special Congregation for the preparation of the Syllabus. In Vienna, where he held a chair in the University, he had already published the first part of a work, *The Pope and Modern Ideas,*[2] and no sooner did the Syllabus appear than he published his second part, accredited by a brief from his Holiness.

In this Schrader not only hailed the Syllabus with clear insight into its aims and spirit, but he did for it what was necessary to render it intelligible to ordinary readers. Over against every condemned proposition, he set down its counter proposition, the one which the Pope would bless and not curse. This process, continued through the whole of the eighty propositions, enables any one to obtain a view of the principles on which it was proposed to reconstruct society. Such a view, however, is obscured by the terminology, which often suggests, to the general reader, either a vague idea or an inoffensive one, when, to the trained reader, the idea is definite, and if he be not an Ultramontane, startling.

In England, the labours of Father Schrader escaped notice, and in Germany aroused the solicitude of only a wakeful few; but in Rome they were so much valued that when the secret

---

[1] *Civiltà*, Serie VI., vol i., p. 172, 173.
[2] *Der Papst und die modernen Ideen.*

preparations for the Council were organised he was called up, that the firm hand which had drafted his propositions might be employed in preparing formulæ.

Though the Syllabus is not even in profession a proclamation of the glory of Christ, or of the Christian verities, or of the mission of the Church to turn sinners from their sins to God, but is formally a charter of ecclesiastical dominion over civil society, the first fourteen of its eighty propositions are named as if drawn from the domain of philosophy and theology. They, however, lay the doctrinal basis for the political claims that follow. Many have been tempted to think that they were set at the head of the document to induce any politician or man of letters, who might take it up, to lay it down again, as a handful of musty, scholastic crumbs. Such a reader might be pardoned for laying it down when he found all the weight of an anathema hurled against the opinion that 'The method and principles with which the ancient scholastic doctors cultivated the study of theology are not suited to the necessities of our times, or to the progress of science' (prop. 13). He might think that men who could commit the authority of a Church, for all ages, to the *methods* of the schoolmen, were hardly the men to reconstruct even the ruined Pontifical States, much less nations all over the world. He might think further that a society which could narrow its terms of membership till all were excluded who should doubt whether or not the methods of the schoolmen were suitable to our times, was hardly a society to embrace within itself all the future of humanity. But in the celebrated Letters Apostolic, of Dec. 21st, 1863, to the Archbishop of Munich, the case of the schoolmen was put in language almost impassioned. The Church had, really, identified her own honour with that of the doctors, not only by following their methods in most of her schools, but also by celebrating their virtues with loud applause and vehement commendation.[1] And so, as Schrader put it, not only their prin-

---

[1] *Receuil*, p. 498.

ciples, but their methods, are perfectly suited to all times, and to the progress of science.[1] In fact, their methods would give to the Church the control of higher education.

The fifth proposition illustrates the difficulty of judging of the practice of the Church of Rome by her theory, or *vice versa.* She condemns the following :—' That divine revelation is imperfect, and therefore subject to a continuous and indefinite progress, which corresponds to the progress of human reason.' Persons not of her own communion would say that, except for the last clause, this might express the ground on which the fabric of Roman doctrine, properly so called, is built. Believing too much almost always springs from believing too little. He who believes enough about one God does not want assistant divinities. He who believes enough about one Mediator does not want to multiply the number. He who believes enough about one revelation does not want new revelations. Both the Councils of Trent and of the Vatican keep up the theory of only developing revelation. Practically their proceedings are pervaded with this principle, ' That divine revelation is subject to continuous and indefinite progress.' The popular effect of this is that new *quasi* revelations are of frequent occurrence.[2]

It is, however, at the fifteenth proposition that the framers of the Syllabus emerge into their natural element. In it the opinion condemned is that every man is free to embrace and profess that religion which he may esteem true, following the light of reason. This, with the few other propositions under the head of Indifferentism and Latitudinarianism, prepare the way for a section, in which communism, clandestine societies, and Bible societies are bound into one bundle. This again introduces the two great sections, that on the Church, and that on the State. These together comprise thirty-seven propositions. A section on ethics and one on marriage follow.

[1] *Papst und mod. Id.,* p. 61.
[2] Friedrich, in his *Mechanismus der Vatikanischen Religion,* p. 12, says that these revelations no longer need to come from God, but may come from other persons, especially from Mary.

Marriage is treated not at all in respect to the morals of wedded life, or to the sanctities of the connubial and parental relation, but in respect to those questions which affect ecclesiastical authority and its relation to the civil. The concluding sections treat of the temporal sovereignty, and of modern Liberalism.

Who would look for Liberalism under the improbable heading of *Naturalism?* yet both the *Civiltá* and the *Stimmen,* proceeding on lines laid down by Bishop Pie of Poictiers, elaborately showed how the *fundamental heresy* of all those condemned was Naturalism, because, viewed in the light of the Encyclical, all those errors converged in the 'denial of the supernatural character of the Church.' Of this mother of modern heresies two political varieties are specified, and two philosophical; but it is shown that the political varieties are those which the Pope particularly condemns because the others are so absurd. The philosophical varieties are simply deism and pantheism. Political Naturalism, on the other hand, is Liberal Catholicism in two degrees : (1) Denying the authority of the supernatural order (the Church) in public and temporal affairs, while admitting it in private and spiritual affairs ; (2) Asserting the right of men according to their private judgment to yield or to refuse obedience to the authority of the supernatural order. The first of these two errors leads to the drawing of a distinction between the duties of a citizen and those of a Christian, and also to the assumption of a right to tell the Church her duty by excluding her authority from a circle of practical affairs. The second error leads to the confiding of instruction and legislation to the State, and to making religion merely the affair of individuals. Hence does it lead also to secularised or lay States. Political Naturalism embodies itself in Liberal associations ; Philosophical Naturalism in secret societies.[1] Had we been left to say who were condemned under these heads we should probably have named Spinosa and Renan ;

---

[1] *Stimmen,* heft i. at length, and *Civiltá,* VI., i., pp. 273-289.

but the true expositors compel us to think of Montalembert and Mazzini.

Under the section treating of the Church, the first proposition affirms the important principle as to the Church being a perfect society. Yet this is put into a sentence containing explicitly or implicitly a number of propositions, some negative, some affirmative, and nearly all of great ambiguity. The error condemned is, 'The Church is not a true and perfect society completely free, nor is she invested with rights proper to herself and permanent, conferred by her divine Founder; but it belongs to the civil power to define the rights of the Church, and the limits within which those rights are to be exercised' (prop. 19). This, be it remembered, is the proposition condemned. Keeping in view the ambiguity of the several predicates, the following points are to be noted:—1. The Church is a perfect society. 2. The Church is completely free. 3. The Church has the direct authority of Christ for her rights. 4. The State cannot define the rights of the Church. 5. The State cannot even limit the exercise of those rights.

Care must be taken to note that no distinction is made between spiritual and temporal rights, or between universal and national ones; nor yet between the exercise of rights by the Church as a voluntary community in a State, and as an establishment of the State. And too much attention can hardly be given to the fact that no epithet limits the term civil power, such as 'Catholic' civil power, or 'Christian' civil power. The term is taken in its widest extension.

It follows from these premises, as Vatican writers often demonstrate, that liberty to the Church means the right of putting all ecclesiastical law in force, and calling upon the State to execute such law. For if the latter refuses to do so, it limits the exercise of the Church's rights, or in other terms, the Church is not left free to carry out her decisions.[1]

---

[1] 'The Council of Trent requires that all, without distinction, and therefore princes, should observe the Canons, for, so far as ecclesiastical affairs are con-

The broad denial of the right of the State to define or limit the rights of the Church, without distinction, is meant to cover, and, to Vaticanists, does cover, the right of the Church to define the limits of her own authority as to its domain and as to its exercise, and consequently the right to define the limits of the authority of the State, both as to its sphere and its exercise.

Yet, what is, at first sight, simpler to superficial readers than denying the right of the State to define the rights of a Church? It is a right of a Church to believe, to pray, to worship, and to preach. Is the State to define such rights? It is a right claimed by one Church to pray any day to 'new patrons,' whom, as Moses said, 'Thou hast not known, thou, nor thy fathers;' yet is the State to assume the function of defining such rights? But one Church also claims the right of employing mercenaries and foreign auxiliaries to force a few millions of men of a fine race, in a fine country, to submit to her chief pastor as their king. She also claims the right to set her priests, in any country, before the princes of the nation; and the right, not merely to ask for an alteration of the law of the land, but to declare it void,—the right even to tell subjects when and where they may lawfully break law.[1] Now, both classes of claims are covered by the one word 'rights,' and the State is confidently warned off from a fort, or from the pamphlet of a seditious bishop, as if that ground was lawful

cerned, the Canons rest upon the eternal, unchangeable dogma of the Church. They are a supplement to the gospels, epistles, and prophecies, directed, like them, to the salvation of the human species. In order that the Church may give a practical application to her laws for the life of men, she needs the power of jurisdiction, and also against the refractory and the transgressor of her laws, the power of punishment.'—*Phillips*, ii., 559.

[1] 'It is not allowable either that the temporal authorities should make a law, in reference to an ecclesiastical subject, on which the Canons have not determined anything; or, that through their law they should change Canons that are in existence. Every law of the kind opposed to ecclesiastical rules, or enacted in addition to them, if not desired by the Church, or expressly recognised by her, is hence in itself invalid.'—*Phillips*, ii., 563.

Church ground; indeed, as if it was holy, like the shrines of faith and worship sanctified by our Lord and His apostles

Perhaps the general drift of the famous formula is most fairly represented by taking the words of one of those who have the greatest influence on its practical interpretation. The following proposition is found in a set of *Theses* propounded by a Jesuit, before a Jesuit college, which forms one of the few recent tracts left by the fathers of that order in the *Collegio Romano:*—

'The Church of Christ is a perfect society, wholly independent of every civil power in its substance and its operation, possessing power peculiar to itself, both legislative and judicial, as well as compulsory, which is exercised by spiritual and temporal penalties, personal and also substantial.'[1]

Father Bucceroni may also be taken as fairly conveying the whole effect of the Syllabus on the relations of the State to the Church, when he says that 'Catholic civil society is bound to yield to the Church, even in temporal affairs, if the advancement of a spiritual end calls for it;' and 'religion should be so positively protected that the *judgments of the Church should never be obstructed.*'

The State has not to grant the powers above mentioned to the Church, but to recognise the Church as a corporation wherein they are, by divine right, inherent. It is for the heads of the Church to define the limits of their own domain, and it is for the heads of the State to permit them within those limits to rule as representing God. In resenting the prohibition of Napoleon III. to promulgate the Syllabus in France, the *Civiltá* spoke thus of the error which misled politicians :—

'It proceeds from the belief that it is the civil authority which permits the Church to exercise within its territory her jurisdiction over the faithful. Nothing is more false. The faithful, wherever found, are subject to the Church by the will of Christ, and not by the will of the State. They must necessarily be governed by two authorities, by the civil and the ecclesiastical, each freely acting within its proper circle; yet the first in

[1] Theses ex universa Theologia quas in Collegio Lavalliensi Societatis Jesu defendet P. Januarius Bucceroni ejusdem societatis. Die II. Juli, 1872. § xxiv.

subordination to the second, as the interests of the body are subordinate to those of the soul. The Christian people, to whatever nation they belong, be they Italians, Germans, or French, if subjects of the Emperor as to things temporal, are also subjects of the Pope as to things spiritual, and more of the Pope than of the Emperor.'

Laughing at M. Langlais, who in the French Courts argued that the Pope in treating of the very foundations of political institutions had gone beyond his proper sphere, that of faith and morals, the *Civiltà* said :—

'According to our weak way of thinking, the legitimate argument would have run thus : The Pope has a right to give a decision only within the moral order : the Pope has given a decision as to such and such propositions ; therefore those propositions belong to the moral order.'[1]

In attempting to judge of the effect of any clause, the reader cannot be too often put upon his guard against loose Protestant interpretations. Any interpretation but the strictly Papal one is totally misleading. The nearer we come to the force of the terms in Canon Law, the nearer do we come to their real import.

For instance, in the condemned proposition 20, ' The ecclesiastical power ought not to exercise its authority without the consent or permission of the civil government,' we must ask, 1. What is the ecclesiastical power ? and 2. What is its authority ? Clearly all Protestant answers to either question would be illusory. The ecclesiastical power, in any given place, is the prelate who there represents the Pope ; and his authority is just what the latter may have given to him, whether it affects doctrines, morals, institutions, laws, land, the bodies and souls of men, or the allegiance of subjects.[2] So, it is no question of the right of a congregation to worship, or of a preacher to preach, or of a priest to perform ceremonies according to his conscience, nor yet of a Church to define and propagate its own doctrines, and frame its ritual, or to exercise spiritual discipline

[1] VI., i., 652, 653.

[2] ' Partiales ecclesiæ praefectos, seu pastores essse episcopos, quorum scilicet potestas iis terminis definitur, qui ab Romano Pontifice sive immediate et expresse, sive mediate ac tacite designati fuerint.'—*Tarquini, Institutiones,* p. 117.

over its clergy, but simply a question of one impersonated authority in presence of another, the one representing the Pope and the other the Crown.

'The possession of the prince originates in human jurisdiction, founded in facts occasioned by man's social nature; but the possession of the Pope originates in a divine jurisdiction, and is founded on the essential dependence of man upon God. *The authority of the Church is the authority of Christ Himself, who governs the faithful through His vicar here below.* Every baptized person, then, is more the subject of the Pope than he is of any other earthly governor whatever. This subjection is spiritual, but just on that account does it embrace the man more fully than any material subjection; for the principal part of man is not the body but the spirit.'—*Civiltá*, Serie VII., vol. vi., p. 293.

Not many will need to be reminded of the vast import of the simple word 'immunity.' As applied to the clergy it means complete exemption from civil control and civil law. The *Civiltá* puts this in an engaging form.[1] The clergy are placed outside of lay jurisdiction by divine right. They stand to the civil magistrate in the relation that ambassadors of a foreign prince hold to the tribunals of the country. They are subjects, but subjects of their own king, and only under his jurisdiction. 'So the holy ministers are ambassadors for God. As such they are not judged by those to whom they exercise their embassy, but they are judged by God, through the medium of him whom He has set up to hold His place upon earth.' The Pope may place a priesthood in a certain measure under civil law by conceding certain rights to the civil power. Or he may abandon a condemned priest to the secular arm. But he is himself '*the supreme judge even of civil laws, and therefore is incapable of coming under any true obligation to them* (p. 663). In him, therefore, immunity, partial only in the clergy, reaches its fulness, for none can place him under that law or that authority over both of which he sits as judge. None surely will confound the idea of supreme judge of the law with that of the highest judge under the law. Our Lord Chancellor is the latter, but not the former.

[1] VIII., l., 662.

A few passages from the standard work of Phillips on ecclesiastical law will clear these points, and that in an interesting form. The author was a layman and a German, both of which circumstances are mentioned by the *Civiltà* as indicating that in advancing ecclesiastical claims the learned canonist will be moderate.

'Above all others, above priests, kings, princes, fathers, sons, and teachers, stands the bishop as the representative of Christ, which is indicated by his anointing. If this is true with regard to all the pastors of the Church, how much more is it true with regard to the successor of Peter, who stands immediately in the place of Him who "did no violence, neither was any deceit in His mouth." . . . As the substitute of Christ, he is set not only over all princes, lands, and nations, but also over all bishops. He has to give account of them all, and for them all must he lay down his life as the Good Shepherd for the sheep. As none other is like to him in the burden of duty, so is none other like to him in the fulness of honour. It is certain that on the whole earth there does not exist any dignity greater than his, and if due honour is to be rendered by all Christians to bishops as the holders of the spiritual power, so must all hearts still more submit themselves to him whom God has elevated above all the bishops. Hence is it especially the duty of those who are clothed with the temporal power, to let this their subordination appear by homage. Since they must be conscious that the splendour of their crown is far outshone by that which they received in baptism, wherein they were called to be fellow heirs with Christ. The pseudo-Ambrose was not so far wrong when he asserted that no fellow can be found for the honour and dignity of a bishop ; for in comparison with it, the splendour of kings and the crowns of princes are but as lead to gold. We may see kings and princes bending their necks at the knee of priests, and, kissing their right hand, commend themselves to their prayers. What Christian king, as Gregory VII. remarks, when he comes to die, does not humbly implore the help of the priest ? but no one upon the bed of death ever calls for the assistance of the king.

'One essential difference between the spiritual power and the temporal power lies in this, that the former can never be imparted to a layman. He must, first of all, through a special qualification, be elevated to the higher grade of the clergy. No law can take away this difference, no power can change it. Therefore princes, no matter how great their earthly might, always abide laymen. Even if a prince has succeeded in subjecting to himself the entire globe, he is nevertheless no teacher, but a scholar of the truth. He is no shepherd, he is only a sheep of the flock. He is no father, only a son of the Church. Her must he love as his mother, yea, more than the mother of his body, for the latter gave him birth only that he might return to dust again, whereas the Church gave him birth that he might be fellow heir with Christ for ever. As from Christ he has received no spiritual power, but only a temporal, *which means an inferior power*, so must he, like all other laymen, be in subjection to the holders of the spiritual power, for in respect to all the laity, the authority of the Church must ever be the same, without any regard to their different worldly standing. Christ does not distinguish between sheep and sheep ; thus clearly indicating that they do not belong to His fold who do not acknowledge the spiritual authority of the Church as over them, in particular that of His supreme representative.

'Hence all kings and princes are subject to the divine laws and the canons of the Church ; and if they fail in regard to them, the spiritual power must judge them.'—*Phillips*, ii., 622-625.

' Innocent III. rightly appealed to the Divine order in this matter when he said, "Because our power is not from a man, but from God, so can no one of sound mind be ignorant that it pertains to our office to admonish every Christian in regard to every mortal sin, and if he despises the admonition, to compel him by ecclesiastical punishment." This must especially take place when the temporal ruler, by means of his falling away from the Church, threatens to lead his subjects into the way of perdition ; and in this case the spiritual authority steps in on two grounds,—out of regard both to the prince and also to the people. The prince, when he makes a bad use of his power, hastens to his own condemnation ; hence it is the duty of the Church, and in particular of the head thereof, to preserve him from it, because the Pope has an account to render for him also. The Church has likewise the same care in regard to the people ; being answerable for them too, she must strive to keep spiritual evils far away from them.

' Now as to the means of which the Church with this view can avail herself in regard to the temporal ruler. First of all, the following present themselves—request, exhortation, admonition, and censure. But if all these are resorted to in vain, because the prince despises the Church and does not hear her, then what Christ has said with regard to all applies to him—'' He that despises you despises me, and he who will not hear the Church shall be to you as an heathen man and a publican." In such a case, the Church, as she naturally concedes no right of self-decision to her subjects, excludes even a prince from her community, in order that she may bring him back by this indirect way, since he would not come back by the straight one. But if these steps are without result, if the prince still goes forward incorrigible, stiff-necked in the way of perdition, and draws his people along with him in the same path, then must the Church resort to the final means which lie at her command for the deliverance of that portion of her flock. If she does not succeed with the prince himself, she must hold back those sheep from the abyss, and nothing else remains for her to do but to let him who despises the means of redemption, walk upon his way alone. In order to this she must undo the bond which binds the subjects to him; for however holy that bond may be, still it cannot have the power of obliging men to open disobedience against God. It was not the custom for any vassal to serve his liege lord against the supreme lord, and should service against God be permitted? Here lies the boundary of obedience to the temporal authority, and the power which has received the full authority to bind and to loose, can, in such a case, decide when the ruler, hardening himself in rebellion against God, is no longer entitled to conduct his subjects. This was, moreover, the proceeding which the Church on several occasions adopted. For instance, the third Lateran Council released from their oath the vassals of lords who had passed over to the sect of the Albigenses, and the fourth threatened those with the same punishment who should tolerate heretics within their dominions. The Council of Lyons, in the year 1245, solemnly pronounced the deposition of Frederick II. That explanation is altogether groundless which would assert that in these cases the Church proceeded only after it had obtained permission from the princes;[1] and that in the last case Innocent IV. pronounced the sentence, not with the consent of the Council, but merely in its presence. Such an assertion is quite incapable of proof. The words of the judgment say directly the contrary, for Innocent IV. expressly declares that he does this after having carefully deliberated over the affair with his Brethren and the holy Council. No choice then remains but either to acknowledge that the Church has a right to adopt such proceedings, or to assert that the Church made herself guilty of an usurpation and of inducing the subjects of those princes to commit a wrong.'—*Phillips*, ii., 632-636.

In reading the following abstract it is to be remembered that we aim not at giving a complete but a summary view of the effect of the Syllabus on the relations of Church and State, and that we do not necessarily disapprove of each separate claim specified. Of course neither the disabilities of the State nor the powers of the Church here indicated are embodied in the existing institutions of any country. They are only the disabilities on the one part, and the powers on the other, which would be embodied in the institutions of every country did the

[1] Cardinal Manning asserts (*Vat. Dec.*, p. 85) that 'in every case of deposition, as of Philip le Bel, Henry IV. of Germany, Frederick II., and the like, the sentence of the electors, princes, States, and people, and the public opinion and voice of nations, had already pronounced sentence of rejection on those tyrants, before the Pontiffs pronounced the sentence of excommunication and deposition.'

tribunal of the Pope acquire the supremacy which it claims. We must not, however, on that account suppose that any sentence of the Syllabus is merely an expression of opinion. Every sentence is a formal and supreme judgment, fixing the state of the law. We need hardly remind careful readers that denying a proposition does not necessarily mean asserting its *contrary.* But it does at least imply asserting its *contradictory.* Schrader indeed says that it is the contradictory of the condemned proposition that is to be maintained. But his own counter-propositions do not adhere to that rule. What they assert is sometimes the *contrary* of the condemned proposition. To explain these technical terms:—One asserts that all Englishmen are shopkeepers. You deny it. That denial does not pledge you to assert that no Englishman is a shopkeeper; which proposition is the *contrary* of the other. But it does pledge you at least to assert that some Englishmen are not shopkeepers; which proposition is the *contradictory.* Two contraries may be both false; of two contradictories one must be false and the other true.

SUMMARY OF POINTS ASSUMED IN THE SYLLABUS AS TO THE DISABILITIES OF THE STATE, AND THE RIGHTS AND POWERS OF THE CHURCH.

Disabilities of the State.

(N.B.—The numbers attached to the respective propositions indicate the articles of the syllabus in which they are contained.)

The State has not the right to leave every man free to profess and embrace whatever religion he shall deem true. (15.)

It has not the right to define the rights of the Church, nor to define the limits within which she is to exercise those rights. (19.)

It has not the right to enact that the ecclesiastical power shall require the permission of the civil power in order to the exercise of its authority. (20.)

It has not the right to treat as an excess of power, or as usurping the rights of princes, anything that the Roman Pontiffs or Œcumenical Councils have done. (23.)

It has not the right to deny to the Church the use of force, or to deny to her the possession of either a direct or an indirect temporal power. (24.)

.It has not the right to revoke any temporal power found in the possession of bishops as if it had been granted to them by the State. (25.)

It has not the right to exclude the Pontiff or clergy from all dominion over temporal affairs. (27.)

It has not the right to prevent bishops from publishing the Letters Apostolic of the Pope, without its sanction. (28.)

It has not the right of treating the immunity of the Church and of ecclesiastical persons as if it were a privilege arising out of civil law. (30.)

It has not the right, without consent of the Pope, of abolishing ecclesiastical courts for temporal causes, whether civil or criminal, to which the clergy are parties. (31.)

It has not the right of abolishing the personal immunity of the clergy and students for the priesthood from military service.[1] (32.)

It has not the right to adopt the conclusions of a National Church Council, unless confirmed by the Pope. (36.)

It has not the right of establishing a National Church separate from the Pope. (37.)

It has not the right of asserting itself to be the fountain of all rights; or of asserting a jurisdiction not limited by any other jurisdiction, say that of the Pope (39). N.B.—*The absence of any distinction between legal rights, of which the State alone is the fountain, and natural rights, of which the laws that create legal rights are but the recognition, is characteristic and pervasive.*

It has not the right even of an indirect or negative power over 'religious affairs.' (41.)

It has not the right of *exequatur*, nor yet that of allowing an appeal from an ecclesiastical court to a civil one. (41.)

It has not the right of asserting the supremacy of its own laws when they come into conflict with ecclesiastical law. (42.)

It has not the right of rescinding or annulling concordats or grants of immunity agreed upon by the Pope, without his consent. (43.)

It has not the right to interfere in 'matters pertaining to' religion, morals, or spiritual government. (44.)

It has not the right to judge any instruction which may be issued by pastors of the Church for the guidance of consciences. (44.)

It has not the right to the entire direction of public schools. (45.)

It has not the right of requiring that the plan of studies in clerical seminaries shall be submitted to it. (46.)

It has not the right to present bishops, or to depose them, or to found sees. (50, 51.)

---

[1] The word is generally translated 'clergy' in English. But it is not *cleri* but *clerici*, which includes divinity students, and is commonly translated in Italian by *chierici*. In Italy the class which would have been exempted under cover of the student's right would have been very numerous.

It has not the right to interfere with the taking of monastic vows by its subjects of either sex, or to fix any limit to the age at which it may be done. (52.)

It has not the right to assist subjects who wish to abandon monasteries or convents. (53.)

It has not the right to abolish monasteries or convents. (53.)

It has not the right of determining questions of jurisdiction as between itself and the ecclesiastical authority. (54.)

It has not the right to separate itself from the Church. (55.)

It has not the right to provide for the study of philosophy, or moral science, or civil law eluding the ecclesiastical authority (57). N.B.—*Moral science includes politics and economy.*

It has not the right to proclaim or to observe the principle of non-intervention. (62.)

It has not the right to declare the marriage contract separable from the sacrament of marriage. (66.)

It has not the right to sanction divorce in any case. (67.)

It has not the right to prevent the Church from setting up impediments which invalidate marriage. It has no right to set up such impediments itself. It has no right to abolish such impediments already existing. (67.)

It has not the right to uphold any marriage solemnised otherwise than according to the form prescribed by the Council of Trent, even if solemnised according to a form sanctioned by the civil law. (71.)

It has not the right to recognise any marriage between Christians as valid, unless the sacrament is included. (73.)

It has not the right to declare that matrimonial causes, or those arising out of betrothals, belong by their nature to the civil jurisdiction. (74.)

RIGHTS AND POWERS OF THE CHURCH.

N.B.—*In many cases, the propositions under this head show the powers of the Church directly corresponding to the disabilities of the State expressed under the previous head.*

She has the right to interfere with the study of philosophy, and it is not her duty to tolerate errors in it, or to leave it to correct itself. (11.)

She has the right to require the State not to leave every man free to profess his own religion. (15.)

She has the right to be perfectly free. She has the right to define her own rights, and to define the limits within which they are to be exercised (19.)

She has the right to exercise her power without the permission or consent of the State. (20.)

She has the right to bind Catholic teachers and authors, even in matters additional to those which may have been decreed as articles of belief binding on all. (22.)

She has the right of requiring it to be believed by all that no Pope ever exceeded the bounds of his power; also that no Œcumenical Council ever did so, and further, that neither the one nor the other ever usurped the rights of princes. (23.)

She has the right to employ force. (24.)

She has the right to maintain that whatever temporal power is found in the hands of a bishop, is not beyond what is inherent in his office, and has not come from the State, and therefore is not liable to be resumed by it. (25.)

She has the right to claim dominion in temporal things for the clergy and the Pope. (27.)

She has the right to make bishops promulge the Pope's decrees without consent of their rulers. (28.)

She has the right to require it to be believed of all, that the immunity of the Church, and of ecclesiastical persons, did not arise out of civil law. (30.)

She has the right to require that temporal causes, whether civil or criminal, to which clergymen are parties should be tried by ecclesiastical tribunals. (31.)

She has the right to alter the conclusions of a National Church Council, and to reject the claim of the Government of the country to have the matter decided in the terms adopted by such National Council. (36.)

She has the right to prevent the foundation of any National Church, not subject to the authority of the Roman Pontiff. (37.)

She has the right to reject any claim on the part of the State to either a direct and positive or an indirect and negative power in religious affairs, and more especially when the State is ruled by an unbelieving prince. (41.)

She has the right to reject the claim of the State to exercise a power of *exequatur*, or to allow appeals from ecclesiastical to civil tribunals. (41.)

She has the right to exclude the civil power from all interference in 'matters which appertain to' religion, morals, and spiritual government. Hence she has the right of excluding it from pronouncing any judgment on instructions which may be issued by any pastor of the Church for the guidance of conscience. (44.)

She has the right to deprive the civil authority of the entire government of public schools. (45.)

She has the right to refuse to show the plan of study in clerical seminaries to civil authorities. (46.) ·

She has the right to fix the age for taking monastic vows both for men and women, irrespective of the civil authority. (52.)

She has the right to uphold the laws of religious orders against the civil authority; the right to deprive the latter of power to aid any who, after having taken vows, should seek to escape from monasteries or nunneries; and the right to prevent it from taking the houses, churches, or funds' of religious orders under secular management. (53.)

She has the right of holding kings and princes in subjection to her jurisdiction, and of denying that their authority is superior to her own in determining questions of jurisdiction. (54.)

She has the right of perpetuating the union of Church and State. (55.)

She has the right of subjecting the study of philosophy, moral science, and civil law, to ecclesiastical authority. (56.)

She has the right of enjoining a policy of intervention. (62.)

She has the right to require the sacrament of marriage as essential to every contract of marriage. (62.)

She has the right to deprive the civil authority of power to sanction divorce in any case. (67.)

She has the right to enact impediments which invalidate marriage, the right to prevent the State from doing so, also the right to prevent it from annulling such impediments when existing. (68.)

She has the right to require all to receive the Canons of Trent as of dogmatical authority, namely, those Canons which anathematise such as deny her the power of setting up impediments which invalidate marriage. (70.)

She has the right of treating all marriages which are not solemnised according to the form of the Council of Trent as invalid, even those solemnised according to a form prescribed by the civil law. (71.)

She has the right of annulling all marriages among Christians solemnised only by civil contract. (73.)

She has the right of judging all matrimonial causes, and those arising out of betrothals, in ecclesiastical courts. (74.)

She has the right to require that the Catholic religion shall be the only religion of the State, to the exclusion of all others. (77.)

She has the right to prevent the State from granting the public exercise of their own worship to persons immigrating into it. (78.)

She has the power of requiring the State not to permit free expression of opinion. (79.)

The importance of questions affecting marriage and betrothal is threefold. (1) Immense revenues accrue to the Court and bureaucracy of Rome from the system of dispensations for marrying within the degrees forbidden in any one of the three separate scales of consanguinity, affinity, or spiritual affinity, *i.e.*, affinity contracted by sponsorship at baptism or confirmation. (2) The grant, every five years, of a QUINQUENNIAL FACULTY to the bishop to issue such dispensations as affect those distant degrees within which dispensations do not pay a tax, or to the poor who cannot pay, holds the bishop in perpetual dependence on the Curia. (3) The whole system of impediments and dispensations subserves the end of extending the control of the priesthood over domestic life through the reluctance felt in families at the time of a marriage, as at that of a death, to cause scandal by a difference with 'the clergy.'

Phillips says (ii., 639) that in modern times the union of Church and State is frequently compared to wedlock,—not an inapt figure, but one calling for care lest it be taken in a wrong sense. 'That would be the case if in this union the female partner was taken for the Church, and the male partner for the State. If we employ this simile, we must think of the relative positions as just reversed.' This seems reasonable. The legal position of a married woman, a *feme covert*, would appear not ill to correspond with that of a State bound to the husband, who calls himself a mother.

CHAPTER VI.

The Secret Memoranda of the Cardinals, February 1865.

THE Cardinals who, in the beginning of December, were commanded to prepare notes on the expediency of holding a Council, did not hurry, but by the beginning of February fifteen such notes were in the hands of the Pope. Their Eminences discussed the subject under four heads : 1. The present condition of the world; 2. The desirableness or otherwise of resorting to the ultimate remedy of a General Council ; 3. The difficulties in the way of holding one, and the means of overcoming them; 4. The subjects of which a Council might treat.

Cecconi gives only a summary of the contents of these notes, and we cannot but regret that it was not published before the conflicts of which the Council has been the occasion. It might have been, in that case, just the same as it is now; but our confidence in its frankness would have been greater, because a change has taken place in the manner of Ultramontane authorities when expressing themselves since 1870, and especially since 1872, as compared with 1869 or the early part of 1870, on what the world calls political, and the Curia generally calls social, points, and more particularly on the grand future of the struggle and triumph of reconstruction. Bearing, however, this change in mind, we may welcome the summary of Cecconi as of real value; for, however incomplete, it is authoritative, so far as representing what the Court wishes to be made public. It is, moreover, not tainted with infirmities often found in declarations on this side of the Alps, which render them frail authorities, whether for a student or a parliamentary committee; infirmities often appearing in English and German translations, as well as in original utterances.

The most eminent consulters, or, as our historian loves to call them, the purpled (*i porporati*), showed how the present age was remarkable for progress in invention. This formed its favourable side. But then such progress served only temporal ends. The ' Christian government of the world,' as it existed in former ages, had given place to a system based on the principle that society, as such, had nothing to do with God. The points in the sad spectacle of this ' social apostacy,' which most distressed the Cardinals, were as follows :—Education was withdrawn from the supreme vigilance of the Catholic Church, and consequently ran into manifold errors; the doctrines of naturalism, rationalism, and various forms of pantheism prevailed, from which sprang socialism and communism.

Coming to political affairs, some of the writers mourned over the prevalence of revolutionary principles in general, some over freedom of worship and of the press in particular, and some over the tyranny of the State, which controlled education and charitable institutions,—thus appropriating to itself all the social forces. Some, again, lamented the violation of the rights of
. the Church in regard to laws affecting marriage, to those on the

holding of land, to the temporal sovereignty of the Pope, to the religious orders, and similar topics.

The practice of magnetism, clairvoyance, and spiritualism is deplored by their Eminences as one great plague and shame of our epoch.   Freemasonry, viewed 'in its true aspect,' not as a benevolent association, but as an institution having for its ultimate aim the erection of a pretended church universal of humanity on the ruins of all religion, is said by several of the consulters to be the arm which carries the modern theories into practice, and therefore is viewed as one of the most potent enemies of the Church.

The next point noted is the influence exerted even upon Catholic teaching by the Reformation and by rationalism.   It is shown that in philosophy, as taught in some countries, the ancient system of the schools had been set aside, and, as all sciences are affected by philosophy, it not unfrequently occurred that authors and professors attacked the pure doctrines of the faith.   Some of them even evinced a disposition to regard Rome as being ignorant of the relations of Catholic science to heretical and rationalistic science, or, at least, as not appreciating the necessities arising out of such relations.   Nay, they even displayed some unreadiness in submitting to her authority.

The countries here referred to are those where Roman Catholic populations border upon reformed ones, or are mixed with them.   South of the Alps and Pyrenees, all that came to be taught at the Vatican soon counted among 'the pure doctrines of the faith.'   But the standard of real Christian antiquity erected in reformed countries, and the tendency evermore to recommence drawing from the wells of doctrine at the river head, could not but make Romish scholars, in places influenced by such countries, slower to follow every fresh innovation. Content to accept Trent as antiquity for the Romish as distinguished from the Catholic portion of their creed, and venerating the ages a little further up, as if they were the truly ancient ones, many of them, nevertheless, were not prepared with grace and comfort to put on new dogmas, new 'devotions,' and new principles of morality, evolved under their own eyes.

The counterpart of an unchanging standard of faith existing in reformed countries is fearless freedom of research; for they who steer by fixed stars are not alarmed about finding themselves at sea, knowing that, however broad the ocean, the stars will guide them to a shore. The northern Catholics were not uninfluenced by this tendency any more than by its counterpart, and often found themselves, as the late discussions have shown, little flattered by the state of science, even of theological science, in ruling circles in Rome.

After this serious notice of the doctrinal differences hitherto tolerated within the bosom of the Church, the Cardinals proceed to urge the lamentable fact that, owing to the want of 'harmony' between the civil and ecclesiastical authority, many precepts of the canon law had fallen into disuse. Hence the state of discipline among the clergy was deficient in uniformity, uncertain and lawless. This expression 'in harmony' is often employed to denote that state of law which is believed to be the normal,—indeed, the divinely-appointed one; that is, the state in which the civil law recognises the canon law, and provides for its due execution.

On the second point, that of the desirableness of holding a Council, nearly all the Cardinals were agreed. ' In the present confusion of principles and systems, the whole episcopate assembled in Council, pointing out the way of eternal salvation to nations and sovereigns, and also the true relation between the natural order and the supernatural order, with the rights and duties of governors and governed, would be a luminous beacon scattering the darkness that covers the world. Perhaps, in the presence of such a spectacle, heretical and schismatical societies would lay aside old prejudices, and would be drawn to a reunion.'

We only interpose a word to say that perhaps there are even yet among us some who do not know what is the supernatural order and what the natural order. The former is the order of government, by the supernatural institution of the Church, for eternal ends; the latter the order of government, by the natural institution of the State, for temporal ends. With this explanation it is obvious that the 'true way of eternal salvation' for nations and sovereigns is to submit the natural order to the supernatural, which will guide it aright. The terms may be greatly varied; the political order, the civil order, the external order, and so on, coming in by turns.

However, the unanimity of the Cardinals was not complete. One advised that the calling of a General Council should be reserved for times when some great difference within the Church demanded a settlement. A second thought that the delicacy of some of the points to be handled, and the want of that external support which the Church formerly possessed, outweighed ·any prospect of advantage. A third could not pronounce between advantages and disadvantages, but gladly left the decision with the Sovereign Pontiff, whom God always assisted with special light.

Cecconi's statement as to the general agreement of the Cardinals appears to clash with that made by persons in Rome, who ought to be well informed, and who affirm that, at first, nearly all the Cardinals were opposed to the Pope's desire, and only yielded to his ungovernable longing to have his own infallibility proclaimed. Lord Acton says the Cardinals gave their counsel against the project, and that the Pope proceeded heedless of their opposition.[1] Both statements may be correct; for even if the Cardinals had opposed the project when informally talked about, they might yield when the official initiative taken by their wilful sovereign convinced them that it was to be. One of the counsellors of Ali, the fourth caliph, when rebuked by Abdullah Abbas for giving bad advice in contradiction to good, previously given and rejected, replied, 'When a person, either through folly or obstinacy, is found to reject counsels

[1] *Zur Geschichte*, etc., p. 3.

which are obviously salutary, he must expect to receive counsels of a complexion precisely the reverse.'

On the third point, namely, that of the difficulties in the way of holding a Council, the Cardinals held that great prudence would be required. The decrees of the Council would be received with indifference by the ungodly and the worldly, or would be made the pretext for new trespasses against the Church. Then, as to governments, would they permit the bishops to attend? Would they not prohibit the execution in their territories of decrees not conformed to the interests of those who held the power of the sword? Again, what would be the use of new canons if the civil power would not further the execution of them, or would even thwart it? And besides all this, the political horizon was clouded, and the Council might be interrupted. So far for external difficulties.

As to internal ones, points noted were, the long absence of the bishops from their flocks, the risk of dissensions in the Council, and of consequent scandal,—a risk which appeared the greater as the thorny character of some of the questions to be treated was considered. The Cardinals also felt that there was some danger that a desire might arise on the part of the bishops to extend their own privileges, already too great, so much so as even to be hurtful to the practical uniformity of ecclesiastical government, as well as to the firmness of ecclesiastical discipline, and to the union of the bishops with the head of the Church.

The considerations mentioned as outweighing these difficulties might seem very slight, but viewed in the light of later attempts, one of them, dismissed in a few words, was of great significance.

Perhaps the absence of bishops from their flocks would not be of such long continuance as some expected. This is sufficient to show that even at that early date the hope of an expeditious assent to what the Pope desired formed an element in the calculations of the Court. But the final argument relied upon, as an answer to the difficulties, is the hand of God fighting for the Church.

On the most important point of all, the subjects with which the Council should deal, the summary of the notes given by Cecconi is so meagre as to suggest the idea either that the views of their Eminences must have been crude, or that they did not care to put on paper such views as were matured; always supposing that the summary really represents the whole of the contents. After a few generalities, the first particular subject named for condemnation is the liberty of the press, after which are named civil marriages, impediments to marriage, mixed marriages, and such like, with questions of ecclesiastical property, and the observance of fasts and feasts.

Only two of the Cardinals mentioned the subject of Papal infallibility. A third named Gallicanism and the necessity of the temporal sovereignty. Only one mentioned the Syllabus. From the facts last named, Cecconi triumphantly infers that they who say that Rome designed to concentrate all power in the hands of the Pope, have lost their cause. We need only remark that, by his own testimony, the Cardinals who mentioned infallibility and the Syllabus were those who were against the meeting of a Council. And perhaps this fact, coupled with that of no allusion being made to these subjects by those who desired the meeting of a Council, might suggest to cold critics an inference opposite to the one drawn by the official historian. We must, in justice to him, however, say that he does not expressly deny that the measures were then in contemplation by which Rome has actually concentrated all her powers in the hands of the Pope.

The omission to name the Syllabus in this instance is one of a series of acts of reticence in respect of that document which are at least curious. It is not mentioned in the Encyclical which accompanied it. It is not mentioned by the official historian at the time of its issue; and when, as we shall hereafter see, the Pope solemnly confirmed it in the presence of five hundred bishops, the act was not mentioned by the Court organs. Further, the Syllabus was not mentioned even in the very document by which the collective hierarchy expressed their solemn adhesion to it. Nor was the adhesion to it by letter of the prelates then absent mentioned till, as our tale will show, all this was brought out by the friction of events.

Points in these notes to be borne in mind, as throwing light on the future of our history, are, that those who desired a Council hoped it would be a short one, and were of opinion that the powers of bishops were too great ; and that the rela_ tions of the supernatural order and the natural order must be regulated, *i.e.*, reduced to rule. These two commonwealths, commonly called the Church and State, had hitherto adjusted their relations, at least wherever Rome represented the supernatural order, by the rough method of trials of strength and skill. The object of reducing their relations to rule would be to restore that harmony of action which, according to the Curia, formerly existed in happy ages, but had been lost in the changes of time. Naturally, this desired harmony could only be restored by each abiding, according to rule, in its own place —the lower under the higher, and the higher above the lower.[1]

---

[1] 'Only three cases are conceivable. Either the Church and the State are perfectly cò-ordinate [by *coordinirt* Phillips clearly means co-equal], or the State is subordinate to the Church, or the Church subordinate to the State. . . . The divine commands of obedience towards authority, given by the apostles Peter and Paul in their epistles, and so earnestly impressed upon all mankind, are sometimes made to apply to an obedience which even the spiritual authority owes to the temporal. First of all, in relation to the well-known passage in the Epistle to the Romans, it is very evident that it cannot have this meaning. It does not speak of the subordination of one power to another, but of individuals who personally are to be subordinate to the higher powers. But as the Church is not excluded from these higher powers, —indeed, relatively to others, must be held as a *higher* power,—this passage would much rather prove the opposite. It clearly, however, proves the truth that every soul must be subject to the ecclesiastical power, which in the strictest sense of the words cannot be said of subjection to the temporal authority. For otherwise there could not be several States in the world independent of one another.'—*Phillips*, ii., 608.

CHAPTER VII.

A Secret Commission to prepare for the Council, March 1865—First Summons
—Points determined—Reasons why Princes are not consulted—Plan for
the Future Council.

IN March 1865, Cardinals Patrizi, Reisach, Panebianco,
Bizzari, and Caterini were appointed a secret commission to
make preparations for the proposed Council. It was in the
deepening grey of an evening in Lent that the red coaches
drove down the Via della Scrofa carrying those Cardinals to
their first meeting, in the palace of the Vicariate. Rome did
not know that this represented the first move in the preparation
of one of those world-representing displays which had some
part in bringing on her ancient decay, and a greater one in
gilding it over; displays which, while changing in the accidents
of form, have retained the essential character of a sense-sub-
duing pageant, and retained also the purpose of binding the
city to an autocrat. The significance of the display now contemplated was to consist in showing both Quirites and Italians
that the world bowed down to the tiara, and so to bind Rome to
the Pope for ever.

The Cardinal Vicar, Patrizi, a man of sixty-seven, was not,
like his colleagues, to use the familiar Roman term, a 'creature' of Pius IX. He owed his hat to Gregory XVI., and had
already worn the purple for more than thirty years, sustaining a
reputation for steady work and large generosity. As a specimen
of the forms of the Court, we translate the circular of invitation
to the meeting, which forms the first document in the collection
of Cecconi (p. 322) :—

'MOST REVEREND EMINENCE,—I have the honour to inform
your Most Reverend Eminence that the first meeting of the
Special Congregation, of which I have already orally apprised
your Eminence, delivering at the same time a printed document
relating to it, will be held on next Thursday the 9th inst., at

the hour of half-past six, *post meridiem,* in the house of his Most Reverend Eminence Cardinal Patrizi, Vicar of his Holiness.

'Bowing and kissing the sacred purple, I have the honour to declare myself, with the most profound obedience and respect, your Most Reverend Eminence's most humble, most devoted, most obedient servant,

'PETER, *Archbishop of Sardis, Pro-Secretary.'*

Formal as is this circular, it avoids specifying either the title of the Special Congregation, or the object of the meeting. Monsignor Peter Giannelli, though signing himself Archbishop of Sardis, probably had no greater personal connection with the Lydian capital than had Crœsus, in his day, with Canterbury. He did not, however, kiss the sacred purple in vain, for in the spring of 1875 he was invested with it, at the same time as Cardinal Manning.[1]

At this first meeting of the Commission, Giannelli read a memorandum intimating his belief that France, Italy, and Portugal would prohibit their bishops from attending a Council, —more particularly Italy; but as Germany, England, America, Spain, and others, would not do so, a considerable number would be able to assemble. This indicates a consciousness that political distrust of Rome was felt most strongly in Roman Catholic countries.

In this memorandum the Archbishop twice raises a point which afterwards excited heart-burnings. 'All are aware,' he says, 'that the number of Italian bishops, in proportion to those of any other nation, is very large, and they, in consequence of their greater proximity to the chair of Peter, have always proved faithful to its traditions, so that their presence in councils has at all times been considered as the strongest support of the Apostolic See. But it would be unjust to blame the Holy See for counting on such support, as if it resorted to a worldly policy.'

After hearing this memorandum the Cardinals proceeded to

---

[1] Cardinals in signing a letter to the Pope to whom they owe their elevation, add to other terms of obedience ' and creature.'—*Frond,* vol. ii., p. 13.

consider the following questions, and gave to each the answer indicated :—

1. Is the summoning of an Œcumenical Council under the circumstances necessary, and opportune ?

Affirmed.

2. Should Catholic princes be previously consulted ?

Negatived.   Nevertheless, when the Bull of Convocation has been issued, it would be well and becoming for the Holy See to adopt suitable procedures with the princes.

3. Should the Sacred College be consulted before the issuing of the Bull of Convocation, and if so, how?

Affirmed ; but in the manner to be determined by the Most Holy,—or, in common speech, in such manner as the Pope may please.[1]

4. Should a Special Congregation be appointed to direct affairs relating to the Council ?

Affirmed.

5. Should the Directing Congregation, after the publication of the Bull, consult some bishops in different countries as to the subjects proper to be treated, both in doctrine and discipline, regard being had to the variety of countries ?

Affirmed.

The reason which led the Cardinals to negative the idea of consulting the Catholic princes is supposed by Cecconi to have been a fear lest obstacles to the holding of a Council might be raised, and also lest the proceeding might be interpreted as a recognition of the supremacy of the State (p. 29).

On the 13th of March these resolutions of the Commission were reported to the Pope, by whom they were approved with one slight modification.   Instead of a consultation of certain select bishops after the convocation of the Council, he appointed that it should take place before.

The first step in carrying out these resolutions was the appointment of a Directing Congregation, which was composed of

[1] '*Juxta modum a Sanctissimo statuendum.*'—*Cecconi*, p. 29.

the Cardinals of the Commission, with a few others, the number eventually being nine. That body was in existence two years and a half before the hierarchy generally received an intimation, in a Secret Consistory, of the intention to hold a Council.

At the meeting of the Directing Congregation on March 19th, the sketch of a plan for the labours of the Council was presented by one of its members, not named. He proposed that the work should be divided into four branches, and that each should be assigned to a different committee.

1. DOCTRINE, to be committed to the Inquisition, presided over by a Cardinal of the Inquisition; the committee to be enlarged by the addition of some members not attached to the Holy Office. This committee could be sub-divided into sections.

2. ECCLESIASTICO-POLITICAL AFFAIRS, to be committed to the Congregation for ecclesiastical affairs, enlarged by consulters and others.

3. MISSIONS and ORIENTAL CHURCHES, to be committed to the Propaganda and the Congregation of Oriental Rites.

4. DISCIPLINE, to be committed to the congregation for bishops and regulars, with the addition of consulters, canonists, and theologians.

Each committee was to be presided over by a Cardinal, and all were to report to the Directing Congregation, with which should rest the ultimate authority.

The language in which the probable value of communications from outside the governing body is indicated sounds like what statesmen might apply to professors : 'Their ideas, for the most part scientific or abstract, can be reduced to a concrete form by discussion, with the aid of those present in the Commission.'[2]

The plan thus sketched was approved; and the meeting recorded its resolution, that, in dogmatic divinity, such errors must be kept in view as had arisen since the Council of Trent. If the point had needed proof, this statement gives it, that dogmatic definitions were intended from the first.

---

[1] *Cecconi*, p. 322. [2] Ibid., pp. 31 and 322.

CHAPTER VIII.

Memoranda of Thirty-six chosen Bishops, consulted under Bond of Strictest
Secrecy, April to August, 1865—Doctrine of Church and State—Antagonism
of History and the Embryo Dogma—Nuncios admitted to the Secret—And
Oriental Bishops.

ON the 10th of April his Holiness sanctioned a letter to thirty-six select bishops of different countries, intimating under the most binding secrecy his intention of holding a Council in the Holy City, at some time yet undetermined, and requesting them to communicate their views as to the subjects proper to be treated.[1]

In August, nearly all the answers had arrived. Out of the thirty-six, only three bishops cast doubts on the wisdom of the project; all the others were rejoiced.

The letters of the thirty-six, according to Cecconi, expressed views on the present condition of society coinciding with those of the purpled in Rome. The thirty-six generally remarked on the absence of any special heresies. So far as reported, their suggestions touching religion were only for a reassertion of such rudimentary truths as a mother might think about when disturbed by the wayward notions of her boys. When we come to particulars, the subjects which our author finds specified are: the right of the Church to hold land; her independence of the State; her right to control education; her right to judge what promotes and what hinders religion. Among other matters noted, the chief are: the obligation of the faithful to adhere to the decisions of the Church, and in particular to those of the Holy See, and the necessity of the temporal sovereignty of the Pope, with 'similar points.'

Any one of these claims, almost any word in them, raises questions of some gravity. For instance, what does the simple word 'independence' mean? We already know that it cannot mean separation from the State, nor dispensing with pecuniary

[1] *Cecconi,* p. 324.

support from the State, nor indifference to protection from the forces of the State, or to patronage from the State in offices and dignities. It does not even mean being without the right to call upon the State to execute the decrees of the Church, both in enforcing what she deems helpful, and in restraining what she deems hurtful to her interests.

Seeing, then, that independence does not mean any one of these things, what can it mean? It is for us to watch and gather up the meaning as we go along. At present we may say that perhaps the Church is to be independent of the State in some such sense as a general is independent of his commissaries. He could not well get on without them, but their place is neither in council nor in fight; he is to use them, but not to consult them, except to learn what service he can get out of them, and what he cannot. In one particular the analogy fails : the general does not look to the commissaries for either rank or pay. Or, to take a familiar transaction in the history of Church and State, the Church independently defined what was heresy, independently taught that the suffering of death was its proper penalty, independently spied out the suspected, independently tried the accused, and independently handed over the condemned to the temporal arm for execution. The necessity for calling upon the temporal arm to do this office could not properly be called dependence, any more than a similar necessity on the part of our judges for the office of the sheriff may properly be so called.

After Cecconi has apparently concluded his summary of the suggestions of the thirty-six, a sentence is slipped in, saying, that among the verities which ought to be propounded by the Council, some mentioned Papal infallibility—'a doctrine admitted in all Catholic schools, with a few exceptions.' Hereupon departing from his general rule, and adopting marks of quotation, he gives the words of one particular bishop, without naming him. These bear directly on the point most agitated before and during the Council. Such English readers as know much of the controversy, will probably risk a guess as to the author, and it may be that persons in Munich will hardly stop at guessing, but will say they know. It plainly was no Bavarian, not even a German, neither of whom would fall into such an expression as ' Munich in Bavaria.' 'At present there are but few who impugn this prerogative of the Roman Pontiff; and they do so, not from a theological point of view, but the better to assert and maintain the freedom of science. It would seem that a school of theologians has sprung up with this object, at Munich, in Bavaria, in whose writings the principal aim is to lower the Holy See, its authority and its mode of government, by the aid of historical dissertations, and to bring it into contempt, and above all to combat the infallibility of Peter teaching *ex cathedra.*'

This language intimates that the science for which especially freedom was claimed at Munich was history, which wants no other freedom than that of learning the truth and telling it, that of detecting lies and forgeries and exposing them. Even the Court historian feels the significance of this announcement of the mutual antipathy existing between history and the embryo dogma. Why infallibility should be looked upon as more closely related to freedom of enquiry than even to theology itself, is due to subtle affinities of thought, which it requires some familiarity with the subject to be able to appreciate.

It is important to remember that all the claims hitherto mentioned are set down by the thirty-six under the head of doctrine, not under that of the relations between Church and State. They are, therefore, not merely advantages to be accepted or waived according to circumstances, but inalienable rights divinely inherent in the supernatural order.

Among the 'isms' designated for anathema by the chosen thirty-six, those which have any bearing on divinity proper could be named by most ordinary readers. One 'ism' to be condemned is regalism, or the doctrine that the king is supreme in his own country; another is liberty of conscience and of the press; and of course the bishops no more forget magnetism, somnambulism, and freemasonry, than their purpled superiors of the Curia.

We ought not to omit the fact that the thirty-six mentioned the Syllabus and Encyclical as tracing the lines along which the Council would do well to proceed.

Two points brought out under the head of discipline, are, the mobilisation of the clergy, and the educational rights of the Church; strong condemnation being levelled against mixed schools.

The same points which had been already touched, under the head of doctrine, reappear under that of the relations between Church and State, but this time rather in a political than a dogmatic aspect. In the former case we were in the region of eternal truths: here we come down to that of allowable or desirable measures. For instance, as to freedom of worship and of the press, the question is how far a *de facto* liberty may be tolerated, it being assumed that liberty *de jure* cannot exist. Of course we again go over solicitudes for the independence and autonomy of the Church, for the control of education, for the right of jurisdiction, and that of immunity; and especially for the subordination of the social order to positive revealed religion, which means of the heads and laws of the State to the heads and laws of the Church. The Council will be called to rebuke Cæsarism, and the pagan deification of the State, and to offer to political powers as at present existing, the *conditions on which they may satisfy* the requirements of God, of Christ, and of His Church, and so merit a blessing from on high, and perhaps find *true stability here below.*

This last sentence indicates the substance of a vast deal of writing as to one practical purpose of the Council, that of bringing the movement for the reconstituting of society to a crisis, and compelling governments either to fight or surrender, no longer leaving them any chance of parleying or running away.

'Having laid down true principles respecting ecclesiastical property, immunity, and the Christian character of the civil power, the Council can easily enact that the temporal power of the Roman Pontiff cannot bo lawfully disturbed, as if it was an impediment in the way of the good of the country, seeing that, on the contrary, it is the only example now existing of the political order being, in a regular form, subject to Christian law, and can be easily adapted to all the concessions and improvements demanded by the present state of things. This would raise the point of once more asserting the necessity of the temporal power, and of solemnly ordaining penalties against the spoliators.'[1]

In this passage we may catch the Vatican meaning of such a phrase as 'the Christian character of the civil power,' which we soon find explained, where the States of the Church are spoken of, as the only existing example of the regular subjection of the political order to Christian law. The seven hundred thousand persons then dwelling within those States were the only creatures under heaven enjoying the benefit of a government in which the relations between the natural order and the supernatural order were not irregular.

After the secret preparations in Rome had been continued for nearly twelve months, the circle of confidential advisers was further extended. On November 17th, 1865, the Cardinal President of the Directing Congregation communicated the intention of his Holiness to the nuncios in Paris, Vienna, Munich, Madrid, and Brussels ; and requested them to name canonists and theologians of sound principles, exemplary life, and distinguished learning who might be called up to Rome to serve on the preparatory committees.

The next extension of the circle was to the Oriental bishops, who were consulted by Cardinal Barnabo, the Prefect of the Propaganda. They hailed the prospect of a Council, hoping that it might at length remove barriers which held the East in separation from Rome. Of these barriers they name both ancient and modern instances. Among the former the worst appears to be 'national spirit,' and among the latter we find Protes-

---

[1] *Cecconi*, p. 42.

tantism and the everlasting Freemasons. 'Nationalism' is a trial to the Papal Church in the west as well as in the east. Cardinal Manning, in the Pastoral issued just before the Council met, said :—

'The definition of the infallibility of the Pontiff, speaking *ex cathedra*, is needed to exclude from the minds of Catholics the exaggerated spirit of national independence and pride, which has, in these last centuries, so profoundly afflicted the Church. If there be anything which a Catholic Englishman ought to know, it is the subtle, stealthy influence by which the national spirit invades and assimilates the Church to itself; and the bitter fruits of heresy and schism which that assimilation legitimately bears.'[1]

The clearest instance of the national spirit invading and assimilating the Church to itself occurred in decaying Rome. The military and absolutist spirit of the empire supplanted in the ministry and organisation of the Church the original spirit of humility and brotherhood. The spirit of the national pomps supplanted the primitive superiority to sensation and display. The spirit of the governing classes set up side by side with the simple code of Christ a new code, meant avowedly to restore the old Roman domination of law, under the form of a spiritual empire. The spirit of that domination claimed to impose upon other churches the will of the Church of the capital, and did not scruple to call her the mother-church, and to support her claims with lie and forgery oft repeated. But after the Pope, conspiring with the minister of the Frankish king, and rising with him against their two sovereigns, had erected himself into a petty prince, the national spirit of the empire began to narrow down to the municipal one of aboriginal Rome. Ever since that time the municipal spirit has increasingly become the spirit of the Papacy. Whatever that power has effected, it has never been able to make itself a nation. Aiming at a universal empire the spirit of its rule has become more and more close, local, bureaucratic as that of any wee Italian republic of the middle ages. Men must not only act and move, but must also think

[1] *The Œcumenical Council*, p. 52

and speak, according to rules excogitated by certain guilds within the Aurelian walls.

There is a curious but striking contrast between this professedly supernatural institution and one which scarcely claimed a regular place among natural institutions. Coming up amid the decline and corruption of an empire older, richer, and more populous than had been the empire of Rome, the East India Company, in a couple of generations, made a nation out of some hundreds of States among which had raged yearly conflicts. That nation still contains many thrones, but within its circle, and in spite of their jealousies, no less than two hundred and forty millions of men, a family immensely greater than Rome ever cursed with war or blessed with law, now live in peace and freedom such as were unknown to the ages which had aforetime passed over their country. On the plains around the presidential cities of India, where a century ago Mahratta, Moslem, and Rajpoot were wont to ravage, now reigns peace at seed-time and peace at harvest. Security sits and sings on every tree, and Industry, building her nest in every bush, sends out broods that, free from fear, busily cover the land. What a contrast with the endless whirl of war which in what are called the Ages of Faith—ages when the spells of the chief priest in Rome had power over semi-barbarous chiefs—ever eddied on the plain around Rome, a glorious plain, growing waste and more and more waste, while kings came, now to be crowned, now to put a Pope in prison, and while Italians and foreigners rose and sank by turn in the alternating surges,—foreigners, however, most frequently coming into the fight at the call of a self-asserting but mongrel and parasitical government, which claimed to be the heaven-sent superior, not only of commercial corporations like the East India Company, but also of the very kings and emperors whom it played off against one another, and on whom it had always to rely. A national spirit indeed! Such a national spirit as we see in reformed countries, and as was once in an inferior degree seen in the Gallican nation, is large, tolerant, and magnanimous compared with the tight, pretentious municipal spirit unconsciously depicted by Liverani when he enumerates the small men from small towns, puffed up with the name of cities, who, in the Curia, swell themselves out with notions of world-commanding importance,—notions rendered possible only by their own helpless narrowness.

CHAPTER IX.

Interruption of Preparations for Fourteen Months, through the consequences of Sadowa—The French evacute Rome—Alleged Double Dealing of Napoleon III.—*Civiltá* on St. Bartholomew's—Change of Plan—Instead of a Council a Great Display—Serious Complaints of Liberal Catholics.

IT was on May 24th, 1866, that the Directing Congregation held its third meeting, Monsignor Nina acting as secretary in the absence of Giannelli, who was indisposed. But, soon afterwards, dark clouds enveloped the Vatican, and ere the congregation could again meet fourteen months had passed away.

On July 3rd, 1866, a shell burst at Sadowa which struck in three different directions, and in each case the blow was heavy. Austria fell from the primacy of Germany, and from her place among Italian States. Italy, acquiring Venice, entered into full possession of herself, Rome alone excepted. The disjointed members of Germany moved to union under Prussia, like bone coming to its bone.

These were deplorable reversals of Papal policy, unfriendly both to the temporal dominion at home and to the spiritual dominion abroad. By the instrumentality of France and Austria it had been possible, for ages, to keep Italy and Germany parcelled into small States, easily played off against one another, inimical to great national organisations or high national sentiment, and glad of an alliance with a small State possessing an organisation by which it could interfere almost

everywhere, and in almost everything. The long-continued
success of the policy directed to this end seemed to stamp it
as almost miraculous. · Had Germany united under the Hapsburgs, ready to keep Italy disunited, it would have mattered
less to Rome. But her uniting under the Hohenzollerns, and
aiding Italy to become one, was doubly dangerous. Reconstruction as going on in Italy and Germany must be met by
reconstruction on a universal scale.[1]

On November 4th, 1866, the people of Venetia carried their
suffrages to the feet of King Victor Emmanuel, while Austria
and France sullenly acquiesced. The king said, ' Italy is made
if not completed,'—a hint which the Vatican both understood
and resented. Five weeks later, at four o'clock on the morning
of December 11th, Mr. Gladstone, whose name had already left
a beneficent mark on the history of Italy, was watching by the
gaslight from a window in Rome as the French troops wound
round the corner of a street, and he felt that the seed of great
events lay in that evacuation![2]   That day the flag of red, white,
and blue which for seventeen years had cast a light on the

---

[1] In the *Times* for Dec. 8th, 1875, its correspondent in Rome, giving extracts
from Monsignor Nardi's review of an article by Mr. Gladstone in the *Church
Review* on the Church in Italy, quotes the following : " 'Mr. Gladstone fulminates
at length against the temporal power. He is not afraid of Austria or Russia,
nor even of Germany, but he is afraid of France. He says the audacious pretension of restoring the temporal power is not the only one with which the
Vatican threatens the civil liberties of Christendom. The re-establishment
of the temporal power 'would unquestionably compromise the very existence of the German Empire.' " We have quoted these words because we can
believe them true. According to Mr. Gladstone, to restore the Pope would be
to destroy the Germanic Empire. We dearly loved the ancient Germanic
Empire, born of the Catholic Church, and heir of its spirit and majesty. It
was a grand and noble association of princes and of cities, paternally ruled by
a head, who received his crown from the hands of the Pontiff. Marvellous was
the prosperity it enjoyed, and that prosperity would have become greater, even
perennial, but for the unrestrained cupidity of Prussia. The old monarchy was
Christian, but this is pagan. Would, indeed, that it was at least pagan ! but
what is more cruel, to the blind ignorance of the Gentiles it substitutes the
cunning perfidy of the heretics. Mr. Gladstone is not wrong here. If this
terrible monarchy were to spread and dominate all Europe, not only would the
temporal power rise no more, but the spiritual would be threatened with death.'

[2] *Quarterly Review*, No. 275, p. 293.

Vatican and a shadow on the Tiber, was lowered at St. Angelo. The Pope felt that it would soon be succeeded by the red, white, and green. So that, as if by a historical parody on the old furor of the circus, the rage of parties in Rome was once more lashed up by the blue and the green respectively.

'Do not deceive yourselves,' said the Pope to General Montebello, when he presented himself to take leave, 'the revolution will come hither: it has proclaimed it: you have heard it, you have understood it and seen it.'

The *Civiltá Cattolica*, alluding to the 'soporifics' administered at this irritating moment by French journalists and diplomatists, asked whether France would hold the same language to Italy, now menacing the Pope, as she had held to Austria and Spain when preparing to assist him, namely, that 'any departure from the principle of non-intervention would involve a war with France.' She had not so spoken to Italy, and would not do so, for had not Billault said, 'It is not possible to turn French bayonets against Italy.' This being the case, France might hold her peace and not tease the respectable public with soporifics.[1]

When Napoleon III., in the discourse from the throne, alluding to the fear of Rome being taken from the Pope, said that Europe would not permit an event which would throw confusion into the Catholic world, the *Civiltá* bitterly exposed his double dealing. Some would take this language as a pledge to uphold the temporal power, but others would see that it was only a shuffling of the responsibility off the shoulders of France on to those of Europe. Had he said France will not stand it? No, but that Europe will not allow it.

It would be about this time that Viscount Poli and Arthur Guillemin, a lieutenant of zouaves and a zealous crusader, sitting over a cup of coffee saw five gentlemen enter the coffee-house who were not Romans, but superintendents of a railway then being constructed. One of them laid on the table a nose-

[1] *Civiltá*, Serie VI., vol. ix., p. 126.

gay, so arranged that the colours formed 'the cockade of a king hostile to the Pontiff,'—doubtless red and white camellias, forming, with their green leaves, the colours of Italy. Guillemin, who was in uniform, heard remarks which showed that the gentlemen knew what the flowers signified. He rose, seized the nosegay, dashed it to the ground, and trampled it to pieces. Then, as the others grumbled, he drew out his revolver, laid it by his side, and went on sipping his coffee, and chatting with the Viscount.[1]

The *Civiltà* was at this time publishing a series of articles on the massacre of St. Bartholomew's, sometimes calling it 'the slaughter' and sometimes 'the executions of Paris;' and calculating that there might have been some two thousand Protestants put to death in the capital, and, say, eight thousand in all France!

Among his other crimes, Bismarck stayed the preparations for the Council by the campaign of Sadowa. The most reverend Court historian evidently has no sense of any need for giving the world other reasons for the total interruption of those preparations than the political troubles. Yet one who learned Christianity at the feet of Christ would not readily see why the studies of holy men in the mysteries of divine revelation should depend upon a battle in Bohemia, or on the flitting of a French garrison. Surely, divines might go on searching into naturalism, rationalism, pantheism, somnambulism, and freemasonry, whether Germany was uniting or splitting up again. Nevertheless, studies in regalism and Cæsarism, in the regular subordination of the natural order to the supernatural, and in the best measures for replacing the political system of Europe on the *divine basis*, or, as we should say, for subordinating civil and restoring ecclesiastical jurisdiction, were liable to be influenced by the flights of the eagles. And the augurs who were tracing the lines for the foundations of the reconstruction, found in the

---

[1] *Civiltà*, Serie VII., iv., 418.

movements of the eagles of Prussia and France omens that counselled delay.

According to the original design, the Council was to be opened on the day observed as the eighteenth centennial anniversary of St. Peter's martyrdom. But, owing to these sad interruptions, when 1867 approached the secret preparations were not sufficiently advanced. Such, at least, is the only reason given by Cecconi why the Council was postponed.

The Pope, however, was resolved to cover St. Peter's day with glory. So his own thrice sacred anniversary, that of 'the Immaculate,' and of the Syllabus, was once more signalised by the issue of letters to the bishops of the whole world, citing them to Rome for the 29th of the ensuing June. They were not only to celebrate the centenary of Peter's martyrdom, but to take part in the canonisation of some twenty additional saints, and also to attend certain consistories. The second name upon the list of the 'new patrons in the presence of God' about to be created was that of PETER DE ARBUES, 'Spanish inquisitor and martyr,'[1] of whose canonisation we shall hear again. This invitation was dated three days before the French evacuated Rome. As trusty bayonets were failing, additional celestial powers were to be called into the firmament.

All this time the Liberal Catholics were becoming increasingly uneasy at the prospect of the dangers on which the Church was drifting. They had hoped to see her first embrace and then dominate modern culture and liberties. This was a dream of O'Connell, of Lammenais, and of Gioberti. At this aimed the erudite and steadfast German Catholics. But every new utterance of the Court, whether in official document or inspired organ, showed that it was determined upon dragging the Church in an opposite direction. According to the policy to which it had fully committed itself, the Church was to conquer, not by adopting the modern age, but by restoring the middle ages. The dominion of the Pontiff over the whole earth as spiritual despot

---

[1] *Cecconi*, p. 133.

and temporal suzerain was the ideal to which everything must give way. Montalembert, who had been flattered by the opening career of Pius IX., as sailors say they are flattered by what they call foxy weather, expresses himself as follows : 'I began as early as 1852 to wrestle against the detestable political and religious aberrations summed up in contemporary Ultramontanism.' He showed that when in 1847 he defended the Jesuits of the Sonderbund against Thiers, as he did with equal eloquence and want of foresight, he did not utter one word of the modern doctrines, and that for a good reason, because, he says, 'No one had thought of setting them up when I entered on public life.' Indeed, he affirms that, in 1847, Gallicanism was dead, but that it had been revived through the encouragement given to extreme pretensions during the pontificate of Pius IX. He then quotes an important letter addressed to himself, in 1863, by Sibour, at that time Archbishop of Paris :—

'The new Ultramontane school is conducting us to a twofold idolatry —idolatry of the temporal power and idolatry of the spiritual power. When you, like myself, made a splendid profession of Ultramontanism, you did not understand things in this fashion. We defended the independence of the spiritual power against the usurpations and pretensions of the temporal power ; but we respected the constitution of the State and the constitution of the Church. We did not sweep away every intermediate power, or every gradation of order, nor yet every legitimate resistance, nor all individuality and spontaneity. The Pope and the Emperor were not then—the former the whole Church, the latter the whole State.'

Montalembert goes on to say that the old Ultramontanes had recognised the right of the Pope, in a great crisis, to rise above all rules ; but they did not confound the exception with the rule. These cares and apprehensions were for the time concealed, and were only brought to light by the anguish of that moment when the final leap downward was about to place a gulf that could never be recrossed between Rome and all things free and equal. But when the expression did come, it bore with it the record of previous irritations.

'The Ultramontane bishops,' said Montalembert, 'have pushed everything to the extreme, and have argued to the utmost against all liberties, those of the State as well as those of the Church.

'If such a system was not of a nature to compromise the gravest interests of religion, in the present, but much more in the future, we might content ourselves with despising it; but when one has the presentiment of the ills which are being prepared for us, it is difficult to be silent and resigned.'

CHAPTER X.

Reprimand of Darboy, Archbishop of Paris, for disputing the Ordinary and Immediate Jurisdiction of the Pope in his Diocese—Sent in 1864, Published in 1869.

WITHIN a twelvemonth of the issue of the Syllabus, letters of significance were passing between Paris and Rome. One of those letters throws light on the steps taken to grind down any bishop who dared to assert, as bishops used to do, some authority for their own office, independent of the direct and universal meddling of Rome. That some prelates were still tempted to this offence we have seen hinted by the Cardinal consulters, in the original notes upon the question of holding a Council.

One of the most considerable figures in the hierarchy was Darboy, Archbishop of Paris, to whose name a historical death has given tragic immortality. When the preparations for the issue of the Syllabus must have been far advanced, in 1864, he had drawn upon himself letters of censure from Rome. To these he had replied both publicly in the senate, and privately, in a manner which showed that some remnants of old French doctrines yet survived the modern influence in primary schools and episcopal seminaries. And wherever any sense of the ancient office of a bishop did survive, there was constant irrita-

¹ Letter quoted in the *Unità Cattolica*, March 10th, 1870. *Friedberg*, p. 118-121.

tion in the condition of dependence to which the system of *quinquennial faculties* reduced the men who, bearing the old name, held the modern post under the bureaux in Rome.   Only a few weeks before the Magna Charta of reconstruction was promulged, on October 26th, 1864, a letter was addressed to Darboy which fills no less than ten octavo pages of small type in the documents of Friedberg.[1]   Besides its solid value as instruction, this epistle has the interest of a sharp lecture. Furthermore, its very language coloured the most important of the Vatican decrees.

We shall here supply only an outline, which, however, will give to any attentive reader a key to certain points disputed between the two schools into which the Church of Rome had the advantage of being divided, before the Vatican Council.

The quarrel arises on the old subject of the 'exemption' of the regulars from episcopal control, and the direct action of the Curia in a diocese, over the head of a bishop and under his feet. Readers of Church history will be tempted to think lightly of the Pope's candour when he speaks of Darboy's complaint as a new one, but however this suspicion may touch those who furnished the materials for the letter, it does not attach to the Pope personally, for he is not usually supposed to read history, though he often sets it to rights.

If inaccurate in his facts, Pius IX. is orthodox in his policy, for just as bishops must be independent of the government of the country, so must the regulars be independent of the bishops, that power to set wheels in motion may be carried from the engine-house in Rome into the midst of a nation by two perfectly independent shafts.   When the Church is a national one, a bishop has some stake in the country, though slight compared with his stake at the Vatican ; and he must, at all events, keep up relations with the authorities.   The former circumstance brings temptations to a 'national spirit,'—one of the standing evils cried down by the Curia.   The latter circum-

[1] *Aktenstücke*, p. 257-267.

stance may make it convenient that the bishop should not always know what is really the course of action being prepared. In both points of view the regulars can be utilised. Darius took care to have three separate powers in each province, all directly dependent on the Imperial Court alone.[1] And from his days highly organised Asiatic governments have had, besides the apparently omnipotent lieutenants, confidential agents in every province, depending directly on the metropolitan authorities.

The Pontiff commences his letter by reminding his venerable brother that he made professions of devotion to the Holy See on his elevation to that of Paris. Then he tells him that certain of his letters replying to animadversions of the Pope, show him to hold views opposed to the divine primacy of the Roman Pontiff over the whole Church. Darboy had asserted that the power of the Pope, in a diocese other than his own, was not *ordinary* and *immediate*, but such as should be interposed only as a last resource, in cases of manifest necessity. He had represented the intervention of the Pope, by the exercise of *ordinary* and *immediate* jurisdiction, as turning a diocese into a mission, and a bishop into a vicar apostolic. Moreover, he had said, in the French senate, that when such intervention took place at the private instance of individuals, it rendered the administration of a diocese all but impossible ; and he had added that regulars, Nuncio, and Curia all aimed at bringing about such intervention as an ordinary thing, and that he would resist it and call upon the bishops and people to do so. He had even spoken of submitting letters apostolic to the government, and of having recourse to the lay power ; nay, he had gone so far as to mention the *Organic articles,* though he could not be ignorant of how the Holy See had always protested against them.

The Pope could scarcely believe that his venerable brother had uttered such things, and was moved with wonder and anguish at finding him avowing the condemned opinions of

[1] Rawlinson's *Ancient Monarchies,* vol. iv.

Febronius, which a bishop ought to abhor. In denying the 'immediate and ordinary' jurisdiction of the Pope, he had denied the decree of the fourth Lateran Council. The words 'feed my lambs, feed my sheep' mean that believers all and singular are to be subject to Peter and his successors, as to the Lord Christ Himself, whose vicar upon earth the Roman Pontiff truly is. Every Catholic would reply to the charge as to a diocese being turned into a mission, and a bishop into a vicar apostolic, by saying that it was as false as it would be to say that prefects, judges, or provincial magistrates were not ordinary magistrates, because a direct, immediate, and ordinary power was held by the king or emperor.

St. Thomas Aquinas, continues the letter, had said 'the Pope has a plenitude of pontifical power, as a king in his kingdom, but bishops are received into a share of the solicitude, like judges set over particular cities.' As a Catholic bishop, Darboy ought to know that all had a right to appeal to Rome, none to appeal from her. Such a complaint as that the interference of Rome rendered the administration of a diocese almost impossible had never been made either in past ages or in the present one. Bishops of a religious mind derived from such intervention consolation and strength before God, the Church, and her enemies. Before God, because it, in part, exempted them from responsibility, in giving account of their stewardship. When Darboy spoke of appealing to bishops and people, he ought to have known that the same had been done by Febronius, and that it was an offence against the divine Author of the constitution of the Church.

The Archbishop had not been informed against, proceeded the Pope, by the regulars, but, from other quarters the fact came before his Holiness that the Archbishop had exercised the right of visitation over them, on which he had been admonished, and of this admonition he had been pleased to speak, in the senate, as of a sentence delivered without the cause having been heard. It was hardly to be believed! The Archbishop knew the

Decretals, and knew how, in all ages, the Popes had written in the same manner to bishops when they became aware of something in their sees which was not quite right. Without this procedure, the government of the whole Church would be rendered too difficult for the Vicar of Christ, and any other course would hardly comport with episcopal meekness.

As it was a question of the visitation of regulars, it must be remembered that the right of exemption had long been enjoyed by the Jesuits and Franciscans in Paris, and that the Apostolic See had exercised its own special or 'privative' jurisdiction. The present case, therefore, was one of violation of possession, *i.e.*, of the possession of the right of exemption enjoyed by the regulars, and of the right of privative jurisdiction enjoyed by the Apostolic See. True, Darboy thought that a presumption of right administration ought to be admitted in favour of one in charge, until the contrary was proved. But that was opposed to the principle of St. Bernard, who held that it was the glory of the Papacy to rescue the weak out of the hands of the strong. Darboy had alleged that, by the law of the Council of Trent, regulars could not have canonical existence in any diocese without consent of the bishop, which consent had never been received by the monks in question. But, having been long on the ground, they had acquired a prescriptive right, by virtual, if not by express consent of successive bishops. And as to the fact that the civil law forbade them to possess land, of what use were such laws in ecclesiastical adminstration? In these most turbulent and miserable times of noxious, odious rebellion, civil law might even deny to bishops their civil standing.

The Pontiff cannot dissemble his extreme surprise and annoyance that his venerable brother had attended the funeral of Marshal Magnan, the Grand Orient of the Freemasons, and had given the solemn absolution while the insignia of freemasonry were on the bier, and brethren of the condemned sect wearing its orders were present. The sect aimed at corrupting all minds and manners; at destroying every idea of honesty, virtue, truth, and justice; at diffusing monstrous opinions and abominable vices, fostering detestable crimes, and undermining all legitimate authority; yea, at overturning the Catholic Church and civil society, and at expelling God from heaven.

His Holiness cannot pass over the fact that it has come to his ears that an opinion has been expressed to the effect that acts of the Holy See do not compel obedience unless the civil government has given authority to carry them out. This opinion is pernicious, erroneous, and injurious to the authority of the Holy See and to the interests of the faithful. The supreme authority of the Apostolic See can never be subordinated to the rule or will of the civil power in any matter which in any respect touches upon ecclesiastical affairs and the spiritual government of souls; and all who glory in the Catholic name are bound to obey the Church, and to show her due reverence and devotion. Furthermore, the Pope's venerable brother had incorrectly asserted in his speech that Benedict XIV. in his Concordat with the King of Sardinia had agreed that the royal sanction should be required before pontifical acts were carried into execution; and that according to the instructions annexed to the Concordat, they were to be submitted to the senate, except when they dealt with matters of dogma or morals; which false assertion the venerable brother would not have made had he weighed the words of the instructions. The letter concludes with protestations of the Pope's affection for his venerable brother and his flock.

This epistle, after being long held in reserve, was launched into publicity, at a time when Darboy's influence was threatening to be inconvenient in the Council, and when the French government had requested a cardinal's hat for him.[1]

It is, perhaps, not superfluous to remark that the terms 'plenitude of power,' as denoting the prerogative of the Pope, and ' *received* to a share of the solicitude,' as denoting the origin and nature of the bishop's authority, are not merely happy phrases,

---

[1] *Ce Qui Se Passe au Concile*, p. 16.

but scientific terms fitted to express the Papal theory of the Church constitution as opposed to the Episcopal theory. The Episcopal theory, holding that the office of all bishops is of divine institution, regards the Pope, not as the source of episcopal authority, but as supreme and ultimate arbiter. According to the Papal theory the authority of the bishop is an emanation from that of the Pope, who, as monarch, unlimited by any co-ordinate authority, retains in his own hands not only extraordinary but ordinary, not only ultimate but immediate jurisdiction over every subject within the bounds assigned to a bishop. The latter is a prefect, not only liable to be discharged or imprisoned, but liable while retained in office to have any matter taken out of his hands and settled contrary to his views. This is the theory which, like a scourge of not small cords, is employed to flog Darboy, while the incongruous epithet ' venerable brother,' dangles at the handle,—a vestige of a past age and an exploded theory. An emperor does not call his prefect ' venerable brother.'

A portion of the letter, which will well repay study, is that indicating the attitude of the Curia to all authority not immediately within its own hands, even if in the hands of its 'prefects.' Against any such authority it will receive the reports of its private agents, and treat those reports as having the status of a legal appeal. It will act, if need be, without hearing the accused, and maintain that none shall appeal from it, though all may appeal to it. This is the case even with the episcopal authority; what, then, is the case with the civil? It is swept aside as an unclean thing ; ' of what use are such laws in ecclesiastical affairs?' If Archbishop Darboy, strong in his character, strong in his see,—the largest in the Roman Catholic world,— and strong in his influence at the Tuileries, is thus treated when complained of by the Jesuits, what must be the case with small prelates who venture to provoke their power ?

As to the Freemasons, one is tempted to wish to be in their secret, for then one would possess a rough test of Papal infallibility. If they do not aim at overturning all government, and expelling God from heaven, infallibility does not carry far. The fact that a Grand Master of the Masons, the Marquis of Ripon, has renounced them to embrace the infallibility which so depicts them, does not tell in their favour.

One anachronism of this epistle is the word 'primacy,' which imbeds as in crystal the original pretensions of the Roman bishop, presenting them in contrast with those advanced in the letter. As the claim of primacy had been developed out of a position in the capital, so out of primacy was developed authority, out of authority essential superiority, out of essential superiority sovereignty limited by many checks, and out of that, finally, sovereignty absolutely unlimited.

The time for the great assembly was now approaching, and, meanwhile, the Papal organs were enlivened by the prospect of a war between France and Prussia, on the question of Luxembourg. When this hope was deferred the readers of the *Civiltà* were informed that nevertheless every possible preparation for war was being pushed forward by the French on the largest scale, and with greatly improved arms.

On the 9th of May, 1867, the deputies Angeloni and Crotti were called up in the Italian Parliament to take the oaths and their seats. Angeloni did so ; but Crotti, a well-known member of the Ultramontane aristocracy, after pronouncing the words ' I swear to be faithful to the king and constitution,' added, 'saving always divine and ecclesiastical laws.' This formula was at once recognised as being that which had been published in Rome by the *Penetenzieria*, with the declaration that the repetition of it was the only condition on which Catholics could accept seats in the Italian chambers. Called upon to take the oath in the form prescribed by the law of the land, Count Crotti stood firm by the higher law of the *Penetenzieria*, and the Chamber disowning his *salvis legibus divinis et ecclesiasticis*, refused to admit him.

<hr />

[1] Serie VI., vol. x., p. 384.

CHAPTER XI.

Great Gathering in Rome, June 1867—Impressions and Anticipations,—Improvements in the City—Louis Veuillot on the Great Future.

THE whole earth had been moved in the hope of not only exhibiting a pageant outshining former ones, but also of carrying the dogma of Papal infallibility by an ecclesiastical *coup d'etat*, or, as it is called, by acclamation, without the delays of a discussion.[1] Had this been accomplished the legislative form of a General Council would have been rendered futile for the time to come, or at the most, would have been but a grander method of working the institution of 'consultative despotism,' to adopt the strict definition of Montalembert. The invitation had been enthusiastically responded to. The spectacle of the Papacy menaced with the loss of Rome was touching, and the belief was cherished that a great demonstration of the interest felt by the Catholic world on its behalf would contribute to ward off the peril. Besides these motives, another in full activity was the ever powerful one, especially powerful with Romanists, the desire to see a pageant; and this sight was to surpass all the former displays of Rome.

The city put on its best, the churches were newly embellished, the streets decked in festive array. Bishops came from all the ends of the earth, till the thoroughfares were mottled with the toilets of five hundred. Priests crowded in till, it is said, twelve thousand breathed the sacred air of the city, every one of them proud to tread that spot of our unruly earth, where the priest was king of men.

Besides the clergy, came such multitudes of pilgrims that, according to Cecconi, the population of the city was almost doubled. The Romans saw their familiar rite, the worship of the statue of St. Peter—*l'adorazione della statua di San Pietro—*

[1] Acton, *Zur. Ges.*, p. 14.

performed on a prodigious scale. In modern as in ancient Rome, adoration has its degrees; all worship does not imply the ascription of supreme, but only of celestial honours. No Pontiff in the days of the Republic ever pretended that Quirinus was creator of the world and father of eternity. He was the protecting divinity of Rome, but with very limited powers in comparison with Peter, carrying no sceptre equal to the keys.

Such of the visitors as had seen the city in former times, if not too much pre-occupied with the sanctity of the place to observe such matters, would find several improvements. Side pavements had been allowed in the main streets. Gaslight had, after long and painful efforts, been admitted. The Papal idea of street-lighting had been ecclesiastical and pictorial. M. Fisquet treats the subject in his folio on ceremonies (*Frond*, iii., 251). Besides all the Madonnas in the churches, there were, he says, as many more on the fronts of the houses,—of the latter, 1421. Those in shops, galleries, etc., could not be numbered. Nearly all had silver crowns, earrings, diamond brooches, or at least filagree ones. One thousand and sixty-seven lamps were lighted before them every day. True, it had been said that this was brought about by the Popes to save expense in street lighting. The street roughs broke lamps if they shone only for the 'temporal end,' but as soon as the lamp was lifted into the supernatural order, by being lighted before the Madonna, it became sacred. M. Fisquet quotes *Bernardin Gassiat* to show how enlightened such government was. In former times, that is, 'in the ages of faith,' the cities of Italy, at night, 'were,' he says, 'like vast cities of the dead, full of mysteries, and without any security. If it is to be supposed that the institution of lamps before the Madonnas was due to the initiative of the Papal police, it would be a fine argument in proof of their devotion to the cause of civilisation.'

However, even Rome had been pushed into some approaches to other sorts of civilisation. Railways had entered the walls. The personal liberality of the Pope had effected several improvements, both in public works and charitable institutions. The French had done a great deal for the cleansing of the streets, although the filth of some of them, and the indecency of some of the bye ones, were still beyond belief to any one from England. The Pope's army, which as late as 1860 was an odd-looking array, was now a sightly and active force, composed mainly of foreigners, in large part French. And, finally, it had become possible to tell the time of day.

Formerly, mid-day had been one of the mysteries of Rome. It seemed as if the right of private judgment, banished from the churches, had taken refuge in the steeples, for each particular clock went off at some mysterious impulse, and struck twelve at a noon of its own. Naughty Romans said that the impulse proceeded from the vitals of the priest, whom discipline forbade to breakfast till the time for saying masses had expired, which did not take place till noon. When, therefore, each separate rector had, out of the depths of his consciousness, evolved the truth that it ought to be twelve o'clock, he told the sexton to make it so ; earlier or later, according as the consciousness was more or less keen. Thus for good part of an hour, they do say often longer, the air continued thrilling with the tidings that it was just noon of day. The same naughty Romans ascribe the change to General Baraguay d'Hilliers, while in command of the French garrison. Having vainly endeavoured to get a standard of time established, he presumed, with French audacity, to carry the case by appeal from the sacristy to the sun. Placing a gun on Fort St. Angelo, with a burning glass upon it, he stole the tidings from another world, which were not to be got from the temples at hand.[1]

One of the most powerful of the pilgrims was M. Louis Veuillot, who as editor of the *Univers* had for very many years done much to second in literature the work done in schools, of

---

[1] This was first told me by a Roman tradesman, in presence, among others, of a very good-natured canon, who joined in the general laugh at my innocent surprise. This year (1875) an ex-officer of the Pope's service added, 'Ay, but the priests bribed the artillery men to steal half the charge of powder, and to

reviving antipathies and superstitions which were in danger of
dying out in France. His notes of this visit form part of his
two octavos. As soon as he reaches the foot of the Alps, at
Susa, he begins to scold Italy and the Italians, takes every
opportunity of doing so, and goes out of the country scolding
worse than when he came in. He says (vol. i., p. 48),
' Florence, where the intellectual life of revolutionary Italy is
concentrated, has not a man, not an artist, not a pamphleteer,
not a caricaturist, to show to the world. It is a vile workshop of
vile counterfeits, a factory of despicable mouldings.' According
to him, the Italians persecuted the pilgrims. It was the old
cry, ' The Christians to the lions;' but, irate as he is, he lets it
appear that the persecutions could not have been deadly, by
adding, ' There are three kinds of lions in Italy—the custom-
house officers, the bugs, and the innkeepers.'

But if Italy and the Italians were exceedingly evil in the
eyes of M. Veuillot, he found compensation in the perfect
loveliness of Rome and the Romans. At a table in the
open air, and in the shade, by St. Carlo on the Corso, ' What
think you,' he asks, ' did I pay for a cup of *café au lait*, a
roll, and two figs dropping pearls of honey, such figs as
Augustus loved ; and for a large glass of beautiful water,
with the animated spectacle of the street, and the view of a
balcony decorated with brilliant cloths ? Twopence halfpenny ;
and it was a halfpenny too much,—the halfpenny of progress.'[1]
The very cabmen are loudly praised, and the cabs carry 'ideas;'
the press, especially the *Civiltà*, is of course far above the
French level. But the Pope was the grandest spectacle of all.
As he entered the Basilica, preceded by a train of five hundred

---

turn the gun toward the Campagna, so that the report should scarcely be
heard.' Probably the last statement is a mere rumour, not representing any
actual transaction, but indicating, really enough, the state of mind of the
people as to what their masters were likely to do. I have heard it said that
Sir James Hudson used to declare that when first appointed to Turin he could
walk all round the city while it struck twelve o'clock.

[1] *Rome pendant le Concile,* vol. i., p. 16.

prelates, it made an impression of power greater than if four
millions of men had defiled past, armed with the most perfect
artillery.[1]

Naturally, however, the imagination of M. Veuillot was most
fired with the prospect of that historical future which was
about to open on the human species. Darkness still covers the
chaos after the cataclysm, but the breaking of the light draws
nigh. A change of tone henceforth marks the utterances
of reconstruction. In 1850 and the succeeding years, princes
were to be favoured agents, and concordats a salutary instrument in restoring the polity of the kingdom of God. But,
alas, how ineffectual had these proved! The time had come
for the true bearers of the commission which gives 'all power
in heaven and in earth,' to assert their own prerogative, and
gradually to file away all interloping authorities which existed
only for a temporal end. The news of a projected Council
has reached the ears of M. Veuillot. His first word is, 'Rome
is officially taking the reins of the world into her hand.' Other
expressions scattered up and down his animated pages are as
follows :—

> The day that the Council is convoked the counter-revolution will
> commence. . . . Pius IX. will open his mouth, and the great word, Let
> there be light, will proceed out of his lips. . . . It will be a solemn
> date in history ; it will witness the laying of the immovable stone of Re-
> construction. . . . At the voice of the Pontiff the bowels of the earth will
> be moved, to give birth to the new civilisation of the cross. . . . Here is
> the great reservoir whence the future will pour out and overflow the
> human race. . . . These days in Rome are a revelation of the state of the
> world, and the starting point of a renovation. . . . The pilgrimage of
> Catholic Europe to Rome in 1867 will have consequences of which the
> *Moniteur* [alluding to remarks in that journal] will be informed here-
> after, and of which the world will become aware when the *Moniteur*
> would wish them to be unheard of. . . . For centuries Rome has not
> seen the Pope in such splendour, nor has he so manifestly appeared in his
> character as head of the human race.'

The following expressions further elucidating the same train

[1] *Rome pendant le Concile*, vol. i., p. 35.

of thought are found scattered over papers printed after the
Council had been called, but we give them here :—

'The order of things which lasted above ten centuries has ceased to
exist. The middle ages are terminated. The 29th of June, 1868 [the
date of the Bull convoking the Council], is their final end, their last sigh.
Another era is beginning. . . . The Church and the State are already
separated in fact. It is not well. The Church is now a soul without a
body, the State a body without a soul. Some in both Church and State
rejoice at this. Let them haste and make ready. Strange toils are
coming. There must be clearing away and rebuilding, and the workmen
will not agree. . . . "One flock and one shepherd,"—these words reveal the
sole political secret of the human race. Europe is on the brink of an abyss
for not having extended the benefit of unity to the world, and not having
conserved it for herself. . . . There are no more Catholic kingdoms, no
more Christian nations. . . . What place could princes take in the
Council ? what part could they play in the government of mind or
manners ? They have no longer the right to speak to men of their
eternal salvation. . . . The Church does not expel them, but takes note
that they are outside. . . . The rupture is declared ; that rupture gives
her the world to reconstruct, and she sets to work. It is entering on a
desert where for forty years the people had to wander to renew themselves. We can foresee relentless pursuits, and catastrophes which will
spare nothing. . . . As the State is out of the Church, we have scarcely
any longer a place in the State. What are we Catholics in France ? A
conquered people. . . . What is about to come to pass is not a thing
unheard of. Noah beheld it. . . . It is not to create division that concordats are destroyed, but to re-establish unity ; it will no longer be a
question of alliances but of conquests.'

These dispersed but not unconnected utterances of one
whose opinions rule so many of the pulpits and schools of
France, and who stands so high in the favour of the Vatican,
are not without importance. His forecast of the future is
remarkable :—

'If we dare to cast our eyes further into the future, beyond the far
extended smoke of battle and of demolition, we behold a gigantic and
unheard of construction, the work of the Church, which by lovelier and
more marvellous creations will reply to the infernal genius of destruction.
We behold the Christian and Catholic organisation of democracy. On
the ruins of faithless empires we behold the multitude of nations arise
more numerous, equal among themselves, free, forming one universal
confederation, in the unity of the faith, under the presidency of the
Roman Pontiff, equally the protected and the protector of every one ;

a *holy people,* as once there was a *holy empire.* And this baptised and sacred democracy will do what the monarchies have not been able or not wished to do ; it will abolish the idols everywhere, it will cause Christ to reign universally, and there will be one fold and one shepherd." [1]

We presume that a *Christian* democracy, in the Vatican sense, means a democratic despotism, with the Pope as suzerain, whether the chief of the State be a monarch or a president after the model of Ecuador, or, better still, a prince-bishop. The *Christian* organisation would be that now going on in unions, leagues, and confraternities, guided by the regulars. The increased number of nations which are to replace empires would seem to indicate a preference for small States—perhaps 'spiritual States,' whose fall is often lamented. The idols to be abolished would be, all heresies, schisms, and modern liberties. The natural order would be absorbed in the supernatural.

M. Veuillot is of course one of those who look on the modern liberty of the press as a great curse. We might suppose that this opinion rests upon the violent examples of political folly and moral corruption exhibited by certain sheets in France and Italy whenever legal fetters do not impede free writing. But not so. It is a notorious fact that rabid papers are favourites with the priests, but moderate ones are odious to them. ' You will never find the *Opinione,*' said an educated Roman, ' in the hands of a priest, because it is moderate. You will often find the *Capitale* in their hands, because it is destructive.' We may insert here what came to hand long after thsee pages were written, as an illustration of the kind of press that is to be quenched. The *Times* of January 26th, 1876, in the letter of its Paris correspondent, gives a morsel from the *Univers,* in the style of M. Veuillot. The *Times* had said something about an interview of the Marquis of Ripon, as a new convert, with the Pope. The *Univers* devotes to that article ' a column and a half of invectives,' and thus winds up : ' The *Times* is now the giant of the press, and prospers in both hemispheres. But the

[1] Vol. i., pp. 65, 66.

day will come when the two worlds will want no more of its agony column, or of its bad literature ; and its last compositor, inactive before his immense poison machine, suddenly idle, will wait in vain for copy which will never come.' Will the compositor look out of the top window in Queen Victoria Street to see if Macaulay's New Zealander has arrived on London Bridge ?

CHAPTER XII.

The Political Lesson of the Gathering, namely, All are called upon to recognise in the Papal States the Model State of the World—Survey of those States.

'*OPPORTUNENESS of the Centenary of St. Peter for reviving the True Idea of the Political Order among States,*' is the heading of an article in the *Civiltà Cattolica* for 1867. The first words are, ' He who comes to Rome finds St. Peter become a king;' a proposition of which we should modify the predicate, saying, He who comes to Rome finds a king, professing to be St. Peter. ' He (*i.e.,* Peter) has joined the tiara of the Pontiff to the crown of the Prince.' Why did not the writer say the 'tiara of the apostle'? That would be too great an offence against antiquity. It is the tiara of the Pontiff, as if Peter had taken over that office from Nero.

However, these are but the introductory notes. The writer proceeds to expound the political effects of baptism. Christianity has not changed the civil power as to its substance, but as to its relations, by making a change in the subject of power. That subject is no longer mere man, but man made Christian by baptism. As such he is brought under the new law, with which no act of his must ever come into conflict. This doctrine— which frequently reappears as the theological basis of reconstruction—is more fully stated by M. Veuillot: 'They will not deny that the true human race is baptised humanity. . . . It is, then, baptism which constitutes humanity, and all that has not been introduced into the Church by baptism is, in reality, only a sort of raw material, which as yet awaits the breath of life' (p. cxii.) In order to prevent any conflict between baptized man and the law of the Church, the *civil power must be subject to the Church.* Suarez is quoted to the effect that as a man would not be rightly constituted unless the body were subject to the soul, neither would the Church be rightly established unless the temporal power were subject to the spiritual. And hence, the political conclusion is firmly drawn: ' The ideal of such a subordination is realised in the pontifical government. Because, owing to the peculiar character of him who here holds the temporal power, it cannot rebel against the spiritual power, civil law can never here set itself against evangelical law, nor is any political act possible which should offend against morals.'

The last affirmation will appear boldest to those who best know what political acts had been done in the Roman States, and in the present reign. No one of these acts could offend against Christian morals! for the all-sufficing reason that Peter had become the king, and Peter does no wrong. Thus we find infallibility, as received in the Court creed, covering measures of taxation and police, as well as lotteries and monopolies,—an abuse of the doctrine made still more obvious by what follows, in which the infallibility of the government is grounded on its immaculate conception, and consequently perfect nature. Since in the Pontifical States ' the laws must be sanctioned by him who holds the place of God on earth, him whom God has given to us for guide and teacher, they can never be in conflict with the divine will.[1] The infallible Depositary of evangelical interests can never sacrifice them to earthly ones. Though in such a government the two powers [spiritual and temporal] are distinct in form, they are in complete harmony and duly co-ordinated one

---

[1] ' I have no need to declare myself ready to repel and reject that which the Pope cannot do. He cannot do an act contrary to the Divine law.'—*Cardinal Manning, Vat. Dec.,* p. 41.

with the other, presenting to lay States the perfect example of the Christian civil power.'

It is granted that lay States can never equal this example, but they ought to imitate it. By their very conception they can never be free from the original taint, owing to which it becomes possible for 'the temporal power to rebel against the spiritual power.' Not only is it possible, but, by their nature, they are predisposed to that sin of sins. But all rulers of lay States are to know that in becoming subjects of the Church the subjects of civil power have been changed, though the substance of civil power has not been changed. We do not stay to inquire what may be the substance of civil power, after its subjects have been lifted above obedience to it by another human power, higher than itself in all things wherein the two may come into collision. Christianity has, thank God, its higher law. That is, it holds man as the offspring of God, and as redeemed by Christ to a nobler life, and a holier than can be prescribed by any civil authority. But in the State it owns no authority but that of the sovereign as supreme, whether he be called king, imperator, or president, and that of those who under him administer law. The higher law of the Papacy, on the contrary, lies in setting up as supreme judge a human ruler over the civil ruler, and in holding the *changed* subjects of the civil power bound, in all cases of collision, to obey the supreme judge.

In conclusion, the faithful are told that the centenary of St. Peter, by bringing together people from all parts of the world, will give to them the opportunity of beholding 'a State in which peace, morality, and justice reign. It is like an oasis amid the desolation of the desert; and it is so because the political order is in full harmony with evangelical law.' It is, therefore, inferred that all those who look upon the immaculate and infallible State will return home to testify how great is the folly of that separation of Church and State which many propose; and also to testify that 'the only way to conduct the nations back to civil well-being, is by making their laws over again, in a

Christian sense, and harmonising political order with the Gospel.'[1]

The reader will by this time begin to attach a meaning to such expressions as 'evangelical interests,' 'harmonising political order with the gospel,' and the like, rather different from that which he would give to them in reading theology or any political writing but that of the Vatican. There the desire to enlist religious veneration for political arrangements, has led to a secularising of sacred language, which is now developed into a highly finished art. If nations are to 'make their laws over again, in a Christian sense,' the Court of Rome has made Christian language over again in a political sense. The approaching pilgrims, in comparing the oasis into which they were about to enter, with the deserts from which they had emerged, would be able to judge by the experience of centuries as to whether, where Peter reigns, the lifting up of the subject above lay government into the supernatural order had led to the elevation of the laity to supernatural goodness, or to the lowering of the clergy to the level of political officials.

Two writers, as dissimilar as Addison and Edgar Quinet, had, in some degree, anticipated the comparison here challenged, each speaking from a point of view suited to his own day and mode of thinking. The Englishman remarks how great is the difference between Roman Catholic populations where they touch upon reformed countries and where they are under the unbroken influence of the Papacy. Ignorance, superstition, and crime gradually deepen till the Alps and the Pyrenees are passed, when all these become strikingly worse. Addison might have added to this observation the further one of a contrast between Roman Catholic populations which border on Protestant States and those which border on Mohammedan ones. Contrast Belgium, Bavaria, Leinster, with Andalusia, Sicily, Croatia!

The Frenchman says that there was only one model country

[1] *Civiltá,* Serie VI., vol. x., p. 525 *et sqq.*

in Europe. This was correct; for France had never cast out the influence of the Reformation, or made away with all the Protestants; and had, moreover, been the hot-bed of what Quinet calls the philosophers. Italy, again, had always been a stronghold of the so-called philosophers, although all the Protestants had been consumed. In Spain, however, as he points out, the Inquisition had really fulfilled its mission; both Protestants and philosophers having been annihilated, schools and letters having been reduced to order, and the whole nation having been made to move for more than two hundred years on the Papal lines. The consequence was the total ruin of religion in the country.[1]

The comparison to which strangers were challenged by the Curia had the great advantage of being a comparison of good, not of evil. If the Papal States are to lay States as the oasis to the desert, proof actually lies before us of something more than human superiority—of something amounting to a higher dispensation. If the Papal States are but moderately superior to others, proof of any higher dispensation fails; but proof of human superiority remains. If they are only equal to lay States, even proof of human superiority fails. If they are inferior, proof fails both of divine commission and of human superiority, and proof arises of the presence of greater human fault.

The only true book of Positive Philosophy yet (we do not say of Positive Science) is the blessed old Book of books. It brings everything to the test of fruits. It puts the extraordinary man to the test before ordinary men. Priest, prophet, and king must produce—not allege, but produce—credentials. If they have an ordinary commission they must prove it by ordinary qualities such as God would employ and bless, if an extraordinary commission by extraordinary qualities, and if a supernatural one by supernatural powers. Moses put the prophet under the test of the written Word (Deut. xiii. 2, 3); and Paul put the apostle and even the angel under the same test, if he claimed

[1] *Ultramontanism et la Société Moderne.*

to say anything to us in the name of God. And that test was to be applied by common men. This is the horror of priestcraft. This is the strength of Christianity. He who refuses the ordained appeal to the Word, and to fruits, and to the verdict of every man's conscience, writes his own description as a false prophet.

The message God sends to men wants, above all things, private judgment—awake, earnest, and searching, that its credentials may commend themselves to every man's conscience in the sight of God.

We shall not, therefore, set out to compare evil, but good. We shall not enquire if there are more waste acres in the Papal States, more filthy huts, more wretched villages, more mean little towns called cities, more blighted prospects, talents thrown to waste, and families brought to decay, more liars, thieves, drunkards, blasphemers, and libertines, more depraved homes, more guilty conspiracies, more strikers, robbers, and assassins, more beggars in the streets, more idlers and extortioners in office, more wretches in prison, and more dead men in graves dug by the law, than, say, in our own far from immaculate or infallible England. We shall only look for the opposite of all these, and more of it,—so much more as would furnish proof of a special dispensation of God's loving-kindness to men.

In one particular, such of the pilgrims as had heard of the desolation of the Roman Campagna would feel surprise, somewhat similar to that often felt by travellers in the Desert of Sinai. The latter, expecting to find extended plains of burning sand—a Sahara—find a country like another, only that it has no vegetation. So when pilgrims on the Campagna found green plains basking under a lovely sky, they would wonder how men could call it waste. Only by degrees would they realise the fact that there were no farm-houses, no labourers' cottages, no hamlets. In Arabia vegetation has failed, and with it animal existence. This region is a degree less desert: the herb enjoys life and supports the beast; only man has failed.

Travellers from the north are under the illusion of the light.

Its richness invests objects with a beauty of which the most brilliant part would be lost under duller skies. Travellers coming from countries equally well lighted, come also from scenes where Islam or heathenism is dominant, or else from new countries, which cannot well be compared with one that has enjoyed so long a reign of civilisation. Those from new countries would be pre-occupied by signs of antiquity; but if not priests, they would feel the lack of any token of modern victories of mind over matter, or of character over circumstances. To those from the East, again, the antiquities are remains of a comparatively modern age. If they had lived under Turkish rule, they would have been so accustomed to see circumstances govern, and matter take its own way, that they really would feel that they were rising into a more vigorous civilisation. And they would be the only ones who, on any grounds but such as satisfied M. Veuillot, could come to that conclusion.

Beyond what *we* call the east, lies a farther east; and it would be the duty of any one who read the challenge of the priest-kings, and came from a part of India which had for a century been under British government, to compare the population now beneath his eye with the heathen population under Protestant rulers. The comparison ought to embrace numbers, industrial activity, security of life and property, education and civil rights. Account should be taken of how much time the one government had enjoyed to develop the benefits of its rule, and how little the other; as also of those preceding conditions the advantages and disadvantages of which each in its place had inherited.

But which of the two more rapidly brought order out of anarchy? Which sooner consolidated hostile States into a peaceful family of nations? Which gave to the greatest multitude the blessing of sitting every man under his vine and under his fig-tree—none daring to make him afraid, none, whether he differed in rank or race, in religion or in politics? Yet the Company was not immaculate, and not infallible.

An observer coming from the south, and entering the States of the Church by the line of the Sacco, finds a rich vale bordered by the Volscian and Hernian Hills. He looks for houses standing apart, for hamlets and villages; but finds none. Charming sites for a mansion and park, and rich sites for farm-houses and hamlets, are without inhabitants, the people to till the land coming down from villages perched upon the hills, in some cases at a distance of miles.

A trained observer seeing the plain forsaken and the villages in military positions on the heights, would at once say, as he would in Syria,—The land has not learned what rest is! It has not yet experienced, for any continuance, that lot of conscious security in which the family suffices to itself, the lonely house is safe, and the village needs neither wall nor steep. The valleys of Tuscany or Piedmont tell a better tale of law and government.

When, at wide intervals, an inn or what is called a *Tenuta* occurs, perhaps it is announced by a few fine children, ill-clad and begging. The house has an expression of fear. The windows are few and small, and the yard, instead of a fence or low wall, is defended by a high one. There are no stack yards, no farm store and treasure spreading securely and ornamentally around as if conscious of strong, benign protectors. There is no grass-plot, no gravelled or flagged walk, no flower-bed before the door, no flower-pot in the window, no garden. The house has never blossomed into the home. It is, after all these ages, but a shelter from weather and violence.

Entering, you find dirt to a degree neither easy to believe nor pleasant to describe, which grows worse and worse the longer and more minutely you observe. The furniture consists of a few stools, a rough table or bench, with a sack or two of straw for a bed. The few utensils, whether of earthenware or metal, are, like the stools and bench, poor in quality, rude in form, and ill kept. Scarcely ever is there against the walls a print or photograph, an engraved sheet, a clock or plaster bust.

You look in vain for book, periodical, or journal. The idea of children's picture-books, or of a cottage library, is out of the question; and the Bible is not to be seen. If there be a picture of the Madonna or the patron saint, it is, in point of art, far below the pictures which often light up the cottage of our humblest labourer. If there is a book, it is a wretched dream-book teaching how to succeed in the lottery. No polished chest of drawers, no white dresser, no fire range bearing witness of taste and 'elbow-grease,' no pretty crockery, no easy-chair. You may perhaps see a man asleep on the bare bench and another on the floor.

As you let the picture print itself, with all its inevitable comments, upon your mind, it calls up comparisons with what you have seen in the unlettered countries of the world—not with the homes that grow up around a family Bible. Here the arts which bring Art home to the multitude have found no entrance. Engraving, printing, carving, ornamental work in metal, wood, or pottery, gardening, or artistic husbandry, are graces that have not crossed this dirty threshold. The æsthetics, which have had some part in the government of the country, have never developed the blessed æsthetic of home.

Turning from the house to the inhabitants, you must take care not to build a comparison on misleading data. We are not to look for the clear northern complexion here, or the burly Teuton physique, and must not put down dark full eyes as sensual, a hooked nose as cruel, or a sallow complexion as gloomy and plotting, without further proof. On the other hand, you are not to take the brightness given by the light and the crispness given by the air, to all tissues, especially animal ones, compared with the flaccid condition of the same tissues in our humid air, as anything more than what it is. Things which in England would look only clean, would here look bright.

Physically, you find a race of great capacity. The frame, if wanting the compactness of the French and the solidity of the English, is large and shapely ; such as after a few well-fed and well-housed generations would probably be one of the finest in the world. There is a certain sluggishness, which is generally called laziness. Perhaps it is not so much laziness as a lack of that physical elasticity which comes with successive generations of hopeful effort and good condition, but sinks away under hopelessness, or the effects of poor food and bad air. The natural intelligence is quick, and the manners generally polite, often winning. The pleasant word and the obliging act are both ready. But when did these carters and labourers wash? Was anything ever done to cleanse these garments, partly of goatskin with the hair attached, and partly of heavy cloth? We do not call raids now and then to keep vermin under, an effort at really cleansing. And the heads of the women and children! Whatever the prevalent æsthetics have accomplished, they have never awakened the sacred æsthetic of the human person, which is not to be confounded with the lower æsthetic of dress.

Turning towards the villages, the observer is again reminded of Syria, where he may have been led on by the prospect of a beautiful city set on a hill, and found a squalid village. Self-defending construction, as in the case of the lone house on the plain, reappears here. No outlying cottages before the village, no detached ones within it, no gardens or orchards behind. The backs of the houses form a continuous high wall, pierced with small windows, constituting an irregular but not despicable work of defence. Again you find the absence of any bit of green, or of flower-beds before the house, or of flowers in the window. The home is nothing outside the threshold, the village nothing outside the walls. Where are the English greens and gardens, the Swiss artistic structures, the fountains, bees, and flowers? Where the umbrage and bloom of an American village, founded not many years ago on the wild? There is no trace of that æsthetic of nature which would have been awakened had the fathers and mothers of these labourers, for the last few generations, gone forth at morning with the language of the Psalms in their memories, and also the language of Him whose touch turned the bird and the lily into spirit links, drawing up the heart of toiling man to the bosom of an all-providing and all-adorning God. We have seen a quotation from a Cardinal to the effect that there are more works of art in Perugia than in all the provincial towns of England. When our towns are as old as Perugia we shall better compare their art treasures. Meantime, the gardens of Nottingham alone would put those of all the Papal States to shame, excepting such as are attached to palaces.

Before entering the houses one feels as if it would be unfair to compare them with those of English villages in our more cultured and sunny counties. But we may take a Yorkshire manufacturing village, near collieries. There the ground is dirty with coal slack; the air dirty with coal smoke and heavy with damp vapours; the houses are of the colour of baked mud, called brick; the sky is low, and more brown than grey. Nature and art seem to have combined to make the house dirty. Here, on the contrary, the ground is as dry as a board, the air bright, the walls of warm-coloured stone, the sky lofty, luminous, and blue. Nature has done everything to suggest cleanliness, and also to reward it with such brilliant effect as we can only see in the brightest moments which summer lights up within our English homes. And as to manufacture, its grimy fingers have never touched the place.

Yet under the unfavourable conditions you find tidy women, with tidy children, by tidy fire-sides. The floor, seats, tables, drawers, dresser, walls, all show that the domestic arts of ornament, in however humble a style, are represented. The cottage child sits with its book on its knee; and you are not afraid to look into the corners. The Bible and hymn-book are probably upon the shelf; and if you do not know that the scene of the cotter's Saturday night is actually enacted there, you feel that it might be.

Under the favourable circumstances, on the other hand, floor, stairs, wall, furniture, utensils, and the persons of the women and children are kept in such a style that one of the women from the Yorkshire cottage would not like to pass a night in the place. And you must not look into the corners. Any stray picture which may be on the walls, only serves to remind you, by contrast, of the wonderful development of illustrative art in England, Germany, and America, and of its penetrating influence in the homes of the remote and poor. Here, sometimes, you may find, even in the village church, prints and dolls, the former of which in England would be considered poor, and the latter tawdry in the village shop. Yet in the same church there may be some real work of art, which has for generations had every opportunity of forming the public taste.

So long as we employ sense-culture as the instrument of thought-culture, it goes on ever extending its sphere. It renders itself the medium of expressing what it had been originally the instrument of imparting. Then it becomes the stimulus and organ of new developments, combinations, and creations of mind. But when sense-culture becomes the substitute for thought-culture, it soon reaches its limits, and, revolving within them, enslaves thought to sensation. Seeing for the sake of a sight, and hearing for the sake of a sound, are as useful in the development of the mind as are play and exercise in that of the body. But when people are trained to look on sights and sounds which terminate in themselves, as the solemnities of civil and religious existence, as the events of a community instead of its diversion, the habit of doing so naturally turns first to valuing things, next to doing them according as they will show or sound. If trainers keep down thought-culture and stimulate sense-culture, the trained will come to appreciate everything, not by the higher æsthetic of reason or of faith, but by the lower æsthetic of impression.

Turning from the dwellings to the fields, the observer is filled with delight. In one place we have rich meadow land ; in another a variety of fruit trees, reminding one of the time when Goth and Norman, in their respective days, sent specimens hence to their kinsmen in the north, as proof of the Paradise they might find.   In a third place we have manifold and bountiful crops of grain.

Still the impression is renewed here which is made upon one by Devonshire in contrast with the Scottish Lowlands ; that is, one soon feels that the charm of the place lies more in the richness of nature than in the grace of culture.   In Devonshire, where nature has done so much more than in the Lowlands, each successive observation brings home a deeper impression that mind has done less.   In the Lowlands, on the contrary, where nature has done less, mind has done more.   There, from father to son for generations, the mind of the plough-boy, the sheep-boy, and the cow-boy, has been cultivated, in some degree That culture has gone out to the plough and the harrow, to the spade and the hoe, to the implements of sowing, reaping, and thrashing ; to the soil, the furrow, the ridge, the field, the meadow ; to the grass, the bush, and the standing corn ; to the sheaf, the shock, the stack, and the farmyard ; to the hedge, the garden, and the grove.   In consequence, the face of the country has a highly educated expression.

While the lower culture of the average mind has been thus impressing itself upon the face of the earth, the few elect minds have been first raised, by its elevating force, above the more sluggish mass, and then floated far away.   Some are in the pulpit and some in the surgery, some in the professor's chair and some at the bar, some in the colonial council and some on the bench, some guiding the bank and some the factory, and some making the world wonder at themselves and at the little land that produces so many of them.

The Reformation found their fathers at a vast disadvantage as compared with the Volscian, the Latin, and the Sabine heirs of eastern and southern civilisation.   But the return to the ordinance that every father was bound to teach his own children, —an essential part of Christian legislation for a community, as good for the father as for the child, as good for the public as the family,—produced the parish school, and, silently but not slowly, led the rougher northman far away in front of his elder and more polished brother. The latter retains what belongs to the race ; and if similar spiritual and mental conditions should, in mercy to Italy, be brought in, he will perhaps one day take his place in the van again.

Nine years later than the time of which we write, the *Civiltà* for 1876, pp. 260, 261, speaks so as to illustrate the auspices under which the Italian race, as compared with the Scotch, has been of late centuries left to develop :—

'We do not say that it [elementary instruction] is injurious to the farmer and farm-labourer (*contadino*), or the sempstress, to the carter or the laundress, to the porter or the vegetable seller, but, on the contrary, it may be of much use to them in life, if they employ it well.'

After showing that mere elements are not education (as if any one said they were), the writer proceeds :—

'Let us not be told that popular instruction will have to go beyond this and include grammar, spelling, history, geography, and other literary branches. For in that case, of two things, one ; either the learners, picking up only bits, will lose them, for want of exercise, sooner, perhaps, than they acquired them, or they will digest or profit by what they learn ; and in that case, all who acquire such knowledge no longer like to belong to the people, but seek to rise, change the jacket for a coat, the ragged hat for a cylinder, and seek to exchange the mattock, the whip, or the plane, for the books of the clerk, the accountant, or the official. Hence it is very rare that one of the populace schooled in the modern fashion knows anything after he has reached a certain age, beyond reading and writing, and accounts, if indeed he has not lost half his baggage of A B C in the field or the shop. The ordinary effect, then, of this instruction, is to set up the pride of knowledge in an ignorant populace, which thinks itself learned if it can distinguish *h* from *z*, and does not confound a 6 with a 9, and to displace a number of poor, presumptuous unfortunates from that position in which Providence placed them by birth, and to tempt them to seek bread and fortune in the over-thronged bureau of the State, of the municipality, of companies, or families, with the double advantage of filling town and country with starving idlers, ready to sell themselves for every enterprise for which they can be bought, and to constrain States and corporations to increase the number of *employés* to appease the herd of these hapless *instructed ones*, who rush in hundreds to storm the first little post vacant at any manger, whatever it may be. Is this a result to be spoken of as so immoderately profitable to the people and helpful to society? One that merits being exalted to the stars by any one who, though not a Liberal, has still a grain of good sense in his head? . . . In the notion of the Liberals,' proceeds the writer, 'this sort of popular instruction must be inseparable from the liberty of the press, which would be of little use if the people were not spoiled by its effects. And indeed if the liberty of the press was done away with, two-thirds of the arguments which lead Liberals to prepare an educated people would fall to the ground. . . . That this instruction proves profitable to a great number of the common people as to their material interests, we cheerfully concede. But it is none the less true that it proves extremely dangerous, in a social sense, by the abuse which the dominant Liberalism makes of it, and by the wicked ends to which it directs it.'

This is a good example of those who wish to keep education in the hands of the clergy, in order to prevent the people from being educated above their position. The proprietors of estates where such ideas triumph, inherit from the fathers who made them triumph, estates that have never been educated above their position, never educated according to their capacity; while heritors of Scotch estates, whose fathers paid for educating the people according to their capacity, find that the estate comes into their hands educated up to its capacity, so that the money spent by the ancestors on the rough diamonds and coarsely-cased pearls, concealed in the *pows* of shoeless urchins, is returned to their descendants in the rent-roll, and proves to be the best family investment they ever made.

The land in these Papal States, like the people, is nobly capable; but our present enquiries turn, not upon the future, but upon proof of immaculate and infallible government, for the last thousand years or more.

Fixing, then, our attention on the works of man, we find cause repeatedly to wish that we had some measure for exactly determining how much progress has been made, amid these lovely scenes, by the human mind since it passed from under the dominion of Pagan Romanism into that of Papal Romanism. At present we have not the means of accurately settling this question, and perhaps we never shall have, though honest research may yet sufficiently elucidate it for a practical judgment. So long as Christianity worked by its legitimate forces, those of the Spirit alone, with its legitimate instrument, the Word alone, it cast out the cruel and obscene spirits of Paganism, silently, but not slowly. In individuals and in families real Christians were made. This continued so long as the ministers of Christ ministered like their Master, reading the Word of God, and preaching it, but no more thinking of performing 'functions,' like the heathen, than He did; so long as they had neither place nor name in the posts graded and rewarded by human powers; so long as they enjoyed no consideration but what was won through wisdom, goodness, and spiritual fruitfulness; so long as their whole inheritance was not a profession, but a calling, which renounced the world, not by cutting God's holiest human ties, but by abandoning, for life, every hope of title, pomp, or power. So long as this spirit reigned, and whenever it again reappeared, they could point to numbers, whom they found vile but left created anew in Christ Jesus unto good works.

But from the time when Christianity became a public power, the courtier, the priest, and the crowd began to flow into the Church, and carried part of their heathenism in with them. For a long time the Christian element dominated not only the names and theories but the forms of the Churches. Gradually, the heathen element invaded the forms, not by any means in Rome only, or, in earlier times, worst in Rome; but all over, and perhaps worst in the East. When, however, the device of the Emperors was parodied,—and as they had assumed the office of Pontiff to confirm the civil dictatorship, the Roman Bishop assumed the temporal supremacy to confirm the spiritual dictatorship,—all the three paganising forces of statecraft, priestcraft, and popular superstition came more vigorously into play; with the result stated by Gregorovius: 'So that Church which arose out of the union of Christianity with the Roman Empire, drew from the latter the system of centralisation, and

the stores of ancient language and education ; but the people
utterly corrupted, could not yield her the living material for
the development of the Christian ideal.   On the contrary, it
was just they who in early times defaced Christianity, and
permeated the Church, scarcely yet established in the Empire,
with the old heathenism.'[1]   It was, however, on the new
system of conversion that the people could not yield the material for developing Christianity.   On the old one they had done
so.   When the Church waits for converts till the Spirit of
God brings her penitents, she will always find material (often
raw and foul, but capable) for doing all her work.

But we find the first step in an enquiry as to the progress which has been accomplished, challenged by the Vatican
philosophy, which decries modern improvements like the railway, telegraph, steam engine, and so on, as 'material progress.'
When we ordinary mortals say 'mental progress,' we mean a
progress of mind ; but when the Pope says 'material progress,'
does he mean a progress of matter ?   No ; then what does he
mean ?   Perhaps to suggest some such idea as the progressive
ascendancy of matter over mind ; but if so, it is unfortunate for
him, as a philosopher, that the inventions he despises represent
the advancing ascendancy of mind over matter.   And very
unhappy is it for mankind that all his influence goes to employ
matter in colour, form, and movement, to make man a creature
of sensation, and to stay the operation of reason and of faith,
exchanging reason for sentiment and faith for sight.

Suppose that an observer before passing from the valley of
the Sacco into that of the Anio looks at a historical place like
Palestrina, situated on one of the noblest heights of the land; a
point whence Pyrrhus and Hannibal, in succession, looked with
the longing of warriors across the Campagna to the distant
Rome; and whence the Temple of Fortune, emulating Egyptian
proportions, and overspreading a whole hillside, dominated the
plain, and held forth its lights to the far off sea.   This city has

[1] Vol. i., p. 14.

a Cardinal Bishop, and a palace of the great Papal-princely family of the Barberini, and yet is what a homely Englishman would call a nasty village. If such a one had to pick his steps up the alleys that serve for streets, in the afternoon, when the issue of the cow-houses is flowing down them, he would rather be at home. The people are civil and apparently industrious, but the energy of the children goes out in begging. The decay and dirt which conquer all, furnish to an English eye a plain instance of material progress—matter gaining upon mind. The palace is neither kept up nor abandoned as a ruin, but, as if to set the town an example of thriftless filth, it is used partly for an æsthetic exhibition, containing as it does one wonderful mosaic, with frescoes and portraits of the Pope and Cardinals of the family, and is partly given up to—matter. If it were only a ruin, one could name many which the proprietors keep tidy, and even ornamental; but it is a question whether the law ought not to punish any prince who employs a palace to set such an example. For the rest, the people follow it with seeming content. Just as confidently as a skilled observer would conclude that Middlesborough or Cincinnati bore witness against any claim to great antiquity, would he conclude that Palestrina bore witness against any claim to supernaturally good government. How much lower was the place when it was heathen?

Taking the way to the valley of the Anio the observer finds, at the foot of the dividing ridge, the well-placed town of Olevano. One visiting it after a heavy shower can see at what a disadvantage the appearance of our towns is put by our humidity. Could its streets have been much meaner or filthier, its children much more given to begging, its women much more untidy, its houses much less like places to call homes, in the days of Pagan Rome? And this is the result of a government and religion given to æsthetics! Compare the fountain with that of a Swiss Protestant village. Few would have heart to go through with the comparison, extending it to the feet, gowns, necks, and heads of the little maids and matrons who group around the two fountains. One is stopped in the attempt to compare, by pity for a fine people who have been so handled, —and that in the name of God. And when dressed up, what maids and matrons they are! See one of these women as a wet nurse in Rome! she is a picture ; and when out with her mistress walks the Corso as if she had constituted herself and the baby into a procession.

From the ridge between the two valleys, by Civitella, the stranger has one of those prospects of which no previous travel blunts the charm, and no subsequent travel blunts the memory. Here he finds well-made men ploughing, and women with busts worthy of Sabine mothers carrying stones. Looking at the plough, he finds it only a few degrees stronger and better than that used by the ordinary Hindu ryot. It is very far behind the improved ones to be seen in northern Italy, and would be a real curiosity to Bedfordshire or Lincolnshire ploughmen. The Sabine farm of Horace lies near peaks within sight; the ploughs upon it may have been inferior, but certainly not much so. Then those women, with big loads of stones piled upon their stately heads! Surely if that does not mark material progress, it marks social stagnation. It was probably just so when Nero built his villa, not many miles off, at Subiaco, except that then the women who did such work would not be the wives and mothers of the free, but slaves. We have here a clear gain from Christianity in the disappearance of the curse of slavery, as also of other cruelties which the name of Nero suggests, but which lay in the habits and religion of his time, though exaggerated in his person. The cart matches with the plough; the want of taste in its form and colour, in the harness, and in the keeping of the oxen or horses, would give a northern farmer, of either the old school or the new, a text for a soliloquy. Can the carts which, in heathen days, rolled on polygonal pavements of basalt along the eight-and-twenty highways into Rome, have been much inferior to these ?

Turning to the domestic animals, one observes the sheep, the pigs, the goats, the poultry, comparing them with the breeds produced in England. The only animal that shows signs of culture is the ass, which, on the average, is decidedly superior to ours. As to the others, it is plain that man has done little by his dominion over them to make them either more beautiful or more useful. The idea of making them happy seems hardly to occur to the people. In towns ladies' lap-dogs are cultivated, but the pastoral æsthetics seem left in deep sleep.

If the observation of implements is extended to those of the handicrafts, it confirms the impression of want of taste made by those of agriculture. Where are the beautifully finished and beautifully kept tools of which the English workman is proud? Compare any workshop or factory here with one in America,—which country, for want of Madonnas and 'functions,' is pitied as being steeped in insensibility to all that is fair! But tools are not things to make a show, and the noble æsthetic of labour has not been fostered. Labour is not part of the supernatural order, only of the natural; it serves but temporal ends. And who made the natural? And who dares to teach man, created in the image of God, that the daily duty appointed to him—duty to himself, his family, his country, and his race—serves but temporal ends? If neglected, are only temporal ends frustrated? When our Father sends us what fills our hearts with food and gladness, is He working nought but temporal ends? Labour —human labour—is, in the eye of Christ, the normal, the divinely ordained action of a spirit which is the offspring of God, operating through a frame built to be His living temple. Away with those who to win a spell-power and a merit in part saving for so-called 'good works,'—that is, for practices not founded in nature nor enjoined in Scripture, practices without sanction, either divine or human, except the word of priests,—would unlink from its connection with the immortal prospects of man the allotted labour which dignifies the day of the lowliest who but fulfils his part! For what is helpful to sanctification commend us even to the stones on the head of the female hod-

man, rather than to the beads at the waist of the novice nun!
Albeit the former is a coarse toil not to be seen without a blush
by man born of a woman, yet is it a real lift at the load of life—
a load natural and therefore divine; whereas the other is neither
work nor play, not tending either to lift the load of life or to
cheer on the labour of lifting it, but tending only to weaken all
the powers by rendering the mind a slave of charms. Least of
all is it spiritual or supernatural. It is simply manipulation
applied by the master with sensational skill, and in the subject
suspending thought on sensational routine.

The French, alluding to the absence of any sense of the
beauties of nature in their literature until recent times, speak
of the days 'before nature was invented;' and in the company
of average Italians one is reminded of that phrase.

You will find that the names of wild flowers are unknown to
nearly all townsfolk—coachman, priest, pleasure tourist, and
trader all alike; and perhaps, till you meet with a rustic, you
may vainly enquire even for the name of the genesta, though
covering hillsides with very beautiful yellow. If it was a vest-
ment only half as fine you could learn all about it. It is little
better as to the names of peaks, or the course of streams, or the
points of beauty in a panorama. The people seldom go to a
hilltop, but will turn out at night to see a mountain illuminated
with Bengal lights. They take a man for an astronomer if he
has an eye for the constellations, but a whole town will flock to
see catherine-wheels.

How far do the villages of the thrice beautiful Sabina exceed
those of our Lake District or of Wales in that poetic property
of all villages, 'innocence'? The last thing we should do is to
set up our own as a standard. One of the first services for
which we ought to thank a foreigner is pointing out remaining
blots in our national life. Not that talk such as Hergenröther
and similar writers indulge in deserves either thanks or answer.
But if you hear the friars talk of the villagers, and the villagers
of the friars and police, the townsfolk of the countryfolk,

the doctor of his practice, and the priest of the refractory, you will hear mention made, with incidental ease, of crimes which, if committed in the Lake Districts of England, or in the tourist's haunts in Wales, would fill the journals for weeks. And how often here does scandal name the priest before all others!

Do the towns in Papal territory contrast with those in 'Lay States' as the oasis does with the desert? Suppose the observer to stand before Subiaco, seated amid Sabine peaks in the smiling valley of the Anio,—a favourite haunt of artists, and worthy of their favour. A marble arch marks the entrance to the town ; a summer palace of the Pope crowns it. The heads of the place are themselves headed by a bishop, and the functionaries who in lay States would be called royal, imperial, or by some other epithet indicating the natural order, are here called apostolic, as belonging to the supernatural. A little way off stands the Sacred Cave where Benedict first taught. That is the Lupercal of Roman monasticism. There arose the institution which became the one grand public institution of Papal Italy,—arose out of purposes not only pure, but lofty, though upon plans departing from those both of Moses and of Christ. These made the love of God in the individual a spiritual force to leaven the family, and made the family the basis of all institutions. The monasticism of the further east made spiritual life a dainty too delicate for the fireside. The Christian system made each new convert a moral agent acting within the social fabric. When Christians adopted the Oriental system, each new convert was abstracted from the social fabric, was taught to turn his or her back on the family, and to call being in the family being in the world, and renouncing the family renouncing the world. Out of a life of three-and-thirty years spent among men, our Lord has left us scarcely another trace of thirty of those years than this, that He spent them in the family; thus elevating its sanctity to a level to which no craft can raise an artificial family, made up by the grouping of one sex into a household and calling it a 'religious family' because it is a family of 'religious.'[1] This convent of Benedict still preserves its celebrated gardens, boasted of as a beauty for the whole earth,—including the bed of roses, the lineal descendants of those which were transformed from thorns by miracle.

This city, then, according to the Papal theory, is a city favoured among the favoured ones, flourishing in a realm where no act of authority can take place contrary to Christian morals, seeing that temporal and spiritual power unite upon one head, like the circling crowns upon the tiara adorning the marble arch. This claim is set up, in good earnest, by those who have ruled the city for ages, and who maintain that he who, summer after summer, was honoured in its palace with more than human worship, was none other than the representative of God upon earth. Be it remembered that we speak of the time before the temporal power fell !

On the principles of Christianity, if this place has for ages enjoyed a spiritual government free from religious error, and a temporal one free from moral fault, and has, in addition, been blessed with the presence of the representative of God upon earth, we shall without fail find it a scene of enlightenment, righteousness, and bliss. It must in these respects be far before places where frail human nature has been in the hands of churches liable to err, and of governments which commit faults every day: such, as Rome and ourselves are agreed, exist in all Protestant countries. If, on the other hand, they who have here been stewards of the unrighteous mammon have employed it ill, who will entrust to them the true riches, who will give to them the keeping of his soul ?

At the entrance of the city, on a morning in May, the sound of chanting floats down the street, and a procession of clergy moves along, passes under the marble arch, and proceeds to a church in the suburbs. Then the priests bless the fields to secure good crops, as is done by the priests in India.

---

[1] The principle here alluded to is elucidated in an instructive manner in *Nazareth and its Lessons,* by the Rev. G. S. Drew.

The observer has here to mark a point of clear superiority over what our reformed countries could show. We could not organise such a procession in a mean provincial town, and indeed scarcely anywhere. The men are not only robed for a procession, but they know how to march in procession; and they carry it through as if accomplishing a procession was a considerable service to God and man. Their artistic march is really imposing, and to get it up probably does not require so much effort as it would do to teach every labourer that, winter and summer, his great Father takes thought for his daily bread, that He will send a blessing in answer to his own cry and that of his little ones, and will not leave it suspended on any performance of priests, nor yet will He withhold His bounty even from the unjust and the evil.

In contrast with the branches of æsthetics illustrated by previous observations, this procession shows that one branch has been cultivated by the governing class—the æsthetic of ceremonial. No people are more highly educated in the art of sight-seeing, and in the manners which become it, than the people of Rome. Consequently, in crowds at a 'function' they are not only good-humoured (as indeed nearly all crowds are), but they are also gentler and more perfectly at home than almost any other crowd. "Rough" is a blemish hardly seen in an eastern crowd, and not in a Roman. If an Asiatic or a Roman who meant next day to have your life met you in a crowd, he would be very civil. Spectacle as an instrument of government is one thing, and as a means of spiritual and moral elevation for the multitude another. As an instrument of government its power is great; but every success it gains with the crowd increases their disposition to look at appearance rather than substance, and to act on sensation rather than upon conviction. It thus tends to make them less capable of being governed by reason, and consequently more liable to be governed by force.

The streets of the city paraded by this procession are not beautiful, and had they been steeped for a few years in a smoky, moist Lancashire atmosphere they would be exceedingly ugly. They are not clean, but dirty, below the condition of any country town in the Protestant parts of Ireland. They are not busy, but have a listless air, as if people had little to do and not much heart in doing it. The signs of enterprise and of improvement which in towns under good governments silently tell the tale, are not to be seen,—signs which already, in 1867, might be traced in most of the towns of the New Italy. The well-dressed portion of the people is small, and the proportion of those poorly but tidily dressed extremely small. A gala costume even of the poor is fine, for whatever is for effect is studiously done. Many men and women, evidently not in abject poverty, but capable of dressing up for a state occasion, are not tidy, but badly the reverse. The number of ragged adults is great, and that of ragged children very great'; it is hard to estimate that of the beggars, for even young women employed, and not very miserably dressed, will take advantage of a passing stranger to seek a penny; and as to the children, begging appears to be a recognised branch of street life.

A young gentleman from Rome, tall and handsome, on the point of getting into a carriage with his companions, anxiously enquires if the road to Palestrina is safe. Have there not been attacks of brigands lately? The fact is not denied, though he is assured that all will be well. In any talk about quarrelling, the use of the knife—that is, the dagger-knife—is alluded to as a common incident. When any occurrence illustrates the amount of confidence felt by the people in the honesty or truthfulness of one another, it seems generally low on the first point, and almost *nil* upon the second.

They who would answer to our working classes are quite equal to them in natural intelligence, and perhaps superior in manners, but far inferior in cleanliness, vigour, and independence; above all, in self-control. Polish attends ancient races, and comes only with time. Any one who has been formally entertained by a Bedouin Sheikh may have seen a specimen of manly bearing coupled with politeness which among us would imply education. Intellectual and moral decay may set in and proceed far without undoing the polish of better times. Indeed, polish may be all the more cultivated as a veil for the decay. The dwellings, furniture, and food of the working class are immensely inferior to those of ours. The smithy and the carpenter's shop strongly illustrate the general principles already indicated. The tools seldom display taste, and show but a backward state of improvement; while the work is not neatly done, and is remarkably wanting in finish. This work is only for use, not for great occasions. The workshops of the tailor and shoemaker are very poor, and disorderly; but more care is taken with the finish of their work,—it is not only for use, but also for appearance.

If the working classes show no sign of having been blessed with a government better than that of all mankind, does any sign of it appear among the trading classes? Beginning at the upper strata of finance and commerce, a merely English eye would look in vain for tokens of their existence. Where are the equipages in the street, with well-conditioned servants and horses, and harness kept to admiration? Where are the houses outside the town, standing in their own gardens, with wealth and plenty in their surroundings, evincing a relish for the beauty of home and of nature which belongs to a higher æsthetic than any taste for pageant?

Coming down to the shops, perhaps an episcopal city in the 'oasis' would so impress Roman Catholic shopkeepers from Thurles or Tuam that they would think a comparison profane. Their evil lot has been cast in a lamentable portion of the 'desert,' the misdeeds of whose rulers, and the wrongs of whose pastors and people, have often made the hearts of the devout in Italy to bleed. Protestant shopkeepers of Munster and Connaught would not be so awestruck but that they could make a comparison. They would not find under the fairer sky, and the theocratic rule, what they would take for symptoms of

divine superiority.   The shopkeepers of Enniskillen and Porta-
down, not blessed even with a heretic bishop, would smile at
the comparison.

As to the professional classes, they are nearly absorbed in
the clergy; for this is a state in which the only way to 'found
a family' is to begin by taking vows of celibacy, and the only
way to bequeath coronets is to begin by renouncing the world.
The one unworldly profession counts, among its prizes, a triple
crown, scores of princedoms, ministries of state, of finance,
and even of war, embassies, exceeding many palaces, honours
surpassing those of nobility, gorgeous uniforms, lofty titles,
revenues of enormous amount, with powers and dignities bearing
a double value,—one measurable by the standards of the world,
and one immeasurable in the eyes of the faithful.   The bulk of
the land has passed into the possession either of corporations
of clergy or of families founded by priests successful in their
profession.   For if the monastery at first drained the moral
force of the family, by withdrawing its best sons from domestic
life, it before long began also to dry up its inheritance, by
appearing at the deathbed a competitor in canonicals.   The
monastery set up beside the landowners a many-handed and
consecrated rival.   Over the cultivators it set landlords without
either the stimulus of personal proprietorship or the check of
hereditary interests.   Over the land it set corporations of idle,
unskilled, and short-sighted owners.   Thus while Islam 'sapped
the family system by polygamy, did the Papal system sap it by
the opposite extreme of celibacy.

The Mosaic economy is generally taken to be more carnal
than the Christian; but Moses, leaving Egypt, where the king
and the priests were the only landowners, enacted that the
priests should not hold land, and though married men, should
have only a house and 'a cow's grass.'   Here, on the contrary, the priest, though renouncing the world in some spiritual
sense, comes a hundredfold more into possession of it in a
material one.   If mind shows its dominion over land and sea,

over adamant and wind, over time and space, the feat is labelled
for contempt as 'material progress.' If ministers of the
Gospel become immersed in the management of manors, provinces, taxes, lotteries, and even of brigades, the fall is certifi-
cated for reverence as 'spiritual' ascendancy. In Israel the
royal tribe was one 'of which no man gave attendance at the
altar,' and the priestly tribe one of which none came to the
throne. Here the priest is king, and the temporal prince kisses
his foot. A favourite image is that of the mystic David, pastor
and king in one. Here is the cure of *political* NATURALISM.

The clergy of the Pontifical States included the two widest
extremes of professional life to be found in Christendom—that
of show and dressiness beyond what our courtiers or soldiers
display, and that of personal meanness and social degradation
to which no professional class among us approaches. Society
seemed to avenge itself for the humiliations it had to suffer
from the Court priest, by the contempt with which it treated
the clown priest. We once asked an advocate if all the priests
did not read the *Unità Cattolica*, and we give his reply, not as
describing what priests are, but as showing what men of education may say of them:—'All?' said the Dottore; 'well, nearly
all that can read.' 'But you do not mean to say that there
are priests who cannot read?' 'Well, not precisely; but
there are many that could not read a journal intelligently, so
as to enjoy it.'

The co-existence of fear with hatred of a dominant priesthood
may be observed in any country where priests have been the
governing class, and perhaps, after the Pontifical States, may
be best observed in India. The Brahmans, however, have not
in the popular eye so direct a command over the lot of the
departed as Rome has secured for her own priests, nor have they
any such pecuniary profit out of the faith of the survivors. On
the other hand, no class of Brahmans sinks so far below the
average of respectability, among their countrymen, as do the
lower clergy of the Roman and Neapolitan States.

But the contempt of the Italians for the priesthood is no more thorough than is their reverence. The man who will not introduce a certain priest to his daughters, will pay him to save the soul of his mother out of the pains of purgatory. To the Monsignore Don Juan, to use a term of Gregorovius, he will manifest profound respect, while in his heart he scorns him. To the not worse but less successful priest, he will manifest contempt and spend some wit upon his vices, and yet, in his heart, will fear his occult power over the souls of his departed kindred. So he hangs suspended between belief and disbelief, swaying in a curved line of incessant yet varying doubt, now approaching to belief of anything, and now to disbelief of everything.

What Rome calls Faith, is not faith either in a philosophical or a theological sense. It is simply submission. Under plea of submission to God, it becomes submission to the Church, which becomes submission to the Pope, which becomes submission to your Confessor. This system, acting on a nation, transfers the basis of character from conviction to submission, from the manly openness of faith to the monkish ambiguity of fear.

The worldly professions have no such lot as the sacred one. This is not a Canaan where Levi has no inheritance among his brethren, but one in which he leaves little for the eleven. The soldier finds a priest over him as minister of war, and an ex-soldier turned priest as king! Except the show corps for inglorious pomp around the sovereign, the military sphere for Romans is narrow, foreigners taking the lead. *Letters are no profession.* The civil service is principally in the hands of the priests. The law exists, and there are men with the titles of advocates and judges. But if we drew any idea of the status and ' chances ' belonging to such titles, from England, it would be altogether misleading. Chief Justice Whiteside has shown how wide the difference is, and he spoke of the great city. In the little one of which we now speak, two English gentlemen, who could not find room in the inn, were directed to the house of an advocate, who played my host with assiduity and good humour, and charged four francs each for dinner, bed, candles, and service. The doctors seem most like men with a professional standing; and if they keep from politics, they have a fair chance of leading a quiet life in obscure usefulness.

As to aristocracy, where are the mansions and parks which in any portion of the United Kingdom would adorn so lovely a valley? There is not one. Some of the Italian nobles have still large fortunes; but most of them, like those of France, are poor. The country house is a house pent up in a close country town; and sometimes a tumbledown house it is. The Papacy has always been a source of wealth to a circle of curialistic families. Yet the Church has steadily competed with the heirs for both their land and gold.

The extinction of the once splendid aristocracy of Spain, with the impoverishment of that of France and Italy, contrasted with the position of our own aristocracy, would afford matter for an interesting study. Is it anything more than one phase of the great phenomenon of the superior stability of all natural institutions in reformed countries? Whatever the reformation adopts or erects has to find a basis in reason, not merely in sentiment or appearances. Consequently, whether it be monarchy or republic, aristocracy or commercial enterprise, municipal rights or parliamentary privileges, it becomes reformable, and therefore capable not only of enduring, but of growth. The Roman nobles, having no political functions, cannot, except for purposes of parade, be called an aristocracy. Macaulay said much in a word when, in one of his letters, he remarked that the utmost a layman could aspire to was to be a Lord of the Bedchamber.[1] To these nobles are equally unknown woolsack or red bench, cabinet or privy council, vice-royalty or embassy, governorship or lord-lieutenancy, the seat of the magistrate or the command of the yeomen. Even the term Lord of the Bedchamber covers a false conception. To us that office implies

[1] *Life*, by Trevelyan.

the grand order of an hereditary legislator. The poor Roman noble, however, has no voice in the government of the parish, any more than in that of the nation; no voice even in the 'functions,' which are the one class of events on which he is welcome to talk. And as under the Papal system nobles cannot be an aristocracy, so cannot the people be a democracy —they are a mere populace. To them are unknown vestry meeting and town meeting; in fact, public meeting of every sort, unless at mass, the theatre, and the lottery. To them are unknown jury-box and polling booth. No voice have they in choice of parish officer, town's officer, or national representative. None of them can even wear the alderman's gown or the civic chain, none can rise to a seat on the grand jury, or in the national council—nay, they cannot attain to the powers and rights of a churchwarden or a guardian of the poor. In the city of Rome exists a lay office called that of *Senator.* Its duties and powers, though not spiritual, are all but impalpable. But the scarlet robe and golden toga are illustrious. The office is a grand one in a procession. With the Senator are several Conservators. A Roman might describe their office as that of train-bearers to the ideas of the ruling priests, in a secret town council. But again their robes are superb. They march clothed down to the feet in crocus and in carnation.

Yet is the whole world called to take this state of things as the model of the subordination of the layman to the priest. 'The ideal of that subordination,' we are told, 'is realised in the Papal government.' The ideal! This absorption, then, of the State into the so-called Church, this suppression of king, nobles, and people under the priest, is not an abnormal and monstrous *lusus ecclesiæ*, but is the ideal of the new 'political order.' Any one can understand it—the king merged in the prince-bishop or else a vassal of the priest; the noble the retainer and jewelled ornament of the priest; the people the helots of the priest. That is the model. Here is realised for us the ideal of *the one fold and one shepherd.* Such talk as

in free countries is sometimes heard from the bishops or
cardinals of Rome, in sound seeming to the ignorant to commend other and noble constitutions, is untrustworthy as the
most treacherous air of the Campagna. The English labourer knows that his son may, like James Cook, walk the
quarter-deck, or, like Robert Stephenson, sit in the legislature.
The Roman noble knows that the utmost his son, if not a
priest, can rise to is to wear pearls and stars at the court of
a priest, and kiss his foot when he makes a great show. Who
would not rather drain away a weary life in the toil that most
debases and least repays, than shine in violet and gold, in scarlet
and in lace, while putting upon this yoke a specious polish, and
trying to allure into placing their necks under its crushing
weight, those whom a purer religion has made free? The Papal
system treats as an abomination the harmonies and balances by
which, as time with wear and tear has proved, it is possible to
combine real democracy, real aristocracy, and real monarchy
into a whole, wherein each of the three elements is mighty, and
none is exclusive because none is extinguished.

The kindly monk who, at Subiaco, shows a stranger over the
Sacred Cave of Benedict, glories in far-famed gardens, which
any peasant from Appenzell could tell him might be equalled in
some private houses in such a village as Heiden. Fame sometimes draws out the dying notes of her trumpet unaccountably
long. The monk is careful to enlist your admiration for several
meritorious works in painting and sculpture, but to Protestants
one gem is shown only by request. It is a portrait of the devil
painted on the wall, in dark passages, and not visible except
when a light is flashed upon it. This done, it appears for a
moment, or longer, as the operator pleases, through one opening,
fitted with real iron gratings, athwart of which the demon
glares out of the gloom upon the spectator. Such a picture is
capable of being put to uses that would meet the strongest
views of those who call for something to strike the senses, and
through them to affect the feelings.

As long ago as the days of the man of the land of Uz, the monotheistic way of depicting a spiritual presence was, 'I could not discern the form thereof;' and, surely, even in that remote time, the æsthetic was higher than that of the Sacred Cave.

They who admire such prostitution of art to degrade theology, or who are forced to reconcile themselves to it, may well disrelish the spiritual medium of teaching, namely, the Word, which, when using things seen to illustrate things not seen, connects the two only by thought, suggesting analogies and attributes, not embodying forms and colours. With its terms serpent, lion, dragon, the Word sets before the reason and imagination a bad being not of flesh and blood, an invisible foe. But such efforts at teaching unseen things through form and colour, as the one in question, only set a man-beast or beast-man before the sensations. Greek art, when at its best, modelled for gods and goddesses the most perfect human forms, but neither stuck wings to their backs nor put plates round their heads to make them more celestial. It did the noblest that idolatry could do.

Here we touch the fundamental difference between the culture of the Pontifical States and that of the reformed nations. In the former sense-culture having been preferred to thought-culture, letters, which with a minimum of sensation give a maximum of thought, have been long neglected, and indeed, in the ages subsequent to the Reformation, discouraged. This went so far that the Italian language had to coin a word to denote the condition of its historic race. When first the control of the Papacy over the teaching of the Peninsula was broken, seventeen millions of Italians were described as *analfabeti*, unalphabeted. Letters were for the learned, and were but sparingly dealt out to the poor. The eye and the ear were to be kept as much as possible in the region of sensation, and to be led as little as might be into the realm of thought.[1]

[1] Any one who shares the marvellous views of Hergenröther, as developed in the *Stimmen aus Maria Laach*, will think this opinion incorrect, and a

The idea having once been admitted that, because many were ignorant, the image was to be resorted to as a substitute for the Word, in teaching things unseen, it became natural to use living form and colour, as well as inanimate, and so glided in dress and action for better scenic effect. Then the ease of performing, compared with the labour of instructing, and the pleasure of spectacle, compared with the effort of learning, led on to further departures from apostolic usage, till men, finally, turned their back on the principle which had been consecrated in divine revelation from the day when the great voice sounded upon Sinai; we mean the principle that the mind of God instructs the mind of man through that medium which has a maximum of the spiritual element and a minimum of the material,—the Word. ' Ye heard a Voice, but ye saw no similitude,' is the appeal of the Parent Spirit to the spirit of the offspring. For the latter the ear, by the Word, becomes the avenue of access to an infinite universe of thought, as the eye, through light, becomes the avenue of access to an all but infinite universe of form. And by letters, the eye, too, learns to join the ear and to travel away on the wings of the Word, so finding a second access to the higher realm by a medium where sensation is as nothing and thought is all.

The Jesuit Father Raffaele Garrucci, in his uncompleted ' History of Christian Art,' gives, in an interesting form, the principle accepted and acted upon. He bases it, however, on one of those historical foundations to the construction of which only Jesuit historians are competent:—

good deal more. But he was writing for Germany. The *Civiltà* of 1876 vol. ix., p. 260, dealing with the figure now generally mentioned, says :—' Who has not had his ears stunned with the lamentations of Italian Liberals, because there are still found in the peninsula perhaps fifteen millions who do not know their letters? Oh, ignorance of the alphabet, according to these gentlemen, is the horrid gangrene of the country, the hotbed of crime, the disgrace of the nation ! ' In the *Opinione* for February 12th, 1876, is stated the result of the five years' conscription, in the province of Rome, from the time of its annexation to the kingdom of Italy to that date. It gave 58·30 per cent. of *analfabeti*. That is, roughly, 60 per cent. who knew not the A B C, and these were young men. A lower percentage of women is instructed.

'The first successors of Peter were not wanting in the culture necessary to teach painters and sculptors how to give expression to the sense
of the prophets. . . . . St. Clement belonged to the house of the Flavii,
and was reputed as of great learning in science and every liberal art.
. . . . Those great pastors proceeded with ardour in introducing the
Christian arts, from zeal for the honour of God and the good of Christian
society. . . . . All confessed that written books (or scriptures) do not
suffice, for they are read by few, and understood by fewer. They also
confessed that what is heard by the ear does not make a deep impression
on the heart, and therefore saw, that if painting and sculpture were
introduced, they would furnish aids to the faithful by means of which
the mind could understand, the memory could retain, and the will could
put in practice the instructions and examples given.' [1]

The weak point in the historical substruction here laid under
Christian image-cult, is that the foundations are not carried
further down than the Roman family of the Flavii.   Clement
might really have heard from them how much the image was
to be preferred to the Word, as a means of teaching the doctrine
and practice of religion, because it had the sanction of the
venerable systems from which Rome borrowed, the systems of
Greece, Egypt, and the great East, whereas there was no nation
which adhered to the Word except the Hebrews, including the
Christians.

It would seem, then, that Clement received the principle of
the superiority of the image to the Word from the Flavii, who
received it from Pagan Romanism, which received it from
Greece, which received it from Phrygia and Phœnicia, which
received it from Chaldea, which received it———. . But the clue
does not lead us in the direction of 'Apostolic tradition.'   If
Clement did not receive the principle from his Hebrew predecessor Peter, and yet did introduce it, he brought in an innovation without any other tradition to sustain it than that of
Pagan Rome.

As the historian lays all the weight of the innovation upon
Clement, he is bound to give us an account of Peter describing

[1] *Storia della Arte Christiana nei primi otto secoli:*   da P. Raffaele
Garrucci.   Vol. i., p. 6.

to his disciples the manner in which his blessed Master had gathered the Hebrew painters and sculptors, and instructed them in the art of embodying His principles, which could be but imperfectly expressed by the Word, especially fundamental principles, such as 'God is a Spirit, and they that worship Him must worship Him in spirit and in truth.' The spectacle of Peter himself so engaged with the Roman artists, would have been worth describing, and it is a pity that no ancient writer, or even painter, perpetuated it. There are bold things in fresco on the walls of the Vatican. Perhaps some generation will see a painting of Peter among the *models* on the steps of *Trinità de' Monti.*

We may doubt if Rome, and much more if Clement, can be proved guilty of being the first to begin the return to heathen forms, under the idea of Christian adaptations. Aaron came before Jeroboam ; the priest, who yields to the superstition of the crowd, before the politician, who innovates to strengthen his position. Both the one and the other appeared in Christianity as in Judaism, only too early; but the city of Rome did not lead the way in either kind of corruption, though eventually in both she outstripped all.

Perhaps there is no town in Italy where one more naturally dwells on the respective offices of the Word and the image than in Subiaco. As it was here that the first Roman convent sprang up, so was it here that the first printing press was established in Italy. But the Swiss printers who set it up soon removed to Rome. How hard is it to find a book-shop in a country town in the Papal States, and when found how clearly does it tell the tale that it cannot thrive ! The book has been for priests, lawyers, and gentlemen ; the picture has been the book of the populace. Where that is the case the cottage is a stranger to that wedlock of picture and book to which many a lettered life owes its earliest inspiration, and to which society owes many a shining career. It is not too much to say that in an American village, where a work of high art was never seen, more has often been done by engraver and printer to make painter and sculptor friends and teachers of the people than in towns of the Papal States a thousand years old, which for centuries have possessed some considerable works of art.

Had the Word been relied upon instead of the image, for religious teaching, Subiaco would for centuries past have had several book-shops. The walls of the houses would have been covered with instructive prints, employing art to represent visible things, and to illustrate thought, not to portray invisible beings. The human frame would have been regarded with re-spect, as a temple to be kept clean, and not lightly maimed or destroyed. Two laws would have become written on the public sentiment—that the person of man was never to be idolised, and never degraded. Every child would have had a mother capable of teaching it the words of the Gospel, and would have found schools where it could be taught whatever its faculties fitted it to learn. All the domestic arts would have been more highly developed, and the glories of nature would have awakened ten-fold the response in the human soul.

Moreover, these peasants and shopkeepers would have been the descendants of fathers who, for many generations, had been in the habit every week of attending worship, not as a spectacle, but as an exercise of faith, reason, and attention. Not only does faith come by hearing, but also reflection, reasoning, and habits of judging. They who join in reading the grand and solemn Scriptures, in mother tongue, and who also hear from a preacher every week a series of things, some of which they believe, some of which they do not believe, and some of which they hardly know whether they believe or not, learn insensibly to reason. Where they are taught not to accept what they hear merely because it is said, but to search the Scriptures to see whether these things are so, and thus to form their own judgment, for which they will have to give account, any capability of thought they may possess is likely to be called into play. The very habit of hearing connected, intelligent, and, above all, expository or argumentative discourse, is in itself a considerable step towards mental training, and an exercise of self-restraint. A population for ages accustomed to scriptural worship and earnest preaching, must grow into a thoughtful one, ready to govern itself and easy to be governed by reason, but that cannot be permanently oppressed. A people accustomed to hear preaching must become in time a reading people. One accustomed only to worship by spectacle, with little teaching, learns to be impatient of reasoning and amenable to watch-words. The one becomes a people calling for the author, the other a people calling for the actor. The one learns to sift what is said, and to treat as tricks any attempt to pass off impressions for reasons. The other learns to fit church to theatre and theatre to church; at both imbibing love of show; in both being made governable by sensations rather than by convictions, in both being trained in the æsthetic of toilet, of posture, and of etiquette, losing meanwhile the æsthetic of deliberation. The breaches of taste in the French Chambers by men of exquisite taste in dress and all nick-nacks, and of finish in rhetoric, as compared with the high taste of our own deliberative assemblies, is one illustration of what we now hastily indicate. The southern races are they especially which need a religion of spirit and reason, not one of material display and sensuous stimuli. Just as historians till very lately have overlooked national food and beverage as among the political forces, apparently assuming either that food and beverage had no part in forming national character, or that character had none in shaping events, so have they overlooked one of the most pervasive of institutions—that of preaching. It is not till after long observation tested by many examples among different races that the evidence appears of how great is the effect of that one institution upon all the processes of political life as contrasted with the effect of a religion of performances. Preaching is pervasive in place, reaching town and country; pervasive in time, recurring every week; pervasive through life, beginning to act on childhood and continuing to act on old age. Had the altar been substituted for the pulpit in Scotland, or in New England, in the days of the Stuarts, Scotland might have been as Sicily, and New England as Mexico.

But what has the ministry of the Gospel done to train this southern population in habits of reasoning? The stated religious services have been a series of sensations—sensations of smell, sound, and sight. Sensations of *smell,* in the odours of incense. Sensations of *sound,* contrived to give a maximum of sensation with a minimum of thought. Language itself has been turned into musical noises emptied of any meaning for the people. Every variety of sound exciting sensation, but not conveying thought, has been employed, from the boom of the great bell to the tinkle of the little one, and from the diapason of the organ to the piping note of the boy! Sensations of *sight,* conveyed through the threefold channel of movement, of form and colour, of light and shade. *Movement*—of vestments, banners, vessels, processions, incense-mists, and ever-changing artistic human action. *Form*—animate and inanimate, representing things seen, and professing to represent, not only things unseen, but also mysteries which angels desire not to look at, but to look into. *Colours*—in glass, wood, marble, silver, gold, cloth, damask, muslin, silk, embroidery, precious stones, and all manner of paint. *Light and shade*—graduated or contrasted, from the undefiled sunlight down through every variety of dimmed light, tinted light, painted light, candle light, to gloom and even darkness.[1]

Here such influences have not been disturbed, consequently we might expect a people with little reading and less reasoning, careless of quiet thoroughness, or of anything which makes no strong instant impression, feebly drawn to the true beauty of nature, not available as a decoration, but dazzled by artificial beauties, especially when turned into costume; looking on

---

[1] Frond, in his *Avant-propos* to the folio of M. Fisquet on the *Ceremonies of Rome,* says:—'When all the senses with which man is endowed concur to the same end, the effect produced becomes irresistible: the sanction of the outward worship is in its proper nature' (*Frond,* vol. iii., p. 5).

a gorgeous pageant as a great event, consequently eager for spectacle, and overjoyed by a set of vivid sensations, accepting an impression for a reason, and an effective scene enacted by priest or ruler as a credential of authority, and as some considerable atonement for its abuse. Such a population is naturally hard to govern and easy to oppress.

Following the smiling valley from Subiaco to Tivoli, one would, in 1867, probably see youths in the uniform of the zouaves, lounging on a bank, near one or both of the towns. Foreign mercenaries! would the Italians say. Foreign, certainly, and some of them mercenaries; but some, even in the dress of a private, would unmistakably show the gentleman —no mercenary, but a crusader who, in answer to the cry raised after Castelfidardo, has come from afar to fight for St. Peter, to 'die for religion.'

Even in this mountain valley the villages still keep to the heights. Where is the squire and his generous hall?—no room here for his magisterial office or commanding influence! Where is the farmstead, full and cozy, warm nest of fruitful brood sure to store a land with golden eggs? When the squire was quenched under the mitre of the abbot, the farmer was smothered in the cowl of the friar. Where are the parsonages and manses, homes where thought-culture is generally at the maximum, and external show often at the minimum, Christian families rooted in nature, blessed by divine ordinance, where woman is doing what the Mother of our Lord was doing at the head of her house—families holier a hundred times than the 'religious' family, artificially substituted for nature and gospel? If from the list of bright names written up in England since the Reformation were blotted all that were first inscribed in the family Bible of parsonage or manse, that list would be more shortened than most men would imagine.

One visiting Tivoli on the day of a great feast would see the people at their best. The wonder is how, out of such interiors, such costumes can emerge, and how they do show in the untarnished air and golden light! Such freedom of the air from colouring matter we never enjoy, unless it be far west or south, beyond all the chimneys, when the Atlantic breeze is blowing. Such richness of light is with us unknown. And this must always make a difference in the æsthetic sensibility, at least so far as colour is concerned. Models for artists are here easy to find, almost as easy as among the peasantry of Galilee when out for an Easter holy-day on Mount Tabor. But here every now and then occur evidences of the artistic gift, and of artistic culture, which there would not be found.

From the Villa d'Este at Tivoli, with its grandiose, ill-kept gardens, the prospect across the Campagna, when the distant city and its unique dome are limmed against the sunset sky, is one of rare enchantment. Suppose that on these Sabine or on the Alban Hills you ask some intelligent inhabitant if these are not the Delectable Mountains, the summits of the true Celestial Empire, where no act of moral wrong has been done by the authorities for, say, the last ten hundred years. Perhaps you might hear such a statement as we once heard. It was from a gentleman in the pay of the government; but he knew that he had not to speak either to a priest or to that denationalised creature which Romans soon detect under the English form, a *convertito*. The statement may not have been correct. But it was such as under our unblessed, lay government is never heard. It was such as under a good government could never be invented. Such a statement, professing to be made from a man's own knowledge, one never heard in Europe, except in Naples under the last two kings; but one might hear such in Egypt, and one could easily hear such, many years ago, in the Mysore, from old men talking of the times of Hyder Ali.

The desolation of the Campagna is the true and terrible material progress. Here physical impediments to health and life have conquered, not being encountered by moral and mental force. What natural riches are here! If England has wealth in its coal, how much has Italy in its sunshine? How much has that saved in the last thousand years in clothes, bedding, and fuel? How much in the wear and tear of buildings, and of implements? How much has it given in ripening what we can never ripen, and in ripening quickly and perfectly what we can ripen but slowly and in part? How much has it both saved and given in diminishing the physical temptation to intemperance? This soil, this sun, and in addition the tribute of nations, poured out here for ages in all the endless forms of Peter's gain,—where is all that wealth gone? Here we are amid the riches of nature, to which successive centuries have brought riches of tribute, and yet are we wrapped around by silence, vacuity, and fear. Sleep not here! whispers every friendly voice. Wealth of matter, poverty of man! The Papal government is sometimes accused of bringing the malaria. No; it only let it come and let it stay. Like many who will not believe in invisible mind, it would not believe in invisible matter. The miasma was the hand of God, and was not to be fought against. The Papal government is also accused of bringing all the foreign hordes who wasted this once glorious plain. It did not always bring them. It only brought them so often that had it been done by any faction in the heart of a country not being priests, mankind would have sunk the memory of the faction under eternal disgrace. Now, the sickly Campagna labourer, the thing like a Fijian hut which to him is home, and the buffalo, seem a meet monument to the memory of Saracen and Lombard destroying, and of Cardinals plundering till only the grass was left. Who would have the heart to ask himself, Is this the proof that the oasis of priests, amid the desert of Lay States, is a garden planted of the Lord? Who, with the grand and benign theocracy of the Bible in view, in which heaven and earth have a common King, as angels and men have a common Father, in which blight to a community below is proof of disfavour on high, though trial to an individual may be proof only of discipline,—in which the care of our heavenly Father for our clothes, our food, and all our little daily needs is made the divine means of engaging our trust and love to the infinitely awful yet infinitely loving One, in whom attention to individuals is not distraction any more than filling the lungs of little children one by one is division to the air, and to whom the rule of a whole nation is not effort any more than speed is hurry to a sunbeam;—who having in view a theocracy which ever sets before common men open evidence of the hand and care of God, telling those who please Him, 'Blessed shalt thou be in the city, and blessed shalt thou be in the field: blessed shall be thy basket and thy store,'— a theocracy which makes godliness prove its promise of the life that is to come by its profitableness in the life that now is, a profitableness not always traceable at the moment or in the individual, but always in the community and in the long run;—who, having in view this revealed government of our Father who gives us bread, could ask if this city is the 'city where God dwells,' seeing as he does the power that here rules sitting surrounded by the signs of its balefulness?

Roughly speaking Rome is about the size of Dublin. All the Catholic world sighs over the woes and desolations inflicted on Ireland by Protestant cruelty. Where has Rome set up a suburb like Kingstown, Dalkey, or Bray? Where sown a tract of country with rich smiling homes like those which spangle the emerald from Dublin to the Wicklow hills? Where in the oasis could a bishop on returning to Belfast point to a creation of wealth and beauty made in Papal times equal to Holywood, or the Antrim shore? And could his colleague of Cork dare to make the people who look on the lone banks of the stream from Rome to the sea mourn for those who hang their harps by the 'pleasant waters' that flow within sound of the bells of Shandon? Had the Roman Curia reigned there, the vale would now be insecure; a wretched village or two, with skele- tons and clouts by way of relics in tawdry churches, would crown the heights; instead of villas, mansions, and cots, a monastery or two walled up to heaven would hold the best points on the hills, inviting artists, but perhaps ill rewarding them, while nursing idlers within and beggars without. And had Rome less reigned at Cork than she has done, a scene many degrees livelier and richer than that which now surrounds the fair city would have noted the response of intelligent industry to the boons of a very bountiful Providence. No such scenes of life, beauty, and comfort have been created in the States of the Papacy during the whole period of its existence as those which smile on the banks of the Liffey, the Lagan, and the Lee. If the Italians were wise they would carefully photograph the interiors of the houses approaching the city, and keep for future time authentic proofs of what the Popes left. Say the wayside public-house at the Saxa Rubra, the hut, where the labourers sleep on the floor, just beyond the tomb of Cecilia Metella, the farmhouse (if we must use so respectable a name) outside the Salara gate, and so on. The men, women, and children, the clothes and bed-clothes, ought to be taken too. Yet this solitude around the city, like that which fences Mecca, has had much to do with the spell of the place and with its power over the superstitious. Priestcraft was true to itself in the instincts which down to our own day resisted everything that would remove that immemorial veil. It is another form of the dim religious light and other similar tricks upon thought.

Inside the capital of the oasis!—capital of a region where for a thousand years, at the very least, no act morally wrong has been done by authority, true bower of a peerless Eden! Let no Englishman say that these pretensions are not to be treated seriously. We should all have said so thirty years ago. But now men from any nation in Europe, some blaming us, some vaunting over our return, will tell us that of late years more has been done to accredit these pretensions by a portion of the English clergy than by any educated class in Europe, and that

more to adorn and sanction these pretensions has been done
by a portion of the English aristocracy than by any privileged
class in Europe. This is one instance more of the fact that
not interests but principles are the safeguards of mankind.

Is the city, then, morally the perfection of beauty? Is it so
rich in the Christian graces as to accredit the claim to be the
central seat of an infallible power, the one spot on earth where
it is directly touched by a divine authority? The priest at
once tells you how holy the city is : there are eight basilicas,
more than four hundred churches, and more than two hundred
convents. Yes, but perhaps the 'religious family' fabricated
by teaching woman that her holy place is not the family which
God founded, and in which every man has his own wife and
every woman her own husband, may not in operation have
proved a better thing than the Christian family. Poor creatures
put into an artificial family where duties ordained by God are
made void, and ties set by Him as strings in the harp of nature
to make holy melody, are rudely unstrung,—a 'family' in
which many of the things called *good works* are neither virtues
nor graces, but vain repetitions of fantastic forms,—a family
where the obedience called for is not obedience to any
natural authority or to any divine law, but to arbitrary will ;
where the submission called for is not submission to the blessed .
though unfathomable providence of the All-knowing, but submission to a human superior, the most artificial ever invented ;
where what is called authority is an arbitrary command without
a root in nature, or a shade of sanction in Scripture;—communities of poor creatures such as these, we say, may not in
the long run have proved centres of holiness. When we ask
if the city is holy, we mean nothing about basilicas, or churches,
or convents ; but we mean, are the people like Jesus Christ,
like a people prepared as a fit population for a sinless heaven?

We shall in reply give nothing but a statement on one side
from the *Civiltà*, and one on the other from the prelate Liverani,
so that neither heretic nor foreigner, nay, not even a layman,

shall disturb the testimony. The *Civiltà,*[1] after the occupation of the city by Italy, showed that one of its characteristics had been the perfect subordination of all civil arrangements to evangelical law. *Christ reigns, Christ governs.* This motto had in Rome a worthy and complete application. Not only individuals, but the family, the city, laws, policy, all social institutions, felt the salutary influence. In the metropolis of Christianity, marriage, education, instruction, the administration of justice and charity, public and private manners, had to be regulated by Christian laws and evangelical principles :—

'Such to a nicety was Rome. It was called the holy˜city, that is, the city more than any other consecrated to God and forming the expression of the kingdom of God upon earth. And the effect of this Christian order was seen in the very virtues of the civil population. The Roman people was not second to any other in piety towards God, and in propriety of conduct ; and not only so, but it seemed the most dignified, the gravest, and the furthest removed from vulgarity and tumult.'

The prelate on the other hand says,—and we begin at the Vatican (p. 87):—

'Thus came it to pass that the Court of Rome, that is, the house of the lieutenant of Him of whom it is written, " *The evil shall not dwell with Thee, neither shall the unjust remain within Thy sight,*" turned into a sink of scandal and a sewer of every foul iniquity (p. 87). . . . It was always to me a mystery how the Roman clergy, rich in gold and lands till most of the Agro Latino is in their hands, with their splendid temples and sumptuous ceremonies, with their retainers diffused among all classes, with control of the charities, the pulpit, the confessional, the confraternities,—how it is that with all these elements of power in their hands I hear from one end of Rome to the other the cry, Death to the priests ! (p. 87). . . . The particulars hitherto related disclose [in the Court] an iniquity only too deeply rooted, and even turned into blood and nature ; they disclose sores both inveterate and envenomed, hard to cure and hard to eradicate. It was this that made Clement VIII. say to Bellarmine, "I have not strength to contend with such a flood of bad habits ; pray to God to release me soon, and to shelter me in His glory." Also the brave Marcellus II. was accustomed to repeat a sentence of Onofrio, which I do not wish to copy' (133).

---

[1] VIII., i., 132.

As to the people, we shall give but one word. Liverani, remarking on objections raised against modern Italian rule by the 'good press,' because certain houses existed in the cities, says :—

'It reminds me of a pleasantry of the old rector of the parish of St. Angelo in *Pescheria*, who one day said to me that when he took charge of the parish he found one house bad and one not so, turn and turn about; but he soon found that they were all alike. This editor is ingenuous and innocent as if he wrote in a land of angels, instead of in the place where not long ago a prelate-judge abused his office to the point of using violence with arms in his hands against the sister and daughter of the convicts, so that he was prosecuted before the Vicar and before the Holy Office, and removed from the bench ; but after a few years, the good nature of the prince being overcome by powerful intercession, he was reinstated in another judicial office.'

We shall not go further into this subject than to add that one of the bitter reproaches cast upon the Italian senate by the *Unità* was that when the most noted and most respected living man in Italian literature and politics, Mamiani, said, speaking on the conscription, that at all events the morals of the barrack-room were better than the morals of the convent, the senate received the statement with loud applause.

However correct or incorrect may be the views of the several witnesses from whom we have heard a word, there can be no hesitation in pronouncing that any attempt to show evidence of divine superiority utterly fails—so utterly as to be more than ridiculous. But if there is not divine superiority, there must have been false pretensions. The one or the other is inevitable. If the States of the Church have not for the last thousand years been ruled by the representative of God, they have been ruled by one who was himself deceived and a deceiver of others.

CHAPTER XIII.

Solemn Confirmation of the Syllabus by the Pope before the assembled
Hierarchy, and their Acquiescence, June 17th, 1867.

THE twenty-first anniversary of the accession of Pius IX.
occurred shortly before the day for which the great assembly
of 1867 was convened. As the Court historian omits all mention of the Syllabus when first issued, so does he also omit to
say a word of its definitive confirmation by the Pontiff on
June 17th, 1867, and of its formal acceptance by the episcopate.
We are indebted for the details in this case to an author who
published before the events of 1870. Important as the transaction was, we cannot find that at the time any of the ordinary
organs of the Vatican notified it to the world. Many of the
learned disputants in the controversies which were soon to arise,
took ground which showed that they were unaware of this
decisive event.

It was Archbishop Manning who related how Mass was celebrated in the Sixtine Chapel, and how the Pope retired, at its
close, to robe in the Pauline Chapel. Here the Cardinal Vicar,
Patrizi, followed by the whole of the Sacred College and the
bishops, presented an address of congratulation, concluding
with hopes for many years of additional life to Pius IX., that
he might behold the peace of the Church, and her triumph.

As recorded by the Archbishop, the terms employed by his
Holiness in reply were of historical importance.[1] It will be
remarked that the watchwords, deprecated by the Pope, are
not those of heretics, but of statesmen—Unity and Progress ;
and no Italian or German could doubt what were the unity
and progress decried :—

'I accept your good wishes from my heart, but I remit their verifi-
cation to the hands of God. We are in a moment of great crisis. If
we look only to the aspect of human events, there is no hope ; but we
have a higher confidence. Men are intoxicated with dreams of unity and

[1] *Centenary of St. Peter,* p. 6.

progress, but neither is possible without justice. Unity and progress based on pride and egotism are illusions. God has laid on me the duty to declare the truths on which Christian society is based, and to condemn the errors which undermine its foundations ; and I have not been silent. In the Encyclical of 1864, and in what is called the Syllabus, I declared to the world the dangers which threaten society, and I condemned the falsehoods which assail its life. That act I now confirm in your presence, and I lay it again before you as the rule of your teaching. To you, venerable brethren, as bishops of the Church, I now appeal to assist me in this conflict with error. On you I rely for support. When the people of Israel wandered in the wilderness, they had a pillar of fire to guide them in the night, and a cloud to shield them from the heat by day. You are the pillar and the cloud to the people of God.'

Here the bishops learned, with the full weight of pontifical authority, that the Syllabus was 'the rule of their teaching.' Some explained the Syllabus as affecting discipline, and therefore liable to alteration. The *Civiltà* and the *Stimmen* had always asserted that it was purely doctrinal, and therefore above all change. In pronouncing it the 'rule of teaching' the Pope settled that vital point. Some, again, had been tempted to think that the Syllabus might be laid up, like an ancestral weapon ; they were undeceived, and given to know that it must be tested in war. Such were placed in the dilemma of having to offer resistance to the sovereign thus surrounded, or of having to observe a silence which must ever after carry the effect of consent. Even if they did not feel with the Pope, that the foundations of universal society were crumbling in unprecedented decay, they did keenly feel with him that the foundations of his own temporal power were crumbling. Every doubter held his peace, and the Pope's act became virtually what, as we shall see, in a few days it became formally,—the act of the whole episcopate.

The Pope is not fortunate in quoting Scripture, often showing that he takes glosses for the text. He imagines that the 'cloud by day' was not a pillar before the host, but an extended field of clouds overshadowing the widespread multitudes, and not merely the tabernacle.

BOOK II.

CHAPTER I.   •

First Public Intimation of the intention to hold a Council, June 26th to July 1st, 1867—Consistory—Acquiescence in the Syllabus of the assembled Bishops— The Canonised Inquisitor—Questions and Returns preparatory to Greater Centralisation— Manning on the Ceremonies—O'Connell on the Papist Doctrines—The Doctrine of Direct and Indirect Power.

THE 26th of June, 1867, was the day of the Secret Consistory, to which not less than five hundred bishops from all regions of the earth lent their splendours. The Pope in his allocution deplored the evils which had overtaken the Church, and, as he supposed, in equal measure had overtaken all society. And now, at length, did he reveal his intention of convoking such an assembly as had not been witnessed for three hundred years. He had firm hope that from a General Council the light of catholic truth would shine forth and scatter the darkness which enveloped the minds of men; and that the Church, like the battle-array of an unconquered host, discomfiting her enemies, rolling back their onset, and triumphing over them, would spread abroad over the earth the dominion of Christ.

Though journalists and bishops at the time bravely reproduced this martial figure, the Jesuit historian Sambin (p. 13), writing after the battles of 1870, makes the Pope say that the

Church would gain her fairest triumphs by converting her enemies.

. The very name of an Œcumenical Council, uttered in the tones of Pius IX., instinct with personal and official hope, caused among the assembled prelates a movement of effusive joy. They felt that such a Council would prove 'a marvellous source of unity, sanctification, and peace.' On the 1st of July, assembling in the great hall over the portico of St. Peter's, with all possible accessories of form, they presented to his Holiness what they called a Salutation. This had been drawn up by Archbishop Haynald of Colocza, assisted by Bishop Dupanloup, Archbishop Manning, and others. It had been proposed to proclaim Papal infallibility in the document itself; but this set the French prelates up in arms.[1] Though stopping short of that goal, the bishops go far in their approaches to it. Their minds had been filled with joy on learning from the 'sacred lips' of the Pontiff his intention of calling a General Council. The language of the address, naturally reflecting that of the Pope in the Pauline Chapel, showed that the Church was not occupied just then with spiritual but with 'civil humanity,'—of which, indeed, no longer satisfied with being Mother Church, she is now to be declared the mother.

'May the unmeasured benefits assured to society by the Roman Pontificate,' say the bishops, 'be, by this deed of Thy providence, once more displayed to the world, and may the world be convinced of the powers of the Church, and of her mission as the *mother of civil humanity!*' They were persuaded that a Council would have the effect of showing that everything tending to consolidate the foundation of a community, and to give it permanence, is fortified and consecrated by the example of authority, and of the obedience due thereto, presented in the divine institution of the Pontificate. Princes and peoples would not, 'in the face of such a display, allow the highest sanction of all authority, the august rights of the Pope,

" Acton's *Zur Geschichte*, pp. 13, 14.

to be trampled upon with impunity, but would see him secured in the enjoyment both of the liberty of power and the power of liberty.'[1]

No one skilled in the language of the speakers will take the last words as meaning less than liberty to exercise all powers which the Pontiff held to be committed to him, and power to guard every exercise of that liberty.[2]

The words in which the bishops confirm their testimony of 1862 to the ' necessity' of the temporal power are few and firm. They then proceed to cover the space between that time and the present. ' With grateful feelings do we recall, and with fullest assent do we commend, the things done by Thee subsequent to that time, for the salvation of the faithful and the glory of the Church.' This is a waymark showing that the old doctrine still ruled the practice of the Court, though long banished from its theory. The acquiescence of the bishops was practically necessary to give the ultimate sanction to the acts of the Pope.

This link, binding the authority of the episcopate to the past of the Pope's action, is followed by a festoon of rhetoric which, however, also covers links in a chain. And then comes the solemn adhesion of the assembled hierarchy to the condemnations collected together in the Syllabus—' Believing Peter to have spoken by the lips of Pius the things which have been spoken, confirmed, and pronounced by Thee, for the safe keeping of the deposit, we also declare, confirm, and announce ; and we reject with one heart and voice those things which Thou hast adjudged to be reprobated and rejected, as being contrary to divine faith, the salvation of souls, or the good of human society.'[3]

---

[1] *Acta* (Freiburg edition), p. 35.

[2] ' The Church must be able to exercise a perfectly free activity in every single case lying within her domain, from the first inception of any ecclesiastical law to its practical application. According to the principles of divine law already explained, the State authority, in relation to this matter, can have only the one duty to fulfil (which, because of the honour connected with it, becomes a right), that of protecting the Church against all obstructions and hindrances.'—*Phillips, Kirchenrecht*, ii., 560.

[3] *Acta* (Freiburg edition), p. 33.

So it was done. The Pope had called for the express submission of the episcopate to his own acts, hitherto variously
understood and discussed, and they had given it in round terms.
Dr. Manning, in characterising their document as 'The Address
or Response, in which they united themselves in heart and mind
to their supreme Head,'[1] might well speak of 'the gravity and
moral grandeur of that act,' for with him vastness always seems
to prove grandeur, and an act of vast moral consequence this
surely was. We shall hereafter see the fact tardily come to
light that absent prelates. were called upon to give in their
adhesion by letter, and did so.

On either the Papal or the Episcopal theory, the Syllabus had
now the status of Church law, and had become to all the clergy
'the rule of your teaching.' On the Papal theory, because it was
the formal act of the Pontiff for the teaching and ruling of the
whole Church; and on the Episcopal theory, because the collective hierarchy had not only tacitly acquiesced but openly accepted
it. But full as was now its authority, the Syllabus was still,
in spite of the care bestowed upon it, amorphous, liable to
strange twists of interpretation, especially by pupils trained for
Rome.

Yet it is worthy of special remark that the Syllabus is not
mentioned in this Salutation. They who knew nothing of the
scene in the Pauline Chapel might read even the passage above
quoted without knowing that it was a formal adhesion to that
instrument in particular, although how they could take the terms
as not including it we cannot see. Of the scene in the Pauline
Chapel the organs of the Court said not a word. More than two
years later, however, the *Civiltà* said, 'There is no doubt that
the prelates had the Encyclical and Syllabus in view, since in
these two documents are contained all the things which the
Pope has *spoken, confirmed, announced,* and *reproved* in matters
of doctrine.'[2] And even as early as one year from the time,
we shall find that the double authority of the Bishop of Rome,

---

[1] *Centenary of St. Peter,* p. 5.   [2] Serie VII., vol. vli., p. 537.

and of all other bishops, was declared to be outraged by Darboy when he practically disowned the Syllabus.

The next point touched by the prelates was one lying near to the heart of the Pope. They had been moved with joy on beholding the loyal faith, love, and reverence of the Roman people for their most indulgent prince. 'Happy people and truly wise'—*Felicem populum ac vere sapientem.*[1] So, whoever had doubted as to the Model State, it was not the five hundred. Were they sincerely ready to make the people of their respective nations 'truly wise' by bringing them to look on that government as the model?

The bishops evidently knew that they were initiating a movement which would test the combative qualities of both Pope and prelates. Every discerning man among them must have felt what Archbishop Manning expressed, 'This event may be taken, I believe, to be the opening of a new period, and to contain a future which may reach over centuries.'[2]

Under anticipations so serious do these old men, addressing a very old one, thus conclude :—

'Courage, most Blessed Father! Guide the bark of the Church with a firm hand, as has been Thy wont, certain of gaining the port. The Mother of divine grace, whom Thou hast saluted with fairest titles of honour, will defend Thy course, by the aid of her intercession ; she will be to Thee the star of the sea. . . . . Thou wilt have the celestial choirs of the saints favouring Thee ; those whose glory Thou hast, with diligence and apostolic toil, sought out, and also hast proclaimed to the exulting world, both aforetime and in these recent days. May the princes of the Apostles Peter and Paul stand by Thee ! . . . . At the helm now held by Thee once stood Peter. He will intercede with the Lord that the bark which, by the aid of his prayers, has for eighteen centuries traversed the deep sea of human life, may under Thy command enter the celestial haven, all sail set, and laden with richest spoil of souls immortal.'[3]

It is to be remarked that in this passage Peter is not honoured, like his successor, with capitals to all his pronouns. Again, he and Paul are coupled together as if they might have

---

[1] *Acta* (Freiburg edition), p. 34.   [3] *Acta* (Freiburg edition), p. 36.
[2] *Centenary of St. Peter*, pp. 12, 13.

been somewhat on a level.   Perhaps in both points the bishops made an unconscious concession to history, but in the state of things now initiated, such jots and tittles were to become symptomatic.

One allusion in the Address, which would pass with a smile in England, had great significance for the mind of Pius IX. It is that made to his claim to peculiar aid from the Blessed Virgin, because of the higher exaltation which he had procured for her, and also to his claim upon new saints whose titles he had made' out.   In the case of the Japanese saints, we have already seen how practical were his views.   He was fighting for the territory of his predecessors, and, finding that he had not hosts enough on earth, he reversed the ordinary process of binding on earth and leaving it to be ratified in heaven, and now bound in heaven, by creating 'new patrons in the presence of God,' leaving it to be ratified on earth by a corresponding increase of forces.

The vision of these new heavenly auxiliaries dazzled the imagination.   Even the professor of history in the university speaks of the awful moment when the Pope raised them to their thrones as 'the sublime rite, during which heaven and earth hung upon the lips of the Pope.'[1]   The expressions of confidence in these new-made powers, as champions in the thickening struggle for that patrimony which, though costing so much blood, forgery, and intrigue, so much dependency on foreign arms, so much slaughter of Italians, had been retained through evil report and good report, irresistibly remind one of Licinius when menaced by the advance of Constantine, under the auspices of one God only.   Licinius feels the advantage he has in the numbers of gods on whom he can rely.

'This present day,' he, as reported by Eusebius, says, 'will either declare us conquerors, and so most justly demonstrate our gods to be the saviours and true assistants, or else, if this one God of Constantine's, who comes from I know not whence, shall get the better of our gods,

[1] *Frond*, i., p. 82.

which are many, and at present do exceed in number, nobody in future will be in doubt which God he ought to worship, but will betake himself to the more powerful God, and attribute to Him the rewards of victory. And if this strange God, who is now a *ridicule* to us, shall appear to be the victor, it will behove us also to acknowledge and adore Him, and to bid a long farewell to those to whom we light tapers in vain. But if our gods shall get the better—which no person can entertain a doubt of—after the victory obtained in this place we will proceed to bring a war upon those impious contemners of the gods.'[1]

Even if this does not describe what Licinius really said, it does represent the view of the early Christian, as to the heathen mode of thought, putting confidence in a multiplicity of celestial patrons, in the lighting of tapers and such like.

The name of Arbues, the Spanish Inquisitor, has been mentioned as being second on the list of those now to be canonised. Professor Sepp, of Munich, long known as a Catholic theologian and Oriental traveller, says in his *Deutschland und der Vatican* (p. 52) :—

'Nothing was more calculated to degrade the Church, and render her unpopular, or to bring a flush of shame to the cheek of every Catholic, than this revival of the most disagreeable recollections of history. Had Arbues contended against the burning of heretics, we should have welcomed him, in the name of God, as a saint. But history gives us no information about the man except that he discharged the odious office of a Torquemada, and that the long-persecuted 'Jews brought him to an untimely end. The most that can be said for him is that he died for the idea of the Inquisition; and for that he is to be set up on our altars.'

Many another Liberal Catholic blushed with Sepp. Baron Weichs, in Vienna, cried, 'A single example will show you the difference between the spirit which reigns here and that which reigns on the banks of the Tiber. While here we speak of abolishing the penalty of death, there they canonise an Inquisitor, covered over with the blood of the victims whom he had immolated because they worshipped God in their own way.' The *Civiltà* exclaims, 'And men of this sort are to be reputed Catholics, and to make laws for Catholics. *O tempora ! O mores !*'[2]

---

[1] Eusebius' *Life of Constantine*, lib. ii., c. 5.
[2] Serie VII., vol. vii., p. 23.

In the Pope's reply to the celebrated address of the five hundred, the principal point naturally was the expression of his satisfaction at the approbation given by so many of the pastors[1] of Christendom to the doctrines and condemnations he had propounded; for 'the Christian nations would be confirmed in their obedience to the Holy See.' This language is not to be loosely interpreted. It is not souls that are to be confirmed, but nations. They are to be confirmed in obedience; and in obedience to the *Holy See.* Perhaps, by this time, the reader can, in part, grant to such a phrase the magnificence of meaning which it had in the ' intentions of the Pontiff.'

After this all-important point, the Pope felt that such a testimony to the necessity of his temporal power was splendid. He was pleased with the praise of his loyal Romans. But he took occasion to couple the names of Peter and Paul in a more correct form than that into which the bishops had fallen. It is 'Peter, prince of the apostles,' and 'Paul, doctor of the Gentiles.' In return for the metaphor of the ship he gave them that of the tower. Human pride, repeating ancient presumption, had long attempted by factitious progress to build up a stately tower, the top of which should reach to heaven, whence God Himself was to be pulled down at last. The Council was the mightiest force to combat these attempts, and he solemnly declared that it should be placed under the patronage of the most blessed Virgin, and that, in whatever year convoked, it should be opened on the day dedicated to the Immaculate Conception![2] If those who think that a representative legislature is a lawful and even a noble erection will only note the Tower of Babel every time it reappears in the speech of the initiated, they will in time catch a hint of its meaning.

The Cardinals of the Holy Office had drawn up a list of questions on points of Church discipline, which was delivered

---

[1] The reader will already have observed that in the Vatican dialect ' pastor' means 'bishop,' almost universally.

[2] *Acta* (Freiburg edition), p. 47.

to the bishops while in Rome, and afterwards sent to many, probably to all of those who were absent. Lord Acton points out that these questions do not touch the depths of existing wants.[1] And Michelis seems to look upon them as a blind, to cover the real point at which the Council was to aim. They are, however, clearly framed to elicit facts bearing on uniformity of discipline, and especially on points of administration in mixed questions —that is, questions wherein both civil and ecclesiastical authority are concerned; for instance, schools, mixed marriages, civil marriages, domestic relations, and the like. The returns which the answers would supply would be of great value in the study of plans for reconstruction, and would seem to be of more practical importance than Lord Acton imagines, for the purpose of governing a mobilised clergy through bishops turned into prefects, by orders from one bureau, and of impressing through them a uniform movement on both institutions and families, in matters affecting national law.

The five hundred bishops soon dispersed to the four corners of the earth, carrying into their respective spheres enthusiastic descriptions of the beautiful, the grand, the splendid, the superb, the glorious, the unutterably majestic ceremonies which they had just witnessed, and no less enthusiastic hope of 'the greatest event of the age' when the princes of the Church should assemble around her head to overawe her enemies and build her up anew. We do not use the epithet 'divine,' but it is perhaps right to say that the *Civiltà* described the appearing of the Pope 'upon the portative throne, in all the majesty of his divine rank . . . the Pope-king, the supreme representative of the twofold authority which rules the nations in the name of God.'[2] It of course celebrates the 'standards which represented the glory of the Princes of the Apostles,' and does not forget the 'twenty thousand wax candles.'[3] Pius IX. was not reduced, like Licinius, to say, 'We light tapers in vain.' So far as the bishops were concerned, the tapers were not lighted

---

[1] *Zur Geschichte*, p. 4. [2] Serie VI., vol. xi., p. 165. [3] Ibid., p. 234.

in vain. They greatly enhanced their faith in the cause, and their zeal for it. Indeed, with twenty thousand wax candles a Pope could make his flock see almost anything: .

The place which the ceremonies were designed to fill in the movement for reconstruction was not better indicated at the time by any one than by Archbishop Manning. He reminded his clergy that in the solemn adherence of the bishops to those acts of the Pontiff, whereby he had condemned errors and enunciated truth, they did not confirm those acts as if needing confirmation, or accept them as if needing acceptance, or imply that they had been 'of imperfect and only inchoate authority until their acceptance should confirm them.' Nothing was further from the thoughts of the pastors, proceeded the Archbishop; 'they recognised the voice of Peter in the voice of Pius, and the infallible certainty of all his declarations and condemnations. . . . They did not add certainty to what was already infallible.'[1] The infallibility, he contended, belonged to all the approbations and condemnations alike—not, as some 'blindly say,' by virtue derived from canons, councils, or ecclesiastical institutions, 'but from the direct grant of our Lord Jesus Christ, before as yet a canon was made or a council assembled.' This is a somewhat crude statement of the doctrine which all the Irish and French Catholics we ever knew in our younger days resented, when ascribed to themselves by Protestants. They called it the doctrine of the 'Papists,' and contended that Protestants wronged all such Roman Catholics as were not Papists, by calling them so, indiscriminately. What we call 'temporal authority,' what the Jesuits have taught Rome to call 'spiritual authority over temporal affairs,' was one point, and the infallibility of the Pope was a second point, on which the Papist was at issue with the Liberal Catholic. In this sense Montalembert and O'Connell were not Papists. The latter says :—

'I am sincerely a Catholic, but I am not a Papist. I deny the doc-

---

[1] *Centenary of St. Peter*, pp. 33, 34.

trine that the Pope has any temporal authority directly or indirectly in Ireland. We have all denied that authority on oath, and we would die to resist it. He cannot, therefore, be any party to the Act of Parliament we solicit, nor shall any Act of Parliament regulate our faith and conscience. In spiritual matters too the authority of the Pope is limited : he cannot, although his conclave of Cardinals were to join him, vary our religion either in doctrine or essential discipline in any respect. Even in non-essential discipline the Pope cannot vary it without the assent of the Irish Catholic bishops. Why, to this hour the discipline of the General Council of Trent is not received in this diocese."[1]

The utterances of Archbishop Manning, though sweet to the ears of those who had the dispensing of the purple in Rome, were, nevertheless, hard on those who, as children, had learned that such doctrine was no part of their creed. In his day Alban Butler had proudly said, 'But Mr. Bower never found the infallibility of the Pope in our creed, and knows very well that no such article is proposed [propounded] by the Church, or required of any one."[2]

It would not be fair to charge upon all Catholics, as doctrine to which they are bound, the loose views of Cardinal Manning, who, as things have turned out, now sets even Protestants upon fixing limits around infallibility as imperatively as he swept all limits out of sight in that rose-coloured moment of 1867 when Rome had just made known that she was officially taking the affairs of the world in hand. Then he had no forbearance for those Roman Catholics who knew that what Dr. Manning called 'blindness' had been the doctrine held in countries to which men might feel proud to belong, and also knew that the countries where it was called blindness had become a drag upon civilisation. Yet, even in the Papal States, Spain and South America, professed theologians, if not writing for Court ends, would have treated the expressions of Dr. Manning as not only exaggerated but as inaccurate. 'Infallible certainty of all his declarations and condemnations' is language which O'Connell would have driven his coach and six, not through, but over.

[1] *The Select Speeches of O'Connell.* Edited by his son, 1862. P. 447.
[2] Life prefixed to the *Lives of the Saints*, vol. i., p. 14. Ed. of 1836.

Dr. Manning went on to declare that he had received the Syllabus at the first 'as a part of the supreme and infallible teaching of the Church.'[1] In this he proved how far he went before most prelates of experience on this side of the Alps and Pyrenees, although he coolly credits them, every one, with having done likewise.[2]

The same spokesman said not more than the Jesuits thought, but much more than the organs of the Court ventured to say, when he went on in the following vigorous and portentous words :—

'Every bishop in the world had the Encyclical and Syllabus in his hands. Upon that summary of the acts of this whole Pontificate, five hundred bishops proclaim their adhesion to every declaration and every condemnation therein contained, and to every other act of *doctrinal authority* since their last assembly in Rome. It is the Encyclical and Syllabus which gives such force and import to the words of the episcopate the other day. It is the basis of their "Salutation," as they style the address. It will be also the basis and the guide of the General Council, prescribing and directing its deliberations and decrees.'[3]

At its proper date we shall see how this declaration is confirmed by the *Civiltà* for the confounding of Montalembert, Darboy, and such like, and, by anticipation, for the confuting of one who on this matter took great liberties with English trustfulness.

The well-defined phrase 'act of doctrinal authority,' which we have put in italics, indicates the rank of the Syllabus according to Manning's model curialistic intellect. It was not a mere act of ecclesiastical discipline, liable to be modified; much less a mere manifesto of ecclesiastical polity. It was a 'doctrinal authority,' fixing eternal principles, to which disciplinary arrangements, concordats, and national laws, must in time be brought into conformity. The Jesuits had always argued that, condemning certain doctrines and not any forms of discipline, it was purely doctrinal. This view the Pope had now confirmed.

Just as the episcopate had been committed in 1862 to the

---

[1] *Centenary of St. Peter*, p. 38. [2] Ibid., p. 34. [3] Ibid., p. 39.

temporal power, so was it committed in 1867 to the Syllabus. Whether a bishop believed that his assent had any constitutional effect or not was now a matter of comparative indifference, for his future action was bound; and the Syllabus was to prescribe the decrees and direct the deliberations of the future Council,—in fact, to be its basis and its guide.

The language of Manning was treated by many Catholics as the menaces of a zealot; but the zealot knew that he spoke for the Pope and the Jesuits. During the conflict now on the point of breaking out, many honest men fought against the supposed design that the Syllabus should receive 'doctrinal authority' from the Council, while in the mind of those in whose hands lay their future faith, the Council was under the doctrinal authority of the Syllabus. The Council might contribute to administration by turning the propositions into canons or constitutions, but could not add to their authority.

The anticipation of Archbishop Manning as to the political effect of the doctrinal change then impending was clearly recorded, and in terms never to be forgotten :—

'Civil governments, so long as their Catholic subjects can be dealt with in detail, are strong and often oppressive. When they have to deal with the Church throughout the world, the minority becomes a majority, and subjects, in all matters spiritual, become free. We are approaching a time when civil governments must deal with the Church as a whole, and with its head as supreme ; and a General Council which makes itself felt in every civilised nation will powerfully awaken civil rulers to the consciousness that the Church is not a school of opinion, nor a mere religion, but a spiritual kingdom, having its own legislature, tribunals, and executive.'[1]

Some seven years after sounding this note, preparatory to a powerful awakening of civil rulers, the Archbishop, having seen some beginning of the results of that policy to which he was helping to hurry on his Church, could say, 'I must add that they who are rekindling the old fires of religious discord in such an equal and tempered commonwealth as ours, seem to me to be serving neither God nor their country.'[2]

[1] *Centenary of St. Peter*, p. 95.   [2] *Vaticanism*, p. 155.

There was one part of the ceremonies which neither Archbishop Manning nor, so far as we know, any bishop on this side of the mountains described at the time. Indeed, had any one of them done so, few of us would then have found in it any important connection with the powerful awaking of civil rulers, and with the fact that the Church is not a mere religion, but a good deal besides. Much that is to come under our eye will, however, show that the ceremony we are about to hear the *Civiltà* describe was one with an edge on it. The chair of St. Peter—not the one with the Moslem inscription described by Lady Morgan, and many others, which might well enough have been set up by the Saracens, or inscribed by them when they had possession, but an old Roman chair—was exposed for veneration. The *Civiltà* had afterwards to relate how, on the evening of a horrible fight in the trastevere, the Crusaders, while engaged in destroying a nest of Garibaldians barricaded in a house, would seize a moment to 'slip into the basilica of St. Grisogono to consecrate their bayonets to God.' This reminds the writer that 'this was one of the practices of the Crusaders, of which every one could see hundreds of examples while the chair of St. Peter was exposed in the apostolic cathedral for the centenary. They laid their swords on the venerable relic, and taking them up again replaced them in the scabbard, to be unsheathed only in the service of God and of religion. We believe that masters of the art of war will not repute as useless such incentives to military valour, not even the Garibaldians.'[1]

The language of O'Connell, as above quoted, was not employed loosely. He spoke as a Catholic, and as a lawyer; but, above all, as a politician. Had his declaration with regard to the spiritual power been less explicit, that upon the temporal power might, though not without violence, have been open to an Ultramontane interpretation. It might have been said that he

---

[1] VII., ix., 54.

only meant that the Pope had no authority in Ireland, which either directly or indirectly sprang from a temporal origin ; for, in the language of the Ultramontanes, temporal authority does not mean authority over temporal affairs, but authority of temporal origin. His statement on the spiritual authority, however, precludes any such interpretation. Even the spiritual authority he declares to be limited, both in doctrine and in discipline: it cannot 'vary' doctrine, and cannot even vary the essential points of discipline, without the consent of the Irish bishops. If spoken to-day, this reserve in favour of the bishops would involve nationalism; and O'Connell's denial of the Pope's infallibility, without the consent of the bishops, would be heresy. Archbishop Manning, with a great many others, sought to prove, before the Council sat, that the latter position was proximate to heresy. So O'Connell and Monta-lembert must always lie under the brand of having lived and died as proximate heretics. The elect champion of the Pope's faith to-day may, if he refuses to change, be the butt of his anathema to-morrow.

To us the words 'directly' and 'indirectly' seem very easy to be understood; yet they have played no little part in the ecclesiastical and political controversies of Rome. O'Connell appears to use them half in a popular and half in an ecclesias-tical sense; still, the popular sense appears to predominate. He calls that authority spiritual which is over spiritual things, and by temporal authority he clearly means authority over temporal things. In thus speaking, he designates authority according to its domain, and not according to its origin. This was just the point upon which Bellarmine and Sixtus V. had their quarrel. There is a curious little autobiography of the great Jesuit Cardinal in the *Collegio Romano.* Writing in the third person, he says that ' Pope Sixtus was incensed against Bellarmine because of a proposition found in his writings, denying that the Pope was the direct Lord of the whole world.' On account of this proposition Sixtus placed Bellarmine's great work, *The Controversies*, in the Index. After his death, the Congregation of Rites had it erased.

In this dispute the popular meaning was on the side of the Pope, but the more astute meaning was on the side of the Jesuit; and astuteness carried the day. The term 'temporal authority' was liable to give offence both to rulers and people ; for rulers do not want a suzerain, and nations do not want two rulers. The term 'spiritual authority' was not so objectionable. It had the further advantage of expressing the origin and the character of the Papal authority, and of both indicating and justifying its claim to be of a higher order than any temporal authority could be. Thus temporal authority came to mean nothing more or less than authority originating in a temporal source, as well as authority used for a temporal end. This obviously could not apply to that authority which the Pope claims over all the states of the world. This universal authority, instead of being called temporal authority, came to be strictly described as spiritual authority over temporal affairs; or if temporal authority at all, not direct but only indirect temporal authority. No matter how secular the affairs over which this authority is exerted, its spiritual character is always sustained by the fact that it did not originate in a temporal compact, and that it never claims to extend to any affair into which the element of sin or virtue cannot enter; but, wherever this element may enter, eternal ends may be affected, and the matter ceases to be any longer a purely temporal one. We do not remember any Papal writer who clearly sets forth the class of human transactions which do not 'involve sin,' as Cardinal Manning expresses it. By this we understand transactions in which one course would be sinful and another course would be virtuous. Such attempts as we remember to indicate actions that are exempt from this quality, are not worth any notice. For instance, Phillips, in matrimonial affairs, draws the line at dowry and inheritance,—a line obviously arbitrary. A child will at once see that both dowry and inheritance may involve moral questions of the highest gravity, —may involve sins and virtues of considerable magnitude; sins, too, in which 'the Church' has a direct temporal interest. It only remains, therefore, for the ecclesiastical authority to say, at any moment, that those questions do not lie on the State side of the dividing line, but on the Church side.

We must remember that the dispute between Sixtus and Bellarmine was not about the domain of the Papal power, but simply about the best way of designating it. Both agreed that its domain extended over the world; over princes, laws, tribunals, institutions, and all actions of governments, corporations, or families, 'involving sin.' But it was not only convenient but necessary that this power, when exercised outside of the Pontifical States, should be distinguished by some characteristic designation from the temporal authority exercised within those States. The wider power came not to the Pope from natural society, but from God; did not reside in a secular person, but in the Vicar of God; and aimed not at the temporal welfare of a nation, but at the extension of the dominion of God, which it is heretical to separate from the dominion of His Vicar. It is, therefore, spiritual power; and the extension of the domain of the Vicar of God always subserves a spiritual end, namely, that of the eternal salvation of the nation in question,—and thereby it subserves the glory of God.

By a process not more strange than what often takes place in the evolution of terminology, in which at least the fittest does not always survive, the terms 'direct' and 'temporal' came to be interchangeable, and also 'indirect' and 'spiritual.' We see no proof that the mystifying influence which these terms produce was the object originally aimed at. The evolution was a difficult one, and, if the result may be somewhat awkward, it has now worked itself clear. We do not say that advantage has never been taken of the mystifying effect of this terminology. In both our own country and others, in both former times and recent ones, advantage has been scandalously taken of it. And advantage will still be taken of it, until the universal conscience resents such courses as an outrage upon the rudimentary duties of citizenship. The use made of the term 'direct' by Antonelli, in his diplomatic fencing with Counts Beust and Daru, will pass under our eye.

Within the Papal States, the authority of the Pope over temporal affairs is direct, aiming at temporal ends. Beyond those States, it is indirect, and indeed is not properly temporal authority, but spiritual authority over temporal affairs. In the one case, the Pope is his own executive ; in the other, he has to set in motion the executive office of the temporal ruler; but his authority over the latter does not extend beyond the limits of affairs in which sin is involved. In every case, however, where a moral question may arise before the mind of the civil ruler, there stands above the ruler the spiritual power of the Pope. As no other question can involve moral consequences of greater weight than one of peace or war, that question becomes one of the first in which the spiritual authority should predominate over all temporal interests, and should control physical forces.

Cardinal Manning has put this matter before the public with sufficient clearness, for those who understand the principles now explained. 'The superior power,' he says, ' cannot be temporal, or its jurisdiction would be direct.'[1] ' A *spiritual* power *indirectly* over temporal things, in so far as they may affect the salvation of men, or involve sin ' (p. 72). The principal point is clearly put by the Cardinal (p. 76). Speaking of the power of the Pope, he says, 'If temporal, it would not be of a *higher*, but of the *same, order*.' The emphases are the Cardinal's. He also says (p. 54), 'If princes and their laws deviate from the law of God, the Church has authority from God to judge of that deviation, and to oblige to its correction.' In the next quotation, it is again the Cardinal who emphasises the proper designation of authority, direct from on high (p. 55). ' The authority which the Church has from God for this end, is not *temporal*, but *spiri-*

[1] *Vat. Dec.*, p. 76.

tual.' For what end ? For that of *obliging* princes to conform to the law of God. Here we emphasise *oblige.* It is to be remembered that the law of God always, in Papal language, means that law as expounded by the Church. The Cardinal says again, ' When any prince by baptism became Christian, he became subject to the law of God, and to the Church as its expositor ' (p. 66). The authority by which one of our judges obliges a criminal to conform to law, by undergoing his sentence, is not physical, but civil, and the civil authority commands the physical force of sheriff and jailer. It acts with a view to a direct physical effect, to be produced upon the person of the criminal ; but it also acts with a view to an indirect civil effect, of a much higher order, namely, the benefit of the community. Just so the authority by which the Vicegerent of God *obliges* princes is not civil or temporal, but spiritual or divine. If the authority of the judge were physical, it would be no higher in its order than that kind of authority which one criminal often holds over another. So, if the Pope's authority were temporal, it would be merely of the same order as that of princes. His authority might, in degree, be greater than theirs ; but, in order, it would sink to the common level. Being spiritual, it is higher in its origin, higher in its end, higher in its domain, and higher in its application ; therefore, according to a favourite simile, higher in order as much as the greater light which rules the day is higher than the lesser light which rules the night.

NOTE.

DR. NEWMAN ON THE SYLLABUS.

It was eight years after the Syllabus had been formally confirmed by the Pope, and after its ratification by the collective hierarchy had been officially communicated to the Papal clergy in England by Arch- bishop Manning, that Dr. Newman treated of it in his letter to the Duke of Norfolk, in reply to the 'Expostulation' of Mr. Gladstone. The assertions in that reply are among the most unaccountable known to the history of our literature. Still, such as they are, they have been made in a pamphlet bearing the name of an English duke on its title-page, and that of an

English gentleman at its end. Moreover, they were received by our Press—and the fact is known throughout Europe—with perfect gravity.

Dr. Newman (p. 78) asks and answers an important question as follows :—

'Who gathered the propositions out of these Papal documents, and put them together in one? We do not know.' After no more than three sentences he adds : 'The Pope has had the errors, which at one time or other he therein condemned, brought together into one, and that for the use of the bishops.' On the next page he asks : 'Who is its author? Some select theologian or high official, doubtless ; can it be Cardinal Antonelli himself? No, surely ; anyhow, it is not the Pope.' First he tells us that we do not know who put it together, then that the Pope has done it, or has had it done. Again, in the same manner, he first tells us that it is not Cardinal Antonelli's, and then more than once calls it Cardinal Antonelli's (p. 91), as if his authorship of the document was an established point on which arguments might be grounded. Dr. Newman in this manner procures for himself a double set of premises, which he employs throughout, with frequent shifting. His argument now assumes the affirmative, namely, that the Syllabus is the work of the Pope ; and now it assumes the negative, that the Syllabus is not the work of the Pope ; and this is what the English Press with, so far as we know, unanimity agrees to call logical.

'But,' asserts Dr. Newman, 'the Syllabus makes no claim to be acknowledged as the word of the Pope' (p. 80). The very heading of the Syllabus sets up the claim to be accounted the word of the Pope ; ay, and his word in official, public, and teaching acts. The heading is, 'The Syllabus of the Principal Errors of our Time set forth in Consistorial Allocutions, Encyclicals, and other Letters Apostolic, by our most holy lord, Pope Pius IX.' This claim is not incidental, but formal and capital, incapable of being either overlooked or put aside. No man's judgments are here introduced but those of Pope Pius IX., and of his judgments not one here recited is less official than are Letters Apostolic.

'The Syllabus, then,' further asserts Dr. Newman, 'has no dogmatic force. It addresses us not in its separate portions, but as a whole' (p. 81). The first proposition here involves matter for Roman Catholics to dispute about among themselves, and we shall pass it by. The Syllabus may have no dogmatic force, as Dr. Newman says, or may be 'part of the supreme and infallible teaching of the Church,' as Cardinal Manning says, [1] or may be 'the rule of teaching' for all bishops, as Pius IX. says. [2] Which of these may be its true position is a question between the Pope and Dr. Newman. Our present question is another.

The second proposition in the clause just quoted from Dr. Newman is one on which even Protestants may venture to form a judgment. 'The

---

[1] *Centenary of St. Peter*, p. 28.   [2] Ibid., p. 6.

Syllabus addresses us not in its separate portions, but as a whole.' This again comprises two propositions, one affirmative and one negative. The affirmative is true, the Syllabus addresses us as a whole. The negative is not true, namely, that the Syllabus does not address us in its separate portions. To put the whole assertion into a true form it would have to be altered to this effect: The Syllabus addresses us as a whole, and in its separate parts.

The principle upon which Dr. Newman grounds the idea that the Syllabus does not address us in its separate portions seems to be this: each article of it, taken in itself, is composed of the words, literal or virtual, of some person declared to be in error. Now surely it is not necessary to be told that the words which the Pope condemns are those of other people. But why do these words proceed out of his lips? On purpose to receive condemnation ; and they fall from his lips one by one, under sentence, although the formula of judgment is not separately repeated before each one. If an arbiter says, I disallow the following items, and sets down eighty, he does not repeat 'I disallow' before each ; but we should not on that account think of saying that his award addresses us as a whole but not in its separate portions. The words.'I disallow' govern all that follows. Does Dr. Newman mean that there is a single one of the eighty propositions which does not bear the Papal brand, 'error'? It is very wide of the mark—no man in England better knows *how* wide of it—to talk about different brands, some more and some less damnatory, such as 'heretical,' 'false,' 'impious,' or the like.

' There is not a single word in the Encyclical to show that the Pope in it is alluding to the Syllabus ' (p. 82). This is said to refute an allegation of Mr. Gladstone, which Dr. Newman calls ' marvellously unfair.' That allegation is, that the Encyclical virtually, *though not expressly*, includes the whole of the errors condemned. It will be seen by any one who refers to our own remarks upon the Encyclical (pp. 5-7), that had Mr. Gladstone read it as we do, he would not have written what he did. He would have written instead of it something to this effect, that the Encyclical includes the whole of these condemnations, not by reciting them, but by clearly expressed reference. What he did say, instead of being unfair, comes short of what is required by the evidence contained in the docu-ments. The reference in the one to the other is formal. ' In pursuance of our apostolic ministry, and walking in the illustrious footsteps of our predecessor, we have lifted up our voice, and in several published Ency-clical Consistorial Allocutions, 'and other Letters Apostolic, we have condemned the errors of our sad times.' This language proves that Mr. Gladstone, in saying that the whole of the Pope's condemnations were virtually though not expressly included in the Encyclical, was within the limits of the evidence. They are expressly referred to, and those addi-tional ones contained in the Encyclical itself are linked on to the previous ones as a complement, making them a whole. In itself the point is of no consequence whatever, but Dr. Newman has chosen to make it important, and for *his* theory it may have some importance.

'The only connection between the Syllabus and the Encyclical is one external to them both, the connection of time and organ; Cardinal Antonelli sending them to the bishops with the introduction of one and the same letter' (p. 82). Some of the assertions in this venturesome sentence cannot be disputed. It is true that the two documents were sent to the bishops with the same introductory letter. It is true that they were both sent at the same time. It is true that Cardinal Antonelli sent them. Moreover, it is true that in doing so he acted as an 'organ,' and not as the author of one document or the other. But the main allegation, that the only connection between them is one of time and organ, is incorrect. There is this important point of internal connection: the Encyclical expressly refers to the Pope's previous condemnations as given in official forms; the Syllabus begins by reciting as its own heading the terms of that reference, 'The Principal Errors of our Times set forth,' as such in the very same official acts by the present Pope, it even recites the words 'Consistorial Allocutions, Encyclicals, and other Letters Apostolic.'

The Encyclical is signed by Pius IX., as are his Letters. The Syllabus is headed by his name, as are his Allocutions. It quotes from no document which is not authenticated and recognised as his act. The Encyclical contains certain new condemnations necessary to complete former ones. The Syllabus collects together the former ones, which become complete by the addition of the new. The two documents fit into one another, under the hand of a critic, as easily as they fitted into the same covering under the hand of Cardinal Antonelli. These clear internal links are strengthened by a point of external connection omitted by Dr. Newman. The letter by which the organ introduced them to the bishops was not only the same letter, but was also an official statement to the bishops that the two documents were from the same author. Antonelli attributes to the Pope, not only the whole, but the separate portions of the Syllabus; and it is precisely for fear that these portions, severally, might not be every one under the eye of each particular bishop in the world, that the Holy Father has had this collection made of the errors he has condemned.

'All we know,' says Dr. Newman, 'is that by the Pope's command this collection of errors is sent by his Foreign Minister to the bishops' (p. 78). That is not all we know. We also know that the Foreign Minister did not, by the Pope's command, send it as the work of Cardinal Antonelli. We know that he did send it as the work of Pope Pius IX. We know that he recited in one and the same note, once for all, the language common to the two documents. 1: As regards what is condemned—'the principal errors of our times.' 2. As to who it was that condemned them—the Pope. 3. As to the official acts in which he did condemn them, namely, Allocutions, and so on.

The next assertion we have to note is made in a strong interrogative form. ' How can a list of errors be a series of pontifical declarations ? ' (p. 84). We reply, how can it be otherwise ? What does an error mean in the language of such a document ? Not something that may be erroneous, or something that has been secretly judged to be erroneous. It means errors declared to be such by the Pontiff ; a list of such ' errors,' therefore, is simply a list of pontifical declarations. Dr. Newman knows as well as he knows his own name, that every clause of the Syllabus is a pontifical declaration that the words there written express an error.

Alluding to the forty-second of the condemned propositions, namely, that in the conflict of laws, civil and ecclesiastical, the civil law should prevail, Dr. Newman says this is a universal, and the Pope does but deny a universal. A universal may be denied in two ways. First by its contradictory, which may amount only to saying in popular language that the rule is not without exceptions. For instance, if one asserted that no Roman Catholic is a Pope, Dr. Newman would deny it ; yet all he would mean would be that as one single exception to an otherwise universal rule did exist, that fact rendered the universal assertion untrue.

Still this denial of a universal by its contradictory is so wide a way of talking, that the effect of it may be just the opposite of what we have now stated. For instance, if one asserted that every Roman Catholic is a Pope, Dr. Newman would again deny it. But now he would not mean that what is asserted is a rule with one solitary exception ; on the contrary, he would mean that it is no more than the one solitary exception, and that the contrary is a rule absolutely true of every Roman Catholic in the world, except one. Even in this one method, therefore, of denying a universal there may be very wide latitude of meaning. But there is another way of denying a universal, namely, by its contrary ; that is, asserting that the rule is just the contrary of what some one has stated. For instance, one asserts that all men should be Roman Catholics, and another asserts that no man should be a Roman Catholic ; each of them intending to exclude all exceptions, and to lay down an absolute rule.

Now if Dr. Newman believes that when the Pope denies that, in case of conflict, the civil law should prevail, the Pope means no more than that there are exceptions to that rule, he believes what is in flat contradiction to the whole tenor of the Pope's language, and that of his organs year by year,—language cast in forms as forcible as the case admits of. If he does not mean that, his repeated statement about denying universals is, in a technical sense, incorrect, and, in a popular sense, misleading.

Schrader is a logician as well as Dr. Newman. Had he taken the denial in question in the sense hinted at by the latter, he would have given as his counter-proposition the following. In *some* conflicts of the two laws the civil law should not prevail. Does he do so ? No surely. Had he done so, his name and place in his Church would have been different from what they became. Against a universal he sets a universal.

Where the statesman asserts the ascendancy of civil law in every case of conflict, Schrader asserts the ascendancy of the ecclesiastical. His proposition is evidently not the *contradictory*, but the *contrary*. 'In cases of conflict (not in *some* cases of conflict) the civil law does not prevail.'

Dr. Newman's treatment of the Sentence (24) which condemned those who say that the Church has not the right to employ force, is very instructive. First, he says (p. 80), 'Employing force is not the Pope's phrase, but Professor Nuytz's.' And what then? Is this phrase 'It is an error to say the Church has not a right to employ force' Professor Nuytz's or the Pope's? Next Dr. Newman says that what the Pope means is, 'It is an error to say with Professor Nuytz that what he calls employing force is not allowable to the Church.' And what then? What does Professor Nuytz call force but force? Schrader translates it 'outward force.' Dr. Newman does not venture so far as to translate it 'spiritual coercion.' The whole sentence is about temporal power and the use of force—*Vis inferendæ—potestatem temporalem;* it never glances at spiritual censures in the popular sense.

At the next step, Dr. Newman professes to 'set down what the received doctrine of the Church is on ecclesiastical punishments' (p. 80). Does he do so, or make any straightforward attempt to do it? Not by any means. 'Ecclesiastical punishments' is a term of wide extension, embracing great varieties of penalty, from the deposition of an Emperor to the paltry penance of a nun. In all this range of inflictions, the single point touched by Dr. Newman is that of corporal punishment. The selection of this one point proves that he was perfectly aware that both Nuytz and the Pope meant force when they said force; and this fact reduces the talk about Nuytz's sense of that term to what it is.

But having selected corporal punishment as the whole of ecclesiastical punishment, how does Dr. Newman set down the received doctrine regarding it? By quoting a passage which, under the appearance of surrendering something, really claims something additional, according to a common usage with Papal writers (p. 80). Cardinal Soglia, as quoted by Dr. Newman, makes a merit of giving up on behalf of the Church 'the corporal sword by which the body is destroyed, or blood is shed.' This, however, the Church *formerly* never claimed to hold *in her hand*, but *only in her power* and *at her beck*, in the hand of the temporal ruler. But, in giving up the corporal sword, Soglia is not contented to claim for the Church in her own hand what the bull *Unam Sanctam* claims; that is, the spiritual sword. He does of course claim that, but he further claims that the same hand should have and hold also the corporal instruments 'of lighter punishments,' such as imprisonment, flogging, and beating with sticks,—anything 'short of effusion of blood.' The last penalty is the stroke of the corporal sword, and is left to the temporal arm. The Church did not in past time claim two swords in her own hand, the spiritual one and the corporal. She only claimed a spiritual sword according to Boniface VIII. ; and according to Dr. Newman she claims also a cat, a cudgel, and a rack.

Neither in what he writes, nor in what he quotes, on this subject does Dr. Newman allow even an allusion to appear to the question, whether the corporal sword is or is not *in the power* of the Church. He cannot be unaware that untrained Englishmen, in reading the statement of his authority to the effect that the corporal sword is by some writers withdrawn from the Church, would suppose that they taught that it is not in her power. Dr. Newman knows that such an impression upon their minds would be a false one. He knows that Cardinal Soglia does not give any hint that the corporal sword is a weapon which the Church may not employ. Dr. Newman himself does not give any such hint. To ordinary readers, indeed, he seems to resent the assertion that she may employ it; but even in seeming to resent it he does not venture to affirm that she may not do so. Much less does he say, in plain English, that such is the received doctrine. He engages us in chat about flogging and thrashing, and forgets all about where his Church keeps her corporal sword,—the only one we care about. Not that we like even the instruments of flogging and thrashing, much less the instruments of other corporal pains which fall short of the 'effusion of blood.'

'Assuredly,' says Boniface VIII., 'he who denies that the temporal sword is in the power of Peter, ill attends to the words of our Lord, when He said, "Put up again thy sword into his sheath."' The word here is clear : in the *power* of the Church, not in her hand. Dr. Newman, however, sees only the weapons in her hand, and does not think of her 'employing' any that is not in her own hand. But the very next words of Boniface save ordinary readers from falling into such a mistake. 'Therefore,' he proceeds, 'both are in the power of the Church, the spiritual sword, namely, and the material ; but the latter to be wielded *for* the Church, and the former *by* the Church.' Perhaps, then, the fence of Dr. Newman turns upon the distinction between employing and causing to be employed. But we, like Dr. Newman, wish to speak with the Fisherman ; and he, in the person of Boniface, proceeds : 'The former (the spiritual) by the priest, the latter (the temporal) *by the hand* of kings and soldiers, but at the beck and sufferance of the priest.' Here the distinction is clear as day. The one sword is to be wielded by the priest; the other, though not in the same way, by the king. The priest's sword is in his own power, and is his. The king's is not in his *power*. It is only in his *hand ;* to make which plainer, the hands of kings and those of soldiers are coupled together in the same ministerial category. It is not at the king's discretion, and to be used on his accountability. It is at the beck or at the nod, *ad nutum*, of the priest. It is not the king's, to have and to hold till God takes it away. It is at the sufferance, *ad patientiam*, of the priest. Moreover, while that sufferance endures, and the king is allowed to hold it in his hand, it is not independent; 'but,' proceeds Boniface, 'sword ought to be under sword, and the temporal authority subject to the spiritual power.'

Yet even the Bull *Unam Sanctam*, strictly interpreted, does not claim all that Dr. Newman's seemingly loose language claims for the *hand* of the Church. The Bull claims in words neither cat nor rack, nor indeed any material weapon,—only the spiritual sword for her hand. By having them in her hand we mean, *as much exempt from civil control as is her spiritual sword*. To have the other sword in her power, at her beck, at her sufferance, and in subjection, is all that the Church of Boniface really claimed respecting it, outside the Papal States. But all of that she did claim. She now, according to Cardinal Soglia, claims, further, to have in her own hand *all instruments of bodily pain short of taking life*. We have carefully spoken of the doctrine, that the corporal sword is not to be wielded by the hand of the Church herself, as what *was* her doctrine. We are by no means clear that it is so now. Part of the preparation for the Vatican Council consisted in teaching, by the high authority of Cardinal Tarquini, that the sword might be directly and immediately wielded by the Church herself, in the person of the Pope and a General Council. The question between Soglia and other writers, as Dr. Newman well knows, turned not upon the use of force, and not upon the consigning of heretics to death, but turned exclusively on the point whether in inflicting upon them the last penalty the Church did right to imbue in their blood her own hand, and not that of the temporal power.

Dr. Newman, at one time, says that the Syllabus does not address us in its separate portions; and at another, shows that every one of its portions refers to an original document, in which that portion is to be found. These documents, he admits, *are* authoritative; but the Syllabus, which culls out the really authoritative parts of them, is not authoritative. We can hardly credit Dr. Newman with making a distinction of the following sort: that one is to feel bound by the Pope's judgments when they lie buried in a clumsy document, and not feel bound by them when they have been culled out by himself, and put simply before us. If Dr. Newman feels free to teach in opposition to any one of the eighty sentences as read from the Syllabus, though bound to teach according to it when read in the original document, what he has written on the subject may have some kind of serious meaning for himself, though incomprehensible to other people.

One other point we would notice. 'When we turn to these documents which *are* authoritative,' says Dr. Newman, 'we find the Syllabus cannot even be called an echo of the apostolic voice.' We certainly do not profess to find that it is so. It is an echo of a voice very unlike an apostolic one. But Dr. Newman means the Pope's voice. Of that voice the words in the Syllabus are not an echo, because they are its own words. Dr. Newman says that, as uttered in the Syllabus, they are not an exact reproduction of the words of the Pope ; meaning by that, as found in the original documents. The words in the Syllabus are the exact words of the Pope used on a second occasion, and sometimes slightly varied from those he originally did use.

Dr. Newman has a passage in his own history which is not to be forgotten, and which ought to have made it difficult for him to stand on points about a variation of language made by a Pope, objecting that it impairs the authority of solemn documents.

There was a moment in the life of Dr. Newman when he still retained the freedom of a Christian man to teach the Catholic faith, ancient, strong, and true. But he was on the point of parting with it,—in the very act of swearing away that blessed birthright of his soul. He had already recited the form of sound words called the Nicene Creed, and had come to the point where the plunge must be made from the rock of Scripture, on which it builds, into the quicksands of tradition. In the modern form of oath which, at that dark moment, he was venturing to take upon his conscience, the first sentences, after parting from the language of the Catholic Church, the first that are the work of Rome, shift to another foundation from that laid under the old, scriptural, abiding verities. The true and noble old words, 'the life of the world to come,' built on the living Rock, are immediately succeeded by such preparation for modern inventions as the following : ' I most firmly admit and embrace the apostolic and ecclesiastical traditions, and the other practices and statutes of the said Church. I do also admit the Holy Scripture according to that sense which holy Mother Church has held and does hold, to whom it belongs to judge as to the true sense and interpretation of the Holy Scripture ; nor shall I ever receive or interpret it except according to the unanimous consent of the Fathers.' .

This new thing in a creed was said by the Pope to have been ordained by the Council of Trent. If Dr. Newman had taken the trouble to see how far the terms to which he had to swear were an 'echo' of those of the Council, he would have found that there was a discrepancy, considerable in words, but, in practice, monstrous. The Council decreed that no one should interpret Holy Scripture against the unanimous consent of the Fathers. That decree was confirmed by the Pope. It had thus acquired all the warrant of infallibility, and the most solemn guarantee for being irreformable that Rome had it in her power to give. This decree was ' of faith.' How long did it continue to be ' of faith'? Only until the Pope prepared his Bull, collecting the dogmatic decrees into a novel creed. Then it was altered. The men who, henceforth, were to be the priests of Rome found themselves called upon to take oath, not as the Council willed it and worded it, that they would never interpret Holy Scripture against the unanimous consent of the Fathers, but that they would never interpret it except according to the unanimous consent of the Fathers. This was another will and another wording altogether.

The latter amounts to little less than an oath that they would never interpret it at all, except on very few points.

To make the scope of this alteration clearer, let us suppose the case of Dr. Newman himself, while yet in the enjoyment of that ministry of the English Church which he afterwards threw away. Had he then been required not to preach anything contrary to the unanimous opinion of the bench of bishops, he might have felt tolerably free. But had he been required never to preach anything except according to the unanimous opinion of the bench of bishops, he would have felt—Why, I can hardly preach at all. Yet this vast change is made in a creed while its articles are passing through the process of being culled from the original documents, and presented in a collected form. In this form it was imposed by oath upon the consciences of men for ever. One and the same Papal hand signed its infallible certainty and irreformable permanency in one shape, in a little time afterwards altered its tenor, destroyed its certainty, reformed its scope, and then signed its infallibility and its irreformable permanency in the new shape. And an Englishman who swallows this camel in the creed stands between us and the light, straining out a gnat that he says has got into the Syllabus.

We have found that the omission to mention the Syllabus by name in the Encyclical was one of a series of acts of reticence touching that document, all of which must have been the effect of one common reason.

The intention of the language of Boniface to make the king, in the use of the sword, merely a minister at the command of the priest, is rendered clearer by his departure from the words of St. Bernard, whom he is supposed to quote, in order, as Ultramontane writers point out, to confound the King of France by the authority of the greatest of Frenchmen. Those words were: 'The latter is to be wielded for the Church, the former by the Church; the material sword by the hand of the soldier, but only at the intimation of the priest and the command of the Emperor.'[1] This language of Bernard leaves the matter much as historians who wrote before Christ habitually put it, namely, that the soldier did not smite with the sword until the king commanded, and the king did not command until the priest told him that the omens allowed it. But Boniface changed all this. He did not allow anything to appear about the king commanding. He simply takes the soldier and the king together as hands to the priest, who is the power that gives the command, to which they are to give effect. Thus the doctrine of physical force steadily develops itself in Papal politics, as does that of materialised worship in Papal theology.

But what is the real teaching, as to the use of physical force, of Cardinal Soglia, who is soberly put forward by Dr. Newman before the English

[1] *Soglia*, vol. ii., p. 216-17.   Edition of 1875 by Vecchiotti, sold at the Propaganda.

public as justifying him in crying out against Mr. Gladstone for accusing the Church of claiming the right to use force? We shall not say one word about it, but leave a few sentences taken from Soglia's chapter on the coercive power of the Church and on ecclesiastical penalties to speak for themselves. We quote from an edition of three octavos, sold at the *Propaganda.* Dr. Newman quotes from a single duodecimo published in Paris. His edition is Cisalpine. Moreover, Soglia wrote before the present pontificate and the new developments of doctrine. Our edition (the sixteenth, 1875) is expressly prepared for use in seminaries.—Page 216 : ' The Church, exercising her power in the external tribunal, has been long accustomed to chastise offenders even with prison, exile, confinement in monasteries, whipping or flagellation, with fine, and other similar penalties ; which, inasmuch as they affect the body, are commonly called corporeal.'—Page 219 : ' We affirm that in the inherent authority of the Church, by which she can coerce offenders with salutary penalties, is certainly contained the right of awarding such temporal penalties as consist in fine, exile, prison, whipping, and other things of the same kind.'—Page 222 : ' If a case occurs in which severer punishment appears necessary, the ecclesiastical judge may not himself resort to it, but he is to hand over the delinquent to the secular power to be punished according to its will. Besides, it is evident that the crime of heresy itself was brought under the cognizance of the ecclesiastical tribunals up to the point when the heretics, being convicted, and found obstinate, were first punished by ecclesiastical censures, and afterwards, being subjected by the lay power to capital penalty, were exterminated.'—Page 222 : ' The Church never pronounced a sentence of blood. Even the Inquisition smote heretics with the spiritual sword, and prison, but the lay princes subjected them to the last capital penalty.'—Page 217 : ' Perhingius believes that the Church does possess the right of inflicting capital punishment, but that she is not accustomed to exercise it, or to carry it out by ecclesiastical ministers and judges, but through lay ones, and by means of the temporal power, because the latter is more becoming, and more appropriate to the claims of the Church.' What follows would, by internal evidence, seem to be added by Vecchiotti, but no intimation is given to that effect.—Page 217 : ' He [Cardinal Tarquini] held that there is no kind of penalty with which the Church may not in her own right punish offenders; and thus temporal goods, reputation, rights of office and of heritage, and life itself, are subject to the ecclesiastical power. Otherwise the Church could not compel disobedient rebels, or avenge herself for their crimes, nor could she cut off rotten and noxious members from the body.' Soglia, or rather his continuator, speaking of the moderns, Tarquini and ' other doctors,' and their doctrine of physical force, says (p. 217), ' They derive it from the character and constitution of the Church herself, or from the nature of a perfect society and its end. Hence, just as in a perfect civil society, the right of execution *jus necis* belongs to the lay power for the good of the commonwealth and of the citizens, so do they assert that none can deny that by stronger reason the same right resides in the ecclesiastical power for the spiritua' good of the faithful.'

CHAPTER II

Six Secret Commissions preparing—Interrupted by Garibaldi—A Code for the Relations of the Church and Civil Society—Special Sitting with Pope and Antonelli to decide on the Case of Princes—Tales of the Crusaders— English Martyrs—Children on the Altar—Autumn of 1867 to June 1868.

WHILE in the provinces the bishops were kindling enthu-siasm for the coming assembly, and for the movement of reconstruction in general, in Rome six Commissions were at work, under the Directing Congregation, making secret prepara-tions for the Council. Each of these Commissions had of course a Cardinal at its head. The first, that for Theology, was under Cardinal Bilio, a monk, and a native of Piedmont, only forty years of age, and but lately raised to the purple.[1]   Rightly or wrongly, as Vitelleschi says, he is credited with the principal share in the preparation of the Syllabus. Others, however, are named for the same honour. We ourselves heard a member of the original Congregation for the preparation of the Syllabus assert that it was Passaglia who first suggested it. Passaglia was a great Jesuit theologian, who lost position by declaring against the temporal power. The second Commission, for Ecclesiastico-Political Affairs, was under Cardinal Reisach, a man of sixty-five, an accomplished Bavarian, but so denationalised in manner and spirit, that his countrymen sometimes accused him of affect-ing to have almost forgotten German. For some years he left Rome to hold high place in his native country. As Archbishop of Munich he did much to supplant the old national faith by the Vatican one, and to unsettle the previously existing relations of

---

[1] *Cecconi*, p. 62.

Church and State. Under his eye the popular catechism of Canisius was changed. The answer, 'The Pope by himself is not infallible,' had done good service for centuries ; but now it had to make way for a new one : and eventually the whole book was transformed by the French Jesuit Dcharbe.[1]

When Reisach had rendered his presence in Munich so un-welcome that the King applied to the Pope for his removal, he resigned the archbishopric, but the Pope raised him to the purple, as Resident Cardinal. Now he was to be the first Presiding Cardinal in the Council.

Cecconi's description of the task assigned to Reisach and his Commission, shows how it went to the root of the enterprise of reconstruction. He speaks of it as '*this first attempt to indite a code of laws concerning matters affecting the relations of the Church and Civil Society*' (p. 301).

The Commission next in importance was that on Ceremonies. If the theological one had to formulate the principles on which the world was to be governed, and the ecclesiastico-political one had to draft the rules and frame the executive machinery by which those principles were to be carried out, the Commission on ceremonies had to devise the scenic effects with which the move-ment should, to use a frequent expression of Roman, French, and even of German Catholic writers, be put upon the stage— the *mise en scène.*

Oriental Affairs, the Religious Orders, and Ecclesiastical Discipline, were the subjects committed to the other three Commissions.

A seventh, of which the official history makes no mention, was, according to Vitelleschi (p. 26), an object of great public attention. It was for Biblical matters, and the revision of the Index. Its President was Cardinal de Luca. But it inclined to a more liberal procedure in regard to the Index, gave

---

[1] An interesting account of this change is given in Sepp's stirring speech in the Bavarian Parliament on the Mering case, *Deutschland und der Vatican,* pp. 182-185.

offence, and after a few meetings, was discontinued. The official organs, as the same author says, buried it in oblivion, though its labours were of great public interest.

The renewed preparations had not proceeded long before they were once more interrupted by political events. From August to December the Directing Congregation could hold no meeting. General Dumont had been sent back to Rome, by Napoleon III., to inspect and harangue those French soldiers who now formed a principal part of the so-called pontifical, or œcumenical, army. The national Italian party was excited by his presence and his speech. France forced them to feel that foreign occupation was discontinued only in name. Garibaldi, supported only by feeble forces, moved upon Rome with the reckless valour which had succeeded in Sicily. The movements of the Italian Government to restrain him were altogether inefficacious. The efficiency and zeal of the little army of ' Crusaders' had been utterly underrated by the Italians. The Dutch, English, Swiss, German, and French youths who fought for the crown of martyrdom were a different material from the soldiers of Ferdinand or from those of the old Papal corps. They faced great odds, and did right daring deeds. But they were too few. The ready French were once more called in. On the 3rd of November they secured for Pius IX. another respite by the battle of Mentana; but the Pope's own historian does not even name the French. For all that is said by Cecconi, not a foreign mercenary might have been in the Pontiff's pay, not a foreign regiment might have been sent to his relief. Indeed the word 'foreigner,' as applied to any baptized person bearing arms for the Pontiff, is offensive language,—another fruit of this degenerate age. In opposition to certain 'ill-advised' Catholics, who thought it a pity to have recourse to foreign arms, the *Civiltà* cries : ' Foreigners?—the word is a great and odious lie ! At Solferino the French were foreigners; at Mentana they were in their father's house.'[1] So does the one

[1] VII., iii., 559.

belief that the Pope is the appointed lord of the world change the lights that fall on every national movement. We only saw the fact that at Solferino the French killed Teuton invaders of Italy, and that at Mentana they were the invaders who killed Italians. We shall find French mothers of 'martyred' counts calling him for whom they fell, 'our King.'

When the lance of Garibaldi was thus, for the second time, shivered against the shield of France, who would have said that when next lifted it would be in her defence, after the armies that had for twenty years upheld the temporal power had gone into captivity?

The martial value of the religious motives and principles which animated the Crusaders, as contrasted with the Garibaldians, became a favourite theme for sacred pens. The Crusaders showed by their bearing that they were 'conscious of serving the majesty of the God of battles.' They lost no passing opportunity of renewing their strength at the altar.

'The proud lads, in full equipment of war, bowed the knee before the altar, offered up their lives to God, and consecrated their bayonets to St. Peter; or hastily receiving the Sacrament, they arose with joy and seized their pieces, which had been laid down by the rails of the sacred table. Happy he who with his eyes beheld such elevation of thought, such constancy of purpose, such sanctity of Christian war march triumphantly through the Roman territory.'[1]

On the 8th of October, the correspondent of the *Times* at Berlin stated that Napoleon III. had bound himself to leave Victor Emmanuel free as to Rome, provided the latter would help him in case of war with Prussia. Earlier than this, in the month of September, the Austrian bishops found themselves menaced with an abolition of the Concordat, and had to make a formal appeal to the Emperor against such a step.

'We have at this time of day,' said Baron Weichs, 'to decide whether we shall be an independent State, or whether, as in Japan, we shall have two sovereigns; the one, subordinate, residing at the Burg in Vienna; the other, the omnipotent Master, having his throne in Rome, at the Vatican, or, more properly speaking, at the Jesuit establishment.'

[1] *Civiltà*, VII., x., 161.

The *Revue des deux Mondes* had spoken of these words as wise, even as very wise, and the *Civiltá* replied, 'To us they seem to be nothing but buffoonery.'[1]

In November, Napoleon III. proposed that the European powers should meet in a Congress, to decide upon some solution of the Roman question. After this proposal had failed, his Minister, M. Rouher, pronounced, in the Assembly, his celebrated 'Never!'—the French would never permit Rome to be occupied by the Italians. This exclamation is often printed by the 'good press' in the largest capitals.

A fortnight after the day of Mentana the activity of the Commissions was resumed, and invitations were sent out to the theologians already selected in different countries, to come to Rome and enter on their labours. The Nuncio at Munich had not recommended any one from the renowned faculty of that city, but had sought his men at Wurzburg. England was represented by Monsignor Weathers, and the United States by Monsignor Corcoran. On October 2nd Cardinal Caterini wrote to Bishop Ullathorne of Birmingham, instructing him, in the Pope's name, to invite 'the priest John Newman.' Three weeks later the bishop replied, enclosing Dr. Newman's answer, which, however, is not printed. According to the bishop, Dr. Newman said that a journey to Rome would be perilous to his life, and though deeply touched with the kindness of the Holy Father, he believed that the latter would not desire him to come at the risk of his life, especially as nothing would be advanced by his presence in an august solemnity of such moment, unskilled as he was in matters of the sort.[2]

In concluding his letter the Cardinal 'cordially kisses hands to the bishop, who in return kisses the hand of the Cardinal, 'in token of reverence,' but he does not 'kiss the sacred purple.'

The language of Dr. Newman, as reported in this correspondence, shows that he had but faint light on the part which mere

---

[1] Serie VII., vol. vii., p. 22.   [2] *Cecconi*, pp. 370, 371.

divines were to play in the Council. Probably he was misled by history into supposing that their part would be public and considerable. His place, had he gone, would have been upon an unseen commission; his share probably anything but an important one; and, as likely as not, his opinion might have been asked only in writing, and upon a question of Oriental affairs, instead of upon theology, as was that of his famous fellow oratorian Theiner. Of the very few German scholars invited to Rome who were not of the Jesuit school, one was Haneberg, who, according to Michelis, was so little consulted that he was soon back in Munich, to avoid idling away his time.

In March the Pope intimated his intention of issuing in June the Bull of Convocation; and then the purpled had to consider who should be summoned. The most serious doubt arose as to those useful fictions called *bishops in partibus.* They have much of what goes to make a bishop—the orders, robes, title, and consequence, everything but the office. Their want of this is delicately expressed by Cecconi—they have no determinate flock; which in lay language means no flock at all. The number of these Court followers had been so increased that Sepp illustrates the case by that of a government creating a batch of peers to carry some measure.

But such peers do not depend for their living on the men who want their votes. Even the Cardinals had not the courage to assert that creatures like these had a *right* to sit in the Council. They did raise the question of right, and left it formally unanswered; but their next question was, Is it expedient to invite them? They boldly affirmed that it was expedient.

In May 1868 it was decided that the only proceeding to be observed with respect to Catholic princes was that of communicating a copy of the Bull of Convocation to each Court. But should the princes be invited to attend? This question 'was much debated among the purpled consulters, and was negatived.'[1] Our author explains :—

---

[1] *Cecconi*, p. 122.

'In former times, when Catholic princes, as such, openly professed Catholicism, when the civil and ecclesiastical laws harmonised with one another, and States executed the decrees of the Church, the presence of princes in Councils was not only fitting, but in some sense necessary. But at present where is the Catholic kingdom? Where harmonious laws! Where is ecclesiastical legislation respected on principle? On the contrary, does not the pretended separation of the State from the Church form the rule which guides every act of governments and of parliaments, as to which, nowadays, sovereigns are nothing more than the executors of their will? Are, then, those to be introduced into the august Council who, in the main, would represent nothing there but *the very principles which the Church, assembled in the person of her pastors, is called to condemn, and, as much as in her lies, to destroy.'—Cecconi,* pp. 122, 123.

This passage needs no exposition, but it will repay re-reading. The words we have put in italics contain an expression of the purpose and the policy of that movement in which the Council formed the legislative episode ; and those words may be pondered again and again. The decision thus taken was logical, for no one is a Catholic prince 'as such' who does not place the law of his land under canon law ; or, in proper language, who does not maintain 'harmonious laws,' recognising politics as lying in the domain of morals, and therefore as being under the spiritual authority. When the controversy on the Syllabus began, the *Civiltà* had enjoyed a triumphant laugh at M. Langlais, a distinguished French advocate. M. Langlais had argued that the Encyclical would not have transgressed its proper boundary had it treated only of faith and morals, but that having touched the foundations of political institutions, it had transgressed that boundary. The *Civiltà* cried :—

'There exist then, according to M. Langlais, foundations of political institutions outside of the circle of morals ! outside, consequently, of the circle of manners ; or maybe, outside of the circle of human actions. . . . His argument assumes that the political order cannot be at the same time moral, or at least founded in the moral order, and assumes further that it must be separate from it, else he could not say that the Pope, simply by entering upon the political order, had gone out of the moral order' (VI., i., 652-653).

It is not said that Antonelli in particular took alarm. But it is said that fears arose lest the 'novelty' resolved upon should prove perilous; therefore the subject had to be reconsidered in the presence of the Secretary of State. Thus for once we see taking his place with the Nine the spare, well-knit, olive-tinted son of Sonnino, with his compelling lip and sharp eye, never at rest and never disconcerted ; with his rare tufts of hair, black enough for the tuft of a Brahman; and with his broad brow, on which sat thought, but thought less sagelike than lordly. The danger that might follow the brusque exclusion of princes was so felt that the former decision was on the point of being reversed. This shows Antonelli's ascendant. But his colleagues had a resource. Only six days before the date fixed for publishing the Bull, a special summons, not from Giannelli, but from Antonelli himself, called together the Commission at a quarter past eight o'clock in the evening, to a meeting to be held 'in presence of the Most Holy' (*coram sanctissimo*)—*i.e.*, before the Pope.[1]

Before the Most Holy ! Thus are we placed in presence of the Eleven, and the kings are on their trial. The Nine are joined by the two men so dissimilar and so indissoluble, Pius IX. and Antonelli, in whom, as an official biographer puts it, he early discerned 'the man of God,' appointed as his succour and stay in his divine office. At the head of the Eleven sits the portly, goodlooking Pope, the beau-ideal of an important squire in a remote place—full of will, spirit, and self-confidence, with more art in governing than he has got credit for, at least in that domineering and deluding which avails with priests. He would be as hilarious as a squire who never put to death anything more precious than a pheasant, and never cursed even a gamekeeper with any intention that his curse should be bound in heaven.

Pius IX. would now feel all the weight of his office. He was sitting as Supreme Judge, to decide upon the claims of the kings of the earth. Were they worthy or were they not worthy to be received into the Council which was to lay ' the cornerstone of reconstruction,' the Council in which the prerogatives

[1] *Cecconi*, p. 532.

rightfully claimed by his predecessors of blessed memory, but from which the Church, slow of heart to believe, had hitherto withheld her formal sanction, were at last to be openly acknowledged in his person? The Church had, however, over and over again acknowledged the right of kings to a place and a voice. But having become mere constitutional kings, were they worthy to retain their ancient place? The historian does not intimate that any question of right was ever raised. He intimates only that strong fears were expressed as to possible danger from the proposed exclusion. The deliberation was long and anxious.

No one could doubt what view Pius IX. would take. The kings were clearly guilty. They had consented to the voice of their people against the voice of the Church. They had abolished harmonious laws. The internal tribunal was reduced to a voluntary confessional; the external tribunal, in most places, was removed, and everywhere subordinated. Even as to the Supreme Tribunal, who hearkened to the words, 'Know that thou art the Father of princes and of kings, and the Governor of the world?' Admitting all this, the smooth man of Sonnino would show that if all the kings were offended, Garibaldi, or personages more formidable, might take their seat in Rome, instead of a Council. Hard words for a Pope to hear! When the call for Trent went forth, the only doubtful crowns were two lying away between civilisation and Cimmerian night in England and Sweden. Now on every hand the word was, There are no Catholic princes. That old English crown was now represented by two monsters of power, the British Empire and the United States. Two other monsters had come up, Prussia and Russia. Spain was fallen, Poland was extinct, Italy was hostile, Austria was enfeebled, France was strong but not sound,—there were no Catholic States. The social system was indeed in ruins. It was only by clearing away that the foundations for reconstruction could be properly laid; but clearing away was attended with danger. The princes were not to be invited, but they were to be allowed to claim admission. The Bull was then and there altered in this sense.[1]

We have already seen what is the Vatican view of constitutional States, when told by the Vatican historian that they are the thing to be combated, and if possible destroyed. The Vatican view of the forthcoming Council is implied in the same utterance,—it was the force to combat and destroy constitutional States. On the ruins, however, was to rise a nobler structure, and more secure. We have already seen the Church called 'mother of civil humanity,'—an extension of the term 'mother of the faithful.' We are now to see the Pope called 'father of the nations,'—an extension of the term 'father of the faithful.' As such, seeing that the nations under their present form are in a dying condition, he is the saviour of society.

The introduction to the Pope's Speeches says :—

> 'It was by a manifest counsel of the Omniscient that the true Father of the nations, the only saviour of moribund society, was led to collect all his forces, and by proclaiming the dogma of infallibility, to establish the supreme teaching authority, as an imperishable centre around which the misled generations might rally in the midst of catastrophes.' [2]

Of the terms here used that most transformed by religious belief is the phrase *supreme teaching authority*. To a Protestant it means some great power of interpreting the Bible. To an Ultramontane it means the power of interpreting the law and mind of God, held by His Vicar, and exercised either in statutes or in institutions; and thus it becomes really a supreme legislative and rectoral authority over rulers. We shall in the sequel see its real meaning clearly stated.

Meanwhile symptoms of the coming conflict began to appear. Catholics of all classes looked forward to great events for the Church and the nations. In proportion as they were well informed, did their estimate of the gravity of impending events increase. Those who did not share the hopes of the hidden Council, or who recoiled from the dogmas likely to be decreed,

---

[1] *Cecconi*, p. 121-124. [2] *Discorsi*, vol. i., p. 24.

felt anxious.   The press began to pour out pamphlets and reprints, enabling all to read up on the question of Councils.

It was by a Cæsar at the height of military and political success that the first General Council was convened.   This new Council was called by one retaining as much of the Cæsar as lay in the office of Pontiff, and the ambition of universal supremacy, but at the depth of political and military failure.   When Constantine sent the good Bishop of Cordova with his letter to the disputants in Egypt, he was grieved by theological dissensions within the Churches.   'Restore to us peaceful and serene days, and nights void of care, that the pleasure of the pure light and the joy of a quiet life may in future be reserved to us also.'[1] Pius IX. likewise longed for quiet days and nights, but he was disturbed by the unity and progress of Italy and Germany, not by bishops sparring with words, to use the phrase of Eusebius.

'The Crusaders of St. Peter' was the title of historical tales now regularly appearing in the *Civiltà*, which continued for years.   The object was to make the blood of Mentana the seed of a great œcumenical army.   Every incident was described with vivid conception and boundless faith in the destiny of the Papacy, with faith too in the duty of all to rear up sons for the Crusade, and faith that those who fell escaped purgatorial pains and found direct entrance among the beatified.   The military virtues of the rosary, of certain medals, and of the scapular, were always kept in view.   One word might express the appeal to the crusader himself—To the fight newly shriven, from the fight straight to heaven.

The following are passages scattered here and there :—

'It was a sight to rejoice the angels in heaven, that of these brave men laying down the carabine to perform the little office of the Virgin, and then turning from the little office of the Virgin to take up the carabine. . . . The congregations of Mary often met at the foot of an olive to recite the holy rosary. . . . No one faced danger without acquiring [by absolution] that daring which is inspired by a pure conscience and by the bread of the strong. . . . On march the fatigue was lightened by reciting the

[1] *Life of Constantine,* by Eusebius, lib. ii., cap. 72.   London, 1709.

prayer which had so often conquered the foes of the Church, the rosary.
. . . . The masters of war know that on the field of battle the last army
to deserve ridicule is an army fresh from confession and communion. . . .
A young gentlewoman gave birth to her first-born. "How long it will be,"
she said, "ere he can carry a musket! But Pius IX. can do anything. He
can make a zouave even now of my Eugenio." Melted by such faith, the
Pope wrote a benediction on a paper "consecrated to him" by the infant.
The venerated word was placed in the domestic sanctum, and in return
for it " the zouave at the breast will do a soldier's service." Some weeks
later, on receiving from him a first oblation, the Pope again wrote a word
for "his soldier in swaddling clothes." The family were overjoyed at
being permitted within five months to kiss two Papal autographs. The
mother wrote, "Eugenio was asleep. I ran to put the Papal benediction
on his head and forehead. He immediately broke out in a smile, and to
me he looked like an angel. I could not restrain my tears. He still
slept, but bounded for joy as long as I kept the blessed letters on his little
head. . . . Should the avengers of Mentana try their hand, the Zouave
will lisp his first word crying *Viva Maria !*"'

Arthur Guillemin said to his crusaders as he led them to the
attack at Monte Libretti, fresh from absolution, 'You are all
in the grace of God; do not count them, they will fall into our
hands.' They marched into battle, some with the rosary round
their neck, some with the Carmelite scapular on their breast,
and some with the cord of St. Francis round the loins, just
like that model of a crusader St. Louis. The young Count de
Quélen, who fell heroically at Monte Libretti, had just received
a letter from his mother. 'If thou art to die, my good Urban,
die like a hero, like a soldier of God.' After his death she
writes to a friend in Rome :—

'My beloved son is dead—died for his God. Oh what a comfort is that
thought amid this desolation ! He fell like the brave, defending the
Church and our venerated Pontiff. Was it not a signal favour granted to
him by that Lord who is so good that He put it into his heart to shed
every drop of his blood for Him, and by this very means to bring him to
paradise, where Urban henceforth—yes, I dare believe it—enjoys the
vision of his God, and is beatified for all eternity, with beatitude unmixed?'
[Thus it was plain that having fallen in battle he had, as the writer of
the story says, 'seized the palm of martyrdom, as he, following St. Louis,
called it,' and so had escaped the pains of purgatory.] 'If,' continues
the mother to her friend, 'you go to a reception of our holy and vene-

rated Pontiff and King, assure him, I pray you, that I am happy that my son has shed his blood for him.'

When the body arrived at Quimper, two hundred priests and a crowd uncounted from the surrounding Breton villages came, 'rather to venerate than to pray for the departed.' The houses were draped in black, the black was decked with the French and the Papal flags; on the coffin lay his sword, twined with laurels and crowned with vermilion. The bishop pronounced the panegyric 'magnifying him as a martyr for religion.' Mrs. Stone, a volunteer sister of charity, went from Rome to Nerola to visit the wounded prisoners in the hands of the Garibaldians, and especially Alfred Collingridge. The dying crusader said, 'The Lord has given me the favour I asked—to die for the Holy Father. Oh, yes, may God accept of my death and my blood for the triumph of Holy Church and for the conversion of England!' He complained that his rosary had been taken away, and Mrs. Stone supplied him with her own. Later, to Monsignor Stonor, another Englishman, he expressed the same sentiments, and it is immediately added that he 'impressed most tender kisses on the medals of St. Michael the Archangel, and St. Ignatius, to whom he professed special devotion.' St. Michael was then patron of the Church, and patron of all her warriors, and St. Ignatius is eminently a fighting saint. Alfred Colling-ridge, from Oxford, 'was the first of the English who laid down his life in the Crusade of St. Peter.' The writer prays, 'May this first English blood shed on Roman soil rise up before God, and descend again in a dew of mercy on the land of Britain!' Of Alfred's countrymen were present, his own brother George, two Watts-Russells, David Shee, and Oswald Cary, 'all soldiers of St. Peter' (VII., v., 155 ff). The father hearing from George of the death of Alfred, had only one regret, that he could not himself step into his vacant place.

When Arthur Guillemin fell he was unhappily consigned to a grave in common with Garibaldians; because it 'was not then possible to separate in the grave the friends of God from

His enemies.' Six months later, Fathers Wilde and Gerlache, with others, piously sought the body of the martyr to restore it to his native Aire-sur-la-Lys, by express desire of Pius IX. Canon Druot had come to Rome to claim it in the name of the family, the country, and the Church of Guillemin's birth. The seekers of the relic included an O'Reilly, a Le Dieu, a Bach, a Loonen, and a Mimmi. 'You will find him,' said a peasant, 'with a Garibaldian at his feet.' The first object recognised was a Carmelite scapular. 'It is like mine,' cried an officer; 'two both alike were given to him and me by the Countess Macchi!' Soon was seen the end of the cord of St. Francis, worn by the deceased in imitation of St. Louis of France. As the corpse was borne off to Rome, the people pressed around and cried *Evviva!*—Long life to him! This cry 'strange around a bier,' expressed a 'profound sense of the marvellous,' and threw 'a glittering light upon the idea formed by Christians of those who fall fighting in the modern crusade.' At Rome, in the great Church of St. Louis of France, the bier was surrounded by ambassadors, prelates, and officers, including the Minister of War. At home, the 'precious deposit' was received in an illuminated chapel, decorated, not with symbols of death, but of glory. 'The crowd of pilgrims from the whole of northern France' thronged the town. The bier was adorned with symbols of victory, the work of Roman artists. The coffin was borne by the youth of the town, emulous by changes to come under the coveted burden. A party of pontifical zouaves in uniform attended. From the corners of the hearse rose trophies of the pontifical flag 'garlanded with triumphal laurel.' While yet the corpse lay in the illuminated chapel, a new-born nephew of Arthur was borne in by the mother, who 'piously laid him upon the coffin, as used the ancient Christians to lay their little ones on the sepulchres of the martyrs. A thrill of reverence went through the assembly.' During the funeral procession, the eyes of the multitude 'were fixed with devout curiosity on a piece of his uniform spread out upon the bier, in which was seen the rent made by the wound' (VII., iv., 415).

Aire-sur-la-Lys is not very far from our own shores, beyond Calais.

CHAPTER III.

Bull of Convocation—Doctrine of the Sword—The Crusade of St. Peter— Incidents—Mission to the Orientals, and Overtures to Protestants in different Countries—June 1868 to December 1868-69.

IT was on St. Peter's Day, June 29th, 1868, that the Bull of Convocation was issued. According to the Pope's promise, the Council was to meet on the Feast of the Immaculate Conception, December 8th, 1869.

The language of the Bull was diplomatically vague as to the objects of the assembly, but awfully explicit as to the authority by which it was convened. Not in an *obiter dictum*, but in legislative language jointed to bear the strain of ages, a claim is set up, as Sepp points out, to exercise the authority of the whole Trinity, and, indeed, we may add, whatever further authority Peter and Paul can lend. 'Confiding in and supported by the authority of Almighty God Himself, Father, Son, and Holy Ghost, and of His blessed Apostles Peter and Paul, *which we also exercise upon earth.*'[1] It ought to be remembered that M. Veuillot writes down the date of this Bull as the day on which the middle ages died. The indication of objects, though vague to us, sufficed for the initiated. *Ce Qui se Passe au Concile* says (p. 9):—

'The Pope repeatedly intimates that the Church has the right "to redress the errors which turn *civil* society upside down, . . . to preserve the nations from bad books and pernicious journals, and from those teachers of iniquity and error to whom the unhappy youth are confided

[1] *Acta*, p. 6.

whose education is withdrawn from the clergy ; . . . to defend justice, . . . to assure the progress and solidity of the human sciences." This somewhat confounds things spiritual and temporal ; but those political allusions drowned in the usual digressions of Pontifical documents, passed unobserved.'

If they passed unobserved in Roman Catholic countries, where journalists did know a little of the modes of pontifical speech, how much more in countries like England and America, where at that time it was considered unintelligent to speak or write upon the subject from knowledge, the proper thing being a serene superiority to study, and a judicious expression of opinions caught in the air. Many a clear-headed man would have taken the expression about redressing the errors that turn society upside down, to mean, confronting false principles with sound ones ; and the expression about 'preserving a nation' from bad journals to mean, beating them by good ones; and to such men, of course, 'defending justice' would never mean what it meant to the French priest, but what it means at St. Stephen's.

To obviate the objection that the assembly would be only a synod of the Western Church, and not an Œcumenical Council, the Bull was followed by Letters Apostolic addressed to all prelates of the Oriental Churches not holding communion with Rome.[1] Until the Vatican Council these were regarded only as schismatics, not as heretics. Therefore the Pope invited them to come, and by submitting to the See of Rome to complete the union. This invitation was dated September 8th ; and on the 13th of that month a 'paternal letter' went forth, to Protestants and other non-Catholics. All these, from Anglican Ritualists down to the smallest sects, were grouped together, not being called to take any part in the Council, but to seize the occasion of joining the Pope's Church by renouncing their heresies and submitting to his authority.

Although the approach of the Council excited little attention

---

[1] Archbishop Manning gave reasons for looking upon the motive here assigned as 'a transparent error.'

in Protestant countries, it began to be discussed in Roman
Catholic ones with an interest which rapidly warmed to excitement. The tremendous significance attached by Ultramontane
authorities to the Bull, especially to the non-invitation of
princes, and to the coming struggle with the Modern State,
was enough to rouse Catholics who did not sympathise with
the aims indicated. For instance, a professor of history in the
Roman University writing a folio said, ' By this august act the
greatness of Pius IX. is raised so far above all previous deeds
of his pontificate, that we are compelled to lay down our pen.'[1]
The *Civiltá* put the alternative as between the end of the world
or its salvation by the Council. ' Either, in the inscrutable
designs of God, human society is destined to perish, and we
are close upon the supreme cataclysm of the last day, or the
salvation of the world is to be looked for from the Council and
from nothing else.'[2] Language like this is not to be smiled
at when it goes to the heart of perhaps half a million of ecclesiastics, each one of whom transmits the impression through a
wide circle. The writers were in awful earnest, and held out
to the falling world the hope of an all-sufficing Saviour. The
following passage in the same article may be laid to heart. A
good part of it is quoted by *Janus*, with the remark that it
needs but a step further to declare the Pontiff an incarnation
of God. The portion which we put in italics gives the theological
key to the doctrine of dominion over the species, as in a former
article we saw baptism made the key to the doctrine of civil
dominion over all the baptized :—

'The Pope is not a power among men to be venerated like another.
But he is a power altogether divine. He is the propounder and teacher
of the law of the Lord in the whole universe ; he is the supreme leader
of the nations to guide them in the way of eternal salvation; he is the
common father and universal guardian of the whole human species in the
name of God. The human species has been perfected in its natural qualities, *by divine revelation and by the incarnation of the Word, and has been*

[1] Professor Massi in *Frond*, vol. i., p. 130.
[2] Serie VII, vol. iii., p. 264.

lifted up into a supernatural order, in which alone can it find its temporal and eternal felicity. The treasures of revelation, the treasures of truth, the treasures of righteousness, the treasures of supernatural graces upon earth, have been deposited by God in the hands of one man, who is the sole dispenser and keeper of them. The life-giving work of the divine incarnation, work of wisdom, of love, of mercy, is ceaselessly continued in the ceaseless action of one man, thereto ordained by Providence. This man is the Pope. This is evidently implied in his designation itself— The Vicar of Christ. For if he holds the place of Christ upon earth, that means that he continues the work of Christ in the world, and is in respect of us what Christ would be were He here below, Himself visibly governing the Church. . . . It is, then, no wonder if the Pope, in his language, shows that the care of the whole world is his, and if, forgetting his own peril, he thinks only of that of the faithful nations. He sees aberrations of mind, passions of the heart, overflowing vices; he sees new wants, new aspirations; and holding out to the nations a helping hand, with the tranquillity of one securely seated on the throne given him by God, he says to them, Draw nigh to me, and I will trace out for you the way of truth and charity which alone can lead to the desired happiness."[1]

The Count Henri de Riancey exclaimed that no monarch, even in his wildest dreams, could flatter himself that he could send irresistible instructions into every nation, as did he who alone upon earth signed himself Bishop of the Catholic Church.

The chief pre-occupation of the Count, like that of most good Catholics, was the preservation of the temporal power. No one shall ever reign over the Seven Hills, cried he, but the successor of him who was crucified on the Janiculum. The inviolability of Rome was a law of history,—fine words for a Frenchman. He believed that the Pope meant to force the powers to understand how much was involved in maintaining the dominion of Peter inviolate. The moral neutrality of the Papal States would probably be changed into a neutrality guaranteed by the law of nations.[2]

Such divines as held that the proper work of a General Council was to heal schisms or combat heresies, remarked on the absence of both. Such as were unwilling to see the Church

---

[1] Serie VII., vol. iii., pp. 259. 260.
[2] *Frond*, General Introduction.

straining after temporal power, and placing herself in antagonism to freedom and light, could ill conceal their anxiety. But the Jesuits everywhere hailed the dawning of a wonderful day.

On Saturday the 17th of October, 1868, the Abbé Testa, accompanied by three other priests, went to the palace of the Patriarch of Constantinople, bearing the Pope's letter to the Oriental bishops. The Vicar-General received the four Latin priests, and introduced them to his Holiness the Patriarch, whose hand they kissed. The Patriarch, on his part, embraced them, and expressed his pleasure at seeing them. The Abbé Testa then drew a richly adorned little book from his pocket and offered it to the Patriarch, while one of his brethren told his Holiness, in Greek, that they had come to invite him to attend the Œcumenical Council, and begged him to receive the letter of invitation.

His Holiness motioned to the Abbé Testa to lay the little book down near him, and said, 'Had not the *Giornale di Roma* published the letter whereby his Holiness summons us to Rome to a Council, which he calls œcumenical, and had we not thus learned the object and contents of the letter, and also the principles of his Holiness, we should have received a communication from the Patriarch of old Rome with the utmost pleasure, in hope of finding some change in his mode of thinking. As, however, this invitation is in the journals, and as his Holiness has proclaimed views in direct opposition to the principles of the orthodox Churches of the East, we declare to you, Reverend Fathers, with grief and at the same time with sincerity, that we cannot receive either such an invitation or such a letter, which only assert principles opposed to the spirit of the Gospel and to the declarations of the Œcumenical Councils and of the Holy Fathers.'

The Patriarch proceeded to refer to the Pope's former advances, and delicately hinted that when they had objected that he held principles which were to be regretted, his reply showed that he was so much pained that it was better not to put him to grief a second time. 'In short, we look for the true settlement of the question to history. Ten centuries ago there was one Church, confessing the same faith in East and West, in old Rome and new Rome. Let us go back for that period, and let us see who has added and taken away. Let us suppress innovations, if such there are, and then shall we imperceptibly find ourselves at that point of Catholic orthodoxy from which Rome was pleased gradually to diverge in the earlier centuries, ever widening the gulf of separation more and more by new dogmas and definitions which depart from the holy traditions.'

The Abbé Testa asked what principles his Holiness spoke of.

'Without entering into minute points,' replied the Patriarch, 'we can never admit that wherever the Church of our Saviour extends upon earth any Chief Bishop exists in the midst of her except our Lord, or that there is a Patriarch who is infallible whenever he speaks *ex cathedrâ*, who is exalted above the Œcumenical Councils, to which alone infallibility attaches, seeing that they always held to holy scripture and apostolic tradition.'

The Abbé referred to the Council of Florence, and received a full and courteous answer. The Patriarch at last said, 'If you would see that union realised which we all desire, place yourselves on the ground of history and of the General Councils; or, if that is too hard upon you, let us all pray to God for peace to the world and prosperity and union to the Church. For the moment, we declare, with pain, that this invitation is fruitless and this circular of no effect.'

The four Latins urged that prayer alone did not suffice; if one was sick we not only prayed but employed means of cure. 'When the sickness is spiritual,' replied the Patriarch, 'the Lord alone knows who is the sick man, how he suffers, what is the root of the malady, and what the real cure. I say again there is urgent necessity for ceaseless prayer to the

Lord of the whole earth, that He may guide all to conclusions well pleasing to God.'

The Patriarch then directed the Vicar-General to hand back the little book, and the four abbés took their leave, accompanied to the stair by the Vicar-General.[1]

Speaking of this interview, the *Stimmen aus Maria Laach* said, 'Neither by his words nor his deeds did the Patriarch manifest polish, theological science, or ecclesiastical education.'[2]

The invitation was rejected by the Metropolitan of Ephesus, and the Bishops of Varna and Thessalonica. The Metropolitan of Chalcedon wrote upon it *Epistrephete*—'Be converted'—and returned it. The Patriarch of Antioch sent the letter back, and his ten bishops did the same. So also the orthodox Greek Patriarch of Jerusalem and his bishops (*Friedberg*, p. 70). The Bishop of Thessalonica assigned four reasons, the last of which called forth a laboured reply from the Jesuits of Laach. 'The Pope is a king,' said the Oriental, 'and wields the sword, which is contrary to the gospel.' The reply was that the existence of the small but heroic army of the Pope was not due so much to any will of his as to the nature of his office as chief shepherd of the universal Church. The army and the temporal power, 'without which this office cannot exist,' were manifestly necessary. But then the 'schismatical bishop' asks if bearing the sword is not contrary to the gospel. No; for in the very words of the gospel Christ allowed the apostles to bear two swords.

Having reached this practical point in the teaching of Boniface VIII., the writer goes on to show that Peter was not told to cast his sword away, but only to put it up into the sheath; which clearly meant that he was to bear it. If he was reproved for using it, that was because, though he had asked permission to do so, he had not yet received it; for, in fact, at that point of time the supreme power promised to

---

[1] *Friedberg Aktenstücke*, pp. 250-253.
[2] *Neue Folge, Erstes Heft*, pp. 72, 73.

Peter had not been actually bestowed upon him. But seeing that he was told to keep the sword, are we to suppose that when he did become ruler, he and his successors for all time were to keep it hanging at their sides, as a useless weight? Certainly not; 'he beareth not the sword in vain.' The writer would probably have called any one an infidel who expected a literal fulfilment of the words 'all they that take the sword shall perish with the sword.'

In reviewing the reception given in the East to the Bull, consolation was drawn from the fact that the Armenian Patriarch in Constantinople had raised the brief to his forehead. But the Catholikos of the same Church in the See of Etschmiazin rejected it with decision. The ill-success of these overtures displeased the 'good press.' Pius IX. had been flattered into the belief that he had in great measure ' restored ' the ascendancy of the Pontiff over the East. Even Archbishop Manning had said enough in print to show that he came back from Rome in 1867 with some such idea, and prelates of more experience had done the same.

That ancient dominion of the Pontiff over the East, imagined by Dr. Manning and others, is a vision, formed in a vaporous historic atmosphere. When Rome set out to establish a physical dominion over the world, she succeeded more speedily and more widely against the over-ripe civilisation of the ancient nations, than over the untamed force of the young North. When, again, she set out to establish a spiritual dominion, she did not succeed with any but Romans or barbarians, unless by the power of the sword.

Just as Josephus said, 'Almost all which concerns the Greeks happened not long ago, nay, one may say is of yesterday only,'[1] so all the learned of the East looked down upon Rome. To them she was what Theodoric and his Goths were to her in the over-ripe stage of her own civilisation—stronger, nobler, wiser; but gross and not intellectual. To the West and North, she

[1] *Against Apion*, Book I., cap. 2, etc.

was ancient and lettered, to the East modern, only beginning to pick up bits of poetry and philosophy, and to reproduce them. In smiling at Greek antiquity, Josephus incidentally laughs at that of Rome. The Greeks, he shows, did not even name the place, not Herodotus nor Thucydides, nor any of their contemporaries; 'and it was very late, and with very great difficulty, that the Romans became known to the Greeks.' [1]

Again, just as in Greek history and biography, the extraction of a god, or the travel-study of a sage, invariably leads one East and South, so Rome always points to the East. Evander was from Arcadia. The ship of Æneas and the chair of Peter were both from the East, and there also lay the colleges of Cicero. When, therefore, Rome attempted to push a spiritual dominion in the East, it was like Birmingham turning upon Oxford. Pontiff is a sonorous, ancient word in Westminster. But in Antioch, Tarsus, or Jerusalem, it was only like what *Moolah* or *Guru* is to us. But at the time now spoken of, the chief pastor of Rome was still known by a Christian title.

The Christianity of the East, though half-paganised, never fell before the materialised forms of Rome, but before the monotheistic Semite, with *his* doctrine of the sword. At that date the two swords of Boniface had not been discovered. 'The emerald standard of the race of Fatima,' to quote Gibbon, had long floated over Christian ruins, before the standard of the tiara and keys ever hallowed sack and bloodshed. Omar had objected to be called *Vicar of the Vicar* before ever Pope stained Christian speech, or rather the speech of Christendom, with the term, the Vicar of God.[2]

---

[1] At Tyre, when rowing near the city, and looking through the clear sea water for ruined columns lying on the bottom, I pointed to a building ashore, saying to the guide, 'You have not shown us that.' He quietly replied, 'Oh, that is not ancient. It is only of the times of Alexander.'

[2] Price's *Mohammedan Hist.*, vol. i., p. 59. The word Caliph is explained to mean successor-vicar, giving the full meaning, of which the Latin term gives only the latter part. Price translates the terms denoting the office of Imaum and Caliph, *Imaumet Khaleifut, by supreme authority, both religious and civil, or pontifical and civil.* But true to the law of its development, as being a

The union of absolute authority in both religion and politics was speedily realised in an Arabian Pope, springing from a heathen stem ; but slowly and with difficulty were the two authorities united in a Latin Caliph developed out of a Christian bishop. Investiture of kings, and holding of stirrups, were borrowed from the Eastern Caliph by the Western one.[1]

Representations as to the readiness of Protestants to submit, had led to the letter to Protestants. Bishop Martin of Paderborn had strong hopes of those in Germany, and set store by some odd letters, said to be from Protestant clergymen, which, however, seem to be either spurious, or from men not likely to lead anybody.[2] Archbishop Manning, after several sentences coloured by a pontifical imagination, had said, ' The Council of Trent fixed the epoch after which Protestantism never spread. The next General Council will probably date the period of its dissolution.' [3]

A few consistories in Germany, Holland, Sweden, and America, noticed the document. Dr. Cumming, of the Scotch Church in London, wrote to the Pope expressing his willingness to attend the Council, if allowed to reason upon the questions at issue. The Pope gave no answer directly, but communicated his views to the public through Archbishop Manning. The Pope having apparently been informed that a number of persons wished to have conferences with a view of uniting themselves to Rome, wrote a second letter to Dr. Manning, to the effect

relapse from Christianity by the Jewish side, Mohammedanism was too reverent to call its chief the Vicar of God,—only of God's prophet. Equally true to the law of its development, as being a relapse from Christianity by the Pagan side, the Romish system called its chief the Vicar of God. Originally aspiring to be successor of Peter, he is now, as many Liberal Catholics and Old Catholics have pointed out, habitually spoken of, by the advanced school, as indeed he often was in the middle ages, as the successor of Christ, or the Living Christ.

[1] *Times*, Dec. 10th, 1870. Letter of Special Correspondent from Constantinople, describing the Sultan, quotes his titles : ' This Padisha, Father of all Sovereigns, this Hunikar or Manslayer, Refuge of the World, and Shadow of God.' Price says (i., p. 27) the first four Khalifs-Lieutenants, or Vicars.

[2] These productions are published by Friedrich—*Tagebuch.* p. 453 ff.

[3] *The Centenary of St. Peter, and the General Council,* p. 90.

that though no place could be allowed in the Council for the discussion of tenets already condemned, any persons desiring conference would find learned men designated, to whom they could open their minds. The public has never learned who were the persons thus provided for, or what was their number. Bishop Dupanloup, as will hereafter appear, had taken an impression, from Dr. Pusey, that in England the desire for union with Rome was widespread. The ' good press' of France and Italy often painted it as almost universal. The English Church has been all but buried many times. M. Veuillot himself has seen it vanishing, and already little remaining to its discomfited ministers 'but their money-bags.'

The Jesuit organs, in replying to an article of the *Times* of October 3rd, 1868, displayed more resentment against the ' folly and arrogance' of others, than against those of the original offender. On the part of the *Perseveranza* of Milan, it was 'a colossal and unpardonable error' to imagine that the *Times* might be taken as the voice of the Protestant public of England. Dr. Lee had acted with more intelligence, for he had said that he could not speak in the name of others.[1]

Archbishop Manning declares that 'the indiction of the Council was no sooner published than the well-known volume called *Janus* appeared.'[2] Our information, however, will not bring that volume to light till after a good deal has intervened.

Between the date of the Bull of Convocation, and that of the invitation to the Orientals, the Pope performed two journeys to the Alban Hills, which were celebrated by Court journalists. At Rocca di Papa, where Hannibal is said to have pitched his tents, the little army of his Holiness was, after modern usage, encamped. The Pontiff went on purpose across the Campagna and up the hills, passed through the ranks of his defenders, and himself celebrated Mass for their benefit. This was repeated a

---

[1] *Stimmen, Neue Folge, Heft* I., p. 54.

[2] He first made this statement in 1870, and repeated it in 1875 by quoting it in his reply to Mr. Gladstone. See *The Vatican Decrees*, p. 104.

second time, to the delight of the soldiers. When his next birthday was celebrated, the zouaves made a special display in the Piazza of St. Peter's, of which the *Civiltá* gives a long but lively description. The last formation mentioned is to us new in military evolutions. The zouaves 'formed so as to make the letters composing the august name Pius IX.'[1]

Ever since 1860 the preaching of 'taking up the cross,' of the glory of 'dying for religion,' and of the pure, bright martyrdom of falling on the field for St. Peter, had been rather heavy work. Now the gleam of victory at Mentana lighted up the future. Vistas long and luminous led the eye of the fighting sons of Loyola away to other scenes, where John VIII. as admiral, or John X. as general, or Pius V. rejoicing over Lepanto, with other martial glories of the Papacy, paled before what the Virgin and St. Michael were about to bring to pass. The 'salutary conspiracy and the holy crusade' which we saw the *Civiltá* announce in its program article, had now fairly passed the subterranean stage. Loud and ringing sounded forth to the faithful the call to the crusade of St. Peter. The youth of the Catholic world were assured that not the fall of Richmond nor the capture of Sebastopol, not Solferino nor Sadowa, had moved human society as did the tidings from Mentana. Stories true and often very touching were mixed with fables and with ecstacies.

The tales were those of youths from the noblest houses and from the lowliest cots. The young Duke de Blacas 'dedicated his sword to the tomb of St. Peter, as his forefathers dedicated theirs to the tomb of Christ.' In his death youths are to see the martyr palm for which it is noble to pant, and mothers are to see a privilege which they might well seek in prayer. Peter Jong, a poor Dutch lad, only son of his mother, a widow, who gave him up rejoicing as if God had granted her great grace, fell, it is said, after having slain fourteen Italians. He receives this tribute: 'For St. Peter he inflicted many just deaths; for

[1] *Civiltá*, Serie VII., vol. v., p. 234.

St. Peter he worthily met his own.' It is told how the King of Holland keeps Jong's photograph in his portfolio, and shows it to other intending crusaders as an encouragement. Another Dutch youth writes : ' Mamma, blessed is he who sheds the last drop of his blood. The martyrs of all the centuries descend to meet him and to conduct him to heaven.' This, though Protestants may not know it, is spiritual warfare ! for ' to defend the Church of Christ is a spiritual object.' One proof constantly alleged that bayonet and ball used for St. Peter are to re-establish truth and righteousness is, ' This is the victory that overcometh the world, even our faith.' If those who do not care to read heavy matter would only read in the *Civiltá* ' The Crusaders of St. Peter,' they would learn how Scripture can be quoted, and how the new red cross and rosary are sent round with a cry to arms. They would learn that the ' universal politics of the soldiers of Pius IX.' are to be expressed in the language of a crusader of Mentana—' I have taken up the cross to do penance for my sin. I have come to Rome for my conversion. I serve St. Peter in this force. Blessed is he who dies for religion ! Oh, might I die in the first engagement ! '

The young Duke de Blacas, not having been in action, seemed in dying to think that he should not escape purgatory. Care, however, is taken, in a studiously written biography of a Goldoni who also died before battle, to show that in point of martyrdom, as to the old crusaders, no difference was made by St. Bernard and St. Catharine of Siena between those who died in battle and those who died in the service. Also, that no difference had been made between these two classes of the crusaders of St. Peter by Pius IX. He had comforted a father who regretted that his son had not fallen in battle, by telling him that he had ' the supreme ' consolation, because the son had died in the service of the Holy See. And he had, in his solemn Allocution, compared both classes alike to the martyred Maccabees. The father of Goldoni, pictured as a devout and humane physician, is represented as often putting up the prayer for his only son, ' Oh that

God would inspire him to take up the cross!' Young Goldoni was a diligent reader of the *Unità Cattolica* and the *Civiltà*, from which 'sources of religious and of pure intellectual culture he drew a generous and daring spirit.' Though he died unhappily before battle, his biographer sees him seated among the celestial martyrs, between the Duke de Blacas and the Count Zileri de Verme, with whom do rejoice and glory others who died at a distance from the fight. When Goldoni received his 'call' to the crusade, he started in haste. 'It seemed as if the Spirit of God carried him.' The Archbishop of Modena specially blessed 'our young crusader.' He then received the Sacrament, and so 'heart to heart with Jesus Christ consecrated his life to Holy Church.' Moreover, in parting, 'the young cavalier of Jesus Christ put upon his bosom, as if a breastplate, an image of Mary.' The night before leaving home he, 'in the manner of the old crusaders,' knelt at his father's knee and asked his blessing. While the father 'shed upon him the holy water and the prayer,' Antonio burst into weeping.

Arrived in Rome, Goldoni sought a Jesuit to 'govern his soul.' The Jesuit made allusion to the dangers of his new life. 'I have made up my mind to be a martyr for the Holy See,' replied Goldoni. 'The Holy Father has declared the temporal power necessary to the spiritual. Therefore, fighting and dying for the temporal power, I should indirectly be a martyr for our holy religion.' The Jesuit was overcome at hearing these generous sentiments from a youth so superior. Two days after, the Jesuit and Goldoni met 'in the tribunal of penitence.'

Goldoni soon caught a fever, and in the hospital often confessed. On the Feast of St. John Berchmans[1] he declared that he had obtained from the saint the grace to be with him in Paradise on the day of the Assumption of the Virgin. He reiterated that he should on the day of the Assumption go to heaven to see the Madonna and St. John Berchmans. His good father, called from Modena, arrived in time to bless and pray for his departing

[1] Technically, Berchmans seems to be only a beatified, not a saint.

Antonio. At the last moment he left him, for it would seem that those around thought that the presence of the earthly father would come between him and the heavenly Father. So he lay, with his lustrous eyes calmly fixed on heaven, as if, says the chaplain, 'he was awaiting the appearance of his John Berchmans, who was to present him at the throne of the great Virgin.' At seven o'clock on the morning of the Assumption he passed away.

The reverend biographer concludes this really effective plea for crusaders by re-affirming the position which his tale is meant to establish, that crusaders, even if they die of fever, and not on the field, are exempted from purgatory and pass to immediate glory. Therefore, he says, Antonio Goldoni, crowned with light, and blessed with the blessedness of God Himself, is so far from regretting having immolated his youth for religion, that from this very fact he draws divine delight, and smiles with youth eternal. Every paragraph of this biography seems to breathe the spirit of a man who believes that in charming parents to bring up sons for the crusade of St. Peter, and in charming lads to immolate their youth, he is himself fighting a good fight of faith, and gaining the merits of a crusader.[1]

CHAPTER IV.

Princes, Ministers, and their Confessors—Montalembert's part in the Revival—His Posthumous Work on Spain—Indignation against the New Assumptions—Debate of Clergy in Paris on the Lawfulness of Absolving a Liberal Prince or Minister—Wrath at Rome—True Doctrines taught to Darboy and his Clergy.

IN proportion as this Popery of physical force came into view, did the mental stress of Catholics who had put their faith in finer forces increase.

Chateaubriand, who played a brilliant part in the Catholic

[1] *Civiltà*, Serie VII., vol. iii., p. 656 ff.

reaction which followed the great French Revolution, especially in that phase of the movement which aimed at linking together, in the imagination, Rome and ideas and hopes now dear to mankind, left a work, at his death, which he called 'Memoirs from Beyond the Grave'—*Memories d'outre Tombe.* Montalembert, who played a still more brilliant part in the Catholic reaction which followed the Revolution of 1830, also left behind him a work, to appear after his death. In that work we can trace the pains of a representative mind, showing what must have been those of multitudes at the time of which we now write.

Montalembert saw, in 'the absolutest politics, the retrospective fanaticism, the embittered hostility to all modern ideas and institutions, flaunted everywhere by the religious press,'[1] not only a blot on the cause, which had been his life-passion,—a passion of feminine flame but of masculine vigour,—but also a personal wound. It made his past look like a well-played hypocrisy. He had enthusiastically and victoriously argued for Catholicism under plea of liberty. ' I neither can nor will,' he cries, ' keep silence, as to the monstrous articles published this very year (1868) by the *Civiltá Cattolica* against liberty in general, and precisely against those Liberal Catholics who, like me, have had the *naïveté* in the Parliamentary tribune, to assert the rights of the Jesuits, and cause them to triumph in the name of liberty.'[2] Montalembert next refers to an appeal made by the *Civiltá* to M. Renan, on purpose to show by his testimony that the true doctrine of the Church was well known in 1848, in spite of all that Liberal Catholics said to the contrary :—

' According to the *Civiltá*, the Church cannot co-exist with any modern liberty. M. Renan is the one contemporary writer who, according to it, first comprehended the truth, which in 1848 he proclaimed, that the Church never has been tolerant, and never will be so ; and that a Liberal Catholic, or a Catholic Liberal, could only be a hypocrite or a dolt. Those of us who, in the same years of 1848 and 1849, and that in the name of

---

[1] *L'Espagne et la Liberté.* Bibliothèque Universelle de Lausanne, 1876, p. 626.
[2] Ibid., p. 635.

liberty and toleration, claimed and procured the right of instruction for Jesuits, as for all other Frenchmen, absolutely understood nothing; or, to speak more correctly, *we were not sincere*, we indeed are a just object of derision for Catholics who are not Liberals, and for Liberals who are not Catholics." Alleging that the *Civiltà* sees no better way of serving the Catholic cause, in the second half of the nineteenth century, than by parading in the eyes of Europe the theories and examples of persecution in the middle ages, and by stamping each one of them with the approving name of a pope, or a saint, he cries, As to Spain in particular, they must forsooth bring to light again an admonition of Pius V., deploring the softness of Philip II. in pursuing heretics and insisting on the infliction of temporal chastisements. And as a general principle, they must declare loudly and clearly, that there is no modern liberty which is not irregular and pernicious in itself, and mortal in its effects. That liberty, not absolute and unlimited liberty, but liberty as such and in itself, is a plague, a spiritual plague, much more deadly than a bodily one. All this seasoned with citations, definitions, and theological dissertations, which have been well summed up, in plain French, as follows : "There is no healthy liberty ; all liberty is a sickness. There is no wise liberty ; all liberty is a madness. There is no good and bad liberty of the press ; all liberty of the press is, in itself, essentially bad. There is no good and bad liberty of conscience ; liberty of conscience bears its proper condemnation with it. There is no good and bad liberty of worship ; it is liberty of worship, in itself, which must be absolutely reprobated." And so on, with all the liberties, all the franchises, all the emancipations in which modern society glories.'

On the second anniversary of that mysterious Thursday in February 1848 when King Louis Philippe, of the Tuileries, suddenly changed into Mr. Smith in a street cab on the way to exile, Montalembert and Thiers pleaded in the National Assembly for ' freedom of instruction ' on behalf of the Jesuits. ' It was only,' says our orator, ' in the name of liberty, of modern constitutions, of modern liberty, of the liberty of conscience, of the press, and of the tribune, that we made the claim.' He adds that the victory was won only by Thiers brandishing the text of the Republican constitution in the face of the furious Mountain, a constitution proclaiming equal freedom of worship and association to all. The italics are his own :—

' We were all wrong, it is clear. In sound theology M. Renan alone was right,—he and the like of him who maintained that Catholicism, and above all, the Jesuits, were absolutely incompatible with liberty. Only—we ought to have been told it *then*. It was *then*, and not now, that they ought to have taught us that liberty was a *plague*, instead of taking advantage of it, and that by our help, in order, twenty years later, to come insulting and repudiating both it and us, at one and the same time.

'I have long passed the age of disappointments and passionate emotions, but I declare on reading these bare-faced palinodes I have reddened to the white of my eyes, and shivered to the ends of my nails. I am no longer child enough to complain of the inconsistencies of men in general, or of Jesuits in particular, but I loudly say that this tone of the puppy and the pedant (*ce ton de faquin et de pédagogue*), employed towards old defenders, all of whom are not dead, and in respect of old struggles, which may be renewed to-morrow, does not become either monks or reputable men. It may be perfectly orthodox. In matters of theology I am no judge, but I think I am a judge in a matter of honour and decency ; and I declare it is perfectly indecent.'

Montalembert does not accuse, apparently he does not even suspect, of personal insincerity the particular Jesuits who in 1848 and the following years led him to believe that they accepted constitutional liberty, among whom he especially mentions the celebrated De Ravignan. But he says :—

'Had any Jesuit, of any reputation in Rome, expressed himself in 1848 or 1850, as does the *Civiltà* in our days, most surely not a single Jesuit college would have been opened in France ; and more than that, not one French soldier would have gone to Rome to re-establish the temporal power. So much for the past. And as to the future, without putting on the air of a prophet, one may affirm that in the old world and the new, more Jesuits than one will shed bitter tears when hereafter they find lying in the way of the Company the pages just published by their Roman brethren in the official journal.'

Utterances which we have already given (p. 15) show that even as early as 1850 the *Civiltà* had expressed in brief all that has since been developed ; but it is only by degrees that such utterances, diplomatically reticent, awaken men to their full import. Even those who do see their entire meaning feel it very differently when, in the early pages of a new periodical, it sounds like the note of some excited monk, and when, after a period of years, it comes with the boom of an awful power. We give but one more extract from this unconscious palinode of the high-souled Montalembert, who could not even

then see that the Liberal Catholicism of his ideal was a generous
phantasy, irreconcilable with the Popery of Rome, as much so
as was his beloved parliamentary system in politics with the
Second Empire. No more could he see that Pope and Jesuit
were true to themselves in urging their old and fixed principles,
and had been equally true to themselves in using instruments
like him so long as they struck or stayed their hand at 'the beck
of the priest,' and in disowning them so soon as they set up to
keep a conscience for themselves, 'as if the rod should shake itself
against them that lift it up.' Such a Catholicism as Montalembert dreamed of would have required some broad national base at
least equal to that which France could have proffered ; but on
the municipal basis of Rome nothing could stand but contracted
personal Popery. He and his friend Lacordaire carried to
Rome the large ideas of a great people, and bathed the quaint
figures of the Curia, and the quaint objects of the city, in the
tropical light of their own genius, just as Lamartine had done
with the withered remnants of the East. After such pictures
as Montalembert had drawn in his books, and his speeches, of
his ideal Catholic Church—pictures of which the most brilliant
would seem faint to himself, in comparison with what they
had been as they glowed before his imagination ere they were
reduced to words—it must have been mortifying to have, in
age and sickness, to write as follows:—

'Certainly, a strange way has been invented of serving religion, of
making the modern world accept, comprehend, and love it. One might
say that they treat the Church like one of those wild beasts that are
carried about in menageries. Look at her, they seem to say, and understand what she means, and what is her real nature ! To-day, she is in a
cage, tamed and broken in, by force of circumstances. She can do no
harm for the present; but understand that she has paws and tusks, and
if ever she is let loose you will be made to know it' (p. 641).

As he wrote this sad passage, in all probability there would
rise before his imagination one of the most memorable scenes
in the life of any orator. When glorifying the return of the
Pope to Rome, restored by French force, and deprecating any

attempt at a conflict with the Church, he said that from any such conflict only dishonour could result, as to a strong man would result dishonour from a combat with a woman. And then, turning upon his audience, he said, 'The Church is more than a woman; the Church is a mother," with a gush and a power which produced such a scene as perhaps has hardly ever been witnessed in any parliamentary assembly. And both ideals were quite sincere. The Church of Montalembert's imagination was a mother; the Church of the *Civiltà Cattolica* is a dam, holding to her young while they continue in sheer dependence, treating them as strangers when they can take care of themselves. His Church is the dream of an exceptional few, the Church of the *Civiltà* is the strong reality.

The articles which called forth this protestation of Montalembert, were among the most curious even of the *Civiltà.* They dealt with France—Paris and Darboy. They directly touched the conscience of politicians and princes, displaying, at the same time, the machinery whereby the Syllabus, which to most of us at that time looked like an edict in the air, could be applied to them in their public action. On the 5th of February, 1868, the Archbishop of Paris held a conference of his clergy in the Church of Saint Rocque, and there argued the following case of conscience. By some exceptional feat of the worst of all evil genii, Publicity, the discussion, and its result, were reported in the *Patrie;* and this indiscretion caused the world for once to gain a real peep into the consultations in the judges' chambers, behind the *internal tribunal.*

'A man engaged in politics,' says the case of conscience, 'declares to his confessor that he has no intention of renouncing the doctrines which prevail among modern nations, the principal points of which are, liberty of worship, liberty of the press, and the action of the State in mixed affairs. The confessor asks if he is to grant absolution to a penitent in this state of mind, or to deny it.'—*Civiltà,* VII., ii., 151.

The reasoning ascribed to the supposed penitent is the following :—

'You, as my confessor, have not the right to lay on me as you would on a private man, the duty of devoting a certain day, and of adopting certain means for the conversion of this or that person. Doubtless, I ought, by word and example, to lay myself out for the conversion and edification of my neighbour ; but it rests with me as a free agent to select the means and to discern the opportunity. In like manner, you cannot order me as politician, legislator, or prince, to take, this very day, this or that measure, against blasphemy for example, or Sunday labour, or the license of the press. Lay it upon me to attend to the propagation of righteousness and truth ; but leave it to me to judge of the opportunity, and to choose the means. And, I pray you, consider the grounds of my opinions. In the first place, whenever we speak or act, we have on one side the truth and right, which certainly ought to be respected ; but on the other side we have fitness and opportunity, of which also we must take account, if we would speak to good purpose. Now, in this respect, I know better than any other what I can do, and what I cannot, in my family, or in a political assembly, or in the nation. In the next place, perhaps you do not see the absurdity which would follow the opposite opinion. It would follow that you had the right to decide and *regulate all my actions*, because into every one of them *morality may enter ;* and every one of them may be connected with religion. You would be able to dictate my will, to tell me what vote I ought to give, to determine whether I am to declare peace or war. Mere trifles, you say. But what, in that case, would temporal power be, but a passive instrument of the spiritual power, and a mere machine ? These are the reasons why I stand to my old notions on this point, and have no thought of changing them for others.'

In this case, as thus put, and in the ensuing discussion, we see the confessor of a king or minister preparing to meet his 'penitent.' In the language of Montalembert we see the feeling of a politician in facing the 'tribunal,' under an Ultramontane confessor ; and in the papers of the *Civiltà* we see the glaring eye of Rome searching out every movement of the one and the other.

The case being thus stated, both as to its substance and as to the reasoning of the supposed penitent, the discussion began. Abbé Michaud, of the Madeleine, maintained that the confessor ought to grant absolution. Abbé G——, a Dominican, maintained that he ought not to do so. Archbishop Darboy now and then interfered, to moderate the opposition of the latter. The Abbé Falcimagne interrupted the Archbishop, declaring that he would deny the absolution, for the supposed penitent was unworthy of it. Finally, the Abbé Hamon, Curé of Saint Sulpice, read out four conclusions, which were fully accepted by the Archbishop, and which allowed the confessor to grant the absolution. The *Opinion Nationale* and other journals said that this conclusion showed to how little the condemnations of the Syllabus amounted.

Both the conclusion and the grounds on which it was rested gave huge offence at Rome. What were the grounds? No less dangerous than that the opinions, avowed by the supposed minister or prince, were *probable opinions;* and that a confessor had no right to deny absolution because a penitent held opinions differing from his own, if they were probable opinions, that is, opinions resting on serious reasons and accredited by respectable authorities. But, cried Rome, those opinions are condemned! And the Church of Paris is to say to the world that opinions which are condemned even in the Syllabus are probable! So Monsignor Darboy and all his abettors sank deeper than ever into disgrace.

The *Civiltà* was not content with less than five long articles, making ninety octavo pages. It is in these that the things are set forth which fired the embers of Montalembert's true love of liberty, and damped his dying hope of ever seeing his ideal Catholicism and actual Popery seated on the same throne. We need not quote the passages which are echoed in his indignant repudiation; but we give a few others, which show that, strongly as we have seen him put the case, he was not guilty of any injustice. The Abbé Michaud said that the liberty condemned was not moderate liberty, but unbounded liberty.[1] The *Civiltà* took it for granted that he could not have been sincere.

'We ought to hold, not only that religious liberty is unlawful in itself, and repugnant to the divine command, but also that it is very pernicious to the State Wherefore, no prince or magistrate can prescribe, approve, or introduce it into his dominions, but ought, on the contrary, to throw obstacles in the way of it, and to remove it by all the means of which he

[1] *Civiltà Cattolica*, VII., ii., p. 150 ff.

can dispose; and if he cannot fully remove it without disturbing the State, and throwing it into disorder, it then, and only then, becomes lawful for him to tolerate false forms of worship. . . . The experience of every age teaches,' adds the writer, quoting the Bull *Mirari* of Gregory XVI., 'and even remotest antiquity clearly demonstrates, that the cities which most flourished in opulence, dominion, and glory, came to ruin from this cause only, that is, from immoderate liberty of thought, licence of meeting, and the mania of novelty' (pp. 157, 158).

Still quoting the same supreme authority, it proceeds to say:—

'Similar to liberty of worship, is that worst of liberties, never sufficiently execrated or abhorred,—liberty of the press, which some dare to invoke and promote with so much clamour.' It continues:—'In respect of religion and the press, it is idle to distinguish between two sorts of liberty, one wise and the other unbridled, as the Abbé did. In such matters, all liberty is a delirium and a pestilence. There is no healthy man's delirium ; all delirium is that of a sick man. There is no praiseworthy and harmless plague ; every plague is deadly. . . . Hence, it is never a decent thing to introduce such liberty into a civil community. It is only permissible to tolerate it in certain cases, in the same way that a pest is tolerated ' (p. 160).

The Abbé Michaud had said that, in mixed questions, the State interfered by *the same right as the Church !* Such an utterance savoured of our bad times. It was infected with the idea of the independence of the civil power in regard to the ecclesiastical. This idea was born with Protestantism ; but it has been received by some Catholics, sincere, it is true, though not discerning. What follows is lengthy, but must be given *verbatim :*—

'If this independence was affirmed only of the origin of the civil power, there would be nothing to say. It is certainly of faith that the ecclesiastical power comes immediately from God, without the concurrence of the civil power. If, then, one chooses to say that the civil power, as to its nature, comes immediately from God, without springing from the ecclesiastical power, let him say it. Thus, in respect to this point of origin solely, the two powers may be said to be independent one of the other, just as, in respect of origin, body and soul in man are said to be independent of one another. The body is not a product of the soul, which animates it; nor is the soul created by the body; but just as it would be a capital error to infer that, in the composite human being, the body exists independently of the soul, so is it a capital error to infer, from

what we have conceded, that, in society, the temporal power in no way
depends on the spiritual. It is true that the temporal prince is invested
with supreme power and authority, in his order; but from this it follows
only that he is not subject to any other earthly power. It does not follow
that his authority, sovereign in its order, cannot be subject and is not
subject to another authority of a more perfect order ; that is, the spiritual.
. . . . It is necessary that whoever holds power, even sovereign, for
temporal rule shall be regulated by the Roman Pontiff ' (pp. 161-163).

So far for the independence of the State. Now as to its
right of intervention in mixed questions, and above all, as to
the defining of limits between the two powers:—

'The State ought first to learn, from the Church, what are mixed
questions, that it may not take spiritual matters for mixed ones, confounding both the one and the other with those which are called temporal
ones. Each separate kind of corn must be tied up into a separate sheaf.
The State ought to arrange with the Church every time it puts a hand
to what is temporal in these mixed matters, in order that it may not
violate what is spiritual.'

The *Civiltà* quotes M. Renan, where he shows how the
Syllabus had proved his assertion of 1848. 'The Syllabus is a
luminous demonstration of the proposition I maintained, that
Catholicism and liberty are two things incompatible.' The
Civiltà adds that, in order to know this fact, M. Renan did not
need to be a profound theologian, but only needed to read the
works of any author sincerely Catholic. It points out that the
Liberal Catholics fancy that the Popes, in condemning liberty of
worship and of the press, only spoke of part of the subject, that is,
of some sorts of liberty; and that it was, therefore, some liberty,
not all, that they called madness, poison, and pestilence. But
the Popes, asserts the *Civiltà*, on the contrary, thought that all
liberty of worship and of the press bore those characters (p.
314).

The Abbé Falcimagne insisted (p. 316) that the supposed
penitent should be at once treated as a sick man, and as being
not of sound reason :—

'He comes to submit himself to my tribunal, and at the same time
rejects my authority. To see how far I can yield to his spiritual
infirmity I must see how far the authority of the confessor over the

penitent extends. On this point, I shall cite the words of Domenico Soto, who, after hearing the confession of Charles V., said, "So far, you have confessed the sins of Charles; now confess those of the Emperor." Soto at least thought that the actions of his penitent, although they belonged to the political order, nevertheless came within the cognizance of his tribunal. Our patient is of a diametrically opposite opinion. He will not recognise in me the right of judging him in what touches doctrine and morals indirectly. But I hold that, as confessor, I have a right to judge my penitent, be he a legislator, or even a prelate of the Church, in things pertaining to dogmas and morals, and to prohibit what is contrary to either, whether directly or indirectly. So I can command him to cease from holding presumptuous tenets.'

The Archbishop then asked the Abbé Falcimagne, requesting him to give a direct answer, if he had a right to order his penitent to leave a hundred thousand francs in his will to be distributed among the poor. To this the Abbé Falcimagne made no reply. He said the point now was to know whether the penitent, who would not renounce his modern ideas as to liberty, was or was not guilty of presumption, *temerarius.* 'Guilty of presumption,' replied the Archbishop, 'is that confessor who lays his hands on temporal things, assessing what he has no right to assess.' 'But,' retorted Falcimagne, 'I have the right to judge my penitent as to his disposition; and if he comes to me, and says that he wishes to maintain his principles, and declares that I have not a right to judge him, I tell him that his pretensions are illegitimate; that his reason is disordered by modern principles; and that, if he will not renounce those principles, I cannot absolve him.'

The *Civiltà* thinks that, at this point, they came to the heart of the matter. On one side they began to allege that the confessor could not require his penitent to renounce his opinions unless they were heretical, or were opinions condemned by the Church. A very false doctrine! exclaims the oracle; for, in addition to heretical opinions, a true Catholic must renounce many others,—those, for instance, which are proximate to heresy; those which are presumptuous, scandalous, and all indeed that are offensive to pious ears. The teaching power of our Church is not merely infallible, and not only does it define with infallibility when defining articles of faith, but also when defining any truth, scientific or practical, political or historical, which is connected, in any manner whatever, with dogma and morals; and whoever would be a sincere Catholic must conform not only in respectful silence, but with interior assent of the intellect (p. 318).

The *Civiltà*, however, though the mightiest, was not the earliest champion in the field. Bishop Plantier, of Nimes, a zealot among the zealous, rushed into the columns of the *Univers* to condemn the conclusions which allowed the political penitent to be absolved, and the frail reasons which propped them up. Monsignor Plantier cannot believe that the conclusions are correctly reported, for they contain two propositions that are false, or, at least, much controverted. It seems to be assumed he says, that the Church has not frequently condemned any liberty of worship, or of the press, but an unbounded and absolute liberty, and that it is only in this latter sense that these liberties have been condemned in the Encyclical of December 8th, 1864. This idea is groundless. It is not in degree, but in principle, that Pius VII., Gregory XVI., and Pius IX., have condemned both these liberties viewed as legal liberties. True, they have recognised the possibility of tolerating such liberties in certain modern States as a dolorous but inevitable necessity. They have even allowed Catholics to take an oath of fidelity to constitutions which permit and protect these liberties. In cases of persecuted Churches, like that of Poland, they have even claimed liberty of worship, as a relative progress; but as to the ground and essence of this liberty, the liberty of different forms of worship, and as to the equality of such various forms before the eye of the law, the Pontiffs have never resorted to tergiversation or subterfuge. Restricted, or unbounded, they, as teachers, have never declared this liberty to be substantially legitimate. They have done the contrary. As to the liberty of the press, they have shown even greater severity.

The notion that it belongs rather to politics than to theology to fix for worship and the press the limits of liberty, makes Monsignor Plantier ask if a General Council would adopt that view.

After rejoicing over the sound principles of Bishop Plantier, the *Civiltà* proceeds to quote the opinions of the 'good journals' of Italy, laying stress on the point that the opinions held by the supposed penitent could not be probable opinions, being in fact those which were already condemned in the Syllabus. It proceeds with great vigour to maintain that the Syllabus was the decree, not only of the Pope, but also of the five hundred bishops who had adhered to it last year (1867). Of these, the *Civiltà* correctly says that Darboy himself was one. It next contributes an important item of information, which completes the evidence of the perfect and formal ecclesiastical authority of all the condemnations of the Syllabus, on either theory of the constitution of the Church, the Papal or the Episcopal. After the address of the five hundred bishops present in Rome, all the absent ones, asserts the *Civiltà*, sent in their adhesion by letter, which they hastened to forward to this Roman chair, where, with the living Pontiff, resides the 'spirit of truth' (p. 324). Hence it draws the inference, which is a just conclusion, if we may say so, in the face of a hundred English writers who, following an old tradition, when reviewing what Dr. Newman put upon paper on this subject, called it logical. ·

'This penitent,' says the great organ of the Vatican, 'openly opposes the teaching power of the Church, whether that teaching power is considered as being exercised by the Bishop of Rome alone, or as being exercised by him in conjunction with all the bishops of Christendom. That teaching power has pronounced in the one mode and in the other, and has proscribed those opinions. In both ways has it condemned opinions, not imaginary or belonging to bygone times, but opinions which to-day, and under our eye, are pertinaciously maintained and reduced to practice' (p. 324).

Returning with intense earnestness to this point, it says (p. 543) :—

'The universal Bishop has spoken alone, and further, he has spoken conjointly with the bishops of the particular Churches. To contradict after this, is in effect to separate oneself from the whole of the pastors, and from him who is supreme among them all.'

This is not enough. Some pages later, hesitation, on this question so vital to practical government, is again censured, in replying to the plea that the supposed penitent might be worthy of absolution on the ground of invincible ignorance:—

'We shall never tell him that ignorance consists in this, namely, that after he has read the Encyclical and the Syllabus, and re-read them, he could not understand that the modern opinions, which he retained, have been truly condemned, or that they have been condemned rightfully. This is not ignorance. It is an error and a pertinacity proper to a man not far removed from heresy. In this case, we once more repeat, confession is not the thing wanted. The first elements of the faith, and of the Catholic profession, have to be set straight in this man's head' (p. 547).

It would almost seem as if Montalembert was personally pointed at in the two latter articles. It is not a little curious to learn here that his bosom friend, Lacordaire, long the charm of the French pulpit, was called to Rome in 1850 to answer for his doctrine. The points on which he had to set himself right with Rome were anything but, in our sense, religious ones : (1) The coercive power of the Church; (2) The origin of sovereignty ; and (3) The temporal power of the Pope. He did set himself right. Father Jandel, the General of the Dominicans, exulting over his answer on the question touching the coercive power, says, 'It avenges his memory from the suspicion of complicity with certain opinions which some Catholics would fain shelter under the authority of his name.'[1] Avenges his memory! It proves that whatever Lacordaire believed, he submitted to write as his own the doctrine of Rome, that the Church has power to 'employ external force,' and to inflict bodily pains. And so France sees the memory of her Bossuet held up to reproach, and the memory of her Lacordaire yoked by the Dominican General to his beloved

[1] Serie VII., vol. iii., p. 65.

Inquisition. She sees her Montalembert driven from public life, assailed, yea, reviled, while living, preparatory to being insulted when dead.

Any one acquainted with the high spirit and immense emotional force of Montalembert, can imagine his reddening and shivering at finding the following among the citations from Renan to prove that the sceptic understood the doctrine of ' Catholicism ' better than its professed friends in France :—

'The remedy applied by the Church of Rome to the liberty of worship and liberty of thought is the Inquisition. The Councils have established and approved the Inquisition, the Fathers and bishops have counselled and practised it. The Inquisition is the logical outgrowth of the whole orthodox system, and the quintessence of the spirit of the Church.'

Strongly as our sympathies are with Montalembert and Darboy, we feel that, so long as the Jesuits have to prove that persecution is the doctrine and has been the practice of the Church, they have it all their own way against the Liberal Catholics, till they creep up to the early ages. But their attempt to father the Inquisition on those ages, not indeed in its apparatus, but in its spirit and substance, and then their attempt to prove that the Gospel itself is persecuting, and that our merciful Lord is the author and founder of persecution, is melancholy as the Roman Campagna on the dampest evening, and unhealthy as it ever is on the most miasmatic. Yet the logic brought to bear for this purpose is similar to that by which we find engrafted on the Gospel the Papacy and the other outgrowths of Roman ingenuity.

A good illustration of the doctrine of the sword, and also of that of direct and indirect power, is incidentally furnished in the papers now under our notice. After saying that the power of compulsion belongs indirectly to the Church, but that she avails herself of the authority of secular princes, to whom the material sword directly belongs, the writer adds, 'The material sword is subject to the Church, and Christian

---

[1] Serie VII., vol. iii., p. 50.

princes must wield it at her command. She orders it and points out its use ; they wield it and strike.' Then follows a broad statement, which seems designed to push the authority of the Church beyond the domain of the baptised, 'All men, whatever their station or office, are by divine appointment subject to the Church.' So we are brought to the old conclusion :—

'If princes hold the material sword by their own right, since without it they could not preserve temporal peace in the societies over which they preside, and if, at the same time, they belong to the Church, and hence are, like any other men, dependent upon her, even in regard of their office, they must, with that same sword, aid the Church, that she may not be hindered in procuring eternal peace for men.'[1]

CHAPTER V.

What is to be the Work of the Council—Fears caused by Grandiose Projects— *Reform of the Church in Head and Members*—Statesmen evince Concern.

CURIOSITY as to what the particular work of the Council was to be grew all the more rapidly, because no authoritative indication of it was given. Were the Jesuit tenets of Papal authority and Papal infallibility to be raised into dogmas? Was the Pope to make another offering to the Virgin by proclaiming as an article of faith, that her body had been carried to heaven? By the repetition of such questions, tens of millions partially awoke to the consciousness that they belonged to a religion which knew not what might be its standard of faith next year, much less did it know to what particular tenets it might be committed.

[1] Serie VII., vol. iii., p. 313. In the text we represent the *Civiltà* as saying that the power of the corporal sword belongs *indirectly* to the Church. The original word is 'directly,' but that is probably a misprint. Yet, as the very important qualification 'as a general rule' is immediately afterwards used before the statement that she avails herself of the secular arm, we are not sure that the writer does not mean 'directly.' If so, he is insinuating the doctrine we shall hereafter see advocated. But a quotation he makes from Suarez is express, 'indirectly.'

Then, as to the position of the bishops, were they to be, as the *Stimmen aus Maria Laach* put it, only councillors, or also judges? If the latter, they would first hear the doctors, as did their predecessors at Trent; would next deliberate, and finally would formulate decrees, which decrees, without alteration, would be confirmed by the Pontiff. But if the bishops were no longer judges of the faith, but simply councillors of the one judge, their place would be to argue points, as the doctors had done at Trent, while the decree should be that of the Pope, and they would merely assent.

Again, as to the composition of the Council, were the bishops *in partibus* to be members? Was Darboy, whose diocese counted two millions of souls, to be balanced by some Court creature with a title from Sardis or Ecbatana? or was Schwarzenberg, with Bohemia at his back, to be balanced by an instrument of the Curia, who, independently of his patrons, had not a month's bread to call his own? Were those who represented ancient and numerous Churches, and who were as far free agents as men under Rome can be, to be voted against, man for man, by vicars apostolic, without churches, or with only new and ignorant ones,—men depending on the Propaganda even for their travelling expenses and board?

Finally, as to the mode of procedure, all-important in deliberative assemblies; were the bishops, as they did at Trent, to agree upon their own rules of procedure, to evolve by mutual consultation the questions demanding solution, and to discuss them till all were ready to vote? Or could there be truth in the suspicion that everything was being cut and dried beforehand, and that the Court would impose ready-made rules of procedure, and allow no one but itself to introduce any subject for discussion?

As to the burning question of moral unanimity, would projected formulæ be passed from hand to hand, as was done at Trent, examined in meetings of groups, retouched, and, if need be, remoulded till a form was arrived at in which all but two or three acquiesced? or was it possible that formulæ for new articles in a creed prepared behind the backs of the bishops would be imposed on millions and for ever, by a majority made up with the help of the bishops *in partibus?*

These questions, touching, as they did, the core of the constitution of the Church, began to loom up ominously; but few ventured to give frank expression to their undefined fears. When put into words, those fears seemed to imply distrust of the Pope, greater than was decent. Therefore both divines and politicians fell into the habit of saying that such things could not possibly be contemplated, instead of saying, if they meant Rome to heed them, that these things would not be endured.

All this time, the nine determined men forming the secret Directing Congregation, were coolly looking at the same questions, and, step by step, as we shall see, when events bring out the secret plans, were settling those questions in the sense most dreaded, and going to lengths not, we believe, suggested in any of the anticipatory expressions of fear.

Even at Trent, in an Alpine valley, the pressure of Rome, and the preponderance of its legates, caused frequent complaint that the Council, as compared with ancient ones, had not liberty, being deprived of the initiative and of the self-guiding power without which no multitude of advisers can constitute a legislature. But if this was the case in Trent, what would it be in the city of Rome?

Earnest theologians who had not been converted by the infallibilist propaganda of recent years, were thrown into consternation. Some bishops, able administrators, saw no essential difference between Papal infallibility as a doctrine taught in many of the schools, and believed by great numbers if rejected by others perhaps greater, and the same opinion as an article of faith. In such a view, the men of thought saw the superficial glance of 'practical men,' as they call themselves, who never discover anything but by feeling it, and who live by acting out to-day what others thought out in time gone by.

Little difference! thought the men of foresight. We are going to be compelled to alter our catechisms and creed in the face of the Protestants, going to be compelled to teach the opposite of what we have always taught, going to part with immemorial safeguards against altering the conditions of salvation, or further narrowing the terms of membership in the Church—to part with the necessity before every such change of the open and formal process of a General Council! The proposed dogma is unlike any now in the creed, in the all-important point of being self-multiplying. If it is adopted, we shall be liable to have eternal obligations laid upon our souls, without a week's warning.

Beside fears like these, others perhaps more general were those of quiet Catholics wishing to live in peace and serve their respective nations loyally, who being conscious that even now they were liable to suspicion of a divided allegiance, feared that if the Jesuit tenets became the creed,[1] their political relations would be less comfortable, and their prospects of office not so good. 'At the Vatican,' says *Ce Qui se Passe au Concile,* speaking of the mystery and the uneasiness of this moment ; 'At the Vatican they spoke in low tones of grandiose projects that were to transform the world, and by exalting Pius IX. were to confound the enemies of the Church.' It was those grandiose projects which made good citizens fear for their own future political standing.

Even feelings of this sort, as represented by *Holtgreven,* ought to touch us, being those of silent millions awaiting in the dark the sentence of their lords in Council. He says :—

'When we left the gymnasium, soon after the year 1860, there was no pupil who could say that, even by hint, he had been taught there that the Pope was infallible by himself, and without the consent of the Church. The answer 128 in Martin's *Handbook of Religion* is still too fresh in the memory of all; an answer which affirms that the grace of infallibility belongs only to the collective body of bishops, as successors of the apostles. . . . Persons in office and out of it, clergy, laity, and exalted Church dignitaries, agreed that the pretensions of the Pope to power over kings and nations, in matters of allegiance and such like, were not part of their religion, but arose out of the state of the civil laws in the middle ages. . . . . Thus does the Catholic teacher teach in his lectures on Church history, thus does the student learn; and this view, which captivates the youth, putting his German heart at rest, and rejoicing it, still gives him repose and removes every scruple when, as a man, he lifts up the hand to swear allegiance to the laws of the fatherland.'[1]

Those of the French clergy whose education had been carried beyond the usual round of Latin, logic, and manners, began to manifest misgivings as to the effect of the impending change on men of enlarged culture. It was in March 1869 that the *Unità* published the Pope's famous letter to the Archbishop of Paris, described in a former chapter. The Paris correspondent of that journal, commenting upon it, calls the dignitary who, in the eye of the world, would be his metropolitan and ordinary, ' a pretty fellow'—*bel soggetto*—whom no one would any longer look upon as a candidate for the rank of Cardinal. In the same letter he says that war against Prussia must break out, whether the occasion be the Belgian railways, or complaints that Prussia violates the treaty of Prague.

Fears as to coming changes, in their effect on men of culture, were felt still more deeply in Germany, where the general education of the clergy was higher than elsewhere. Both the German clergy and the nobler of the French were unprepared for what they began, in secret, to call Pius-cult, as it appeared in the language employed by the favoured organs. One word in the prayer for the Pope, recommended by the *Unità*, on March 12th, grated not on Protestant ears only. The *Ave Maria* was for a week to be followed by these petitions: ' Eternal Father, defend Pius IX.! Eternal Word, assist Pius IX.! Holy Spirit, glorify Pius IX.!'.

Perhaps none of the publications now flowing from the press excited greater attention than one which was announced as being from the pen of one of the best known of the Austrian clergy. It was entitled *The Reform of the Romish Church in*

---

[1] *Holtgreven*, pp. 4, 5.

Head and Members. The writer affirms that Rome holds fast to the view that the regal power is conferred by the ecclesiastical. 'The Catholic Church requires you to elevate this distinguished warrior here present to the dignity of king' is the language he quotes from the form of coronation. Not only does this author oppose the attempt to restore laws enforcing unity of creed, but he actually does so on principle, as well as on the ground of expediency. To him it is a humiliating fact that the only two States in Europe which keep the absolutism of the Papal States in countenance are Turkey and Russia. A reason which he urges why the attempt to impose ecclesiastical law upon States should be relinquished is one very frequently urged upon the other side, as showing the necessity for the Church at once to erect what is called the supreme teaching authority. That reason is that now even Catholic kings, being constitutional ones, cannot, if they would, enforce ecclesiastical law by their own will, without the consent of their people. The longing of Rome for the subjection of the States of the world, and for power again to employ the arm of the State in her service, is, he contends, a delusion which will lead only to her overthrow. Moreover, he lays down the startling principle that the Church has nothing to ask but liberty to act in her own sphere *like any private society.* This last position is utterly irreconcilable with all the ordinary theories. He holds that anything granted to the Church by the State beyond what is given to any other private society is an evil, and also that every case, in the past, wherein Church and State have joined hands in order to help one another to gain their respective ends, has turned out ill for both of them. One of the two always manages to subordinate the other. This ecclesiastic takes the relation of Church and State, as it existed in the first three centuries, to have been more favourable to the Church for the fulfilment of her end than would be the subjecting of the State to her power, although that object was so much yearned after by Rome. In the former position of things the Church, he argues, achieved her grandest triumph by the conquest of the dominant heathenism, and with it of the heathen State. In modern times his ideal of the normal relation of Church and State is that existing in America, which he imagines works favourably for Romanism.

The author of *Reform in Head and Members* looks on the system of lower seminaries for boys and higher ones for young men, in which the future clergy pass their youth separated from all society, leading an unreal life, pursuing narrow studies and without knowledge of men, or the possibility of acquiring any breadth of mind, as producing only a race of priests unfit to lead an educated age. He declares that in France, Italy, and Spain the system of close seminaries has destroyed theological science among Catholics. He manifests the ordinary contempt of German scholars for the showy and wordy pupils of the Roman seminaries, and contends that Catholic theology does not bear any comparison, as to talent and learning, with Protestant theology in any country except Germany, where the priests have to study at the universities. He further believes that the lamentable moral condition of the Romish clergy is not a little to be ascribed to the seclusion and unreality in which their youth is passed (p. 161).

'The young priests in whose hands the guidance of the people is to be placed, squander the fair and precious years of youth in enclosures shut off from the world, and out of them do they go forth into life without experience of men or of the world. Then does the world, with all its charms, allurements, delights, and seductions, rush in upon those narrow, inexperienced young clergymen; and alas! only too many of them sink in a sea which to them is new, strange, and untried.'

He demands a thorough reform of this system, insisting that the contempt shown by all respectable Italians for the priesthood is not to be accounted for except on the ground of this wretched system and of its wretched moral and religious results.

Another demand boldly made by this Austrian priest is for the abolition of the vows of celibacy, so far as they are either perpetual or obligatory. He would admit of vows that were both voluntary and temporary.   The corrupting effects of celibacy evidently leave him no hope that it is capable of being rendered consistent with tolerable morality.   He treats this institution as purely local and Romish, regarding its imposition upon the Catholic Church as a great public evil, impossible to be justified. At page 117 he says, ' Upon the law of the Romish Church fall back all those moral abominations, beyond measure and' beyond number, which have arisen out of it, and which will stain the Church as long as that law remains in force.'   When the writer approaches the subject of bureaucratic centralisation, the Catholic rises against the Romanism which has fastened itself on the Churches of other nations.   This system of centralisation as carried out by the Curia, is much too narrow legitimately to claim the name of national.   It scarcely deserves the dignified name of municipal.   While denouncing all nationalities which by reason of some broad base have a claim to such a noble name, like Gallicanism or Josephism, it sets up a number of petty bureau interests, parasites to the Churches under Rome all over the world, constantly sucking in a multiplicity of small charges.   Our author wants to see an end of the system.   He wonders what may be the annual revenue paid into Rome from all quarters of the globe, for indults, dispensations, indulgences, remissions of sins, and the fees gained by all the inventions for what he calls selling poor parchment and bad writing very dear.   He does not, like many writers when they touch this subject, break out into a passion against the huckstering of their religion, but manifests a cold contempt, feeling that the system is low and hollow, and wanting to see it swept out of the way.

The system just referred to is connected with contrivances for withdrawing episcopal functions from the bishops, and concentrating them in the hand of the Pope.   Those functions are let out again in this way.   Such dispensations as *do not pay* any money tax may be distributed by the bishop himself.   This however, can only be done by virtue of what is called a Faculty, granted to him from the Pope. This faculty does not include the heavier cases, which pay a money tax, and for which a constant system of recourse to Rome must be kept up. These latter 'weighty affairs,' which to the Curialist, who abhors nationalism and local organisations anywhere beyond the Aurelian walls, these *causæ majores*, too important to be entrusted to the archbishops or bishops of France, Austria, or Spain, include such matters as these : if a layman hears mass in a chapel in a private house, also if a priest celebrates mass in his own house, or if he celebrates it when his foot has been maimed or broken, or his hand, or his thumb, or fore-finger, or when he loses the left eye or becomes blind, or when he has to wear a wig by reason of baldness, or if his tongue is injured so that he stutters.

The modern contrivance for making a bishop a tenant on a short lease is calmly exposed. Formerly, as the author points out, a bishop used to rule his own diocese; now he is no more than a delegate. We have said that he is allowed to distribute such dispensations for the smaller sins against Church law as do not pay any money tax, but his power to do this, as also his power to perform several other of the acts essential to his office, is no longer conveyed to him with the office itself. On the contrary, for that power he is dependent upon a lease, never given for more than five years, called the QUINQUENNIAL FACULTIES. If at the expiration of one of these terms the Faculties are not renewed, he becomes a mere lay figure in his chair, and would be at once exposed to his clergy and people as under disgrace. By this means is he kept a perpetual pensioner on the favour of the Curia, and in addition to the periodical expiration of the ordinary lease, he is a tenant at will, liable any day to have his Faculties withdrawn by the Holy Father.

'The centralising of the government of the Church in the See of Rome, to effect which it was necessary to destroy the rights of metropolitans and to curtail the jurisdiction of bishops, is a state of things so unjustifiable and ruinous, that the well-being of the Church urgently demands its removal. This absorption of all the powers and rights of Church government is not to be justified either by pleading the necessity of preserving the unity of the Church, or by pleading the supreme hierarchical power, which belongs to the See of Rome. The very necessity of manifesting unity pre-supposes a number of persons entrusted with independent functions of government ; and if the incumbent of the highest power of the Church strips the subordinate functionaries of all authority, he makes himself the sole seat of power in the Church.'

This last conclusion would not disconcert the Curia. In their view to have only one seat of power both for the Church and for the world was the desideratum of ruined society.

This writer would restore worship in the mother tongue.

Such publications betrayed the disquietude attending membership in a body ever liable to change by adopting new principles, but incapable of reform by recalling what has been once adopted.

Statesmen began to feel concern, at least such as did not belong to the class finely laughed at by M. Veuillot, who do not think it necessary to inform themselves on 'the small affairs of the Catholic Church,' although speaking, legislating, and perhaps writing on matters of which those affairs form a considerable element. Might not the Papal authority, already a difficulty to most governments, become, by concentration and increase, a greater difficulty ? Might not the sections of population most susceptible of its impulse, always hard to govern, become really unmanageable ? In February the *Opinion Nationale* of Paris said : 'A decisive struggle is preparing. . . . The Church is collecting its forces for a final contest, and paving the way by proclaiming within itself personal government and dictatorship; in other words, Papal infallibility.'

Naturally such fears were sooner and more seriously felt by Roman Catholic statesmen than by Protestant ones. Though *Von Lutz*, Minister of Worship in Bavaria, spoke after the event, he tersely expressed the apprehensions felt at this time :—

'The Church lays down the principle that the Pope is Prince of princes, and Lord Paramount (*Oberherr*) of all States. Do you think it possible that States will put up with that ? That the State will quietly stand by while the bishop orders the parish priest to preach against the law of the land, and while he deposes him if he will not comply? Or must the State itself drive the parish priest out of his home for refusing to misuse the pulpit, against the State?'[1]

Several bishops in different countries tried to allay such alarms by appealing to the confidence of the faithful in the goodness of the Holy Father, and in the wisdom of a General Council. But fears too intelligent to be relieved by such appeals found voice through Mamiani, once the Minister of Pius IX., under the title *Del Prossimo Concilio Ecumenico.* Mamiani believed that the Curia would manage to procure a decree, midway between dogma and discipline, to be set up as a positive ordinance of the Church, for the upholding of its temporal power. He held it for certain that Rome would come out of the Council with her lordship more unlimited, her illiberal theocratic notions more embittered, and her heart more than ever set on measuring herself with the spirit of the age. She would press down upon conscience with all the weight of the Syllabus, and would more desperately clutch the shreds of the temporal power, already the absorbing care of the Holy See, which indeed would fain make it the absorbing care of the entire Church. Hence, cries Mamiani, the rapidly increasing number of the discouraged and the fearful. Many, he adds, will bend the neck and be mute. Many will secretly cease to be Catholics, and the Council will have sorrowfully to repeat the words, 'not to bring peace on earth, but a sword.'

Poor Mamiani! cried the organs of the Vatican; he, at least, was one of the discouraged and the fearful. If the General Council should not bring peace, but a sword, it would, in that case, only carry on the work of Christ. The Gospel was to bring peace to men of goodwill, but a sword to those of perverse will. Mamiani was not deceived in his forecast, but the prospect ought to give him pleasure, because the effect of conflict would be that the kingdom of God and that of darkness would

[1] Menzel, *Jesuitenumtriebe,* p. 119.

be more clearly distinguished than ever.[1] The kingdom of God is the Church. (See Phillips, *passim*.)

M. Veuillot did not fail to twit his brother journalists on their affectation of treating the Council as a matter of no great 'practical' importance. 'Paris, no doubt, thinks less about the Council than about M. Rochefort, author of the *Lanterne*. Yet, after M. Rochefort, the Council has taken a certain place to which the journalists imagined it could never pretend.'[2] One able journal had postponed the publication of the Bull as not containing anything 'very striking.' Even the *Debats* was amused at the old Church, which fancied that the Council was of any importance.

The great gatherings of bishops in 1854, 1862, and 1867 were, continued Veuillot, but *preparatory assemblies*. The Pope had been preparing the Council for twenty-three years; had even taken eighteen months after issuing the Bull to perfect the preparation; but fifty journalists could pass a sovereign judgment upon it without finding any necessity for thinking about it.

Sneering at those statesmen for whom a question never becomes practical till it has become ripe, he proceeds thus. They study *affairs*, and admit that this satisfies them; and admit that they arrive at the understanding of affairs without understanding ideas. Still, while laughing at such statesmen, he artfully used their words, flowing from ignorance of ideas. He quotes M. Ollivier, who cried, 'The Church says, All I demand is the right of ruling myself in my own way,'—a clear proof that M. Ollivier was treating the affairs without knowing anything of the ideas. He spoke as if the Church claimed to be a private society within the State. M. Veuillot, more instructed, conceived of the Church as impersonated in God's Vicegerent, and understood leaving him 'to rule in his own way,' in a devout and large sense.

---

[1] *Stimmen, Neue Folge, Drittes Heft*, p. 60.
[2] Vol. i., p. 4-18.

Bishop Fessler, of St. Pölten,[1] in a lengthy manifesto, gave a clear intimation that the infallibility of the Pope would probably be defined by the Council. This set many Catholics in Germany on preparing to combat the intention announced, and set still more on saying that as Fessler had been tho first to face tho German public with this intimation, his fortune was made at Rome.

Bishop Dupanloup, of Orleans, put forth his best literary power in what was called, by the *Constitutionnel*, an attempt to bring about a reconciliation between the Council and the principles of 1789.[2] He urged that they greatly erred who looked upon the approaching Council as a menace against modern society, or as a declaration of war with progress. On the contrary, freedom, fraternity and progress, so far as they were true and good, had nothing to fear from this ' senate of humanity.'

Bishop Von Ketteler, of Mainz, declared that the forthcoming Council was the greatest event of our age [3]:—

' At least,' added this doughty pupil of the Jesuits, 'in the work of reconstruction ; for as to destruction, certainly, there have been greater events. As God provided för the Church and the world in the century of the so-called Reformation, by means of tho Council of Trent, so has He in our century, which, still sadder to say, is the century of Revolution, the century of demolition and universal destruction, inspired the High Pontiff with the supreme remedy, the convocation of the Vatican Council. The work of destruction is manifestly hasting to its end. It is time to commence the work of reconstruction, on the ancient foundation laid by Christ once for all. This is precisely the work to which the Council is called.'

These words we quote from the *Civiltá*, to which the whole document seemed highly laudable.[4] But its translation is strong. Ketteler did not use the term ' reconstruction ' for his German audience, but ' construction.' He did not say that God had inspired the Pontiff, but that the Spirit of God again

---

[1] *Das Letzte und das Nächste Concil,* p. 59.
[2] *Lettre sur le futur Concile Œcuménique.*
[3] *Das Allgemeine Concil und seine Bedeutung für unsere Zeit.*
[4] Serie VII., vol. vi., p. 93.

assembled the General Council, the highest Court of Judgment for the Truth on earth. This last form of words had the merit of which our English tongue has within the last few years presented some examples of all but incredible skill,—the merit of suggesting to a Protestant an idea that would not awaken his political fears, and yet of representing to the Jesuits of the *Civiltá* the true doctrine. The Pope himself began to take part in the controversy now gradually rising. The Abbé Belet had translated into French the work of the Jesuit Father Weninger, published in New York. The Pope wrote a brief to thank him, taking occasion at the same time harshly to censure the great Bossuet, as a bishop who, in order to flatter the civil power, contradicted his own proper opinions, and contradicted the original doctrine of the Church.[1]

Pleasant to the military palate of Pius IX. were the words of brave Colonel Allet, in a soldierly order of the day, issued in December, to his zouaves. After recounting, in terse strong terms, their services against the Garibaldians, he says :—

'Soldiers ! all is not over. Great dangers still threaten the Church. Remember that in your regiment you stand, not merely as soldiers marching side by side ; you also represent a principle before the world, the principle of the voluntary and disinterested defence of the Holy See. You are the nucleus around which will unite in the hour of danger the prayers, the succours, and the hopes of the Catholic world. Be, then, true soldiers of God. You have not merely duties, you have even a mission, and you will not fulfil it without union, discipline, moral conduct, and military instruction. A third battalion is formed. Your swelling ranks assure to you a larger part in future struggles. We shall march together to the cry of "Long Live Pius IX. !"'

Funereal solemnities on behalf of the fallen are proudly re-corded as having been celebrated in France, England, Germany, etc. The proudest mention of all is that of Lovaine, apparently because the 'function' was that of a University. The design of the Belgians, it is shown, was not merely to give their suffrage to the souls departed, but especially to show their consciousness

[1] *Friedberg*, p. 487,

that it was for them a glory to have so many volunteers in the Papal army. The Belgian *soldiers* especially showed interest and sympathy.[1]

To these military consolations were added such as a crown and a nation once great could now bestow. Queen Isabella strongly recommended from the throne, and her Cortes almost unanimously voted, that the forces of the nation, acting in alliance with the Emperor of the French, should be ready to defend the Holy See.[2] What was more important, the King of Prussia, in reply to Ledochowsky, spoke clearly in support of the temporal power. The Pope, at the opening of the new year, poured blessings upon France, her sovereign, and her arms, especially on General Failly, whom shortly afterwards he, in taking leave of him, blessed anew.

It was also told with satisfaction how, at banquets, both at Malines and Namur, the health of the Pope was drunk before that of the King of Belgium, and how pleasantly the Nuncio gave the health of the local and subordinate sovereign after that of his master, as the Lord Paramount, had received its meed.[3]

It is not easy for us, whose faith has always rested on the fixed standard of God's Word, to enter into all the feelings of suspense which are to be read between the lines of a lecture by Professor Menzel, then of Braunsberg, now of Bonn, printed for private circulation among his former pupils.[4] He is teaching them the doctrine of *Church* infallibility, but not, as he had hitherto done, in the twofold confidence of persuasion and personal security. Persuasion abides, reinforced by fresh study, and animated by assault. But security is gone. The consciousness that he may never more be allowed to teach this doctrine weighs upon all he utters. Before another session, should his own faith not change, that of his chair probably will. The

---

[1] *Civiltà*, VII., i. 108-109.   [2] Ibid., pp. 228-230.
[3] Id., 622.
[4] *Ueber das Subject der Kirchlichen Unfehlbarkeit.* (*Als Manuscript gedruckt*). Braunsberg: 1870.

Church which he had served, as permitting the membership of those who denied the infallibility of the Pope, had been catholic enough for him.   But now, after pausing since the Reformation, she had actively resumed the process of narrowing the terms of membership by dogmatising new shibboleths.   One had been already added in his own day.   Another now hung overhead, still more momentous, because it not only altered the doctrine of the Church, but altered the standard of doctrine, and was moreover self-propagating,—a seed bearing fruit after its kind.

'This complete subversion of the old Catholic principle, *everywhere, always, and by all*,' cries the poor Professor, 'has found its most doughty champions in the Jesuits of the *Civiltá Cattolica*, with their branch at *Maria Laach*, and in the Archbishops of Malines and Westminster, Deschamps and Manning.'[1]   In the struggling argument of the Teacher of this year, we cannot help hearing, by anticipation, the sighs of the excommunicated of next year; excommunicated for holding fast what he had always taught, with the sanction of the Church, and from one of her chairs!   And as the iron enters into his soul, he evidently feels it hard that an English hand should be one of the foremost in driving it home.

Professors looked from the chair on their classes not knowing what they might have to teach a twelvemonth hence.   Preachers looked from the pulpit on their congregations weighted with the same uncertainty.   Editors wrote that the Catholic faith was thus and thus, feeling that, perhaps, soon they must write the reverse, or else drop the pen.   Heads of families were perplexed as to what they should say to their children, if compelled to believe what they and their fathers had always resented as a false accusation against their religion.   Jurists wondered if they must either break with their clergy, or begin a campaign for reinstating canon law over civil.   Heads of colleges wondered if they must break with the Church, or move heaven and

[1] P. 7.

earth to procure universities 'canonically instituted.' Nobles wondered if they must for the sake of their souls turn against the legislative rights of their order, and seek a polity wherein the noble, as in the Model State under the Perfect Society, served merely as a brilliant to enrich the crown of the priest of God. Statesmen pondered how Church and State could be held together if the Pope resolved to have all 'the liberty of power and the power of liberty.' Kings whose forefathers had compelled nations, by the sword, to wear the yoke of Rome, chafed to think that their religion was to be 'changed over their heads.' But all this time the silent arbiters of the Catholic's destiny were patiently framing ·the decrees. Week by week, and month by month, decisions were being formulated. Men moved and combined to prevent new fetters from being forged for their souls next year; but link was being already noiselessly added to link, by old, cool, and resolute masters. The Emperor set to defend the Gallican liberties for the millions of France, and the Emperor set to uphold the Josephine safeguards for the millions of Austria, had no access to the subterranean forge *Antra Ætnæa,* where chains and thunderbolts were on the anvil, away from the ears of men. Turnus had not less power over the island cave where the arms by which he was to fall were being tempered. But, on the other hand, the Vulcan of the Syllabus had more than one Venus at the Court of each potentate, wooing in his interests, and pleading for his will. The truth, however, was to dawn upon their subjects, from behind gorgeous clouds of their beloved pomps and ceremonies.

CHAPTER VI.

Agitation in Bavaria and Germany—The Golden Rose—Fall of Isabella—The
King of Bavaria obtains the opinion of the Faculties—Döllinger—Schwarzenberg's Remonstrance.

THE proximity of Bavaria to Italy on the one hand, and to
Protestant Germany and Switzerland on the other, had
assisted in giving to the schools of Munich a clearer insight into
the condition of theology south of the Alps, than perhaps any
other learned body north of them possessed, and, at the same
time, in giving to them a juster appreciation of the effect to be
expected in the world at large, from new additions to the dogmatic burden which Catholics must carry, and from the consequent narrowing of the terms of membership in their Church.
For a considerable time, a conflict had been silently growing
up between the theology of the German schools and that in
recent years imported direct from Rome by the new type of
priests there trained. The catechisms—even those prepared
by the early Jesuits—had been gradually altered, till first the
denial of Papal infallibility disappeared, and secondly the
statement of Church infallibility was so obscured as to prepare
the way for further change.

Jesuit establishments had been springing up in defiance of the
law. The Ultramontane press had raged against the unity of
Germany under the leadership of Prussia, writing so as to lead
foreigners to believe that France had only to invade Germany
and she would find the Catholics on her side. A *littérateur*
named Fischer being arrested at Landeck in June 1868, a letter
was found from Count Platen, saying, 'A league of the small
States with France, for the common end of breaking the power
of Prussia, is the duty of all.'[1]

The feelings of the educated classes generally resented such
attempts with indignation. We have seen how Sepp spoke of

[1] Menzel, *Weltbegebenheiten*, band i., p. 123.

the canonisation of Arbues. The painter Kaulbach executed a picture of an *auto da fe* celebrated under the eye of this new celestial patron. A priest preached against the sale of the engravings ; and Kaulbach wrote a letter, which was printed in the *Cologne Gazette,* hailing such reproach as an honour, and appending a sketch of the Roman twins drinking in the milk of the she-wolf. Of his Romulus and Remus, one wore the crown of imperial France, and the other the tiara.[1]

German writers assert that Napoleon III. induced Queen Isabella of Spain, in the spring of 1868, to pledge herself to send into Italy forty thousand men to protect the Pope, in case he should be obliged to withdraw his troops by entering on a war with Prussia. Other authorites say that it was to be in case of a war with Italy. At all events, the most select favour the Pontiff had to confer on the worthiest lady of his Church, the golden rose, was sent to her most Catholic Majesty. The ablegate assured Queen Isabella that it was pre-sented not only as a token of the special goodwill of the Holy Father, but 'as a certain pledge of the celestial protection.' This distinction placed Isabella on a level with the Queen of Naples and the Empress Eugenie, the only two lambs in all his fold hitherto held worthy by Pius IX. of this pontifical seal of stainless whiteness. In acknowledgment the Queen said that if possible it increased veneration and filial affection toward the Holy Father 'in my heart, always rather more his than mine.'[2] If in this event we do not see proof of Queen Isabella's pre-eminent virtue, we cannot but see some criterion of the virtuous sentiment of the Vatican. But to the daughter of Queen Christina the golden rose proved to be the last rose of her summer. In September 1868 this elect lady, after out-living more insurrections than any sovereign in Christendom, was compelled to flee. An Italian writer, as a full account of the cause of her fall, said ' Pius IX. blessed her.' Many Italians

---

[1] Menzel, *Jesuitenumtriebe,* p. 21.
[2] *Civiltá,* VII., i., 740.

say that his Holiness has 'the evil eye,' and that ruin attends all things which he regards favourably. An expression fell from the *Catholique* of Brussels on the news that the crown of Isabella was threatened, which throws light on the Ultramontane dialect : ' Spain will be lost to Catholicism, lost to the cause of order in Europe, and *the last Christian government* will have disappeared from the Old World.'[1]   This drew from Montalembert the remark : ' To wish modern society, or any Christian born in that society and destined to live in it, to esteem the condition of Spain under Isabella II. more highly than that of England under Victoria, and to wish this in the name of the Catholic Church, in the name of the party of order in Europe, is to impute to that party and to that Church the saddest of responsibilities, and the most menacing.'[2]   But in so great a question as the spiritual life of a nation, might the *Catholique* have replied, the personal vices of a sovereign were as a speck on the sun. The thing essential was whether the nation should or should not be held in obedience to the Vicar of God. Should it rebel against him, by statute and by constitution, Christian it could not be. When, in March 1876, the *Voce della Verità,* the daily organ of the Papist party in Rome, spoke of the overthrow of Don Carlos, it spoke of his rule as 'the Christian kingdom,' in contrast to that of Alphonso, not certainly because of the personal virtues of the sovereign—a ground far too narrow—but because Don Carlos would have administered ' Christian law,' that is, he would have taken the law on faith and worship from the lips of him whom God had set up among men to give the law.

Schrader, in the *Papst und König,*[3] gives an allocution of Pius IX., delivered three years after his original triumph in adding to the creed. He rejoices over the inauguration of a column to perpetuate the memory of that event. As this stood

---

[1] Quoted by Montalembert, *Bibliothéque Universelle* 1876, p. 194.
[2] Ibid., p. 195.
[3] P. 18.

near the Spanish embassy, in the *Piazza di Spagna,* he affectionately mentions his dearest daughter in Christ, Isabella, the Catholic queen, and the next female name on his lips is that of the Immaculate Virgin.

But all Catholic political personages were not as good Papists as Queen Isabella.

Montalembert, full of thoughts suggested by the questions rising in the Church, saw in her fall but an incident of the decay of Spain, which, again, was but the most striking example of the condition of most Roman Catholic countries. He wrote what, as we have seen, appeared only after his death. Confessing that the reign of Isabella had lasted ' too long,' he traced the ruin of the country to ' despotism, spiritual and temporal, absolute monarchy, and the Inquisition.' After showing that both municipal and parliamentary liberties had been well developed in Spain in the days when she struggled, rose, and took the lead, he dates the beginning of her fall from the combination of Church and State, under Charles V., to work unitedly in quenching civil and religious liberty. Though no advocate of the separation of Church and State, he says, ' A thousand times better the fullest separation, with all its excesses, than the absorption of the State by the Church, or of the Church by the State.' No better expression could have been chosen than the former of these phrases to designate the effect of the ' Jesuit polity of Church and State just about to be adopted by Rome.

He takes the social and political effects of the Inquisition to have been disastrous:—' That monstrous institution ceased to act only when it had no more to do, when it had substituted emptiness, death, and nothingness, for the life, the force, and the glory of the first nation of the middle ages, the one which we may justly call the pearl of the Catholic world.' Aiming a two-edged thrust at Bonapartist legislatures, and at the character of the coming Council, he says that the ' ill-omened' Charles V. was the inventor ' of consultative despotism, or representative absolutism, of which the Napoleons are wrongly accused of being the originators.' And what he meant by 'consultative despotism' is keenly set in words that might have been written after reading the Rules of Procedure laid down by Pius IX. for the approaching Council : 'The Cortes could no longer exercise a check, nor take the initiative.' For one who had spent his life in battling for the Papacy, but always with the hope of reconciling it to liberty, it was bitter, when death was in view, to write : 'There is not in the history of the world a second example of a great country so ruined, so broken down, so fallen, without foreign conquest or civil war having materially contributed to the result, but by the sole effect of institutions of which it was the prey.'[1]

There is something in this wail of Montalembert which reminds us of a saying of the French historian of Spain: 'From Charlemagne to Charles V. Europe expended much effort and much blood in searching for an equilibrium, impossible to maintain, between the spiritual and temporal power.'[2]

Had the Prime Minister of Bavaria at the juncture in question been a Protestant, he would have been slower in seeing the political bearings of what was taking place. One of the three brothers of Prince Hohenlohe was a cardinal, and otherwise his means of information had been good. Besides, though Bavaria had often served the Papal cause to the hurt of Germany, it had never, like Prussia, given up its *placet* and other guards of the royal supremacy. The Prime Minister submitted questions for the formal opinion of the two Faculties of Theology and Law, in the University of Munich, as to the effect which the definition of Papal infallibility as a dogma would have upon the relations of the civil and ecclesiastical authorities.

The Faculty of Theology, in its reply, after referring to the work of Schrader, and quoting some of his propositions, says :—

'Should these or similar conclusions be adopted ' (*i.e.*, the conclusion of the Syllabus against freedom of religion, of the press, etc.), ' it would lead to great confusion. The counter-principles are so established, both in the theory and practice of all European constitutions, that anything

---

[1] *Bibliotheque Universalle de Lausanne*, 1876, p. 27.
[2] St. Hilaire, *Histoire d'Espagne*, vol. vii., p. 1.

contrary to religious equality and freedom of opinion can scarcely again obtain a footing. Were it laid upon Catholics, as a duty of conscience, to repudiate those principles, undeniably collision between their civil and ecclesiastical obligations would result, and in certain circumstances consequences would ensue, burdensome and hurtful both to the individual members of a national Church and to the collective body.'[1]

The statesmen had asked the divines what was meant by speaking *ex cathedrâ*. The Faculty replied that among those who asserted the doctrine of Papal infallibility, there were some twenty theories on the subject, none of them authoritative or generally received, and all arbitrary ; 'because here it is impossible to frame a theory from Scripture and tradition.'[2]

The Faculty of Law said :—

'Should the propositions of the Syllabus and the Papal infallibility be made dogmas, the relations between State and Church hitherto subsisting would be altered in their very principles, and nearly all the legislation fixing the legal position of the Catholic Church in Bavaria, would be called in question.'[3]

The chief of the Theological Faculty was Dr. Döllinger, whose aged but erect head was to every scholar in the University a crown of glory. The professors were proud of him, and of their attainments made under his eye. In common with the scholars of other Catholic seats of learning in Germany, they habitually manifested contempt for the *Doctores Romani*, the imported pupils of the Jesuits from the *Collegium Germanicum* or other seminaries in Rome,—a feeling which they extended to the great bulk of the men of the Curia.

Döllinger had been a firm Tridentine Romanist, devoutly bearing the burden of the new dogmas which the Council of Trent bound up and laid upon men's shoulders. But being profoundly versed in antiquity, he was not disposed for more accretions of the same sort, and he had long been detested by

[1] Friedberg *Aktenstücke*, p. 300. [2] Ibid., p. 302.
[3] Ibid., pp. 313-323. Archbishop Manning places the time when these questions were put 'about the month of September 1869,' being 'about' half a year too late. as he places the publication of *Janus* about a year too early.—*Vatican Decrees*, p. 114.

the Jesuits, as standing in the old paths and resisting their innovations. Superstitions newly carried over the Alps did not thrive under his eye. As a historian he had not feared to narrate and censure the enormities of Popes.

While these agitations were arising in the provinces, the secret preparations in Rome were being pushed forward. The fact became known that the six Commissions were at work. The names of those serving upon them no sooner transpired than a cry arose that only favourites of the Jesuits were appointed. So few names from Germany appeared that offence was given, even in a national point of view. This feeling increased when it appeared that celebrities of whom the Catholic faculties were proud had been passed over, and that inferior men, known only for devotion to the Curia, had been selected. These feelings were partly theological, partly personal, and yet more strongly patriotic. The Germans knew that a double peril for the Fatherland lurked in the anti-unionist policy of Rome,—peril of disruption from within, and of invasion from France

Dissatisfaction must have run tolerably high when Cardinal Prince Schwarzenberg wrote to Cardinal Antonelli, formally remonstrating as to the selection made. The fact, he submitted, that all those selected belonged to one well-defined theological school, was in itself open to objection. As to the reputation of the favourites, he said, ' I have had fears lest their qualifications should not prove equal to their weighty responsibilities.' He names Munich, Bonn, and Tübingen, as Universities where fit men were to be found as well as at Würzburg, and goes so far as to mention names, among them that of Döllinger.

This letter was politely answered by Antonelli, after a couple of months. He said that Döllinger would have been invited only that his Holiness had learned that he would not accept the duty.[1]

One of the theologians at whom the innuendo of Cardinal

---

[1] Both letters are given in *Documenta ad Illustrandum Concilium Vaticanum,* I. Abtheil., pp. 277-280.

Schwarzenberg was aimed was Hergenröther. Yet Archbishop Manning wrote to *Macmillan's Magazine*, and, after speaking of the men of Munich as if they were of little more account in the esteem of students than in that of ecclesiastical courtiers, told us that if we wanted to learn anything of the true relation of Catholics to national law, we must not go to them, but must study Hergenröther.[1]

CHAPTER VII.

Intention of proposing the Dogma of Infallibility intimated—Bavarian Note to the Cabinets, February to April, 1869—Arnim and Bismarck.

IT was in February 1869 that the fears and hopes which had long been more or less distinctly directed to a given point, were both quickened by fresh light. The *Civiltà Cattolica*, in the letter of its French correspondent, published suggestions that the Council should sit for but a short time, that it should proclaim the doctrines of the Syllabus, and that the infallibility of the Pope should be adopted by acclamation. It was at once alleged that the finger of Pius himself gave this sign. The suggestions thus made explain what the Cardinals consulted in the first instance meant when they hoped that the Council would not last so long as some might think. They had in 1854 induced the bishops to acclaim a new dogma, and in 1867 to accept the Syllabus without demur, and surely they could get any portions of that document which it was necessary, for greater clearness, to formulate into decrees, passed in the same delightful way; and this would be still more desirable for the dogma of infallibility. Archbishop Manning treated the idea of an intended acclamation as a pleasantry ; but he charged the ventilation of it on a wrong time and on a wrong

[1] No. 183, p. 259.

publication. '*Janus* first announced the discovery of the plot.'[1]
It may have been *Janus* who first clearly indicated a certain
English prelate as the man chosen by the party of acclamation
to give the signal. But he was long behind the first to announce the plot. The laity generally were offended and alarmed,
at least those north of the Alps, and many bishops who were
ready to vote for the Curia, did not feel flattered at having
the whole world informed that they were not wanted in Rome
as judges of the faith, but as adornments of a grand pageant.
The translation or assumption of the body of the Virgin was
also suggested in the same article, as a doctrine which it was
desirable to make into a dogma.

As time wore on, the excitement became more intense. In
France, the action of the government, as in most things under
the Second Empire, was ambiguous. It seemed to dread the
impending innovations, and every now and then what appeared
to the world as a menace was half uttered. Yet it was plain
that the Curia was not disturbed. Nothing can be more
tranquil than the letters in the *Civiltà* from its French
correspondent. There is an apparent sense of solid support,
such as no gusts of the popular winds will seriously shake.
M. de Banneville, the acceptable representative of France in
Rome, continued in his post. When the question of the presence of princes in the Council was to be faced, Cardinal
Antonelli had the comfort of treating it with this trusty friend.
It was comparatively easy to convey to him the intimation
which, in a few words, represented, as M. Veuillot had showed,
a radical revolution in Church and State. *There were no more
Catholic States.* The term 'Catholic arms' continued to be
applied, by official writers, to those of France and the other
countries which had reconquered the lost States of the Pope.
But arms are perhaps, like gold and silver to the Brahmans,
substances which never contract pollution. The monarchs were
outside the door. Even France, whose flag at Cività Vecchia

[1] *Privil. Pet.*, Part III., p. 37.

was the only protection of the temporal power, was told that she was no longer a Catholic State,—she, the eldest daughter of the Church; she whom the Pope, in parting with General Failly, had for love of her chassepots—the 'prodigious chassepots,' as they were called—blessed as the 'most Christian nation!' The Curia knew that the hold of the Pope on the priests and schools was stronger than that of the Bonapartes on army and nation; and they were rearing up their champions, while the Empire was wearing out its own.

We have no account of the scene when the French marquis learned that his country was no more a Catholic nation, from the firm but mobile lips of the son of that Sonnino chief whom, it is said, the French had condemned to die for brigandage. He would, however, learn it in tones and with an air which would do all that tone or air could do to divest it of every offensive appearance. Very different would be the language of Antonelli to the representative of a reigning Bonaparte from that of the Curia over a fallen one.

The same number of the *Civiltà* which records the death of Antonelli states the case in the following terms. The Pontiff could not invite powers 'of which one, like Italy, was in open hostility to the Church; of which another had, like Austria, of her own motion, torn up the Concordat; and another had, like France, a turncoat and a perfidious traitor to the Holy See upon the throne.' However, proceeds the apologist, in refusing to invite them the Pope 'did not in any respect approve of the separation of Church and State, but adapted his action to the state of things created by the apostasy of the governments.'[1] A still later number of the *Civiltà* speaks of the 'infernal cleverness' of Louis Napoleon.

The Ultramontane priests enjoyed this disfranchisement of kings; but they were not yet all prepared to find that the Order of Priests was also to be disfranchised. Not a man of them was to be allowed to plead in presence of the Council. The Car-

[1] Serie IX., vol. xii., pp. 397, 398.

dinals, in their close and still Commissions, were preparing to put, not only laymen, but priests and bishops too, more on the footing of a marching army than ever before.

On April 9th, 1869, Prince Hohenlohe addressed a circular to the European Cabinets in the name of Bavaria. It was not to be believed, he said, that the Council would confine itself to purely theological questions, of which, in fact, none were pressing for solution. The only dogmatic point that Rome wished the Council to decide, was that of Papal infallibility, for which the Jesuits in Germany and elsewhere were agitating. 'This question,' added the Prince, 'reaches far beyond the domain of religion, and is in its nature highly political; for the power of the Pope in temporal things over all princes and nations, even such as are in separation from Rome, would be defined, and elevated into an article of faith.'

The smooth reply of the German Jesuit organ was that something of the kind had been said before in the *Augsburg Gazette*. But the circle of Church authority would remain the same, whether the organ of that authority should be the Pope singly, or the Pope in conjunction with the bishops; just as the powers of a national government would be the same in extent, whether in the hands of a monarch or of a republican executive.

This is characteristic. The discussion was not about any proposal to enlarge or contract the theoretic circle of Church power, but about a proposal to declare that the Pope alone, without the bishops, was the depositary of that power. If the theory of Rome was correct, no extension of the circle of power was possible, but the depositary of power was now to be changed.

If, among ourselves, it was proposed to give the power of life and death to the Crown, without judge or jury, we might be told that the power of life and death was the same whether exercised by royal warrant or through the traditionary courts. The circle of power would not be extended.

The Bavarian note did not elicit a practical response from

other cabinets. The reply of Austria was, perhaps, influenced by the fact that Count Beust, then Prime Minister, was a Protestant. His despatch bears marks either of non-appreciation of the import of terms and acts, proceeding from the Vatican, such as would be natural in one not trained to watch them, or of a desire to evade the gravity of the question. He thought it best to wait and to be on his guard.[1] On behalf of Prussia Bismarck also took up an attitude of observation, but with more insight into the reasons for the suggestion of Prince Hohenlohe. The Italian Government had expressed itself in favour of common action, but practically let things take their course. England, naturally, declined to interfere. As to France, she thought herself protected by the Concordat against all eventualities—another proof that her statesmen handled affairs without mastering ideas. Perhaps not one of them had read what Rome had lately been teaching as the true doctrine of Concordats.

The *Unità Cattolica* (June 23rd), however, put this tranquil attitude of France in a different light :—

'Hohenlohe is sold to Prussia, and torments the Catholics of Bavaria to push them to throw themselves into the arms of Prussia, where Catholicism enjoys the utmost liberty, thanks to the fox-like policy of Bismarck. This is known in Paris, and hence Napoleon is said to have looked darkly on the perfidious proposals of the Bavarian Minister.'

Count Arnim, then German Minister in Rome, wrote to Prince Bismarck on the 14th of May, a despatch, in which he showed that ignorance of the practical bearing of the doctrine of Papal infallibility which, appearing in many statesmen, surprised Vitelleschi. This writer says, alluding to specific Canons, the bearing of which the most heedless might see :—

'Rome was wisely content for the moment to sacrifice these Canons for the sake of the dogma of infallibility, which virtually includes them all, and *as many more besides as may spring from the will of a single and irresponsible individual.* If the statesmen who directed the policy of Europe had been more familiar with ecclesiastical matters, and less dis-

[1] *Friedberg*, pp. 325-328.

tracted by other important interests, they would have seen that the dogma of infallibility was a far more serious matter than the Canons, because the effect and limits of these latter are known, whereas those of infallibility are infinite and boundless, as was apparent on all occasions when they could be exercised' (p. 157).

In contrast with this view of the Roman, the German diplomatist wrote :—'The question is not one of those the decision of which, in one sense or another, is of essential importance for governments.' Later, he represents the question whether the Pope is infallible alone or only when united with a Council, as 'an idle war of words, which is without influence on the position of temporal governments.' This sounds as if he repeated what some Ultramontane had told him. Still he admits that the preparations of Reisach's Ecclesiastico-Political Commission may involve the most serious questions for States.[1] Arnim having soon afterwards to pass through Munich, Prince Hohenlohe advised him to see Döllinger ; and it would seem that conversation with him soon gave Arnim light on the difference between an absolute and a limited power of settling all questions affecting morals, so as to bind the consciences of whole nations.[2] Count Bismarck replied on May 26th, declining to apply for the admission of an ambassador, and taking the position that Prussia would maintain 'the perfect freedom of the Church in ecclesiastical affairs, and would firmly repel every trespass on the domain of the State.' He felt that they must avoid what would tend to the mixing up of the two sorts of questions. The duty of Governments was to give plain notice that they would not tolerate any trespasses. He felt that the existence of the Politico-Ecclesiastical Commission showed that Rome was assuming the right to establish fixed rules for politico-ecclesiastical affairs, without giving to the governments interested any opportunity of discussing the points : they were treated as if they were not factors in the case. This fact he considers a sufficient

---

[1] See *Cologne Gazette*, April 19th, 1874.

[2] Manning's *Vatican Decrees*, p. 114, whose authority, *Daily Telegraph*, as quoted in the *Tablet*, October 31st, 1874.

reason why the governments should give timely warning before-hand, rather than wait to make idle protests against decisions once announced. To promote such a united warning, but not to promote the sending of an ambassador, he proposes to communicate with the Southern German governments.[1] These two documents yielded clear proof that Bismarck, instead of seeking a conflict with the Church of Rome, wished to avoid it, and endeavoured to take the most open and practical way of warding it off. Arnim's charge against him of not seeing the danger is an undesigned, but a strong, confirmation of his pacific desires. Certainly he had not then or ever an idea of peace at any price; least of all at the price of surrendering the principle of national supremacy, in any national establishment, be it called Church, or school, or what else.

CHAPTER VIII.

Indulgences—Excitement—The Two Brothers Dufournel—Senestrey's Speech—Hopes of the Ruin of Germany—What the Council will do—Absurdity of Constitutional Kings—The True Saviour of Society—Lay Address from Coblenz—Montalembert adheres to it—Religious Liberty does not answer—Importance of keeping Catholic Children apart from the Nation—War on Liberal Catholics—Flags of all Nations doing Homage to that of the Pope.

ON the 11th of April, 1869, was issued another of those Bulls proclaiming indulgences on which the world has almost ceased to look as one of the forces of history. Nevertheless each of them is a monument to an authority obeyed by disciplined millions, as holding executive power both in this world and the other. Once more were long Latin sentences filled out to tell the faithful that he who had power to bind and to loose proclaimed to them, on the occasion of the Council, full remission of their sins, and indulgence, on condition of their visiting certain basilicas, and saying certain prayers.[2] 'This pardon,' says the

---

[1] *Cologne Gazette*, April 14th, 1874.
[2] *Acta*, p. 18. Freiburg edition, p. 62.

Archbishop of Florence, 'was to extend not only till the opening of the Council, but through the whole of its continuance.'[1] Millions were thus put under the necessity of imbibing the conviction, that sin against our neighbour and our God admits of being cancelled in such a way, or else of seeming to believe what they did not believe, or of bowing and not asking themselves whether they believed it or not.[2]

The excitement steadily rose higher. The *Augsburg Gazette* published articles which aroused general interest in Germany, and attracted attention in England. What had hitherto been treated as mere ravings in the Ultramontane press began to be looked upon as worthy of notice. The priests who, in those journals, preached down Italian and German unity, and lauded France, pointing meanwhile to some swift approaching vengeance, were only excited, not beside themselves. Vague knowledge of great plans awakened hopes, and these led to an exaggerated view of the forces available for a world-transforming struggle. The swords of seventy millions combined against the Hohenzollerns was a splendid dream, and not quite beyond the possibility of realisation. It is often ascribed to Buss, a Professor at Freiburg and Aulic Counsellor, as having been long before this crisis propounded by him in the highest places of Catholic Germany.[3] In its number of January 4th, 1869, the *Unità Cattolica* had an exulting report of a *fête* given by the Papal zouaves to his Holiness, accompanied by the ex-King and Queen of Naples. Telling of the prowess of these troops with their Remington rifles, it said, ' Set four thousand of our soldiers to fire on a body of men some eight hundred or a thousand yards off,

---

[1] *Cecconi*, p. 144.

[2] The extent to which the direct influence of the Curia, as against that of the bishops and parochial clergy, may be increased by the system of indulgences through the various orders of regulars, is traced in *Der Mechanismus der Vaticanischen Religion*, by Friedrich. The power of moral disorganisation contained in that system, and the power of loosening national ties, and of making the Pope the centre of all things to the believer, is also clearly exhibited.

[3] This plan, often alluded to in the German press, is related at length in the *Neue Freie Presse*, June 1872, as quoted by Menzel, *Jesuitenumtriebe*, p. 6.

for only five minutes, and in that time you would have two hundred thousand hit.' On the twelfth of the same month it welcomed General Dumont to Rome, and cited reports of war materials coming from France. On the 16th it hailed the title given to the newborn son of the Duke of Aosta as an omen ' of the victory of the Pope in the year of the Council.' That title was Duke of Apulia, and the first who bore it, in 1059, took an oath of fidelity containing the following words : 'I, Robert, by the grace of God and of St. Peter, Duke of Apulia, and, thanks to the grace of the one and the other, future King of Sicily, will be faithful from this hour forth and for evermore to thee, my Lord Pope Nicholas,'—a general promise, which is subdivided into many particulars. Don Margotti does not tell that Robert was a Norman invader used by Nicholas against Italians, or Lombards already naturalised in Italy. No more does he tell that the gift of the kingdom of Sicily was a gift beforehand, in case Robert Guiscard should conquer it from Greek and Saracen, who then divided it between them.

About this time was inaugurated, with great display of dignitaries, military and spiritual, a monument to two brothers Dufournel, who lie in St. Lorenzo. The monument bears all the emblems of martyrdom which the art of the catacombs can supply. Instead of the usual request to pray for the repose of the soul, into which Romanism fell from Christianity, stands the word of the early Christians, ' They rest,'—here applied because martyrdom had merited what grace was no longer believed to give. Emmanuel Dufournel, on meeting the Garibaldians, shouted to his men, ' Here, lads, is the spot to die ; in the name of the Father, the Son, and the Holy Ghost, forward !' When expiring, he said, ' I am pleased to see my blood flow from fourteen wounds for the glory of Holy Church.' The people of Valentano, where he died, said to his men, ' Let us kiss the bier ; we do not come to pray for his soul, but to commend ourselves to him' (VII., vi., 547). ' Such,' adds the reverend writer, 'Such is the Christian instinct which distinguishes between combatants in any other cause, however just, and the heroes of the Christian religion.' To develop instincts of this sort, it is impossible to conceive writing more skilfully adapted. And these are the men who, at every breath, call the Italians Mussulmans!

The other brother, Diodato Dufournel,—young, handsome, polished, rich,—soon after the death of Alfred, met Father Gerlache at daylight entering St. Peter's : 'I go to say a mass for our dead on the Apostle's tomb.' 'I go too,' replied the Captain, and they entered the crypt. The priest asked the zouave what had caused his strange absorption in prayer. 'Father, I was praying to the Virgin for the favour of dying for Holy Church.' Ten days afterwards he fell mortally wounded during the Garibaldian disturbance in Rome. When the white-headed father arrived, it was too late to see either son alive, but he was instantly received by the Pope. The sovereign tried to fasten on his breast the order of the Piano, but was blinded by his tears. Maria, the sister of Diodato and Emmanuel, came between the two weeping old men, and, guiding the hand of the Pope, fastened the decoration on the breast of her father. The writer concludes by representing the ladies of the house hereafter as pointing out to their little ones the glove, the sword, the fatal ball, and other relics, the victor palm and the exulting angels, and saying, 'Their souls are in paradise, lovely and resplendent, and are interceding for us. Children, kneel down and pray to God that none of our family may degenerate from the example of Diodato and Emmanuel Dufournel!' They are further to tell the children that similar relics of Charles Alcantara and of Bernard Quatrebarbes are preserved; the one in Brittany, the other in Flanders; and that 'in those countries these relics cause a new growth of crusaders continually to spring up' (VII., vi., 552).

Bishop Senestrey, of Regensburg, known as a pupil of the Jesuits and an ardent Ultramontane, made a speech at Schwandorf, which has not yet been forgotten in Bavaria, and was soon heard of in other parts of Germany. He said :—

'We Ultramontanes cannot yield. The antagonism can have no issue but in war and revolution. A peaceable settlement is not possible. Who makes your temporal laws? We observe them only because a force stands behind which compels us. True laws come from God only. Princes themselves reign by the grace of God, and when they have no longer a mind to do so, I shall be the first to overturn the throne.'[1]

Reminiscences of this speech will occur during the sittings of the Council. The offence given by it to Liberal Catholic politicians was more serious than would have been the case with us. We should have put some Protestant interpretation on the expression 'reign by the grace of God.' But Liberal Catholics knew that the meaning of that phrase was very definite in lips like those of Bishop Senestrey. He was not the man to believe that the grace of God would reach royal heads through channels condemned by the Vicar of God. Jurists and journalists might fancy that what the latter bound on earth would be left open in heaven, but not so the Bishop of Regensburg.

To the Germans, who were just rising to a consciousness of their unity, the threats of breaking them up again were cruel, especially when coming from within. 'The foreigner,' said Sepp, 'has always counted on the internal splits in the German oak, to drive in his wedge, and rend us to pieces.'

Political vicissitudes, said the *Stimmen aus Maria Laach*,[2] may possibly change the face of all Germany, and the Lord may, in a surprising way, remove all the barriers which hinder the free action of the Church and break her bonds. One of the complaints against Bavaria, immediately following these ominous words, is that the ruling idea of religious equality gives statesmen the impression that they may interfere in the affairs of the Catholic Church in the same way as they do in those of the Protestant.

At the very same time the rage of the Italian organs of the

[1] Menzel, *Jesuitenumtriebe,* p. 178.
[2] *Neue Folge,* Heft iii., p. 76.

Curia against Italian unity was unbridled. Not to dwell on words written for a day, we have the following language penned, as Count Henri de Riancey says, 'under the radiance of infallibility,' that is, by the direct sanction of the Pope; language put into a work meant to go down in monumental form to future ages, a bound copy of which costs forty pounds. The Count says, 'Naples, Sicily, Parma, Modena, and Tuscany have seen themselves deprived of their princes, capitals, independence, and nationality. These nations, formerly so free, are now the slaves of pro-consuls from the rugged summits of the Alps, coarse conquerors, recalling those of whom Virgil complained. *Barbarus has segetes.*[1] No wonder that with such views the Count looked with horror on the prospect of the Holy City, which 'pastors and people hailed as the country of their souls,' becoming by any possibility 'the capital of that tyrannical unity which is crushing the nationalities of Italy.'

The Archbishop of Salerno, in a pastoral, said : 'The Council will apply a remedy to the gangrened wounds now consuming the social fabric, and will reconstitute society on the basis of the faith. . . . The Church will dictate laws, will dictate lessons, and two hundred millions of men will bow the head in docility and obey; perhaps also with them not a few millions of non-Catholics.'[2]

Bishop Macchi of Reggio, in his pastoral on the Council, made society represent the Prodigal Son : 'We hear society repeat the cry of the prodigal, I perish. Who will save this society? Who will bring a remedy? Who will breathe into it the breath of a new life?' He heard a voice asking, 'But what is a Council that it should be thought the medicine for sick society? . . . Mary is the bow of peace; behold the sun in the Council, which will be the great work of illumination and pacification for the cure of society.'[3] These being the passages selected

[1] *Frond*, vol. i., General Introduction, p. xvi.
[2] *Unitá Cattolica*, Feb. 24th, 1869.
[3] *Civiltá*, VII., vi., 709.

at the Vatican for circulation all over the world, it would seem as if the Pope now felt sure that he had found his sick man.

Bishop Sannibale of Gubbio wrote : 'A few months hence and Rome, the capital of the Christian world, with nations for her children, kings for her sons, and empires for her provinces, will see,' etc., etc.

In contrast to the tone of the Italians is an extract from a German, Dr. A. Schneider, of Cologne. He speaks of the Church re-acquiring her power over public life by first converting individuals, as she did in the beginning. That was said under the Prussian flag (p. 718). From Holland a correspondent writes in hope that the Council will bring the Liberalism which is the plague and danger of the Dutch Catholics, to its end.

The scorn with which talk of recognising Italy was treated at this proud moment, may be judged from the words of the *Unità* for January 27th, in an article headed, *Dying with Italy or Living with the Pope.* The Marquis de Moustier, it remarks, having promised to study a *modus vivendi*, proposed by Menabrea, was seized by mortal illness. In a similar way Morny, Wallewsky, Petri, and Billault were struck with death, by urgent study of means for making revolution live side by side with the Pope. Now Bonaparte was wishing to reconcile two banners, that of Italy bearing a pair of sculls (those of Monti and Tognetti), and that of Christ's Vicar, the way, the truth, and the life.

Parliamentary government, hateful everywhere, was viewed as monstrous in Italy. The *Civiltà* cannot ' accurately study ' the proceedings in Florence, because of ' the ineffable weariness, the disgust, the disdain with which the mind is seized, on reading those speeches, often vulgar, and running over with sophism and effrontery.' [1] It proceeds to say that the famous boons of 1789, *liberty of worship, liberty of meeting, liberty of the press, and liberty of instruction*, led in practice ' to the triumph of irreligion, to the tyranny of the State, to unbridled license in handling through the press the most sacred and inviolable rights,

[1] Serie VII., vol. vi., p. 234-235.

and to the barbarising of the young by more infamous ignorance.'
Yet, at the same time, it records with satisfaction efforts of its
own friends to obtain liberty of instruction, after their ideal;
that is, the State giving up to the priest the control of what is
taught to its subjects with its own money.

The *Civiltà* gloried in the disappearance of the Liberal
Catholic priests, utterly extinguished, as it held, by the Syllabus
and by the prospect of the Council. There might still linger
some slight remnant of Liberal Catholics among the laity. But
Catholics in Italy were now to be noted for their hope, their joy,
and their perfect withdrawal from political life. They were no
more to be found seeking situations from the government, but
were all ardently drawing close to Pius IX. Since he uttered the
' prophetic word,' Let us wait upon events, above all since the
Council was summoned, they had betaken themselves to pious
works and to waiting on the hand of the Almighty.[1]

Clerical immunity from civil jurisdiction is once more
asserted with great solemnity, as ' not only Catholic truth, but
of faith.' Just as Phillips turned the act of our Lord in paying
tribute into an argument why priests should not be required to
pay taxes, so did the *Civiltà* turn the fact of His refusing kingly
dignity into a reason why emperors should leave the Pontiff in
his spiritual action free from ' carnal intrusion,' and also why
he should resort to imperial laws only in the conduct of temporal affairs. The Pontiff is not to be bound by imperial laws,
except in ' temporale,'—he interpreting that term ; but he is to
command in all things that are not temporal.

In its own order, continues the article, the family is independent, but, its end being subordinate to that of the State, the
latter can control the parental power by its laws, and can come
in as judge in any case where the domestic government becomes
hurtful to the public interest (p. 301).

' But this precisely demonstrates the impossibility of saying that it may
do the same with the Church. For it is not the Church that is subordi-

nate to the State, but *vice versâ*, the State that is subordinate to the Church, since it is not the religious end that is inferior to the political one, but, on the contrary, the political that is inferior to the religious. Hence it is not the State that has an indirect power over the Church, but the reverse,—the Church has an indirect power over the State, in what regards the purely temporal order. *And thus she can correct or annul civil laws and the sentences of secular courts, when they are opposed to the spiritual good. She can bridle the abuse of the executive power and the abuse of arms, or indeed* PRESCRIBE THE USE OF THEM, *when it is necessary for the defence of the Christian religion.* The tribunal of the Church is higher than a civil one. Now, the superior tribunal can review the inferior one, not the inferior the superior.'

Hence, it is concluded that the dogmatic teaching of the Bull *Unam Sanctam* settles the matter. If the civil ruler err, he is to be judged by the spiritual one. If an inferior spiritual ruler err, he is to be judged by his proper superior; and if the highest spiritual ruler err, he is to be judged by God only. Hence, the appeal *ab abusu* (*i.e.*, from an ecclesiastical to a civil court) is utter disorder, an appeal lying from a higher to a lower tribunal. It 'takes away the sovereignty of the kingdom of Christ, and subverts its divine constitution.' The right of *placet* and that of appeal form two sores of the Church, more deadly than the old investitures, to abolish which *the Church did not shrink from long and bloody wars.* If the question of investiture touched the 'independence of the Church in the creation of her magistrates,' the *placet* and the appeal touch the independence of the Church in giving laws to the faithful, and applying them to their spiritual government. They are not to be allowed or tolerated. *No physical evil can outweigh so great moral evils.* They impair the fundamentals of the Church and its social structure.

Had we, said the *Unità* of March 3rd, instead of a Chamber of Revolutionists, as Marco Minghetti called the present one, a Chamber of Jesuits, what wise laws, what fruitful sittings, what far-sighted measures would you see! You would see a forced currency disappear as if by enchantment, financial equilibrium established, public morals restored, and crime rapidly diminishing.

But in the same publications which struggled against unity of nations, the loss of another unity was bitterly deplored. 'Catholic unity' in Spain, hitherto existing by law, alas, exclaims the *Stimmen*, exists in fact no longer. By religious unity is meant the state of things which forbids men to worship God except under direction of the Pope. Massimo D'Azeglio exclaimed as to Italy, Religious unity is the only unity we have left. We should say, No wonder!

The attempt to place the unity of Christians not in faith in Christ and manifestation of His spirit, but in subjection to one human being, has had just the same results as had the attempt to place the unity of mankind in obedience to one sovereign, treating all who did not yield as enemies. Human unity is larger and nobler than one throne will ever shadow, and so is Christian unity. The lust of uniformity that erected the Inquisition, fettered the press, sentenced free opinion and free speech to death, reformed the decalogue, and laid bonds upon the Bible, has never given a nation rest, and has only been an endless source of division and scepticism, by teaching men to curse and shun one another even for differences often innocent, perhaps advantageous. The Apostolic Council of Jerusalem, instead of suppressing very grave differences which had spontaneously arisen, set up on a solid and permanent basis the right to differ. This was a divine token of catholicity condemning retrospectively past attempts, and prospectively future attempts, to reduce mankind to uniformity. Azeglio, in the same breath in which he speaks of this 'unity,' calls Italy 'the ancient land of doubt,' where even at the time of the Reformation people thought little of Rome and nothing of Geneva. And the *Stimmen* says that those Spaniards who had broken down 'religious unity' were not Protestants but sceptics.'[1] So that in both Italy and Spain the result of that uniformity which is no unity, was scepticism in religion and decay in politics.

To the race the bond of unity lies in a common Father, and

---

[1] *Neue Folge*, Heft iii., p. 75.

to the Church in a common Lord. In the one case and in the other the maintenance of unity consists not in putting down variations, but in treating them with brotherly regard, as did the apostles in council.

Very great political significance was lent by all the Papal press to festivities in honour of the Pope's fiftieth year of priesthood. The demonstrations of devotion to him at this moment were fervent and grand, and the supplies of money laid at his feet were immense. Great care was taken by the *Civiltà* to ridicule the idea of the *Opinione* that these manifestations had nothing to do with politics. On the contrary, cried the leaders of the 'good press,' humanity, bewildered and almost in despair, was hastening to the feet of the only deliverer. All society needed a saviour, as every rational creature knew. 'The Pontiff is now almost alone in the world, the representative of truth, justice, and good sense.' And hence, the poor world, swimming in error, fraud and absurdity—' the world sees in Pius IX. a true master, a true judge, a true sovereign, and it cleaves to him as the bulwark of society.' The Syllabus suffices to prove that the Pope alone declares the truth : ' the Syllabus which burst like a thunderbolt out of a serene sky, both illuminated and blasted.' Hence all turn to the Pope, who more than ever promulgates the ' ancient truth which seems new.' The Pontiff is the 'living remedy and the constant *protest*' against injustice, iniquity, tyranny, despotism, etc., etc. . . . . 'If there still exists in the world a type and model of good and paternal government, it is found in Rome.' The Pontiff, ' rather than abandon one Hebrew child converted to the faith, braved the Masonic rage of the world.' The nations seem to be saying, To whom *should we go*, but to the Supreme Pastor of the Christian flock ?—*thou hast the words of eternal life.* Pius IX., by rejecting the counsels of the prudent, ' now has become morally the strongest support of order in the world, so that those who have fallen, and those who wish not to follow them, lean upon him.' And not only so, but the 'new queen of the world, Public Opinion, is now altogether in favour of the Roman Pontiff, and protects and saves him, almost of herself alone, against every violence and every intrigue, so that it now may almost be said that all those in the world who are not with Pius IX. from love are with him by force' (VII., vi., pp. 310-311).

Turning again to the subject of constitutional government, the writer proceeds :—

'In fact, it is a truth plain to common sense, that the head must govern; but it is a discovery of modern science that the king ought not to govern. Not governing, however, the king must do something in this world. But what? If he governs in spite of the system, he is a traitor to his oath ; if according to his duty, in a constitutional State, he does not govern, there he is a useless de-nothing. In either the one case or the other he must be dismissed as a do-nothing, or as a traitor. This, in a few words, is the history of all modern constitutional kings.

'This absurd system,' he goes on to say, 'will never be understood by the common sense of the people, who on this account cast their eyes around to seek for one who now really does govern, yet, nevertheless, with the counsels of the wise, and without tyranny; and they find that this is clearly exemplified in the Roman Pontiff, whether as a Pope or as a king ; not, forsooth, with constitutional fictions, more or less observed or violated, but with Christian and evangelical clearness, as morality and propriety demand.

'Yes, morality : for in truth it is not easy to understand how the good conscience of a reasonable person can be preserved, who is placed in the position of being forced to sign laws which other people make, under pain of violating the constitution if he refuses his approbation to that which is demanded by force—not the force of equity and of justice, but of numbers, and even of a casual majority' (pp. 311, 312).

The writer then goes on to argue that the people can never understand how one and the same person can have two con-sciences, one as a constitutional king and the other as a man. This, however, is a necessary condition of a constitutional king, but it is not the case in the Pontifical States, where nobody would ever suppose such a condition of things possible.

'The Pope has only one conscience, and neither majority nor univer-sality of votes and suffrages would ever lead him to sanction that which is contrary to morality, to justice, to equity, and to the well-understood interests of his subjects and of the flock. The Pope can say with truth, "Although all, not I;" and on this account the eyes and the hearts of all in the world who hate fictions and impostures, and who love truth and rectitude, are turned to the Pope thus reigning and governing' (p. 312).

We make no attempt to enquire how many consciences a Pope may have. The *Civiltá* contends that he cannot have more than one. We have heard Romans contend that one is above the number. Liverani (p. 140), alluding with much personal respect to Father Mignardi, the Jesuit confessor of Cardinal Antonelli, who, though not Pope, had much to do with the perfect model of government above commended, evidently thinks that a director of Antonelli's conscience held a sinecure. He asserts that no one knew that his Eminence had a conscience till April 2nd, 1860, when he declared the fact in a despatch to Count Cavour! And this is the language of a prelate!

The more distant prelates were already bidding their flocks farewell. The Bishop of Montreal, in doing so, said that the 'Council was destined to destroy the errors and sophisms which cause so much damage to man and to society.' Moreover, he cited the example of the valorous Canadian youths, who had enrolled themselves among the zouaves to defend the Pope at the cost of their blood, exhorting his clergy with similar courage to contend against the errors pointed out by the Pope.[1] From Jerusalem five priests wrote to announce that they would commence a concert of prayer, on the slopes of Calvary: 1. For the happy result of the Council; 2. For the union of the Oriental schismatics; 3. For the conversion of erring priests. At the same time that it announces this fact, the *Civiltá*, quoting from the *Tablet*, says that in Russia, 'under the appearance of *external unity*, there is great division of religious sects;' and that there is some desire for union with Rome.[2]

Confident in the spiritual and political triumph approaching, the *Civiltá* for May opened with an article[3] on Church and State, which made a great impression. Beginning by proclaiming Christ as the invisible, and the Pope as the visible, monarch of the one kingdom, the Church, it roundly asserts that the Pope's

---

[1] *Civiltá*, Serie VII., vol. vi., p. 229. [2] Ibid., p. 291 ff.
[3] Ibid., p. 229.

right in any Christian country is as real as that of its own prince, and of a higher order. It is not content with one assertion of the closer dependence of subjects on the Pope than on their king. The following is a reiteration, but ought to be read carefully :—

'Without doubt, the relation of each single Christian to the Pontiff is much more intimate than that in which he stands to his own civil government ; because it is a relation formed by a tie which God Himself has immediately and positively bound with His own hand. It is a bond which directly attaches the spirit and leads to the *summum bonum* of man, eternal felicity. In fact, this relation is not distinct from that which binds us to God ; since it is not to be forgotten that the authority of the Pontiff is the authority of Christ Himself, the place of whom he holds upon earth, and whose work he follows out in the sanctification and government of the faithful.'

Returning to the point at which it started, nearly twenty years before, as we saw long ago, this authority again asserts that the State is in the Church, not the Church in the State. The Church is the whole, the State the part. What the family is to the nation, the nation is to the Church.

In June 1869 the Catholics of Coblentz presented an address to the Bishop of Treves, protesting against the innovations proposed by the *Civiltá Cattolica*, and suggesting reforms in a spirit contrary to that of the Syllabus. This was followed by another address of the same purport to the Archbishop of Cologne from the University of Bonn, where the Catholic Faculty of Theology had obtained a very high position. Great interest was excited by the warm adhesion of Count Montalembert to the address of Coblentz. His services, both to the spiritual and temporal power, had been conspicuous. He was now in the grip of a mortal disease. France will always respect his piety and his genius, but she will increasingly have cause to deplore the direction of his influence, as the slow but sure results of priestly power in education develop themselves.

'Twice within the last few weeks,' he writes, 'have I touched the brink of the grave.' So he feels that he may speak of this world as one whose personal interest in it is as nought.

The dying man notes the journals whose words consoled him, among them 'the learned and courageous *Literaturblatt*' of Bonn. Speaking of the address, he says, 'I cannot express how much I have been moved and charmed by that glorious manifesto, flowing from the reason and conscience of Catholics. . . . . . At last I seemed to hear a manly and a Christian tone, amid the declamations and adulations wherewith we are deafened.' He would have signed 'every line' of it, but he felt somewhat humbled that it did not proceed from French Catholics, with whose antecedents it would have harmonised, as well as with those convictions which made them, in the early part of this century, the champions of religious liberty on the Continent.[1]

It was hard for the Jesuits to own that Montalembert stood in their path, to be pitilessly struck down. For the present they tried to reason. Like him, many, especially in Belgium, had imbibed the conviction that civil and religious liberty were good in themselves, and might be made to work favourably for the Church, which they thought incurred great danger by setting herself in opposition to both, and by using her spiritual engines for the overthrow of constitutional government. Such men argued that the perfect liberty existing in England, the United States, and Belgium had many advantages for the Church.

To reasoning of this sort the *Stimmen aus Maria Laach* replied by first of all uttering encomiums on religious liberty, and also on those excellent Catholics who favoured it, thinking it might prove best for the Church. But though this view of the case had its noble aspects, there was another side to it. Experience proved that under such a system the losses of the Church were deplorable. Not to speak of Europe, the case of the United States would suffice. As much as thirty years ago, Bishop England, of Charleston, had said that whereas the Catholics ought to have six millions of the population, they really had less than two. And this terrible loss was ag-

[1] *Friedberg*, p. 88.

gravated at the present day, for considering the enormous immigration of Catholics and the addition of Mexican territory in the meantime, they ought now to number fifteen millions ; but in fact they did not dare to claim more than six. A good authority had showed that the Church lost more souls in the State of Winsconsin in a single year, than she gained in the whole Union. The loss among the children of the Irish was greater than among those of the Germans. This the writer attributes to 'the pestiferous air' of non-denominational schools, and complains that the system prevailing in America deprives children of a well-ordered and continuous Catholic education, such as would protect them, among other dangers, from the necessity of learning English.[1]

This anxiety to keep up the German tongue in America illustrates the cry raised in the German press against that tongue being put out of the schools, both in Posen and in the Tyrol. 'Liberty of instruction' had been so used that whole districts, once speaking German, had been educated into the use of Polish in the one case, and of Italian in the other. In both these countries the same reason which in America made it desirable for Rome to keep up German, turned the other way. In America, the German tongue would enclose a people, in the heart of the country, walled off and apart from the nation. In the other cases, that tongue would be a channel connecting the people with the ebb and flow of the national mind. Even a comparatively small population, kept well in hand, inaccessible to the common thought, and ready to obey every touch of the leaders, may be made a formidable political power. Had Wales been in the hand of Rome![2]

Among the causes of chagrin to Montalembert would be a recent article in the *Civiltá*, directed against the Liberal Catholics by name, and plainly meant to thwart any influence with

---

[1] *Stimmen, Neue Folge*, Heft iv., pp. 59, 60.

[2] Curious examples of this use of education are given by Menzel, *Jesuitenumtriebe*.

which they might have hoped to approach the Council. A pamphlet being taken· as a text, the positions of the Liberal Catholics are stated, as—1. That modern nations deserve more liberty than ancient ones ; 2. That liberty of worship should be conceded, as now inevitable ; 3. That 'the distinction between Church and State ' is not now to be got rid of, and has its advantages ; 4. That Catholics ought to avail themselves of all liberties. On the first point it is replied that modern society has made only material progress, but gone back in faith and morals, and therefore deserves not more liberty than ancient society, but less. On the second point, resenting an allusion of the Liberal Catholic to the fact that Pius IX. had himself granted a constitution at the opening of his reign, the *Civiltà* alleges, first, that it was conceded *in circumstances of imperious necessity;* and, secondly, that it was free from the essential faults which would deservedly brand it as Liberal—'it lacked the criminal principles of liberty of worship, of the press, and of meeting.' Moreover, it issued in the exile of the Prince, 'which seems to be the inevitable result of modern constitutions.' So the Pontiff was obliged to revoke it, and to condemn it to oblivion.

The Liberal Catholic writer had quoted passages, even from Jesuits, to prove that it was lawful for princes, in given circumstances, to tolerate liberty of worship. Certainly, replies the *Civiltà*, it is lawful to tolerate it, if imperious circumstances render it necessary in order to avoid a greater evil. But that is one thing, and admitting liberty of worship as a principle is another. ' What meaning have the words of the present Pontiff when he declares that liberty of conscience and of worship is madness, and the pest of the nations?' What did he mean when he condemned President Comonfort for admitting religious liberty into Mexico? Did Gregory XVI. and Pius IX. talk to the middle ages? Did they tell the present generation what was suitable or not suitable for the middle ages? Catholics may not be able to change the state of things where liberty of worship already exists, but it is in their power to prevent its entrance where it does not, and to demonstrate its criminality, and its moral and social balefulness. The phrase 'a distinction between Church and State,' is soon crushed. What is meant, alleges the *Civiltá*, is a separation. That is condemned in the Syllabus. As to Catholics availing themselves of all liberties, that idea is no patent of *Liberal* Catholics. Of course Catholics avail themselves of all liberties of which they can make use. But to take part in the elections of a kingdom like that of Italy, formed by iniquity, and binding up in itself a perpetual sacrilege, is impossible. The words of the Bull which hurled an excommunication against king and people, are paraded, and the unfortunate Liberal Catholic is reminded that those words apply to *adherents* of the spoliation.[1]

The Paris correspondent of the *Unitá* felt satisfied that the speech of the Emperor, made in June, to the troops in camp at Chalons, on the anniversary of Solferino, meant war. The correspondent of the *Civiltá* was not so sure ; and was bitterly disappointed that the Emperor, when expressly reminded at Beauvais, by the Bishop, of the 'never' pronounced by M. Rouher, and thus fairly offered the opportunity of repeating it, did not deign to say one word pledging himself to keep up the temporal power.

A London correspondent of the *Civiltá* told how the journals had at first affected to ignore the Council, but now began to speak of it. The Anglo-Catholic party were discussing projects of union, and he gives an account of a meeting for that purpose, not naming time or place, but making the Rev. Edward Urquhart prominent. It is said, he adds, that one bishop will go to the Council ; and the Ritualists think that many of their party will do so. There is much cause for hope. Some persons of high station have publicly said that they would submit to the Council, and many say so privately. They do not feel safe in Anglicanism. He dwells on Mr. David Urquhart, and his ideas of what the Pope is to do for international interests.[2]

---

[1] Serie VII., vol. vi., pp. 445 ff.   [2] Vol. vi., pp. 484-5.

The prelate who replaced the Bishop of Montreal in his absence, delivered an address, from which the *Civiltá* repeats these words, that Pius IX. had a mission, and his mission was to recall, to confirm, and to defend in the world, the law of the 'Most High,' the essential principle of authority, and thus to 'save at once both the Church and Society.'[1] But as a while ago we heard of toasts in which the Pope, as universal king, was put before the national king, so now on British ground is held up to admiration the trophy of banners in the Church of St. Sulpice as the fairest tribute of 'New France,' as Canada is called. The flags of all the societies in Montreal, and also those of all nations, were gathered together '*in homage to the standard of Pius IX., to express the obedience of the Catholic nations to the supreme authority.*'[1]

CHAPTER IX.

Publication of Janus—Hotter Controversy—Bishop Maret's Book—Père Hyacinthe—The Saviour of Society again—Dress—True Doctrine of Concordats not Contracts but Papal Laws—Every Catholic State has Two Heads—Four National Governments condemned in One Day—What a Free Church means—Fulda Manifesto—Meeting of Catholic Notables in Berlin —Political Agitation in Bavaria and Austria—Stumpf's Critique of the Jesuit Schemes.

LITTLE more than three months remained before the opening of the Council, when the intellectual movement respecting it received a new impulse. A book, under the title of *The Pope and the Council*, by Janus, issued from the German press; and conjecture at once ascribed the principal authorship to no less a person than Döllinger, although it was assumed that he had availed himself of aid. The profound impression made by this work may be accounted for, partly by the excitement in the midst of which it appeared, and partly by its own force. It combined a minute knowledge of the inner history of the Church, with comprehensive views of the questions, both doctrinal and constitutional, which were now raised.

After a few clear passages from modern utterances of authority, Janus strikes the keynote rather higher than he is prepared to sustain it:—'So they find themselves under a delusion, who believed that in the Church, the spirit of the Bible, and of old Christianity, had got the upper hand of that spirit of the middle ages according to which she was a penal establishment, able to send men to prison, to the gallows, or to the stake.' The Bible and old Christianity are here set up as the standards. But how old? Would a Hebrew seeking to restore religion in the days of Nehemiah, have accepted six centuries after Moses as antiquity? or would he have sought the *old* truth in the law itself? But if seeking the norm of Church order and doctrine in the first six centuries is less scientific than seeking it where those centuries sought it, the historical result is advantageous, as elucidating the total absence of the modern Papal dogmas in those early centuries.

Beginning with the *Magna Charta* which Innocent III. condemned, while he excommunicated the Barons, Janus cites case . after case in which the establishment of free institutions, and especially of freedom of worship, brought down the solemn condemnation of the Pope. The case of Austria in 1868 is the latest. With the quietness of scientific knowledge, he states what at the time would have required, from an English writer, arguments and proofs in detail, namely, the simple but most important fact that 'the oft-quoted word of the Apostle, "We must obey God rather than men," means, in the Jesuit sense, We must obey the Pope as the representative of God upon earth, and the infallible interpreter of the Divine will, rather than any civil superior, or any law of the State' (p. 33).

The tone of Janus is calm, and scholarly, without being cold; and the acuteness of his analysis is such as is found only where clear intellectual insight is united to trained habits of weighing language, with reference to possible interpretations by such casuists as are formed by the Curia and the Jesuits.

He clearly proved that the Church was on the eve of one of the greatest constitutional changes ever effected in any commonwealth. If, in the past, the forged Decretals of the Pseudo-Isidore had facilitated inroads upon the constitution of the Church, how much more would an authentic article of the creed, containing in itself the power of making any number of other articles, and assuming as its basis the unlimited authority of the Pope, pave the way to far-reaching civil and ecclesiastical encroachments! When Archbishop Manning said of Janus that by some it was ' regarded as the shallowest and most pretentious book of the day' (*Priv. Pet.*, iii., p. 114), he greatly moderated the tone of his Continental friends. Most bad things that could be said against a book, or its writers, were said in very bad language. The Archbishop himself could not let it pass without twice calling it ' infamous,' and that in a pastoral.

The excitement in Germany now reached a point at which the bishops began to be alarmed. The 'good press' undertook to extenuate the importance of the changes dreaded, and threw doubts on the probability of their being adopted. The perplexity became greater when, in France, appeared a book in two volumes from the pen of Monsignor Maret, said by some to be the most learned prelate in the country, and who, at all events, was Dean of the Theological Faculty of the Sorbonne. He combated the proposed innovations with French tact and skill, raising a voice, if not for the old Gallican doctrines as a whole, at least for some remains both of them and of the liberties with which are identified the names of the most renowned Churchmen in France since the Reformation.[1] The book made a profound but passing impression. It was called *Religious Peace and the General Council;* but the Jesuit historian Sambin (p. 47) styles it a brand

---

[1] Monsignor Maret boldly quotes Eusebius as saying (Book II., cap. xiv.) that Peter was not only the greatest and strongest of the Apostles, which is like what he says, but that he was the prince and patron of them all, which he

increasing the conflagration. The question raised was that between a constitutional but oligarchical government and a personal
one for the Church.   Maret holds that in her constitution a
check upon the monarch was provided by the 'aristocracy,' that
is, the bishops (vol. ii., p. 107).   The democracy is formed by
the priests and the laity.   But we may point out that this is
very loose language.   *Democracy* means a people with power, not
a populace excluded from all functions of government. The
people in the Papal Church are absolutely stripped of all part
in government. They are a mere populace. The clergy are
disfranchised officials. That Church is a society with a populace, but without a democracy. Before the Vatican Council, it
had a constitutional aristocracy. Since then, the bishops are
nobles without any but delegated power. Maret clearly states
the familiar fact, that in the earlier centuries both clergy and
laity took part in the election of bishops. But when he comes
to speak of the part taken by kings in their election, the facts
glide out of sight, as noiselessly as writers of his school generally
say that they are wont to do in the hands of a Jesuit. A reader
might imagine that kings first got the idea of a right in the
election of bishops by some grant of the Church ; whereas even
the Bishops of Rome were for a long time elected on imperial
or royal order, coming from Greek or Goth, from Arian or
orthodox prince, as the case might be.

Maret quotes Cardinal de la Luzerne as saying that a General
Council, in which the order of priests was not represented, would
be illegitimate though not invalid (vol. i., p. 125) ; and gives
it as the general opinion of theologians that their presence was
necessary.   He also admits that the presence of laymen in the
Councils is attested by a large number of documents.

Maret places this dilemma before the Roman theologians—
Either you will state the conditions of a definition *ex cathedrâ,*

does not say. That is said for him by the Latin translator. The one word
προήγορον, 'spokesman,' or champion, of Eusebius is deliberately turned into
the two, ' prince and patron'—*Principem et patronum.*—*Maret,* vol. i., p. 97.

or you will not. If you do state them, the only condition which is of divine origin cannot be omitted, the consent of the bishops ; and thus you gain nothing, for separate and personal infallibility would still not be defined. If, on the contrary, you do not state the conditions of a definition *ex cathedrâ*, you do indeed gain the absolute, separate, and personal infallibility of the Pontiff, his monarchy pure and indivisible, *but at the same time you effect the most radical of revolutions in the Church.* You overthrow the whole Christian and evangelical institute; you destroy the limited monarchy of the Church; you abolish the divine rights of the episcopate, nineteen centuries old; you suppress the divine counterpoise to the pontifical authority. In a word, *you change the constitution of the Church.* But in changing the constitution, you are obliged to change also the doctrine, and henceforth, in the Holy Sacrifice, we must chant, I BELIEVE THE POPE, instead of I BELIEVE THE CHURCH.

Von Schulte reviewed this work in the *Literaturblatt* of Bonn (v., pp. 2 and 54). Looking at it in a popular sense, Schulte thought it was a book to mark an epoch. It was likely to produce a great effect among the clergy, little among the laity. Time has not justified this anticipation. The fact is, all the younger clergy had been educated out of French ideas and sympathies, and such of the young laity too as had been brought up by priests. Men were but beginning to find how the Christian Brothers, and convent schools, and episcopal seminaries had changed France.

The *Civiltá*, in reply, objects even to Maret's formula, *the Pope with the bishops superior to himself alone.* Such an objection implies that in Council all the bishops add to the Pope nothing at all. So many mitres without any heads in them would add at least as much. We believe, indeed, that great thinkers have doubted whether a judge with his wig is not superior to the same judge without his wig. But the Pope with all the bishops is not superior to the Pope without any bishop ! The Jesuit writer says that he thinks he expresses the mind of

Maret with exactness when he puts it thus, ' *The supreme power resides in the Pope together with the bishops ; in the Pope as supreme, whose strict duty it is, nevertheless, to obey ; in the bishops as subordinate, who, nevertheless, have the right to command*' (*Civiltá*, VII., viii., p. 257 ff).

The choicest auditories of Paris had often crowded noble Notre Dame, quaffing with delight the sparkling eloquence of the Carmelite preacher Hyacinthe. Now the ear of the country was thrilled, for a moment, by a cry from that eloquent voice. ' By an abrupt change,' he wrote to the General of his order on the 20th of September, 1869, ' for which I blame not your own feelings, but a party in Rome, you now accuse what you did encourage, and blame what you did approve, commanding me to hold a language, or to preserve a silence, which would not represent my conscience.'

Placed in this difficulty, he must forsake General, order, and convent. He continues : ' My profound conviction is, that if France in particular, and the Latin races in general, are delivered over to social, moral, and religious anarchy, the principal cause is, not assuredly Catholicism itself, but the manner in which it has been understood and practised for a long time.'[1]

It was to the hands of Father Hyacinthe Loyson that Montalembert committed his work on Spain and Liberty which has already passed before us; and by M. Loyson was it at last given to the public, after others had long refused to let it appear.

St. Peter's Day, always a great day in Rome, was, of course, of surpassing importance in the year of the Council. The *Civiltá* celebrated it in an article very like one of the Pope's Speeches. This article yields an example of a dualism in the government of the universe which must glide in as the unconscious but inevitable complement of the doctrine into which Papal writers fall, in explaining away what to others seems the blight of Providence on whatever they rule according to their own principles. They begin by separating the God of providence from the God of

[1] See the original, *Vitelleschi*, p. 266.

grace. They end by turning the bounties of Providence into the bribes of the evil one. It will be seen that in what follows national prosperity comes from the devil. The increase of our fields, the blessing in our basket and our store, are in reality a curse. This, though unseen to the poor Pope who teaches such things, presents a true and a very hurtful form of Manicheism. It is another proof that they who readily forge and hurl bad names are not safe from the errors which those names when correctly used denote. A lame beggar was sitting and looking up to Peter. But what the beggar wanted was gold, and Peter could not give him gold. But Peter could say, *In the name of Jesus Christ of Nazareth, rise up and walk.* The beggar was Society. There was another who did offer gold. *He* said to Society, Fall down and worship me, and I will give you all the kingdoms of the world, etc. And the societies that got rich did so by worshipping the devil, their own head. Peter, however, can say to Society, Arise and walk.

Peter has often pronounced that word, and just as often has Society been saved. Rise, said Peter to the Roman world, and law from a tyrant became a protector. Rise, cried Peter to the barbarian world, and the rule of the stronger gave place to the defence of the weak. Rise, said he to the German world, and the despotism of dukes and emperors was changed into mild paternity. Rise, he said to the feudal world, and the dissolution of all ties was arrested, and societies hasting to ruin were re-constituted. Rise, he said to savage society, and culture replaced ignorance, gentleness of manners perversity. Peter never spared his ' Rise and walk ;' and that mighty word never failed of effect.

To modern Society, Peter, by the lips of his successor, addresses the reviving word : ' Gold and silver have I none, but in the name of Jesus Christ of Nazareth, rise up and walk.' He, by the Vatican Council, holds out to it the help to rise. The ancient prodigies of that word will be confirmed by new prodigies. The Vatican Council will save modern Society. Good

Catholics have already heard the word of prodigy uttered to modern Society. They see those apostolic hands extended to shrivelled Society, offering it the miraculous cure, by means of the Council. (Serie VII., vol. vi., p. 683 ff.)

What good Catholics saw we cannot say; but what cold history saw was, not lame Society asking gold from Peter, but Peter begging gold from the beggar he was going to cure. The Pope calls contribution 'consolation;' yet he tells the nations who have most 'consolation' that they get it by falling down and worshipping the devil.

In spite of all the secrecy surrounding the preparations, it transpired that Cardoni, Archbishop of Edessa, *in partibus,* had, in the Commission for Doctrine, read a paper on infallibility, and that, with the exception of a single man who had the courage to oppose the Presiding Cardinal and all his colleagues, the dogma was unanimously approved. The opponent, Dr. Alzog, of Freiburg, belonged to the German nation, and to a class of men who were becoming inconvenient—the Church historians.

Meanwhile any bishops who made inquiries as to the intended program were reminded that all were under the oath of secrecy. But there was one subject on which they were not treated so cruelly—the important one of dress. Ten months before the Council, information on that head was requested by the Propaganda for the benefit of the numerous bishops depending upon it. An *elenchus paramentorum,* or inventory of vestments, was sent. The Prefect of Ceremonies then wrote to the Under Secretary of State, requesting that the same inventory might be sent to the several nuncios, for the information of the prelates within their respective bounds. On the 16th of February his most Reverend Eminence the Secretary of State sent off a despatch to each nuncio with the inventory. As to pluvials every prelate was to have three,—a white, a red, and a violet, and so on with other vestments in proportion. (*Cecconi,* pp. 491, 493.)

In June, the Curia had to set up a strong resistance to the

movement originated in Austria for the abrogation of the Concordat. That instrument, which had formed the diplomatic
triumph of Cardinal Rauscher and had crowned the professional
reputation of Schulte, had legally restored to the Papal Church
much of what it calls its liberties; but the clergy complained
that they never practically got all that was promised upon paper.
In the *Frond* biographies of the Cardinals, that of Rauscher
describes the condition of the Church in Austria, under the
Josephine laws, as deplorable! Instead of leaving her, like
Protestant Prussia, to manage her own affairs, without having
defined either what 'manage' or 'her own' meant, Austria,
knowing how Rome interprets, had taken a different course.
There was left, according to our authority, no canon law, but
only such legislation as was imbued with Febronianism and
Cæsarism. Bulls, briefs, rescripts, and even the pastorals of
bishops were subject to the royal *placet*. Marriage was withdrawn from under the control of the Church. The State pushed
into everything, 'and the Catholic Church had none of the
liberties claimed by the tolerance of the age, for all religions.'
Rauscher had succeeded in getting these grievances redressed,
but now the national spirit was rising against his work. His
Concordat bound Austria to concede to the Church 'all rights
and privileges to which by the divine order and by canon law
she is entitled.' Probably the Emperor but imperfectly comprehended what that implied. Rauscher comprehended it. He
was as honest a man as any Papal priest is likely to be. He
was the adviser of the Emperor, and his sworn personal friend.
Any one may tell what such friends do for princes who will only
master what Rauscher managed to bind his sovereign to. The
minister, Von Hasner, put the plea for the abrogation of the
Concordat on ground exceedingly offensive to the Pope and
those around him. When the Concordat was contracted, said
Hasner, Rome was an independent State. Now, it has ceased
to be so, and is sustained only by foreign arms. The reply
from the Vatican was: So long as the Pope is sustained by

Christian arms, he can never be sustained by those of foreigners. The reply of the politician would have been that in 1855, when the Concordat was concluded, the Papal State was as much dependent upon foreign arms as in 1867, the only difference being that at the former time the arms holding a great portion of it were those of Austria.

A paper in the *Revue des Deux Mondes*, by the well-known Belgian Professor Laveley, excited the *Civiltá*.[1] Laveley quoted the words of Baron Weichs, to the effect that Austria was much in the condition of Japan, having one sovereign residing in the Burg in Vienna, and the other, the Omnipotent Master, at the Vatican. To this the reply was that every Christian must take the Church as God has made it, that He has constituted a kingdom, and

'all and every man that is baptized is bound to obey the Monarch of that kingdom. These are subjects of the Pope, and are his subjects just because they are subjects of Christ, in the authority of whom the Pope governs them. For German Catholics, as much as for French ones, or Belgian ones, or Spanish ones, and for all that form a part of the Church of Christ, that which seems strange to the worthy Baron is perfectly true, namely, that they have two sovereigns—the one, temporal, residing in Vienna, Paris, Madrid, and so on; the other, spiritual, residing in Rome, the metropolis of the Catholic world' (p. 22).

After this, by way of shutting up the German politician to the faith, the writer quotes the great German Doctor of Ecclesiastical Law, reinforcing his authority by the consideration that he is a layman.

'The eminently learned Phillips,' he says, 'speaks thus: "In conferring the supreme pastorate upon Peter, God has subjected to him the entire human species, because every man, by right, belongs to the fold of Jesus Christ. In presence of the crook of Peter, the mightiest prince upon earth is no more than the humblest of the lambs." In contradiction to this,' continues the writer, 'modern Liberals adopt the cry, We have no king but Cæsar ; and as for the Vicar of Christ, they would say, Crucify him !' (p. 22). . . .

'If, by divine institution, every baptized man is a subject of the Roman Pontiff, necessarily every nation is governed by two authorities,—by that of the civil sovereign for the affairs of temporal life, and by that of the spiritual sovereign for affairs which relate to the eternal salvation of

[1] *Civiltá*, VII., vii., p. 18-33.

the soul and the service of God. Those two authorities may certainly enter into agreement between themselves, to terminate a contest as to the domains of their respective powers, and to determine the exercise of them. This is the generic idea of the origin of concordats. They are not conventions between two distinct nations, or between the sovereigns of two distinct nations, like international treaties, but they are conventions between two supreme authorities, which, in different orders, rule over the same people—the one in the temporal and the other in the spiritual order. Therefore, they are conventions altogether *sui generis.*

' The two authorities which negotiate such conventions, belonging to two different orders, of which one is inferior and subordinate to the other, it follows that the concordats, although they may be called contracts binding on both sides, so far as *in due proportion* they oblige each of the parties, nevertheless cannot be called binding in the sense of the Regalists, in so far as the conventions might imply a perfect equality in the contracting parties, such as would exist between two parties equal and independent as between themselves. The temporal prince, even as a prince, never ceases to be a subject of the Pontiff. Nor does the political authority of the one cease to be subordinate to the spiritual authority of the other, as the end for which the one rules does not cease to be subordinate to that for which the other rules ' (p. 24).

Going on to state that concordats are particularly concerned with mixed matters, the writer shows that in such affairs the object of a concordat is to fix actual limits of jurisdiction as between the two powers, according to the circumstances of the particular country. Mixed matters, it must be remembered, mean those in which both moral and material interests are involved; such as affect only material interests being temporal, such as involve only moral interests being spiritual, and all into which any moral element enters being at least mixed. The writer proceeds :—

' So far as it affects *purely* temporal things, a concordat may have the nature of a contract, as there is nothing to forbid it. But not so in regard to spiritual things, or to mixed ones, which are also spiritual on account of the spiritual considerations they involve ; for it is simony to enter into a contract with regard to sacred things ' (p. 28).

Then to show that a concordat is not a contract between two princes, but a law given by the superior prince to the inferior in his own land, the definition of Cardinal Tarquini is quoted :— *It is a particular ecclesiastical law, for a certain state, promul-*

gated by the authority of the High Pontiff, at the instance of the local prince, and confirmed by the special obligation of the said prince to maintain it in perpetuity.[1]   The *Civiltá* does not, however, quote Tarquini's words, to the effect that a concordat is to be classed with instruments called privileges.

An illustration of Laveley, in which he imagines the King of France allowing the appointment of the officers of the army to be subject to the King of Spain, is met by saying that no Catholic is a foreigner to the Pope :—

'To be a foreigner to him you must be a foreigner to Christ, whose place the Pope holds, and whose mission he continues upon earth. . . . Do you know what you say when you compare the Pope, in regard to the Catholics of this or that kingdom, to what a temporal sovereign would be to the people of another State ? Catholics, be they French, German, or Spanish, or whatever else, are more subjects of the Pope, as the head of the Church and their spiritual prince, than they are of the king or emperor as the temporal prince ; the ties which bind them as subjects, in the first respect, being, beyond comparison, more intimate and more elevated than those which bind them in the second. It is so by divine ordinance, it having pleased God, the Universal Governor of all, to constitute two authorities in the world for the government of the nations—the one, spiritual, to direct human actions to eternal life; the other, temporal, for the ruling of the same, in order to temporal business and peace among men. . . . As to the comparison respecting officers of the army, if it did prove anything, what do you think it would prove ? It would prove that you cannot concede to the temporal prince any interference whatever, in the nomination of bishops or of other sacred ministers, who are officers of the army of the Church, whose sovereign is not the secular prince, but the Pope' (p. 26).

The next step in this argument brings out a principle which shows how far the idea of sacred things may be extended into what the common political mind would naturally look upon as secular things :—

'Had the matters treated of in the Austrian Concordat been merely temporal, even then the faith of the prince might easily have been engaged, as promoting the spiritual good of his own subjects and in obedience to

---

[1] *Juris Ecclesiastici*, p. 83. In my copy, 4th edition, it is, p. 73, ' Concordatum recte definiatur : Lex particularis ecclesiastica pro aliquo regno Summi Pontificis auctoritate edita ad instantiam principis ejus loci, speciali ejusdem principis obligatione confirmata, se eam perpetuo serviturum.'

Christ the Lord. Having once engaged his faith, he could never with-draw by his own will, both because *the gift conferred upon the Church had in the very act of bestowment taken on a sacred character*, on account of the spiritual end to which it thus became devoted, and also because the prince has not power to withdraw his faith but by an authoritative judgment, and the authoritative judgment belongs to the superior, not to the subject. But the matters concerned were either spiritual or mixed, and therefore directly belonged to the Church itself. . . . The inter-pretation of concordats can only be given by the Pontiff, not by the lay prince, much less can this prince annul them by his own will. . . . Concordats are not contracts (because it is an act of simony to make contracts upon sacred matters), but a particular law made by the Pontiff, and the kind of treaty or convention which is added to the law regards the promise of the prince to procure the execution of it. . Now since the law made by the Pontiff for the spiritual government of a given nation binds that nation, independently of any additional obligation, it is clear that the Hungarians are bound to observe the concordat made by the Pontiff for them also, even though the representatives of the nation have not ratified it. The necessity of ratification by them exists for civil laws, but not for ecclesiastical laws, regarding which no political parliament has authority of any sort. Besides, Hungary would gain nothing by with-drawing herself from the Concordat, for withdrawing from under a par-ticular law she would fall under the obligation of the common law, which is the canon law pure and simple' (pp. 28, 29).

It must be remembered that the Emperor, when he applied his august mind, as we saw Tarquini note, to reform his code under the guidance, not of legists or of courtiers, but of priests (as if they were not both legists and courtiers), was not able to impose his 'evangelical law' on Hungary, but only on his hereditary States. The last word of our last quotation is never, for one moment, to be lost sight of in reading or hearing what Vaticanists say. If we let our English ideas push out of our mind the correct idea which it presents, we read or hear in a maze. The common law is, in the mind of the Church, canon law. That law is as much above national law as the Pope is above the king or president, as much as the Church is above the State.

Another dictum in this article is, 'If the Pope should condemn the fundamental laws of a country, it would be a manifest sign that those laws were erroneous and to be condemned.'

M. Ollivier, who had soberly appealed to the Concordat, as giving real guarantees to the lower of the two parties to it, might well be acceptable to M. Veuillot.

On the anniversary of the Pope's accession, his speech, addressed to the Sacred College, contained the following passage: The two societies of which the world consists, said his Holiness, are, first, the Tower of Pride, *i.e.*, Babel; secondly, the society whose prototype is seen 'in the upper room, on the day of Pentecost, where Peter, the Apostles, and thousands of the faithful of different nations, heard one and the same language and understood it.' Those who wish to form a clear idea of what these two organs of two hostile societies are—the Babel tongue and the Pentecostal tongue—must just keep their eyes open as we go on. (*Civiltá*, VII., vii., p. 130.)

The Pope, on the 25th of June, calling governments before 'his tribunal,' and sitting in judgment, pronounced censure on the governments of Italy, Austria, Spain, and Russia. Italy was discussing a law to subject students even for the priesthood to the conscription. Austria was miserably wronging and injuring the Church. Spain was doing likewise, or worse. And Russia was persecuting the Polish bishops and sending them into exile. The high spirits of the Court at this moment appear in the comments on these sentences. We give a few specimens from the *Civiltá* (VII., vii., p. 135, etc.) :—

'From no other lips could those words burst forth, save from those of him who is set by God as ruler of His Church, with divine power, above all human powers. . . . Only the Pope can thus menace, reprove, and instruct, because he only is set in a region above all human greatness between heaven and earth. . . . When science gloried in being Catholic, and authority in being derived from God, both were, when they spoke, echoes of the word of the Pope. But science and authority have become unchristianised. The Pope has remained what he was—the herald, the oracle of the Lord. . . . The only religion which has the moral liberty of existence from God Himself is the Catholic, and the only worship from which modern liberalism takes away every liberty is the Catholic. The Catholic religion free means, in fact, the use of Canon Law free, the possession and enjoyment of Church property free, the jurisdiction of ecclesiastical ministers free, the rites and ceremonies of religion free, and instruction in the sacred sciences free ' (p. 139).

The article proceeded to show that the Pope had menaced in the same breath one republic, Spain ; two constitutional monarchies, Italy and Austria ; and one absolute monarchy, Russia. This could not be done unless the Pope was king. Then follows a specimen of history as it flourishes under Pius IX. The Roman Emperors used to imprison the Popes, in order to reign in Rome ; and Constantine, *not wishing to imprison* the Pope, abandoned Rome. But a king not Pope, and a Pope not king, never were able to live here together, and never will be able to do so. (*Civiltá*, VII., vii., p. 131, ff.)

Great attention was awakened by the prominence given by the *Civiltá* (p. 210) to a publication of Bishop Plantier, of *Nîmes*. It was 'splendid and profound.' Plantier spoke of the suggestion that the two doctrines of Papal infallibility and the assumption of the Virgin should be defined by acclamation. He alleged that such a mode of definition could be conveniently and infallibly adopted, and asked if the Council should adopt it, what would be the harm ? He ridiculed the idea that the assistance of the Holy Spirit would be given to a decision by vote and not to one by acclamation. The appearance of this in the *Civiltá*, after all that had passed, quickened the fears of the anti-infallibilists and also of the anti-opportunists, lest the Pope should be determined to carry through the definition by acclamation. Plantier declared that the Council would not be a whit frightened by threats to the effect that it would have governments and people against it if it condemned liberty of worship and of the press, with the other vaunted liberties of modern civilisation. This forecast of Plantier was viewed very gravely by the *Literaturblatt* of Bonn (vol. iv., p. 827).

Early in September the bishops of Germany met at Fulda, and issued a collective pastoral. They solemnly deprecated the rumours spread abroad as to the intentions of the Council.

These rumours, however, only echoed the voice of the *Civiltá Cattolica*, and the doubts cast upon their probability soon fell back upon the candour of those who expressed them.   The bishops went on to asseverate that the Council would never define any new doctrine which was not contained in holy writ or in tradition, but would define only principles which were written 'on all your hearts by faith and conscience' (*Friedberg*, p. 276).   The Catholics of Germany took this solemn language in its apparent meaning ; and the persuasion that their bishops would stand fast, and that the Curia would not ride roughshod over such a body, tranquillised most men.   Only ecclesiastics appear to have suspected that the assurance might amount to little more than carefully dovetailed words.   Even the governments seem to have taken comfort from the prospect of such powerful opposition, knowing how pertinacious these same prelates could be.   But Menzel dryly says that they were stubborn with cabinets because they seemed to be afraid of them, but pliant with the Curia, by which they were always browbeaten.

The German bishops, in giving the assurance that nothing but what the faithful believed would be defined, probably hoped that the fact of their having to give such an assurance would weigh, at Rome, as a hindrance to the plans in contemplation. If so, they only furnished one more proof of the truth which we in England have been told by Dr. Newman, that *no pledge from Catholics is of any value to which Rome is not a party.*[1] How easily the language understood by the people of Germany, in one sense, could be turned by the initiated in another, received a shining proof when it was quoted with commendation by Archbishop Manning, in the highest Ultramontane sense. This may have been only a joke at the unfortunate German bishops. If meant as real praise, it was to their reputation a blow in the eye, unfitting them to appear among men whose word can be trusted.[2]   The *Civiltá* elaborately interpreted the

[1] *Letter to the Duke of Norfolk*, p. 14.
[2] *Œcumenical Council and Infy.*, p. 136.

bilingual bishops in its own sense, as a 'triumphant' refutation of the Liberal Catholics (VII., viii., p. 130).

If the German bishops read as little as Dr. Friedrich says they do, they perhaps do not read the *Unità Cattolica*. There is no doubt that it, at least, speaks language agreeable in the highest quarters. In its number for the preceding 1st of May, it commented on the same assurance as having been flung before the French people. 'If the Council,' says this real echo, 'should only define what all believe, the Council would be useless, for in points which all believe all are agreed.' To say, it proceeds, that an Œcumenical Council should express what all the faithful think, is to confound the Teaching Church with the Learning Church. 'The pen falls from our hands, and we have not courage to contend against such nonsense.'

After having put this assurance before their nation, certain of the bishops felt it necessary to address a private appeal to the Pope, drawn up by Dinkel, Bishop of Augsburg, representing the great danger to the Church in Germany which the proposed alterations would involve, and praying him to abandon 'the far-reaching projects which were ascribed to him.'[1] A similar appeal was sent to his Holiness by the prelates of Hungary, in which country a notable commencement had been made in restoring the laity to a part in the management of Church affairs.[2]

In June 1869 a remarkable meeting of Catholic notables was held in Berlin; with an account of which Sepp opens his book. The chair was filled by Peter Reichensperger, since noted for his Ultramontane zeal, and Herr Windhorst, now the Ultramontane leader in the Reichstag, was present, with even Dr. Jörg, of Bavaria, whose allusion, in the winter of 1874, to the attempt of Kullman on the life of Bismarck called forth a remarkable speech from that statesman. These gentlemen, thinking, or professing to think, that their bishops would defeat what the Curia

[1] *Friedberg*, p. 19.
[2] See Lord Acton, *Zur Geschichte.*

had planned, adopted an address expressive of confidence in them, and of their hope that the threatened collision between the Church and their governments and nation might be averted.

Sepp himself went to Prague to present the document to Cardinal Prince Schwarzenberg. The latter read it slowly, thought it over, and said, 'It is far too weak. With Rome you must hold very different language from that.' In further conversation Sepp said to the Cardinal, 'You have in Prague the first canonist in Germany (Schulte), the man who drafted the Austrian Concordat, and surely he can be employed in similar work for the Council.' The reply was: 'You have in Munich the greatest Catholic theologian in Germany, and the gentlemen in Rome will not hear of his being invited' (*Sepp*, p. 4).

In October 1869 the Bishop of Passau addressed a protest to the Central Committee of the Catholic Association, saying that, while pretending to agitate for religion, the Association, influenced from abroad, organised secret clubs, and carefully concealed their movements from the bishops. He was thanked by the King of Bavaria in a private letter, and threatened by the Jesuit organs.[1]

Large numbers of priests had been returned to the Bavarian Parliament, all burning with zeal against Prussia, and against union under it. In 1868 the clerical agitation had gone so far that, in November of that year, President Badhauser, when closing the Landsrath, addressed the members in unwonted language :—

'When the government of the country and its organs, the chamber which represents the people, and the new laws, are daily held up to suspicion, mockery, and contempt, when the peasantry are excited against the townspeople, and when men, throwing off all patriotic shame, feed themselves with hopes of foreign intervention, threatening our German warriors with the chassepots, then must every honourable man condemn such proceedings; for the venom daily instilled will, in time, poison the honest country people, as occurrences in Upper Bavaria, already show.'[2]

---

[1] *Weltbegebenheiten*, i., 330.   [2] Ibid., 336.

Secret associations for Ultramontane objects were formed even among children. Those of the clergy who would have warned the authorities were kept still by secret terrorism. The meeting of the Council and the necessity of overthrowing Prince Hohenlohe were closely connected with this turmoil. And the Liberals plainly said, 'The whole Catholic world is to be fanaticised, to enable the great Catholic powers, after crushing Prussia, as they hope to do, to carry out a grand reaction.'[1]

The *Vaterland* went so far, when Napoleon III. took his last *plebiscite,* as to tell its readers that a French intervention in Germany would soon follow, that it was eagerly looked for, and that all would join France to break the hated yoke of Prussia. Morally, Prussia was already at an end, but it was for France to put an end to her physically. 'Who can tell if we shall have any North German Confederation, Zollverein, or Prussian monarchy in 1871?'[2] Similar hopes of great events often pointed to the year of the Council, or the year after. The *Civiltá* did not scruple to tell Napoleon III. that he owed the new *plébiscite* to Mentana. So far from concealing the Pope's direct action in a question affecting the stability of a throne, his confidential writers exaggerated his influence.

In Austria a struggle had set in against the supernatural order. On the part of the people this struggle was conscious, on that of the Emperor apparently it was somnolent. Yet he was even more interested than any one of the people could be. Laws on civil marriage, education, and registry of baptism were passed by the legislature, and tardily assented to by the Emperor. The Bishop of Linz issued a manifesto saying that he would not acknowledge the new illegitimate laws,—of course under the plea of obeying God rather than man. Turning on the Emperor, he said that he had pledged his faith to the Concordat as a man and as a kaiser. Other prelates, in milder language, set Papal above Austrian law. Finally, as we have already seen, on June 22nd, 1868, the Pope himself laid the

[1] *Weltbegebenheiten,* i., 327.   [2] Ibid., 340.

new laws under his condemnation. While to us that sentence was only a criticism, to the Bishop of Linz it was the judgment of the supreme tribunal, under which kings reign and princes decree justice.

A Catholic meeting against the school law was being held in the church at Schlanders, and while the curate was making a speech Count Manzano, the local authority, declared the meeting closed. Cries of 'Down with him! kill him!' were raised. He was thrown to the ground, beaten on the breast, and barely escaped to the barracks of the gensdarmes.

When the Council was closely approaching, great excitement broke out in Austria against the religious orders. The spark which kindled the blaze was the discovery of a nun confined in the Carmelite convent of Cracow. She had been kept in one cell for twenty years, with incredible privations and in bestial filth. The rage of the public forced the government to go as far as some show of action. Orders were issued for the inspection of convents. Sentences of bishops condemning priests to confinement in ecclesiastical prisons were declared invalid unless the culprit voluntarily consented. The bishops were also required to give in lists of the voluntary prisoners.

These measures were resented as an 'insult to the episcopate.' The Bishop of Brünn won himself an honourable mention in the *Civiltà* by a circular in which he repelled the pretensions of the government, refused the list required, and told the superiors of monasteries to pay no heed to the orders. While this second government was set up, beside that of the country, the voice of Rome cheered it on in taking the upper hand. The same voice railed against the constitutional ministers, the parliament, and the laws.

The combative Bishop of Linz, in a great meeting, said that he did not cast any doubt on the religious feeling of the Emperor, but he was now nothing more than a constitutional sovereign. Instead, therefore, of merely saying that they had confidence in the Emperor, they must come to his aid. This was repeated in Rome, with the explanation that it had been said that the bishop in this appeal for aid to the Emperor was only uttering the sentiments of his Majesty as expressed to the bishop. Thus were bishops commended by the organ of the Papal Court for breaking the laws of their country, and credited with influencing the mind of the sovereign in a sense hostile to the constitution.[1]

The Ultramontane party had frequently, during the year, been encouraged by correspondents in Paris to expect a war of France against Prussia. On March 10th the *Unità* contained a letter expressing fears that Austria and Italy might agree to remain neutral, but quoting a passage from the *Volksbote* in favour of French invasion of Germany. On April 23rd it was said that for a year past the Emperor had allowed no opportunity of rousing the war spirit to pass. A week later a crusading significance was given to the approaching anniversary of Joan of Arc. It was announced that more than twelve archbishops and bishops would attend—among them Cardinal Bonnechose—and that the Empress would grace the scene. On May 1st the fact that the appearance in Paris of Benedetti, the French ambassador at Berlin, was officially said to have no connection with political prospects, was noted for a smile. On the 12th of the same month it was plainly said, 'Every one believes that at the first cannon shot which passes between France and Prussia, a French regiment, as the *Pays* expresses it, will be sent to occupy Belgium.' And on the 13th the display at the festival of Joan of Arc at Orleans, with a great array of prelates, was described as 'one of the noblest ever connected with war and religion, well adapted to excite a nation which aims at uniting the cross with the sword.' On June 19th it was said that the mission of General Fleury to Florence was with reason taken as a sign of approaching war.

Yet, while the Emperor of the French was looked to as leader

---

[1] *Civiltà*, VII., viii., pp. 209 ff.

against the foe whom the Church had marked out for the first victim, every sign of discord in France, every outbreak or disorder, was eagerly paraded as proof of the anarchy to which all countries must come under any regime but that of the Church. At the same time every crime, riot, or difficulty in Italy was magnified and dwelt upon with the same moral. 'Let the Chamber invoke the authority of the Council, and proclaim its canons as the laws of the State,' was the demand of the *Unità* eight months before the Council met (March 21st). And it seems to be a kind of tacit canon, among interpreters of Vatican indications, that the utterances of Don Margotti in Italy, and of M. Veuillot in France, more frequently express the real intentions of the Court than things that fall from more responsible personages. Another saying was, There are three Italys—the Italy of Pius IX., which prays; the Italy of Mazzini, which conspires ; the Italy of Menabrea, which trembles (March 27th). Menabrea was then Premier. Again:—

'The Council is drawing near, and Babylon is trembling, hell is blaspheming, and before long the world will hear the infallible word of truth and righteousness. Hallelujah ! . . . The revolution which for nine years has been bent on marching to Rome is disgraced, senseless, divided. The traitors are betrayed, the robbers plundered, and the rebels plotted against by rebellion. Hallelujah!' (March 28th.)

The *Unità* found that the threefold opposition of governments, rationalists, and heretics showed itself most strongly in May, the month of Mary, which only means that the Immaculate has set her heel on the three heads of the Hydra. Here the mention of governments as one head of the Hydra is no slip of the pen, that is, governments which dwelt in Babylon, as we have just read, or in the Tower of Babel, as it is more frequently expressed. Three days later (May 23rd) the *Unità* cries, 'It is time for Catholics to be up in defence of the Council. It is the only plank of safety for shipwrecked society.' The *Mémoriale Diplomatique* says that 'governments are less and less disposed to interfere in religious questions, unless their rights are infringed ; but such reserve is war against the Council, which *being infallible cannot infringe any right.'* The italics here are our own ; and would that we could print the words on the mind of every rising man in England. That would save vast waste of words.

The courage of the *Civiltá* was stimulated by the French elections in the summer, and its hatred of United Italy boiled over. The ever faithful *Univers* had given the watchword to the electors, ' The temporal power, and liberty of higher instruction ! ' In the cry ' liberty of higher instruction,' we have the popular side of the original call of the *Civiltá* for universities all over Europe, canonically instituted. One hundred and twenty deputies were pledged to the program, and the French electors ought to be proclaimed as having deserved well of Catholicism. ' The illustrious Louis Veuillot,' as the *Civiltá* styles him, had showed that what the Voltairians wanted was the separation of Church and State, from which would follow the decay of Christian worship to such a point that it might be feasible to annihilate it. If the temporal power was done away with, the separation of Church and State would soon follow :—

' Out of this would rise a war worse than civil war, a war of conscience, to be fought out not by discussion but with laws, with irons, with the knife. And for the benefit of whom ? Of Cæsarism, the refuge and the scourge of nations which permit themselves to be separated from God. For France, the fact of the Pope having become a foreign subject would be enough. We should not proceed to the separation of Church and State,—at least, we should not stay at that point long ; we should pass over to the religious system of Russia.'

Noble, Catholic, chivalrous France is contrasted, by the *Civiltá*, with vile Italy. The latter, in a serious catalogue of crimes, is said to have ' reduced the bishops to the extreme of poverty, has at its own caprice impeded the divine word, and showed more than sixty dioceses widowed of their pastors.' The French voters had said, We go to the urn ' as the delegates of the universal suffrage of Christendom.' ' The monstrous edifice of Italian unity must crumble,' says this Romanist, who was no Roman. It is founded on the ruins of the temporal power of the Pontiff, which cannot perish. (VII., vi., 611, ff.)

The plea of the Liberal Catholics for freedom of conscience became more and more offensive to the Catholics. The Fathers of Laach, in censuring the address of the laymen of Coblentz, went so far as to say that the treatment of the Jews in Rome 'showed no want of humanity or civil tolerance.' These educated laymen well knew that the proper condition of heretics, according to the same principles, ought to be much worse than that of the Ghetto Jews. The latter, not being baptized, were theoretically not subject to the jurisdiction of the Church, but the others, as Bellarmine shows, *though not of the Church, belonged to the Church.* Stumpf, writing in the Bonn *Literaturblatt,* did not content himself with questioning the intolerant doctrine of the Jesuits; he directly attacked it. He took an important step further,—one, indeed, which seems like a new life in the Roman Catholic intellect. He told the Jesuits plainly that their exclusive principle of one *fold* rendered religious freedom and unity impossible. Here he touched the distinction between the grand and the huge, which Romanists carefully keep out of sight, and which the sincerest advocates of liberty in their ranks had hitherto overlooked. They took for a grand conception that of the unity of Christians, as consisting in submission to one human head. That conception is narrow and illusory. It fails of grandeur by monstrous disproportion. It is the same thing as making the unity of man consist in submission to one king, a violence to the order of God and to the lofty and blessed truth of a unity lying deeper and reaching higher than any which absolutism can ever confer. Stumpf goes on to declare that the absolute dominion of the Church over the State, although the favourite doctrine, as he admits, in Rome, is in contradiction to the fundamental principle of Christianity. He would no longer be content, as a Liberal Catholic, to plead for freedom of conscience merely as a compromise. He says, We now represent a principle. The theocratic principle menaces society, and that principle will never be satisfied till the acknowledgment of civil rights is made to depend upon the profession of the Catholic faith. He adds that a promise to compromise *till we had the power* would content no one, because the modern world has learned that nothing is settled till the principle is settled. He understands the Jesuit meaning of 'independence,' when the Church is in question, to involve the logical fault of confounding independence with omnipotence. He had clearly in his eye the fact that the two apparent extremes of the Papal and the socialist theories of the State practically meet in the point where one all-absorbing centralised power annihilates the liberty of the individual, and reduces his life to a mechanism. He clearly understands both ideas, and he does not want either. He says, We are determined to have the Church a Church, and the State a State. But this is a postulate which demands, as its condition, individual freedom. This he thoroughly feels, protesting that the individual must be free to fulfil his religious and moral duties in each of the two spheres included within the natural order and the supernatural order, following their respective laws. According to him it was Christ that introduced among men the idea of independence, and that of a limit existing to the power of the State, by distinguishing His own kingdom of love and grace from that of law and compulsion. 'When the Church authorities,' says Stumpf, 'do admonish the rulers of the State, their first counsel should be to consider it their highest duty to protect freedom of conscience. They ought to warn them, before any other kind of unrighteousness, against the use of force, for or against any form of religion which is not inconsistent with the maintenance of moral law;' and he adds, what we shall emphasise, '*privation of civil equality is an employment of force.*' Such, he says, was the counsel given by the early Christian teachers; and though later teachers reversed it, their course is not to be justified before the law of Christ.

Stumpf faces the practical point of the difficulty—Are statesmen to learn Christian principles from standard teachers of Christian morals, and then to apply them in preparing statutes as being themselves responsible before God; or are they to take their instructions in framing laws from the ecclesiastical authorities? He shows that what the *Stimmen* demands is that they should do the latter. That demand he not only contests, but also resents. In that case, he argues, legislators, whenever they had to frame a statute, would have to go to the heads of the Church to seek their directions, and to faithfully carry them out; but, argues Stumpf, it does not follow that because a Church teaches the revealed moral law, she is entitled to pronounce 'authoritatively' upon the righteousness, necessity, or expediency of a law of the State. The word 'Church' here is manifestly used in two senses. That Church which claims to dictate laws to statesmen is nothing more than the bishop representing the Pope. That Church which upholds moral law, on the contrary, includes the Christian judge or minister of State quite as much as the prelate. And in this case the judge or minister is doing the work to which it has pleased God to call him, being set 'for that very thing;' while the minister of the Gospel (if indeed he would not himself consider that description an affront) is leaving his appointed work, the ministry of the Word of God, to do work for which rulers and lawgivers are raised up. The sharp division of the Church into two bodies, the Teaching Church and the Learning Church, is without a shadow of support in holy writ, except that it is the office of some to devote their life to teaching, but such a division is of essential necessity in order to give a foundation for the exclusive jurisdiction of the central power. The *end* of the State, as viewed by Stumpf, is much loftier than that assigned to it in the Papal theory. In the great collection of families called by men a State, he does not see a body politic without a moral mission, existing, according to the ruinous theology of Rome, only for temporal ends,—a body politic which would be unworthy of God or man. According to Stumpf, the end of the State is *the maintenance of general moral order.* This theory does not bind the families of a country, acting in their collective capacity, to prescribe the creed and cult of individuals. No more does it bind them, on the other hand,

to resign all moral aims, leaving every moral question to be
decided for them without any appeal to the common conscience,
to fruits, or to the Bible, by a power which in order itself to
direct the course in every important transaction, would strip the
State of every moral quality, and would also prescribe the creed
and cult of all. The theory of Stumpf holds that the collective
authority of the nation, in the affairs common to all the families
of that nation, is called to regulate action so far as action affects
the common good, but does not hold that it is called to regulate
belief. The separate authority of each house-father, in his own
family, is called to be a terror to evil-doers and a praise to them
that do well. Let but the State fulfil this simple yet glorious
moral end, and it will then secure to all lawful temporal ends the
best opportunity of fulfilling themselves, and will also secure
to the Christian Church all she wants,—room and leave to
lead a quiet and peaceable life in all godliness and honesty,
reclaiming those who do ill, building up those who do well,
and blessing with intercession and with thanksgiving lawgivers and rulers who to her give nought but the greatest of
all boons, good government in the land. Claiming for the
Church the full right of asserting and urging moral principles,
Stumpf, with great solemnity, claims for the legislator freedom to frame law according to his own conscience, and to
his belief in what tends to the maintenance and the perfecting
of moral order. This he has to do without the direction of any
ecclesiastic, but knowing that he must give account to God.
*No omnipotent word of Church authorities can or shall deter us
from this work.* Then he interjects, Would it not be pleasant to
have to consult the theologians of the *Civiltá* and the *Stimmen?*
The Jesuits, he alleges, had no conception of any exercise of
moral power upon one another but in the way of commanding
and obeying. The Church, in the middle ages, by her influence
in secular affairs secularised herself, and lost her moral influence,
which was never recovered to Christianity till the States had
done what the Jesuits call apostatising from Christ, and so

opened the way for a return of true moral Christian influence
The early Church, he truly and nobly points out, was able, in
the face of the omnipotent heathen authorities, to pervade society
with her true moral influences; and he contends that nothing
can give back to the Church her position as the first force in
culture, but the recognition of the independence of the State.

One very curious part of this grave and forceful essay is the
protest of the layman against the twisting of Scripture by the
Jesuits. He puts together a number of the texts upon which
they ring the changes, making them prove their own ideas by
the simple process of putting those ideas into them, and reiterat-
ing them again and again. The first of the texts which he
quotes is, ' Teach all nations.' He, apparently, is not aware that
this is now as handy a weapon with those theologians as ' obey
God rather than man.' In their lips ' teach ' means ' make laws,'
and ' all nations ' means, not *every creature*, but, collectively, all
States. Therefore the words ' *teach all nations* ' are, in the lips
of the Jesuits, a commission to the Pope to give laws to all
countries, or, in highflown language, ' to exercise the supreme
magisterial office.' The Jesuits had saucily told the laymen of
Coblentz to ask the nearest theologian for an explanation of the
relations between the natural order and the supernatural. But
this particular layman gave them as good as they brought.
When men write as he does, they have begun to be Catholics,
have ceased to be Papists, and are, however unconsciously, in
process of ceasing to be Romanists.

The Allocution of June 22nd, in which the constitution and
new laws of Austria were condemned, had proved as distasteful
to Liberal Catholics as it had been agreeable to the Jesuits.
' The Curialistic notion,' says the author of *Reform in Head and
Members*, an Austrian (p. 174), ' that the law of the Church
must be the inviolable rule for all laws and statutes, and
for all and every kind of activity in the life of the State, runs
through it, like a black thread. The Austrian *Magna Charta*

of civil, political, religious, and scientific freedom was called a sacrilegious law. Moreover, the Pope,' he proceeds to say, 'had declared that these laws themselves, together with *all that should arise out of them*, are and ever will be invalid and of no effect. . . . Every enlightened person among the Catholics of Germany and France concealed himself in silence and in mourning at this rude opposition of Rome to the public law of the entire Western world.' Count Beust, in a despatch dated about ten days after the Allocution was delivered, said that 'the Holy See had extended its animadversions to subjects "which we by no means can allow to be under its authority."' We shall hereafter see how clearly and completely Count Beust had now grasped the question as between the Papacy and the life of nations.

As the scholastic basis for the future structure had been in process of elaboration ever since the movement of restoration began, it will repay us to spend a little time in mastering the outline of Cardinal Tarquini's system. It is not very long, and to men who know that principles will in time make institutions, and that treating affairs without understanding ideas is blundering work, it will be interesting. We shall see what in reality is the teaching to which the English public has been strangely pointed as modern and mild—modern, indeed, but carrying the doctrine of the sword and the fagot further than it was carried in abstract propositions by writers of equal rank in old time. While shaping the doctrine by which he wrote his way to the purple, Tarquini might easily have seen that circumstances would often arise in which it would be desirable to keep it back. He can scarcely have foreseen that, almost immediately after his death, he would be represented to the English public by an Englishman, as the modern writer whose mild doctrine on the relations of the civil and temporal authority ought to dispel all idea that Rome held tyrannical or persecuting principles. But the following is the language of Cardinal Manning (*Vatican Decrees*, p. 94) :—

'Our older writers, such as Bellarmine and Suarez, when treating of this subject, had before their eyes a generation of men who always had been in the unity of the faith. Their separation therefore was formal and wilful. Their separation from the unity of the Church did not release the conscience from its jurisdiction ; but if Bellarmine and Suarez were living at this day, they would have to treat of a question differing in all its moral conditions. What I have here laid down is founded upon the principles they taught applied to our times. Cardinal Tarquini, in treating the same matter, has dealt with it as it has been treated here.'

Another of the sayings of Cardinal Manning, as to the civil and ecclesiastical authority, is, 'It is mere shallowness to say that between the civil authority, as divinely founded in nature, and the spiritual authority of the Church there can be opposition.'[1] Any jurist who will weigh the principles of Tarquini which were before the Cardinal will be able infallibly to fix the sense in which there can be no opposition between the two authorities. The principle whereon perfect harmony may be established was well indicated when the *Civiltá* refuted the pretensions of the State to hear appeals from the ecclesiastical courts, or to hear causes arising out of complaints as to some alleged abuse of the authority of the sacred ministry. It alleged that a pretension to such a right rested on the political error of supposing that the State was the only social power.

'This,' continues the *Civiltá*, 'is entirely false. Human society is also subject to the religious authority of the Church, and to its authority much more than to that of the State. For, absolutely speaking, the individual and the family are not under any moral obligation to enter into and to continue in the body politic ; but on the other hand it is most strictly the duty of every man, of every family, and of every nation, to enter into and to continue in the society of the Catholic Church, and to be subject to the authority of its supreme head, under pain of eternal damnation ' (VII., ii., 285).

THE DOCTRINE OF THE PERFECT SOCIETY.

The idea of the Perfect Society is the central one around which the Jesuits construct the fabric of their cosmopolitan system. According to Tarquini (*Institutiones*, p. 3), any company of men, joined together for the attainment of one end, is a Society ; and any such company forms a Perfect Society, if it possesses *within itself means sufficient for the attainment of its end.*

[1] *Vat., Dec.. 46.*

Perfect Societies are among themselves divided into different orders, according to their end. Any Society, the *end* of which is subordinate to that of another Society, is of an order subordinate to the order of the other. Every Perfect Society lawfully claims to have in its possession means necessary to the attainment of its own end. If it be of a superior order, *it may claim those means from a Society of an inferior order;* but if of an inferior, it cannot claim them from a Society of a superior order. Every Perfect Society embraces within itself three powers—the LEGISLATIVE, the JUDICIAL, and the COMPULSORY (p. 8). The power it has over its own members consists in the right of *requiring everything that is necessary to the attainment of its end.* These three powers provide for the three necessary elements of government, namely, propounding the means to the end in an obligatory form (*i.e.,* making laws), applying the means so propounded in the way and in the sense in which they were propounded, compelling, by the use of force, those who refuse to apply them, and checking those who hinder. No Society has any legislative power, *as touching the things of a superior order,* unless it may be *to forward the execution of what has been already determined by him to whom the care of the superior order is committed* (p. 9). It is repugnant to the notion of a law that its acceptance by the people should be necessary to give it the force of law (p. 11). Suarez is quoted as saying that acceptance by the people cannot be required for any reason except two : first, that the power of the prince is imperfect, he having, through the peculiar constitution of his Society, received it under a condition of dependency (*i.e.,* he acts under a constitution), or else because he is, out of gentleness, disinclined to use his absolute power. Tarquini defines a merely arbitrary power as *one without the capability of compulsion.* Of two societies, constituted of the same members, the one which is of an inferior order, that is, which has an end of an inferior order, ought as such to serve the Society which is of the superior order at the least negatively. It ought also to serve it positively in that which the Society of a superior order demands as necessary to its own ends. A Society of a superior order ought to afford aid to the one of inferior order, in so far *as the nature of its own end demands;* but otherwise it is not bound to do so. Negative service is rendered when an inferior Society does not pursue its end so as to offer any impediment to the end of the superior one. The inferior Society cannot, by any right of its own, claim the service of the superior Society. Co-ordinated Societies Tarquini defines as those which are so connected one with another that the end of the one Society is in the nature of means to the end of the other (p. 21). When two Societies are thus co-ordinate, the subordinate is bound, as far as possible, to aid the chief one ; but the chief one is not at all bound to aid the other, unless its own end requires such aid. Two equal Societies would be two which had an equal end ; and when two Societies come into conflict, that one ought to prevail the end of which is the higher (p. 22). The true notion of a Society is that the end is tho predominating element, and the means a subservient one (p. 24). Again, it is not true that the Society ought to prevail which is based upon necessity, and that to give way which is based only upon utility (p. 25). In case of conflict, the right of final judgment belongs to the superior Society; that is, to the one that has the superior end (p. 27). No two Societies can be absolutely supreme (p. 28). *Absolute* supremacy is distinguished from the supremacy of a Society *in its own order*, which is the supremacy it has over minor Societies, or companies, included within itself, and of its own order. [That is, the supremacy of the State over guilds, companies, municipalities, or families.] The conclusion is, first, that the Church is the Perfect Society (p. 30); secondly, that, in relation to others, it is the Society of a superior order, and altogether supreme. Anticipating the objection, though not formally raising it, that the Church has not within herself all the means that Rome claims as necessary to her ends, Tarquini says that any Society has those means if it possesses them virtually, though not really. 'Virtually' he explains to mean that it can, in its proper right, claim those means from another Society, and that the other Society has no authority to deny it, or by its own judgment to determine the matter (p. 30). Any Society, he says, which by its nature is supreme, and is not subordinate to another, is perfect in its nature, and hence ought to have all the means for the attainment of its end within itself. It is absurd that the Supreme Society should be subordinate to another, or should depend upon it. That Society is supreme of which the end is supreme; but the end of the Church is supreme, *ergo*, etc. That Society is not subordinate to another, the end of which is not subordinate to another end ; but the end of the Church is not subordinate to another end, *ergo*, etc. (p. 31).

Tarquini proceeds to demonstrate the superiority of the ecclesiastical society over the civil society, that is, of the Church over the State. The definition of the duties of the State, which affirms that it is *to moderate and defend all the rights of its citizens*, is rejected, as containing more vices than one (p. 45). Such a definition would lead, Tarquini says, to the inference that the State is to protect *all* the rights of its subjects ; hence, even their religious rights. Out of this would arise the error that if any one thought himself injured by an ecclesiastical court, he might appeal to a civil one.

The State is not to hold itself passive as to all matters which pertain to religion and probity. Care for these affects even temporal happiness; but the State is to care for them only in the manner which God has appointed, namely, *in dependence upon the Church* ; otherwise its power would be disorderly. Therefore the true definition of the duties of the State is that it has *directly only the care of temporal happiness, but indirectly the duty of defending religion and probity, yet in dependence upon the Church* (p. 47).

Civil societies are arranged in three categories: 1. Those which obey the Church, or Catholic societies; 2. Those which are indeed under its power, but separated from it, that is, heretical societies; 3. Those which are exempt from its power, that is, societies of the unbaptized (p. 47). Of course the word ' society' here means ' nation.' Under the first head, it is stated that a Catholic civil society, or nation, is composed of the same persons as the Church itself. *It does not form a different body.* The same men composing both societies seek temporal happiness under the civil magistrate, and eternal under the direction of the Church. A Catholic civil society is, therefore, a company of men who so pursue temporal happiness that they confess it to be subordinate to the pursuit of eternal, which they believe to be attainable only under the government of the Catholic Church.

The Church has no power in civil society in temporal things *taken in respect to the temporal end.* The reason of this is that the temporal end is outside of the end of the Church. Therefore in temporal things, *when they relate to the temporal end*, even a Catholic society is independent of the Church. Tarquini quietly asserts that when the Fathers spoke of the independence of the State, they meant it only in this sense. Having thus limited the independence of the State to actions that have no relation to the spiritual end—which is, in fact, limiting it to actions that have no moral quality—he proceeds to define the powers of the Church.

The Church, according to him, rightfully exerts her power in all affairs, even though they be temporal, in which, either by their own nature or by accident, the spiritual end becomes involved, and civil society ought to yield to the Church (p. 49). The proof of this is the one with which we are already familiar—that a Society with an inferior end ought to yield to one with a superior end. Therefore, in all such affairs as would involve conflict between the temporal end of the civil society and the eternal end of the spiritual, the civil ought to yield to the spiritual.

Then follows the usual argument about obeying God rather than man. We may pause to remark that this pocket-pistol which the Jesuits always carry about, is no lawful weapon of theirs. *It was not*, as Liberal Catholics point out, *to the civil authority that Peter made that reply, but to the ecclesiastical.* He made it on a question relating exclusively to faith and worship, and not relating to any civil institution or law of the temporal government. Moreover, in making it, he directly rejected the ecclesiastical authority,—he who, in the eye of ecclesiastical law, was a mere layman. The ecclesiastical authorities attempted to bind Peter's religious freedom, by their ecclesiastical censures, without the warrant of divine law. He appealed from them to God. That appeal is the charter of private judgment, the charter of appeal from the tribunal of priests to the Almighty. It is a strange case to choose as furnishing the charter for priests to take the law into their own hands and to set aside the rulers and the tribunals of their nation, in subserviency to a guild of political priests in another country. Peter did not claim to be exempted from the law of the Emperor, nor did he claim, if he broke it, to be exempted from its penalties. He did protest against the attempt of priests to shackle his rights, as secured by the Bible. Moreover, the priests wished it to be assumed that their deeds were *irreformable.* ' You intend,' cried they, ' to bring this man's blood upon us.' They had done the deed, and it was to be taken as well done. But Peter did not believe in their infallibility. They had no divine warrant for gagging him. The civil law had not given them the right to do so. He stood upon his double freedom, under the Bible and under the constitution ; and, furthermore, the signs he wrought showed that God was with him, while the additional but equally divine proof arose of obedience to law increased by the influence of his doctrine. Teachers whose disciples are practically found harder to govern than other populations or other sections of the population are stamped, by the hand of Providence, as a social blight.

Tarquini next goes over the usual round of Church authorities teaching that the State must be subject to the Church, as the body to the soul. He spends considerable strength in refuting a conclusion often drawn from the words of St. Optatus, who said *that the Church is in the State, not the State in the Church.* Texts of Scripture in Jesuit hands often go in at one end of a set of paragraphs with their natural meaning, and come out at the other end with a meaning exactly opposite. So this much-cited patristic saying comes out of Tarquini's paragraphs thus :—' It is plain, Optatus denies that the Church exists in a State where the doctrines of the regalists prevail.'[1] Another conclusion is that what Optatus did affirm amounted to saying, ' The Church needs the protection of the State against her enemies, not the State that of the Church.' This is orthodox doctrine, not tainted with the errors of the regalists (p. 56).

Our author denies that the Church is *formally* in the State, and does not admit that it is in it even *materially.* It cannot be in it formally, because the end of the Church cannot be contained in that of the State. He cannot admit that it is materially in the State, because the Church embraces the whole world, and further, in the mind of God, the framer of both societies, the Church is prior to civil society. Therefore it should rather be said *that the State is in the Church, not the Church in the State* (p. 57). Tarquini meets the assertion that the Empire was constituted before the Church, and in full possession of liberty, and that therefore it ought not to be disturbed in its possession, by asserting that the Empire did not exist before the Church, which had been constituted from the

---

[1] The words quoted from Optatus are, *Non enim Respublica est in Ecclesia sed Ecclesia in Republica est,* id est in imperio Romano. . . . Ubi et sacerdotia sancta sunt et pudicitia et virginitas quæ in barbaris gentibus non sunt et si essent tuta esse non possent (p. 53). Tarquini assumes that Optatus denies that the Church exists in barbarous States, whereas the latter only says either that such and such institutions of the Church do not exist in them, or cannot exist in safety.

beginning of the world, and also that it was false to say that before Christ the Empire possessed the liberty asserted by the objectors (p. 58). As to the right of previous possession, he argues that in speaking of the Church you speak of a divine institution. What then? Would you set up a right of previous possession as against God? Hence he regards the complaint that the State, in entering the Church, is curtailed in its civil rights, as unreasonable; for no one cares about resigning some slender rights in return for great advantages, and the advantages secured to princes in entering the Church are so great that what they have to resign is not to be compared with them. He denies that the Church, even when taken distributively, is part of the State. If that were the case, the Church would have as many bodies as there are nations. Moreover, as the Church is a society diverse from civil society by reason of the diversity of its end, and much more excellent, it is absurd to call it a part of it.

The objection that in the Jewish religion priests were obedient to the temporal rulers, is met by saying that the end of the Jewish religion was not purely spiritual, but also included the temporal end of instituting a nation which should procure temporal happiness. The further objection that the priests of the heathen were subject to the kings, is first treated as an insult to the Christian religion. Next it is affirmed (p. 61) that the whole aim of the heathen priesthood and worship was temporal good, and as that lies within the sphere of the king, it was fitting that the priests should be subject to him.

Afterwards follows the proposition that the supremacy of the Church over civil society springs out of her nature and out of the divine will; and who will say that this can be abrogated or changed by human facts? This is advanced in reply to the objection that the authority of kings in ecclesiastical matters had often been recognised by Christian bishops. If they recognised it when power had' been delegated to the kings by the ecclesiastical authority, the recognition was just; if otherwise, it was unjust. When, for example, Emperors acted at the request of Pontiffs, or embodied in edicts what the canons had already decreed, the power of the State legitimately came to the support of the Church. The same may be said also of certain edicts of .the kings of France, which were really framed by the bishops themselves.

Then follows the demand that, in doubtful cases, the right of the Church must be preserved *to define what matters really belong to the category of religious matters.* This comes in direct connection with the affirmation that the State cannot be atheistic, which is defined as being indifferent in religious matters. We do not remember that Tarquini ever notes the distinction made by Phillips between an *indifferent* State—that is, one which, like America, does not establish any form of religion—and an *atheistic* one, which would to us be one like France at a certain stage in her great Revolution. For the purpose of the Roman author, the two cases appear to differ so little, as not to be worth distinguishing from one another.

As the State cannot be indifferent, it follows *that civil society is by all means bound to lend physical force to the Church when she requires it for her own necessities,* even though the physical force of society may have passed from individual hands into those of its head. It has passed, carrying its obligations with it ; those, namely, which bind all individuals to give to the Church, whose members they are, whatever is necessary for her, and therefore even physical force (p. 63).

The Christianity of physical force, which Liberal Catholics had hoped to supersede by a Christianity superior to the use of such a power, just as a steamer is superior to that of the animal force of oarsmen, instead of being disavowed by modern Rome, was being rehabilitated both by popular pens in her journals and by scientific writers like Tarquini, and spread with new vigour of argument and enthusiasm.

Even in supplying physical force the prince is not to be free. He is so to defend religion that he shall not anticipate the judgments of the Church, but follow them (p. 65). It is urged that it must be evident that members of the Church, in granting her things necessary for her, are bound to do so, not according to their own judgment, but according to that of her head. *Only the Church can know* what belongs to religious affairs and what promotes the good of religion. Therefore should the prince, in defending religion, anticipate the judgment of the Church, he might easily invert the due order of the subordination of temporal to spiritual ends. As he who sacrifices when he is not a priest commits sacrilege, so does he violate order who disposes of any matter which has not been committed to his charge. Further, as the navigator who determines the ultimate end of the ship gives command to the ship-builder how to construct it, and as the citizen who determines the ultimate end of the weapon gives command to the smith what kind of weapon he shall make, so ought the Church, to whose end 'that of the State is subordinate, to command the State in all things which affect eternal salvation (p. 67).

The reply of Tarquini to the objection that it is not well that man should be compelled by the kingly power to obey the Church, is candid, and when taken in the strict and scientific sense in which it was written, shows exactly under what conditions the Church can suffer a prince to allow religious toleration in his States. ' Account is to be taken of the circumstances of the State. If they are such as *to* forbid the use of power, such toleration is to be shown as is often shown in permitting other crimes (*malefactis*), provided always that the prince holds himself passive and negative, and does not approve anything contrary to the good of the Church' (p. 67).[1]

The breach of ' unity' is thus shown to be a crime ; but if the attempt to suppress this crime by force would endanger the throne of a Catholic prince, or threaten the Church with other evils greater than that of

[1] Quoted by Tarquini from *Auctor de Regin. Prin.*, lib. i., c. 15.

tolerating the crime itself, the moral possibility of the prince resorting to force is taken away, and with the moral possibility goes the obligation. Hence, as any other crime that cannot be put down must be tolerated, so must heresy; but let the circumstances change, and the possibility arise of applying force with success, then with the moral possibility comes back again the moral obligation; and the prince is bound, whenever the Church calls for it, to use his physical force towards all baptized persons. Tarquini, in a note, gives the following summary of principles as to toleration: 1. In the absence of a positive law, toleration is illicit, for two reasons, because it is wicked to co-operate in the superstitions of the heterodox, and because it is wicked to expose Catholics to the dangers of seduction. 2. In order to justify toleration, the same conditions are required as those which would justify co-operation in the sin of another, or such conditions as are commonly held by theologians to render it lawful to expose oneself to the occasion or danger of sin. 3. Nothing is to be determined in this matter without consulting the Pope, both because it touches a weighty question as to the state of the Church, concerning which only the Pope can judge, and also because civil toleration is prohibited by ecclesiastical law. 'Finally, the propositions condemned by our most holy lord, Pius IX., in the Syllabus are to be kept before the eye. They are the seventy-seventh and the eightieth.'

We presume that the obligation to consult the Pope applies both to the case of granting toleration where it did not exist, and to that of abolishing it where it did exist. In our own day instances of both kinds have occurred. The censures of the Popes against those who granted toleration are facts of history. Where are the instances of his censures against any government for doing away with toleration? They exist, but always when the intolerance, real or alleged, was directed against Romanists.

The objection that, by teaching intolerance towards heretics, while claiming liberty for herself, the Church uses a double measure, is met by Tarquini in a straightforward manner. He denies that she refuses *any real right* to the heterodox while claiming it for herself. He admits that she does refuse to the heterodox rights which *belong exclusively to the truth, and are incommunicable to error.* Lunatics cannot have the same rights as sane persons, not even because they do not think themselves lunatics. We have to look at three things: the conscience of the Church, that of the heretics, and the matter in itself.

The conscience of the Church assures her, on divine testimony, that she holds the truth, and that heretics err. As to the conscience of the heterodox, if they are sincere, they will have the same rights as lunatics, to whom the things they do in their madness are not imputed. As to the matter itself, the marks and tokens of the case are so manifest that there is no just person who ought not to recognise the rights of the Church. Heretics either do or do not weigh seriously, and with right intention, the evidences of credibility displayed by the Catholic Church and those of falsity attaching to their own sects. If they do not weigh them, their ignorance cannot be consistent with good faith. If they do weigh them, still less can it be admitted that they persist in their error in good faith. No one is entitled to acquit them before man on the ground of their good faith. Therefore every pretext vanishes for the charge, that in denying them the liberty she claims for the truth, the Church measures with two rules.

Under the special head of jurisdiction over heretics, what Tarquini says is short but not sweet. The one all-important point is, *heretics are bound by the ecclesiastical laws.* The proof of this is that they are baptized. This proof is confirmed by the consideration that no one is released from the obligation of the law because of his own crime. And it is only because of their own crime that heretics are outside of the Church, *ergo*, etc. It is further confirmed by the consideration that if heretics are not subject to the jurisdiction of the Church, they cannot be punished by her for their heresy ; but (as Bellarmine, who has carefully expounded this doctrine, shows) they can be punished by her for their heresy, *ergo*, etc. Therefore, he adds, Bellarmine said correctly that heretics *were not of the Church but belonged to the Church*, both because they are subject to her jurisdiction, and because they are under obligation to return to her. He shows, of course, that there may be circumstances in which the exercise by the Church of her rights over heretics would do harm instead of good, and in such cases the Church must be held to wish heretics not to be bound by her will.

Protestants sometimes speak as if the principles of the Papacy bound its followers to persecute under all circumstances. By no means. The principles of war do not bind a general to attack when, by all the rules of war, that course would lead to the injury of his cause. And just so with the Papacy.

CHAPTER X.

Conflicting Manifestoes by Bishops—Attacks on Bossuet—Darboy—Dupanloup combats Infallibility—His relations with Dr. Pusey—Deschamps replies—Manning's Manifesto—Retort of Friedrich—Discordant Episcopal Witnesses.

IN November 1869 the Bishop of Versailles, writing of Bossuet, said that the fame of the Eagle of Meaux was from day to day declining (*Friedberg*, p. 81). This was but a symptom of the new war against nationalism. Professor Ceccucci, though writing for a French audience, did not scruple to say, ' If Bossuet escaped excommunication, he owed it to the benign and paternal indulgence of the Holy See ' (*Frond,* iv., p. 112). Bishop Dupanloup soon took occasion to show that Innocent XI. sent Bossuet two briefs congratulating him on having written in a manner calculated to win back heretics and increase the propagating power of the Church.[1] And, as we have seen, Bishop von Ketteler could at this very time utilize the name of Bossuet in Germany. If the Church, even before infallibility had been proclaimed, began to be so conscious of its narrowness that it could hardly contain Bossuet, what will it be when a few centuries more have passed over it ?

As the opening of the Council drew nearer, feeling grew warmer in political and religious circles. Archbishop Darboy sketched the impending dangers in a pastoral :—

' You have been told that articles of faith which hitherto you have not been bound to believe, are to be imposed upon you ; that points affecting civil society and the relations of Church and State are to be treated in a spirit opposed to the laws and usages of the age ; that a certain vote is to be carried by acclamation ; that the bishops will not be free, and that the minority, even if eloquent, will be treated as an opposition, and will soon be put down by the majority. . . . It must be owned that much has been done to spread these alarms by writers taking different sides.'[2]

Bishop Dupanloup, when about leaving home for the Council, published a memorable letter. He seemed to regard the desire of the French clergy for centralisation as the origin of the cry for a dogma. The change, however, from a national to a Papal spirit was natural. Was it likely that youths from the schools of the Christian Brothers, passed through an episcopal seminary, would comprehend the national spirit and episcopal convictions of Darboy or even of Dupanloup ?[3] The lower education of

---

[1] Letter as printed in *Otto Mesi,* p. 413, and now (but also in French) in *Eight Months at Rome,* p. 277.

[2] *Friedberg,* p. 287.

[3] The author of *Reform in Head and Members* says (p 156): The theological lecture-rooms of the Sorbonne are empty, and the fame and splendour

the country had been just long enough in the hands of Rome to begin to bear fruit. Dupanloup meant no ill to France when he succeeded in binding Louis Philippe to Gregory XVI. by inducing him to give the priests their way in schools, in return for forbearance in baptizing the Comte de Paris, as the son of a mixed marriage, and of a mother who refused to abjure her Protestantism. But he then did one of the most hurtful deeds to France, and to the future of European peace, that man could have done.

'This letter,' cries Sambin, ' gave an episcopal head to the revolt ; . . . the objection was pointed against the opportuneness of defining the dogma of infallibility, but it was hardly possible to be deceived—the principle of infallibility itself seemed to be attacked. . . . The acts of the sovereign Pontiff were presented in a light so far from the truth, that a feeling of profound astonishment passed through the ranks of pastors and people. They were grieved to see the paling away of the triple halo which had hitherto hovered around the author's brow' (*Sambin*, p. 49).

This was published in France in 1872, after Dupanloup had ' submitted,' and rendered new and conspicuous service to the Papacy. As Dupanloup's pamphlet will be hard to find hereafter, and as it is a representative document, we may give a general idea of the argument it presents.

For two years, says Dupanloup, thousands of printed papers have been circulated in the streets, containing a vow to believe in the personal infallibility of the Pope. Agents have got them signed by persons who did not understand the first word of the question.

He contrasts the confidence and freedom of speech granted to the *Civiltà* and the *Univers* with the secrecy observed toward bishops. Naming Manning and Deschamps as the leaders in the agitation for the new dogma, he adds, ' I say new, because

of France in theological science, in which she once took so high a place, have been extinguished, since the clergy began to receive their education—that is, as much education as was indispensable—in the smaller episcopal seminaries, and their theological training in the greater ones. There is no theological science at all in France now.' He supports this broad assertion by details given by Bouix, a well-known Ultramontane writer.

for eighteen hundred years the faithful have not, on pain of ceasing to be Catholics, been bound to believe it.' Alluding to the freedom which, it was said, the bishops would have in the Council, he asks what freedom was left to them even now, when any who expressed an unwelcome opinion were denounced in the papers, beforehand, as schismatics or heretics. . . . 'After having taught for eighteen hundred and seventy years, the Church is now to come and ask in a Council, Who has the right of teaching with infallibility? . . . When the oak is twenty centuries old, digging to find the parent acorn under the roots is the way to shake the tree.'

The Bishop proceeds, with tact and great earnestness, to plead for the necessity of moral unanimity in defining new dogmas. He relates a fact of interest, and one very closely affecting the person of Pius IX. We have seen that, in 1864, the Pope formally initiated official preparations for the Council; that he had long before 1867 decided important questions as to its constitution and procedure; that he had set commissions to work, consulted bishops in different countries, and ordered nuncios to select theologians; and that it was only political perplexity which prevented the assembly of 1867 from being the General Council.

Yet Bishop Dupanloup, whether then aware of these facts or not, makes the following statement, in which the appeal to the testimony of other bishops as eyewitnesses would rather encourage the impression that he felt as if the statement—very simple if the fact stood alone—was liable to be called in question, because of some relation it might have to other facts :—

'I well remember, and more bishops than one who were present in Rome in 1867 can recall, the fact that one of the most serious anxieties of Pius IX., before deciding on holding the Vatican Council, was, lest questions should arise calculated to provoke stormy discussions, and divisions in the episcopate. But the Pope remembered the sagacious conduct of the Council of Trent and of Pius IV., and proceeded, in the hope that it would not be forgotten at the future Council.'

One of Dupanloup's solemn sayings is, ' I have read and

read again the catechism of the Council of Trent, on purpose to find if it spoke Yes or No about the infallibility of the Pope ; I have ascertained that it does not say a word about it.'

Again, he states that in 1867 one hundred and eighty-eight Anglican ministers wrote to the Pope asking for the basis of a union. In his reply, the Pope spoke of the authority of the Church and the supremacy of the Pope, but he did not speak of his infallibility. Yet journalists, screening themselves behind his name, tried to shut the mouths of bishops by attacks full of violence and gall. This was meant for M. Veuillot, who was not slow to reply.

As to Greeks and Protestants, Dupanloup points out that what is proposed amounts to telling them, ' A ditch now separates us ; we are going to make it an abyss. . . . Two years ago, Dr. Pusey said to me in Orleans, " There are eight thousand of us in England, daily praying for a union." ' . . . When Pitt thought of relaxing laws against Catholics in England and Ireland, he asked several learned bodies what was the real doctrine of the Roman Church on the power of the Pope. ' I have under my eyes the replies of the Universities of Paris, Douay, Louvain, Alcala, Salamanca, and Valladolid.' They all ' answer expressly that neither the Pope nor the Cardinals, nor yet any body or individual in the Roman Church, hold from Jesus Christ any civil authority over England, any power to re-lease the subjects of his Britannic Majesty from their oath of fide-lity.' Such doctrine was calculated to reassure Pitt, as against the contrary doctrine, professed in celebrated Bulls by more Popes than one. But what if the Pope be declared infallible ?

As to Catholic governments, their standing jealousy of the ecclesiastical power would be increased. Had not Boniface VIII. taught that the temporal sword also belonged to Peter, and that the spiritual power had a right to institute and judge the tem-poral? Had not Paul III. released all the subjects of Henry VIII. from their oath of allegiance, offered England to any one who would conquer it, and given all the goods of the dissident English, real and personal, to the Conqueror? Was not that Bull a great misfortune to Christendom? 'I am sad—and who would not be sad?—in recalling these great and painful historical facts; but they force us to it,—those whose levity and rashness have stirred these burning questions.' After the dogma shall have been proclaimed, he contends that from the point of view occupied by governments, 'all civil and political rights, like all religious belief, will be in the hand of a single man.' The journals which claim to be purest in their Romanism 'treat the doctrine, so strongly held by the Catholic sovereigns, as well as others, that each of the two powers is independent in its own sphere, as tainted with atheism.'

The following passage in the Bishop's argument suffices to show that there may be more senses of the statement that Catholics do not owe any divided allegiance, than plain English folk ever dreamed of in their philosophy:—

'We lately read, as quoted with praise in a French paper, the following, which compares those to the Manicheans who deny that the two swords are in the same hand : "Are there two sources of authority and power, two supreme ends for the members of the same society, two different objects in the intention of the Being who orders all, and two distinct destinies in one and the same man, who is both member of a Church and of a State? Who does not see the absurdity of such a system? It is the dualism of the Manicheans, if not atheism." '

We ought to interject the remark that 'the two swords in the same hand' is not strict but popular language. The two are in the same *power*, but only one is in the spiritual hand. Again, the taunt of Manicheism frequently falls from Jesuit pens. Boniface VIII. set the example of calling people something like Manicheans, if they believed in any supreme power in princes on a level with that of the Pope.

Coming to the crucial question, What is speaking *ex cathedrâ*? Bishop Dupanloup shows that the diversity of doctrine on this point is almost endless, and perplexing beyond belief. The lay Professor of Theology in the seminary of the Archdiocese of Westminster, Dr. Ward, formerly an Anglican minister, goes

beyond the great majority. They hold that a condition necessary
to an infallible utterance is that the Pope shall address the whole
Church, but Dr. Ward thinks that this is not necessary.   The
majority think that the intention of binding the belief of the
faithful must be clearly expressed, but Dr. Ward again thinks
that it need not be so.   Phillips, the German doctor, holds
that the Pope need not consult a Council, the Roman Church,
the Cardinals, or any one ; nor is it necessary that he should
maturely deliberate or carefully study the matter by the light of
God's written word and of tradition, or even that he should put
up a prayer to God before pronouncing sentence.   ' Without any
one of these conditions,' says the Bishop, ' his decision would not
be less valid, authentic, or obligatory on the whole Church, than
if he had observed every condition dictated by faith, piety, and
good sense.'   He adds the words of Phillips, that the definition
ex cathedrâ may be verbal or written, and with or without
anathema, but must be given by him to all believing Christians
as Vicar of Jesus Christ, in the name of the Apostles Peter and
Paul, or in virtue of the authority of the Holy See, or in other
similar terms.   The Church, he says, according to Phillips, has
no right to fix any condition or restriction whatever.   We do
not remember these words in Phillips, but if only an inference,
they are perfectly fair.[1]

Citing the cases of Popes Stephen VI., Honorius, and Pascal II.,
Dupanloup shows that heavy facts obstruct the historical path
to the new dogma.

He proceeds to point out that the difference between the
universal infallibilists and the dogmatical infallibilists is very
grave.   The former argue that the dogma, if adopted in the sense

---

[1] Phillips says (*Kirchenrecht*, 2 Band, 3rd Edition, p. 305), ' Why must
we wait for a Council as for a new Messiah, when the representative of Messiah
has come already ? Again (p. 339), ' A General Council may be called or not, but
it alters nothing as to the infallibility of the Pope.'   As to the possibility of the
Pope deciding without reflection, consultation, reading, or prayer, the words of
this oft-cited Doctor are (p. 342) :—' If he neglects to do so, he burdens himself
with guilt, but nevertheless his judgment has just the same force and validity,
and, hence, it is perfectly obligatory on the whole Church.'

of the latter, would involve a peril. A Pope infallible in some cases and fallible in others is, they think, a contradiction. If, as a private teacher, the Pope should err in doctrine, might he not impose his error on the Church? If this is not possible, you have either a Pope who thinks one thing and defines another, or a perpetual miracle! And why distinguish, ask the universal infallibilists, when Christ has not distinguished? 'That thy faith fail not'—that means the faith of Peter in every sense, personal and pastoral. These theologians contend that a Pope could not, even if he would, fall into an error, public or private.

As to the effect of the change on the episcopate, Dupanloup contends that Councils will be rendered superfluous. Hitherto, the bishops have been judges of the faith, real judges, though in union with the Pope,—co-judges, as was said by Benedict XIV. But if the proposed change is made, their judgment before or after will be of little account; as Monsignor Manning has said, the Pope can determine 'without the episcopate, and independently of it.' The bishops, he proceeds, are now Doctors, not mere echoes. With the Pope they constitute the Teaching Church. After the change they will not be a voice, only an echo. Again, he proceeds, 'where Peter is there is the Church,' does not mean that the Pope is the Church, but that he is the head of it. In divisions, we know where the Church is by where the Pope is. Thus we know that the Greek or Anglican Church is not the Church of Jesus Christ, because the Pope is not with them.

Drawing a glowing picture of the services of the French bishops to the Papacy, he says :—

'Ah ! ·I dare to affirm that so much devotion to Rome and to the Catholic world gives to the Church of France the right to be trusted, to be heard.' He adds, anticipating his arrival in Rome, 'I shall no sooner touch the sacred ground, no sooner kiss the tomb of the Apostles, than I shall feel myself in peace, out of the battle, in the midst of an assembly presided over by a father and composed of brethren. There the noises will all die away, the rash interferences will cease, the indiscretions will disappear, the winds and waves will be calmed down.'

The statement, frequently repeated, that Bishop Dupanloup in this letter admitted the doctrine, and contested only the opportuneness of defining it, is incorrect. This was pointed out at the time by Dr. Reusch, of Bonn, in the *Literaturblatt.* Dupanloup once or twice says that he will not touch the question of its truth, one way or the other. He never, directly or indirectly, indicates belief in it. Many of his arguments more than indirectly oppose the very substance of the doctrine. He plainly feels that it is unscriptural, uncatholic, and unwise; but he knows that it is and has long been gospel in Rome.

Bishop Dupanloup was replied to by Archbishop Deschamps, of Malines. Monsignor Deschamps was following the straight path to the purple. He roundly lectured Dupanloup. 'Why should not that trouble me which rejoices the enemies of the faith and of the Church?' 'You have committed an error, Monsignor,' he says, repeatedly. He correctly states that Dupanloup has not confined himself to the question of opportuneness. 'You have handled the principal question, . . . your fears have disturbed your vision.'[1] Dupanloup prepared a rejoinder to Deschamps, but was prevented from publishing it by circumstances which taught him that in leaving France for Rome he had not passed from disturbance to tranquillity, but from regulated conflict to all-triumphant violence, compelling inaction, unless action was on its own side. In Rome, where any movement of an ecclesiastic is often accounted for by the prospect of some ribbon, robe, or perquisite, it was freely said that Napoleon had promised Dupanloup the archbishopric of Lyons if he would head the Gallicans. An English paper repeated this Roman scandal, fathering it on well-informed circles. Certain circles are always well informed as to the motives of men who oppose them.

The pastoral from the banks of the Thames forms a contrast to that from the banks of the Loire. True, Archbishop Manning no longer speaks of the extinction of Protestantism, or the restoration of the Pope's dominion over the East, as probable

[1] *Stimmen, N. F.,* vi., p. 57.

effects of the Council. He even shows some dawning consciousness that the war which he had announced in 1867 with a light
heart, would not be carried through so lightly. In the earlier
part of his treatise he more than once coolly speaks of the
bishops as being unanimous in the belief of Papal infallibility !
Before the conclusion, Bishop Maret's work extorts the admission that he must now call that doctrine Ultramontane which,
two years before, he had asserted to be Catholic. He none the
less eagerly presses for the carrying out of the program. The
Church is far too large. She permits differences of belief, which
are not only unseemly, but dangerous. After an outbreak
of questioning thought and conflicting will, such as had been
occasioned by a simple demand for only one or two new dogmas,
tighter and tighter binding up seems to Dr. Manning to be not
merely becoming, but even necessary.

While panting for additional fetters for his own Church, he
speaks of Protestants as sighing for something beyond insular
narrowness. In fact, it would seem as if he had no perception
of the difference between a big sect and a large creed, or of the
possible harmony between a local organisation and a universal
brotherhood. There is no insular narrowness, much less Pontine-
Marsh narrowness, in the definition of a Church given by the
English Church, whereby she marks her relation to all other
Churches. That definition is large, catholic, and scriptural. It
leaves the English Churchman free from any obligation to
unchurch other Christians, and therefore he may rest and be
thankful, when others feel bound, by the narrowness of their sect,
to unchurch him. He may do more than rest, he may smile,
when he finds those who are already tied up so tightly that they
must unchurch him, crying for a tighter twining of the cords,
and thinking that with increasing tightness they gain increasing unity. The Church of Christ was catholic when she could
number only one hundred and thirty adherents in the whole
world. She will never become more catholic than she was then.
No sect can increase its catholicity by adding millions of igno-

rant and bigoted people, and calling them Christians.   No sect
could do other than make itself more sectarian by adding new
terms of membership, and excluding from its communion all who
will not accept them.   Insular narrowness, when the island is
England, would be, at the worst, infinitely more respectable than
what we have called Pontine-Marsh narrowness.   True, the insular Church would make itself ridiculous if it tried to fasten
itself upon all mankind, and called that catholicity.   Still, it
would have a broader base and a nobler code than the municipal
Church of Rome ever had.

Dr. Manning resented, as a sort of rebellion, objections
taken against multiplying terms of membership, and adding new
conditions of salvation.   To him every increase of narrowness
seemed an increase of unity.   If there are men in the English
Church sighing in a similar way for bonds and anathemas
which, thank God, our island does not forge, they are not the
men inspired by the catholic creed of their own Church, but
men infected by the municipal creed of the Popes.

Like Dupanloup, Archbishop Manning made an attack and
provoked a retort.   He denounced the historical school of
theologians in Germany, and especially in Munich, and was
pitilessly cut up by Friedrich, in the *Literaturblatt.*   The
Archbishop, like Auguste Comte, had reached a point in the
development of theory when it was necessary that it should
conquer history.   Preparatory to the attack on the Catholic
Faculty of Munich, he writes in mother English matter like the
following (p. 10): ' *The day is past for appeals to antiquity.*   If
Christianity and the Christian Scriptures are to be maintained
in controversy against sceptical criticism, the unbroken, world-
wide witness of the Catholic Church must be invoked.'

A number of equally exposed positions are taken up in face
of the Liberal Catholic scholars, and that with all the contempt
which official power often feels for reasoning power :—

' They who, under the pretensions of historical criticism, deny the
witness of the Catholic Church to be the *maximum* of evidence, even in a

historical sense, likewise ruin the foundation of moral certainty in respect to Christianity altogether' (p. 125). 'It is not, therefore, by criticism on past history, but by acts of faith in the living voice of the Church at this hour, that we can know the faith' (p. 126). 'No historical certainty can be called science except only by courtesy. 'It is time that the pretensions of "historical science" and "scientific historians" be reduced to their proper sphere and limits. And this the Council will do, not by contention or anathema, but by the words "It hath seemed good to the Holy Ghost and to us"' (*id.*).

However confused in his ideas of catholicity and of historical authority the Archbishop had become, the struggle he had done something to occasion and to exasperate already began to awake him to the difference between an ordinary addition to the creed and that change of base which he was moving heaven and earth to procure:—

'There is a difference, also, between a definition of the infallibility of the Pope and that of any other Christian doctrine. In the latter case the authority of the Church may be sufficient to overcome any doubt. In the former *it is this very authority, the principle and foundation of all certainty in faith,* which is in question' (p. 31).

These protentous words tell where Dr. Manning had placed himself,—in pupilage to a power which, having left the divine 'fountain of all certainty in faith,' was disputing as to what cistern, of all the cisterns it had hewn out, was the one into which the true spring overflowed. Where will the dogma be found to conquer the history made by the Archbishop's own hand when he wrote those words,—history proving that after he had been for years flourishing before Anglicans his Papal Society as affording absolute certainty in faith, he himself declared her to be in the throes of a combat as to 'the principle and fountain of all certainty in faith'? Where will a dogma be found to conquer the history made at the moment when his Papal Society, in accordance with his wishes, adopted an unchangeable decree, which, *if true*, proves that for all the time of her existence she had not only been fallible but had indeed failed, and that right grievously,—failed as to the doctrine of her head, by withholding from him the recognition of his attributes and rights? If from the beginning the Popes were infallible, the Church, which never consented to recognise them as such till 1870, had up to that year failed in the doctrine of her head, and failed in opposition to her head. If they were not from the beginning infallible, she in 1870 failed in the doctrine of her head, and failed in conjunction with her head. The decree of 1870 fixes her in the fork, and out of it she cannot wrestle: if the decree was true she had been in a fault of faith up to that day; if it was not true, she committed that day a fault in faith.

Archbishop Manning did not fail to hold out once more a warning to the governments. For some months past the tone of the Vatican press had been that of men who felt that they now held the internal peace of many a nation at their mercy; being able to menace almost any government with serious unrest, and some with overthrow. The habit of insinuating such threats seems to be native to the bad air which Dr. Newman truly speaks of as hanging around the foot of the Pope's rock.[1] But the following is too close a copy of those revolutionary vaticinations for the banks of the Thames:—

'The Catholic Church now stands alone, as in the beginning, in its divine isolation and power. "Be wise now therefore, O ye kings; be instructed, ye judges of the earth." There is an abyss before you, into which thrones, and rights, and laws, and liberties may sink together. You have to choose between the Revolution and the Church of God. As you choose, so will your lot be. The General Council gives to the world one more witness for the truths, laws, and sanctities which include all that is pure, noble, just, venerable upon earth. It will be an evil day for any State in Europe if it engage in conflict with the Church of God. No weapon formed against it ever yet has prospered ' (p. 130).

The last words might be enough to account for Cardinal Manning's dislike of history. They flatly contradict it, and it flatly contradicts them ; for by the Church of God is here meant the Church of the Pope. The weapons which have most prospered from the days of the Reformation to this day

[1] *Letter to the Duke of Norfolk.*

are those that have been turned against the Pope. The nations that have most prospered have been those that have declared him a pretender ; and in these nations the reigns that have been distinguished for prosperity have been the most decidedly Protestant. England was long ago put to the choice between the Reformation and the Church of the Pope, and happily chose the good part, and as she chose, so, ever blessed be the God of nations, has been our lot. We will repeat the choice of our fathers, and the lot of our children shall be better and better. And they will have to pity, even more than we are called to pity, those who, having rejected reformation, have placed themselves under a continual terror and a liability to a periodical outburst of revolution.

The great favour in which France, at this juncture, stood with the projectors of the future world, is reflected in the sentence which follows the above threat, and seems to set the lot reserved for wise nations that lend their power to the Pope, in contrast with that of foolish ones that nurse it for good purposes. 'The attitude of France,' says the Archbishop, 'is wise and de-liberate, worthy of a great people with the traditions of Catholic history at its back.' Yet the weapons which France, in the service of the Pope, had for many years been brandishing in the face of Italy, and occasionally dyeing in her blood, did not prosper. In allusion to the fact that France had forbidden the execution of the disciplinary decrees of the Council of Trent (a fact to which she largely owes it that she did not go down so low as Spain went), and the possibility that she might take a similar course with regard to those of the Vatican Council, should they prove unacceptable to her rulers, the Archbishop says, 'The guardians and defenders of the principles of 1789 ought to rise as one man against all who should violate the basis of the political society in France.' Then praying that God might lead the rulers of the kingdoms and nations to a spirit of wisdom and justice at this crisis of *their trial*, he says, 'The Council will assuredly be for the fall and the rising again of many.

If Christian nations be desolated, then would come the alternatives of anti-Christian Socialism or the Catholic Order of the world, purified in fire, and reunited to the centre of stability and justice from which it is now departing.' Thus, there is to be a tribulation, a fiery purge, a fall and a rising again of many, a possible desolation of so-called Christian nations; and all these threats point to the one end of forcing us to choose between the *Catholic Order* and anti-Christian Socialism. This language reflects the substance of many Vatican warnings and forecasts with regard to the Council and its issues.

Friedrich, in the *Literaturblatt* (v., p. 164), replied to the attack on the historical theologians of Munich. He said that the abuses of the middle ages had crept in through the total neglect of history. On the other hand, Protestant theology had risen up and had matured as a strictly historical theology. Baronius had attempted to win this weapon back to the service of Rome, and the Munich scholars had followed in his steps. If archives and original works were to be wrested out of their hands, it meant nothing more nor less than laying down their arms in the presence of their antagonists. Friedrich would not allow the ambiguous expression ' the witness of the Church ' to cover anything more than her infallible utterances.

He said that the Archbishop had a false idea of the way in which a Council should proceed, because he seemed to think that the Church might speak without first using all human means to ascertain the truth. If he thought so, he was under a delusion of which a careful study of the history of the Councils might cure him. The statement of Manning, ' I have already said' that the proofs of Papal infallibility outweighed those of the infallibility of the Church without the Pope, provoked the remark that as the Archbishop had adduced only his own authority, 'I have already said,' we might still doubt the infallibility of the proofs until he had produced his credentials as one inspired. Friedrich says that while blaming others for attempting to influence the Council,

Manning himself tried to impose his authority upon it, in such a manner that it might be fancied that the Council was not to utter the words of the Holy Ghost, but those of the Archbishop of Westminster. Thus he indignantly flings back in the face of the prelate the assertion that it was an attempt to interfere with the freedom of the Council when the Theological Faculty of Munich gave an opinion to the king of the country in answer to questions put by him. The Archbishop, he protests, has no title to deprive theologians of their calling, or of their right to investigate historical evidences or to give their views, so long as the Church has not spoken.

He reminds the Archbishop that, severe as he is against those who do not go as far as himself, even he does not go far enough, for his allies now begin to require people to say, that the Church may define dogmas without having any support in the Bible and tradition, and that indeed when nothing but apocryphal documents are in favour of the definition. And, moreover, that the authority of a General Council (as distinguished from that of the Pope) is only human authority. These innovations, says the sturdy German, we abhor; and then he leaves the Englishman to the care of his Jesuit allies with these words, 'If what everybody here says' (he writes in Rome) 'is true, that the Archbishop, at every opportunity, declares we have only one school to fear, the historical school, I grant to him and grant to his allies that they have the light of history to fear.'

With various feelings the bishops now set forth to bear witness as to the faith of their respective Churches. This was the most dignified of the professed duties of a bishop in Councils, as they used to be. It had some show of a foundation so long as the rule of 'apostolic' tradition was adhered to. Of course, however, that became antiquated. So 'ecclesiastical' tradition was set up side by side with apostolic, as what was so called had been set up side by side with the Word of God.

Of late, however, the words 'Church' and 'Pope' had been approaching to a confused identification. Ecclesiastical tradition had been growing to mean anything to which the Popes had committed themselves.   If the identification of 'Pope' and 'Church' by the multitude was *confused*, not so with the Curia. They perfectly understood the difference between identification from below and from above.   They had no idea of the Church setting up to be Pope, but a great idea of the Pope becoming the Church.   The body, they argued, could not be the head, but the head, though not the whole body, was surely the commanding member.   Still the form of bearing witness to the faith of their respective Churches lingered for the bishops—one of the historical traces of old ideas, underlying sandheaps of innovation.

Darboy set out, from his diocese of two millions of souls, to bear witness that the doctrine of Papal infallibility was not the faith, and never had been, on the banks of the Seine.   Manning set out to testify that it was the faith and the tradition on the banks of the Thames.   Clifford set out from Clifton to declare that it was not the faith on the Avon.   Deschamps went to prove that it was the faith in Malines.   Dupanloup went to prove that it was not, and never had been, the faith in Orleans. Cullen left Dublin to demonstrate that it was, and ever had been, the true faith of Ireland.   MacHale left Connaught, bracing up his fourscore years, to go and bear witness that it was not the faith he had learned, no, nor any of his coevals.   Spalding embarked from Baltimore to testify that it was the ancient faith in America.   Kenrick set forth from St. Louis to protest that this was the reverse of the truth, and to prove that he had never been taught it in Maynooth, and even to tell of the first time when the doctrine was broached within the walls of that college.   Rauscher left Vienna and Schwarzenberg Prague; Haynald left Hungary and Strossmayer Croatia ; Von Scherr left Munich, Melchers Cologne, and Förster Breslau, to testify that the faith and tradition of their Churches had not ignored, but had withstood, the new doctrine.   They had to add that the conscience of the people was so set against it that it was as much as the authority of the Church was worth to attempt to impose it upon them.   Von

Ketteler left Mainz to testify loudly, but with so uncertain a sound that no ordinary man could 'know what was piped or harped.'

On the other hand, the bishops of Spain, Italy, and South America almost unanimously sallied forth to testify that in their Churches the new dogma was an old doctrine.

Their testimony was reinforced by some from more ancient sees. Hassun set out from New Rome, as the Orientals call Constantinople, to bear witness, as Patriarch of Cilicia, that the City of Paul, and the Churches planted by him, had always held the faith and tradition of Papal infallibility. Valerga turned his back on the Mount of Olives, on Sion, and on Bethlehem, to give evidence, in the sight of God and man, that the Church of Jerusalem had always held the faith, and conserved the tradition, that the Roman Pontiff was infallible and his decrees irreformable.

Darboy, in his farewell pastoral, said to the Catholics of Paris, 'In these matters, bishops are witnesses who prove, not authors who invent.'

Had the contest lain between these two forces, the weight of talent, character, and supporting Churches would have decided it in favour of the *status quo*. But bishops sailed from Jaffna in Ceylon, and Jaro in the Philippines, from India, China, and Siam, from Swan River and New Caledonia, to swamp with their traditions those of bishops from Churches which might pretend to have a tradition. The fact that theirs could not set up any such claim was one objection urged against their votes, another being that they were dependent on the Propaganda. With these came also a number of Oriental bishops, in the same financial position, of whom Vitelleschi says that they brought the finest wardrobes and the steadiest votes. In aid of these a thick growth of bishops *in partibus* sprang out of the well-warmed conserves of Court patronage.

Roughly stated, the result was, that out of Italy and Spain old and educated Churches, when represented by prelates trained in their own bosom, generally declared in opposition to the new dogma.   Where they did otherwise, they were often represented by prelates trained *in Rome*, and, like Cullen and Manning, specially selected to imbue the National Church with the municipal theology of Rome, and, in case of need, to impose it upon the clergy.   Those from really ancient cities, like Jerusalem, who supported the Curia, were dependents of the Propaganda.   With these came the occupants of sees created by Pius IX., most of which, from Westminster to Oceania, were represented by witnesses in favour of infallibility.

Many of the bishops had for travelling companion a small pamphlet.   It was called Considerations (*Erwägungen*), and put the case against Papal infallibility in a form and compass seldom equalled, in any composition, for clearness, depth, fulness, and compression.   It was no secret that the author was Döllinger, but he had not chosen to put his name on the title.

In this manner was prepared for the world a drama of many scenes, which has left permanently in the eye of history four great spectacles:—(1) How an ancient aristocracy, claiming to be the senate of humanity, was made the instrument of destroying its own legislative rights; (2) How masters of ceremony, habituated to employ it for both political and religious ends, were made its victims, ceremony being brought into operation to carry away surreptitiously their constitutional forms, and with them their legal privileges; (3) How they who had declared 'ecclesiastical' tradition to be as good a foundation for doctrine as the Word of God, went through the process of building on the sand ; (4) How a Head of the human species, a King of kings and Lord of lords, was erected by priests, and humiliated by Providence.

CHAPTER XI.

Diplomatic Feeling and Fencing in Rome, November 1869—Cross Policies on Separation of Church and State—Ollivier, Favre, De Banneville—Doctrines of French Statesmen ridiculed at Rome—Specimens of the Utterances approved at Court—Forecasts of War between France and Prussia—Growing Strength of the Movement in France for Universities Canonically Instituted.

THOSE who arrived in the autumn months in Rome, perhaps with the hope of preventing the dreaded proposals from being brought forward, or with the intention, if they could not succeed in that, of organising an opposition to them, found to their surprise that the tone of the Curia was very gentle. The Cardinals and Monsignori, for their part, really did not care about infallibility. Indeed, the subject might have been passed over in silence had not such false rumours as to the designs of Rome been set afloat. Lord Acton names Cardinals Antonelli, Berardi, and De Luca, and also Bishop Fessler, the Secretary of the Council, as declaring that the utterances of the *Civiltá* were not to be relied upon, and that if the idea of proposing infallibility had been entertained, it was given up. He also quotes a letter written home by a bishop, afterwards known among the Opposition, saying that there was no ground for the idea that in Rome they meant to make infallibility a dogma. That seemed to be an imagination, spread abroad with no good design. Still, after the agitation which had taken place the Council could hardly pass the matter over in silence. The Holy See would not curb the zeal of the bishops if they resolved to give effect to their persuasion, but would not itself take the initiative. But if anything was done, it would be some moderate measure, that would satisfy all, and give no pretext of a party triumph.

Lord Acton further says, what is confirmed from many quarters, that Cardinal Antonelli feared that the Pope was about to bring upon himself difficulties similar to those which beset the earlier years of his pontificate. Some treat Antonelli's apparent coldness as a *ruse*. But, Englishmanlike, Lord Acton takes the

hypothesis that requires least dissimulation, crediting the foresight of Antonelli with real apprehensions.

Lord Acton also, states that the Pope himself requested the
diplomatic corps to help him to allay the excitement in Germany.
He said to one ambassador, 'The *Civiltá* does not speak in my
name.'   To another he said that 'his approval would never be
given to a proposition which would sow discord among the
bishops.'   To a third his words were, 'You come to witness a
scene of peace-making.'   More than once, when addressing a
group of bishops, did the Pope express himself to the effect that
he would not do anything which could, by any means, raise
contentions among them, and that he would be content with a
declaration fixing a proper standard on the question of tolerance
and freedom of conscience.   He certainly wished Catholicism in
England and Russia to enjoy the benefit of toleration, but the
principle must be rejected by a Church which had to maintain
the doctrine that salvation was to be found in her alone.

Lord Acton expresses a belief that there might have been
some idea of finding a substitute for infallibility in the suppression of freedom of faith and conscience ; with the expectation
that the most prominent hindrance to the new dogma would be
removed so soon as the Inquisition should be recognised as
having one and the same legal position with Catholicism itself.
He thinks that a great step in that direction would have been
taken if the proposition of the Syllabus had been confirmed
which condemns the assertion that the Pontiffs and Councils had
ever transgressed the bounds of their power, or usurped the
rights of princes.   As to usurping the rights of princes, a writer
like Lord Acton is at a disadvantage, compared with one like
Professor Ceccucci, who wrote the history of General Councils,
for the voluminous work of Frond.   Ceccucci settles the point
with an ease of which Lord Acton has no idea.   The Church
'never did usurp political power; that possessed by her has
always been the most legitimate on earth' (*Frond*, vol. iv.,
p. 358).

But one point stated by Lord Acton is that infallibility had been looked upon as a means to an end; and this is the kernel of the matter. Just as, logically, the doctrine of infallible judgment was developed out of that of unlimited power, so, practically, unlimited power must be exercised by an infallible judge. Admit that God has given all power upon earth to one man, and surely you will not deny that, in mercy to His creatures, He will make that man infallible. Admit, on the other hand, that the judgment which bids the secular arm smite this and shield that is infallible, and surely you will own that the secular arm should obey. Liberal Catholics were, not unnaturally, incensed at the writing in the *Civiltà* at a moment when those in power might have been expected to set an example of moderation. The Freemasons were told that the reason why they dreaded the Council was that they would be condemned, and that no respectable persons would join them after that. And the Liberal Catholics were told that their reasons for dreading the Council were much the same. They professed similar principles with those of the Masons, which were sometimes called Principles of '89, sometimes Principles of Modern Society, or Toleration, or Liberty of Conscience and the Press, or Modern Constitutions, or the Rights of Science, or the Boons of Progress, or Liberalism. No wonder that men who had championed the Church of Rome as the Catholic Church, should tremble when they saw her sinking into a sect so straight as to put all these principles under ban (*Civiltà*, VII., viii., p. 285).

On the 9th of November the Pope received the Marquis de Banneville, newly returned to his post as ambassador of France. After many signs of vacillation, the Emperor had finally decided not to ask for the admission of an ambassador. This policy met the views both of the Papal party and of those who desired the entire separation of the Church and the State. The latter had adopted the notion that they took a step towards separation by leaving the Church, while still an establishment of the State, to legislate for the nation over the head of the State.

As early as July 10th, 1868, M. Emile Ollivier, in the *Corps
Législatif*, dwelling on the fact that the Pope, in his Bull, did
not name the Emperor, and that he held all those addressed in
it bound by it simply through its being posted up in Rome,
said: It is declared that, by the simple fact of its being issued
in Rome, every bishop in France is bound and must betake
himself to Rome, on pain of disobedience. The Emperor or the
civil power is not thought of. It is the gravest act accomplished since 1789. It is the separation of Church and State,
proclaimed, for the first time, by the Pope himself.

A joke of M. Pelletan contained a real answer—'All the
better, he renounces the budget.' No, the Pope never did renounce the budget; and M. Ollivier's inference was hasty. What
was signified was, not the separation of the Church from the
State, but, as Montalembert, who had studied the subject, said,
the absorption of the State in the Church. The ordinary ground
alleged by Vatican writers for no longer paying attention to
governments was, that the modern State had separated itself
from the Church. Of course it was not meant that it had dis-
established the Church, but that it had withdrawn legislation
and executive action from under the supremacy of the Pope.
M. Veuillot said: 'Three orators spoke—M. Guérolt, M. Ollivier,
and M. Baroche, who replied. The first is not a Christian, the
second is not a Catholic, the third is Minister of Worship. All
three are good Gallicans' (vol. i., p. lxxii.). In M. Ollivier,
Veuillot evidently recognises his man ; we do not mean his conscious, but his effectual, ally, for the Ultramontanes habitually
find their best helpers in those who, proudly rejecting their ends,
consent to employ their means. He speaks of the greatest fact
of the age as lying in the substitution of the 'indifferent' State
for the Catholic one. The 'indifferent' State recognises all religions and prefers none, and this constitutes ' the rupture of the
necessary union of Church and State.' It will be remembered
that France was not 'indifferent,' but ' Paritarian,' *i.e.*, it recognised four Churches, and paid them all, and of course *preferred*

those before all others by paying them, and among the four it preferred Romanism before the other three by many and great privileges. But the State, as such, had ceased to be ' Catholic.' M. Veuillot does not fail to tell statesmen and journalists that the faith of the Church will conquer them both. It will dominate journals, parliaments, and armies, will raise up great men and martyrs, and will make history (vol. i., p. lxxxi.). He did not fail to hint repeatedly at the coming travail of all mankind, of which he spoke with so much feeling on the first announcement of the Council.

One of his hints was, Should God by the act of the Council ' add some greater splendour to the power of His Vicar, it will be because circumstances are approaching in which it will be necessary to obey more fully, more quickly, and from further away.' [1]

On April 9th, 1869, Ollivier again raised the subject, protesting that the abstention of the government from the Council amounted to an abrogation of the organic articles of the Concordat. Jules Favre said that it was the separation of Church and State, and as such he gratefully accepted it. These consequences were denied by the minister M. Baroche, who asserted, ' After the Council, the rights of France will remain entire.'

This boast passed in France, but not so at the Vatican. The *Unità Cattolica* for April 14th showed that the usual ambiguity of the Bonaparte policy marked the replies of the ministers on this critical occasion. The bishops were to go to the Council with ' their conscience in full liberty,' and yet ' after the Council the rights of France were to remain entire.' ' What,' asks the *Unità,* ' does that mean? Does France want to be free either to believe or to oppose what the Council will define? After having permitted her bishops to take part in an assembly which every Catholic must believe to be infallible, does Napoleon III. mean to hold himself free to prosecute them if they preach the doc-

---

[1] Vol. ii., p. cix.

trines defined, and enforce the discipline enjoined by the Council?'

This straightforward question shows that M. Picard hit nearer to the point than either Ollivier or Favre; for he cried, ' It means a Church free in a State not free.'[1] Even that is not quite the truth ; which strictly is, A State not free in a Church which is free; for the State is part, and the Church whole; or, to recall the image from the early pages of the *Civiltà*, the State is the leg and the Church the man. We have seen it roundly asserted by the *Civiltà* that the Church free means canon law free. That being so, for any man to speak of the State being free, in any modern sense, is trifling. In its expositions of the Syllabus the *Civiltà* had laid down the true doctrine as follows :— *The first condition of an efficient alliance of the laws of the State with the laws of the Church, is the application in every case wherein spiritual penalties are insufficient of the means of coercion whereof the State disposes.* The voice of the pastor has not always efficacy sufficient to drive away the rapacious wolves from the fold of Christ. Therefore does it appertain to the prince invested with the authority of the sword, to arm himself with its force, in order to repel and put to flight all the enemies of the Church (VI., ii., 137). Refusing to stand in this position is, in the esoteric sense, separating the State from the Church. To a conscientious Ultramontane it is as absurd to say that a State in this manner subject to the Church is not free, as it would be to say that a body ruled by its informing mind is not free. That is the figure of speech which recurs at every turn of discourse on the subject.

After it had been determined to ratify the policy censured by Picard, De Banneville had his interview. Most writers describe him as a willing tool of the Curia, and as doing all he could to lead France in the way which it might trace out for her. Lord Acton regards him as honestly hoping to compose a difference between the Italian and German schools of theology,

[1] *Friedberg*, pp. 93, 94.

by the moderating weight of French influence.[1] Banneville's despatch, on the occasion now in question, would rather seem to countenance the former opinion than the latter.[2] But the Pope in the interview did not say a word indicating his personal opinion as to the questions to be decided. He did, however, say that all must be left to the wisdom of the Fathers,—as if all had not been prepared, and doubly prepared. He further said that the rash conjectures of hasty spirits—in manifest allusion to the *Civiltá*—were to be regretted, as also the premature discussion of questions which would have been better reserved to the Council itself.

It is not probable that this deceived M. de Banneville as to the past, for he well knew how the Pope had encouraged the 'premature discussions;' but he might take it as the covering of a retreat from a position found to be too advanced. But a wary man might have felt that perhaps the retreat was only a feint.

What, asked M. Veuillot, would M. Baroche do at the Council as ambassador? Not belonging (as minister) to any Christian communion, he does not represent any. And as to the members of the Council, what is the French State to them? If he produced his *French* ideas on matters of religion, the Fathers would reply with one word—Anathema. The 'indifferent' governments of our day have but one duty in respect to the Council— not to put hindrances in its way.[3]

Had two governments, those of France and Italy, taken M. Veuillot at his word, and said, All we shall do is not to put hindrances in the way, France would have withdrawn her troops from the Papal States, Italy would have said, We sit still, and the 'revolution' in earnest would soon have been afoot, and not far from the walls of Rome.

The despatch of M. de Banneville shows that Pius IX., like

---

[1] *Zur Geschichte.*   [2] *Friedberg,* p. 330.

[3] Here Veuillot treats France as if it was 'indifferent,' but apparently uses the term in a popular, not a strict sense. America is 'indifferent,' France is only 'Paritarian' (vol. i., p. xcvii. f.).

every Italian, knows how to keep his own counsel. Even his renowned saying, I am tradition—*La tradizione son io*—is no more than what M. Veuillot had said in proving that the Pope could not be an innovator—' Peter can no more be an innovator than the Holy Spirit, which reveals tradition to him.'[1]

The tranquillity of the Curia on this occasion was that of perfected preparation. The dissimulation would not provoke a remark from a Roman. The effect of both was to prevent the anti-infallibilists from organising any opposition.

Meanwhile the 'good press' was preparing the world for events. Bishops who, in their pastorals, boldly advocated infallibility, were at the Metropolis marked for praise. The Liberal Catholics were remorselessly written down. The assumption of the Virgin was frequently mentioned as having being taught in speeches or pastorals. Any sign of crusading zeal for his Holiness was celebrated. For instance, in Belgium, at a festival of a college in Mons, in presence of the nuncio, it was told how forty of the youths executed military movements in the uniform of zouaves, raising cries of 'Piux IX. for ever!' 'To Rome!' Gifts of different kinds, but specially those sent in money, were registered and applauded.

•Much attention was attracted by the announcement of a formal call issued by the Academia Romana, of the Immacolata, to professors, men of science, and men of letters generally. The object was declared to be that of obtaining a homage of the intellect and a submission of science to the Church. It was necessary in our day that a formal protest should be made, to the effect that the sciences are subject to her as the supreme teacher. The adhesion of the savants was not to be merely internal. Ornamental cards were issued on which each adherent was to enter his name, with his degree or titles, under the printed words *Tribute of adhesion and obedience to the Vatican Council.* The signer was, moreover, to state what

---

[1] Vol. i., p. cxxi.

pecuniary contribution he would give. It was announced that all these cards would be presented to the Holy Father.[1]

Some examples of the points kept before readers arriving at the Holy City at this particular time may be of permanent interest. The Canadian Bishop of St. Hyacinthe was quoted as writing, ' Sublime assembly, in which the eye of faith contemplates with wonder, poor and simple mortals who, sitting as judges, do not hesitate *to impose the responsibility of their decisions and judgments on the Holy Spirit,* because they know and believe that they form together with Him one tribunal.' The emphases are given as we find them.[2]

A Latin pamphlet on the crisis, by a layman, was ridiculed, and one point, which seemed most comical to the reviewer, was that the author proposed two such queer anathemas ; first, if any one offends against charity, let him be anathema ; secondly, if any one begins war, let him be anathema.

The Archbishop of Lima, being ninety-four years of age, was unable to come in person, but sent his pastoral staff as a present to the Pope. It was of pure Peruvian gold, and of the value of two thousand pounds.

From the thrice-blessed Republic of Ecuador came the Archbishop of Quito, presenting a chalice of gold, rich with precious pearls. He bore valuable gifts in addition. That ' illustrious Catholic,' the President, Garcia Moreno, had, on a public occasion, been presenting prizes to students, when they joyfully laid down their medals to send them as an offering to the Holy Father. On seeing this, the President took from his breast a medal of rare value, all studded with gems, which had been presented to him by the government for distinguished services to the country. This he added to the tribute of the youths, and the Archbishop had the joy of laying the united oblation at the feet of the Pontiff.[3]

---

[1] *Civiltá,* VII., vii., p. 356.   [2] *Civiltá,* VII., viii., 335.

[3] Under Moreno, Ecuador attained the distinction of being often mentioned, with solemn commendation, as the one and the only *Catholic State* in the world ; the one in which the principles of the Syllabus were applied.

From Venezuela the Archbishop brought more than three thousand pounds in money. His people had also laden him with their valuables, ladies having taken off earrings, bracelets, necklaces, and rings to send, as tokens of their devotion to the impoverished Pope.

Had our English journalists devoutly pondered the elaborate description given at this cheerful juncture of a bell designed by a priest, and presented for the use of the Presidents in the Council, they would not have wasted so much criticism as they did on the rhetoric of a speech reported in the *Daily News*, in 1875, as having been made by the Pope, censuring Mr. Gladstone. His Holiness spoke of that gentleman as a viper attacking the bark of St. Peter, or something of that sort. Now the bell in question was described as being symbolic, within and without. The clapper of it was the ship of Peter, round the hull of which was coiled a serpent attempting to board the vessel, but it was finally precipitated with its head down, and the three-forked tongue shooting out.

The doubt of our men of letters as to whether the Pope could use a metaphor describing a snake attacking a bark, illustrates, in general, what Cardinal Manning said of those gentlemen on the particular occasion of the Council:—'When English Protestants undertake to write of an Œcumenical Council of the Catholic Church, nothing less than a miracle can preserve them from making themselves ridiculous.'[1] It would require a miracle to prevent any one from making himself ridiculous who should criticise the Speeches of Pius IX., assuming that his metaphors must have been subject to some rule.[2]

---

[1] *Priv. Pet.*, iii., p. 3.

[2] *Civiltá*, VII., viii., 490. The inscription on the bell in question is as follows:—

> 'Invocata—Immaculata
> Pius Nonus—Pastor bonus
> Per Concilium—Fert auxilium.
> Mundus crebris—tot tenebris
> Implicatus—obcœcatus
> Per hoc Numen—et hoc Lumen
> Extricatur—illustratur.'

We find the revolution called by the *Civiltà* 'the executioner of the Church;' and it is said that the Pontiff in his distress is 'rendered more and more like Christ upon the Cross, whom he represents, and with whom he can repeat, "My God, my God, why hast Thou forsaken me?"' (Id., p. 514.)

The Word of God is shown to be the source of human redemption, and then the following applications are made of this principle : [1]—

'The State indeed must be civilised and modernised by separating it from the living Word in the Church, that it may die. . . . The laws must be civilised and modernised by putting them in opposition to the laws of the Word, that they may be laws of death. . . . Some would wish the Word to reconcile Himself with Satan. . . . Schools must be civilised and modernised by separating them from the schools of the Word, that they may be schools of death. Wedlock must be civilised and modernised by separating it from the consecration of the Word, that it may be the wedlock of death. Public speech must be modernised and civilised by separating it from the influence of the Word, that it may be the speech of death. Everything, in fine, must perish, since everything must be secularised, or torn away from that God who *upholdeth all things by the Word of His power.* . . . The modern revolution, inspired by Satan, would find that all its weapons directed against the Vatican were destined to have no other effect than that of multiplying the victories of the Word of God, who reigns there in the humble person of His Vicar' (p. 522-526).

The certain success of the Council, it was foretold, would result in that *restoration of order,* first in ideas, next in facts, which was the end aimed at by the Holy Father in calling it. This reminds us that almost the same language was used at the time of the publication of the Syllabus, in describing what its effects would be,—first, the silent restoration of order in ideas, and then restoration in facts. A prelate honoured with notice was the Bishop of Le Mans, who was quoted as saying that perhaps among the doctrines which the Church would define would be that of the Assumption of the Virgin. He immediately afterwards assured his flock that in no case would the

---

[1] The term *verbo* is employed, which in Italian has about the same effect as *logos* would have in English writing.

Church invent doctrines, but she would only define those which have always formed part of her creed (p. 599).

In the chaos now formed, according to the bishops, by society, the newspapers would appear to be the roaring winds, smiting all things and rooting up not only ancient trees but even the sacred groves which used to cast an inviolable shade over the shrine of an oracle. ' Lies, calumnies, and outrages of every sort,' were charged against them by the Bishop of Laval, while his brother of Galtelli-Nuovo declared that society was a complete intellectual, moral, civil, and social anarchy. God only, said the Bishop, could save society, and He would save it by the Council.

Bishop Mermillod, at Geneva, was quoted as saying that God had displayed clemency to the age by giving it the remedy of the Council. Speaking as he did to a Swiss audience, he describes the evil of our time in rejecting the supernatural order, not as withdrawing society from under the authority of the Church, which is the most frequent terminology in Rome, but as withdrawing it from under the authority of Christ. Of course to a conscientious Ultramontane, this comes to the same thing, for ' Christ living, reigning, and teaching His Church in Peter,' exercises His authority through ' the living Christ,' as the editor of the Pope's Speeches calls him ; but the sound of the two words in Geneva would be different.

In a work of a French professor, Allemand, which is greatly praised, a portion selected for quotation is that which shows that our Lord's words, ' My kingdom is not of this world,' mean, *It did not originate* from the earth :—

' If the Church is queen, her visible head is king. . . . The Pope is the least imperfect image of the Father who is in heaven. Therefore has this viceroy of souls been invested with infallibility. He sends the bishops as Christ sent the Apostles, and as the Father sent the Son ' (p. 602).

This curious passage seems to ground the infallibility of the Pope on the basis of his personal holiness. This is not, as yet, any part of Papal doctrine. But the selection of it at the Vatican for quotation, while it may be without any deliberate intention, would almost seem to favour the idea that such a notion is not unacceptable.

We find Pius IX. hailed with the title 'The Pope of Prodigies.' The Court, if we may judge by its organs, was deeply affected at the want of faith displayed by many Catholics, who expressed fears lest the Council should define anything that it ought not to define. Did they not know that the Holy Ghost would preserve it unerring? Why then all this solicitude? Could they not trust a body so guided to go right, without their advices and warnings? They treated it 'as an ordinary human assembly.' This sounded like mockery to those who had any idea of how much Rome had done in employing *art and man's device* to prevent the Council from going wrong and to forestall all possible impulses in any direction not predetermined. Had they only known of the long labour and the jealous precautions which we shall see gradually coming to light, the retorts they did make would have been much more indignant.

CHAPTER XII.

Mustering, and Preparatory Stimuli — Pope's Hospitality — Alleged Political Intent — Friedrich's First Notes — The Nations cited to Judgment — New War of the Rosary. — Tarquini's Doctrine of the Sword — A New Guardian of the Capitol — November and December, 1869.

WHILE the chiefs of the Curia and the leading prelates were testing their diplomatic skill, and the former were, on that field, meekly winning the prizes, the rank and file of the hierarchy were flocking in from all the winds of heaven. The Roman nobles in many cases gave up their palaces to the Fathers of the Council. With his habitual personal liberality, the Pope freely offered hospitality to all who would accept it.

This simple act, natural to his station, and still more to his disposition, was smiled at as a good bid for votes. About three hundred bishops made themselves, in whole or in part, dependent for their daily expenses on the bounty of the man upon whose exaltation they were to decide. The *Civiltá*, as if to emphasise their dependence, told how they were lodged, supported, and assisted by him in all the necessaries of life. Hence the mocking name of 'the Pope's boarders,' which greeted any manifestations of opinion on their part. The *Civiltá* again speaks of Pius IX. as having in this case become the treasurer and dispenser of the temporal charity of the faithful ; a proud position for him, but not flattering language for his venerable brethren whose votes were in question. This mention of his charity leads the *Civiltá* to say that, for the last ten years, the annual average of his income from the offerings of the faithful had amounted to four hundred thousand pounds.[1] It is said that his expenses for the entertainment of the bishops amounted to one hundred pounds per day.

A case of history repeating itself is suggested by these allegations as to the diplomatic value of the Pope's hospitality. Dr. Karl Benrath has restored to his place among Italian worthies one of the most picturesque figures of the many-hued life of that nation in the sixteenth century. This was Frà Bernardino Ochino, the all-eloquent General of the Capuchins, whom the blot of the Inquisition had covered from the common eye for three centuries. Ochino, who became a guest of Cranmer and a prebendary of Canterbury, wrote on the banks of the Thames, among other works, one called ' The Tragedy.' Conceiving of the Papacy exactly as all modern Italian Protestants do, as the anti-Christ, and the master-piece of Satan, he traces the rise of this dread power. Besides supernatural sources of ascendancy, he alleges the fact that in early ages the Bishops of Rome entertained bishops out of the provinces when they fled to the capital from persecution, or

---

[1] ' Cento milioni di lire in dieci anni.'—Serie VII., vol. ix., p. 15.

came from other causes, and thus the Roman prelates acquired great influence over the others. Their object then was ' Primacy,' out of which infallibility was in our day to come. Ochino puts into the mouth of the secretary to the Emperor, after he has discovered the Pope's yearnings, the following words : "O Lord God, that there can be so much ambition in the heart of a man ! it is no marvel that he entertains in so friendly a manner all strangers who come to Rome.'

Besides bishops came a mixed multitude—the devout Catholic, the keen politician, the commonplace tourist from every country, the gay sightseer, the American politician, the artist, the charlatan, the Indian civilian on furlough, and the learned official theologian. Few, but intent, came a new class of spectators—Italian Protestants, watching with eyes as open to all priestly arts as men of the sixteenth century, but with a readiness to affiliate each part of a Roman show on its Pagan original, much beyond what was even then common among our countrymen.

The Count Henri de Riancey, beholding the hierarchy pressing to the sacred walls, exclaims :—

' Open then thy gates, metropolis of the world ; open thine everlasting gates, that the Queen of glory may come in ! And who is this Queen of glory ? It is the Church. . . . Make way, then, for the angels of the Churches, spoken of by St. John. Make way for the divine hierarchy, the ranks of which are moving, with order, force, and holiness, terrible as an army with banners ' (*Frond*, vol. i., p. 9).

One of the theologians has published a diary (*Tagebuch*), which will always remain one of the original sources of information on the Council. Its accuracy, like that of the Letters of *Quirinus*, has been assailed, and with not dissimilar result. Strong general assertions and weak proof, except on such minor points as show that the substance is unassailable, leave its accuracy but slightly impeached, and its truthfulness not at all discredited. The author states things which, by our standard, would be held private; but however that may be by the standard of his own country, the things, when once published, take their place among the materials of history.

Dr. Friedrich, a professor of Munich, was appointed theologian for the Council to Cardinal Hohenlohe. He began his diary before leaving home. He found that it was vain to seek in the palace of Archbishop Von Scherr for such works in the original as a set of the Fathers, or a collection of the Acts of the Councils. The Reverend Secretary said, 'You know little of bishops if you think that those people study anything'. This gentleman, who was to be the Archbishop's theologian at the Council, himself read only pamphlets. When Friedrich was on the railway platform, observing the two Archbishops of Munich and Bamberg taking their departure for the Council, the confidential servant of the latter came up to the Professor and said, ' You are not surely coming to Rome as a spy ? ' Answering not the man but the master, he replied, ' Let bishops take care that they do not betray the Church, for just as they are bound to speak to the best of their knowledge and conscience, so am I as a theologian.'

Thus Friedrich evidently expected to have to speak, as it would seem that Newman also did. He did not know how the secret plans had put aside all such possibilities. But, if surprises awaited him as to the new part reserved for the doctors, there were surprises for the bishops also.

Friedrich remarked that, as he travelled farther south, less and less respect was shown to the clergy, till in Italy the difference, as compared with Germany, became painful. At Trent, a scholar warned him to beware of poison, and said that it was well that Döllinger had not gone to Rome, as he would never have returned. The same gentleman said that the wealth of the Jesuits enabled them to buy Italian statesmen, and named one of the successors of Cavour as having been purchased. The theologian, full of the lore of Munich, standing in the quaint Alpine city, on the Adige, with the image in his mind of the doctors who, three hundred years ago, there disputed before the bishops and before the world, would naturally form an exalted idea of the work awaiting him in the grander assembly on the banks of the Tiber. The elegant but small church of St. Maria Maggiore would swell, in his anticipation, into St. Peter's; the listening prelates to a threefold or fourfold array; the doctors, the Sotos and Catarinos, whose dialectics are commemorated by Paolo Sarpi, would be represented by men of several schools. The struggle itself was to be much more concentrated, turning on one vital point. It was not now merely a question as to what was to be taught, but as to who was the divine teacher. It was not a dispute about one doctrine or more, but about the very fountain of doctrine. Then it was not any question between the Church and her enemies, but one between the Church and her head. It was to be decided whether or not she had existed all these years without confessing what a head she had. It was to be decided whether the oracle was the whole Church, or the Pope without the Church. The dispute was awkward. Raising it showed Protestants that Rome, while claiming infallibility, had not yet settled where it lay.

Doubtless the Doctor would brace himself up for the battle by the memories of Trent, little knowing that the Curia had taken care that the bishops should not be agitated by Church historians, like him. Still less did he suspect that the very day when he was quietly leaving Trent, the bishops were in the Sixtine Chapel gazing with dazzled eyes on a new and bewitching 'function,' under cover of which the self-organising powers of a General Council, and the traditionary rights of the hierarchy in maintaining those powers, were being, with incomparable sleight of hand, conveyed out of view, to re-appear no more.

After a narrow escape of being murdered on the railway near Terni, Friedrich reached the Holy City. Such was the throng, already, that he had to pay ten francs for the use of a room for a while in the afternoon, before going to his home in the Palazzo Valentini with Cardinal Hohenlohe. That palace stands in the Piazza of the Twelve Apostles, full of reminiscences of days when Alberich and his descendants ruled the city, and held the Popes, sometimes in prison, but always in subjection to the chiefs springing from Theodora and Marozia.

On the 28th of November, a discourse was delivered in St. Peter's, by Father Raimondo Bianchi, Procurator-General of the Dominicans, which was thought sufficiently important to be printed with the Freiburg edition of the *Acta* (p. 130). If good preaching lies in saying much and suggesting more, in the least time, this sermon is perfection; for it occupies less than four octavo pages. We give a brief outline of it. A note which we have already heard delicately touched by Archbishop Manning, a note at that time as often sounded as any in the episcopal scale, was given forth with full power—'Be wise, O ye kings; be instructed, ye judges of the earth.'

The most imposing view of Christ in the eyes of the faithful, says Father Bianchi, is that which unites His humiliation in the manger with His glories and terrors as a Judge. It is precisely of this view that a representation is now about to be offered in His body, the Church. Amid wars assailing her, amid fears among men of little faith, amid mockings of the wicked, by whom she is treated as dying, if not dead, will the Church arise to judgment, with her youth renewed as the eagle's, clothed with glory and majesty, and filled with the Holy Ghost; while Peter, in Thee, Most Blessed Father, the angels of all the Churches attending him, will judge the whole earth in truth and righteousness. . . . When God sent His Son into the world, He committed to Him all judgment and power. So Christ, founding His Church upon a rock, gave to her all judgment and all power, which He had received from the Father, that all men should honour her, even as they honour Him by whom she was built. He who sits on the right hand of the Father, has made her queen on His throne. What she looses He does not bind, and what she binds He does not loose; for her judgments are ratified in heaven. Now the day of the great judgment draws nigh, and all men will behold the Church, the spouse of Christ, leaning on her beloved, glorious in humility, mighty in meekness, thrice faithful in guarding her treasure of truth, and even the unwilling wicked will be compelled to confess her divine. The signs of judgment appear, as they will at the judgment of Christ—commotion in heaven and earth; some exulting because redemption draws nigh, some shrivelled up with fear; hell raging and trembling. 'Behold, I shake the heaven and the earth and the sea and the dry land, and I will shake the nations also.' . . . The judgment is set, and the nations will behold the Vicar of Christ in great power and majesty, and with him the angels of al the Churches, who will judge the nations in truth ; they, the Holy Spirit inspiring, will judge, and with His fan in their hands will they throughly purge their floor, separating the wheat from the chaff, and, once more uttering words first uttered in Jerusalem, will they say, It seemed good to the Holy Ghost and to us. They will encourage the good, reclaim the erring, coerce and condemn the heretic. They will judge and will restore the Christian and civil commonwealth, and renew the ancient beauty and honour of the spouse of Christ. They will judge, and their judgment will be ratified in heaven, and will endure for ever, an eternal monument of the divinity of the Church, against which the kings and the princes set themselves, and the people imagine a vain thing. . . . Rejoice, O heavens, and be glad, O earth, because our Church comes to judgment. And you, Fathers, the lights and stars of the Church, sing praises, and bless Him who, being appointed Judge of the quick and dead, hath set up you also in His house, committing all judgment to you.[1]

Father Bianchi would seem to have been more deeply im-bued with the spirit of the movement than initiated into the plans of the Curia. He fully comprehended the purpose of changing fulminating words into solid thunderbolts, destined to smite not individuals but nations ; but he did not seem to comprehend the means. The Tridentine episcopal doctrine and the true Papal doctrine jostled against one another in his discourse, as they had long done in the Church. The Council that filled his imagination was the historical one,—a Council framing its own decrees, and speaking in its own name. He, too, had been, not inside but outside the door of the Secret Council, and knew not how far it was from the intentions of ' Peter, in Thee, Most Blessed Father,' to grant the old attri-butes to the so-called General Council.

Such language as the above, on such an occasion, in such a

---

[1] Bryce (p. 177) quotes from the second excommunication of Henry IV. by Hildebrand as follows : ' Come now, I beseech you, O most holy and blessed Fathers and Princes, Peter and Paul, that all the world may understand and know that if ye are able to bind and to loose in heaven, ye are likewise able on earth, according to the merits of each man, to give and to take away empires, kingdoms, princedoms, marquisates, duchies, countships, and the possessions of all men.'—*Holy Roman Empire.*

presence,—language, too, reproduced in a collection of the constitutional and judicial acts of the Church,—would call for
reflection, no matter from whom it fell. Coming from a high
officer of the order identified with the history of the Inquisition, it did not lose any of its suggestiveness. As one
looks at it and into it, with the image of the black and white
Dominican in one's eye, it resistlessly calls up the memory of
the famous picture in Santa Maria Novella in Florence. There
Emperor and Pope sit side by side, their respective officers
around them, and the faithful as a flock of sheep at their feet.
The sheep are attacked by wolves, which, as all the learned
tell, are heretics, and these in turn are beaten off by a pack of
spotted hounds, which all men grant to be the *Domini Canes*,
the Lord's dogs, the Black and White Friars of the Holy Office.[1]

On December 4th the Dominicans appeared again. The
Pope, departing from the usual course, had appointed Father
Jandel as their general ; some say selecting him that he might
amend the theology of the order, the members of which were
known to be weak Immaculatists, and suspected of not being
sound Infallibilists. Father Jandel now broke out in a circular, which twenty years ago we should have smiled at as at
new *gri-gri*, but which now seems to be more like to the red
cross of the Muster. We shall presently see how scientifically
Tarquini had demonstrated that the right of *directly* wielding
the temporal sword did, in spite of all denials, belong to the
Pope and a General Council, and we have already seen with
what fascination popular pens were surrounding the life and
death of the 'soldier of the Cross.'

' We hasten,' exclaims Jandel, ' to announce to you the joyful tidings, and we make speed to convey to you the pontifical
brief which grants new indulgences for the recitation of the
rosary during the whole continuance of the Vatican Council.'
The brief thus heralded looks as if the inspiration of St. Peter

---

[1] This picture is fully described in Bryce's *Holy Roman Empire*, p. 129.
The same idea is reproduced in some pictures in Rome.

Arbues, 'first inquisitor of the kingdom of Aragon,' was beginning to operate. The Pontiff informs the faithful that St.
Dominic, armed with this rosary, as with an invincible sword,
crushed the infamous heresy of the Albigenses. Therefore, in
the present crisis, equipped with the same armour, and *with
the authority of the Vatican Council*, they will be enabled to
' overthrow and extirpate the manifold monsters of error that
prowl around.' To invite all to arm themselves with this holy
weapon, special indulgences are granted to those who will
daily recite ten rosaries, so long as the Council lasts. We
believe a rosary consists of one Paternoster, ten Ave Marias,
and one Gloria; so that each week seven hundred prayers to
the Virgin, seventy to God, with seventy doxologies, would
have to be repeated. The Pope strongly expresses his simple
faith in the efficacy of this expedient. [1]

Father Jandel, not content with the triumph of the rosary
against the Albigenses, cites another triumph calculated to
touch the national Italian party. Their ears had been tuned
to the epithet ' Mussulman ' ever since 1860, when General
Lamoricière unsheathed *his* 'rosary,' and in doing so, used
that epithet in his first general order to the ' œcumenical
army.' Father Jandel informs the faithful that it was by
virtue of this ' holy prayer' that Pius V. obtained the victory of
Lepanto over the Turks ; and, therefore, he is confident that
by the same weapon Pius IX. will vanquish the present foes
of religion, more embittered even than the Turks. In the
battle of Bagnorea in 1867, if the *Civiltà* be correct, the
crusaders of St. Peter—the few forerunners of the great
crusade yet to come—killed fifty-five Garibaldians, with the
loss to themselves only of Heykamp, 'the first of the zouaves
who hallowed with his blood the crusade of St. Peter.' And
on that miraculous day, eve of the holy rosary, surely, says
the writer, many rosaries passed through the hands of those
who so bravely plied the bayonet, and many hung round their

---

[1] *Guérin*, pp. 61, 62 ; *Friedberg*, p. 82.

necks. 'A public address from Rome to these soldiers said :
'You are blessed ·by two hundred millions of the faithful,
who applaud· you as heroes, who call you the favoured
martyrs of the liberty of the Church and of the world.'[1]
Jandel calls his own order, the heirs of the sacred patrimony
of St. Dominic ! Moreover, he quotes from a public appeal
of Cardinal Patrizi, in which the feats of St. Dominic, and
his destruction of the Albigenses by the rosary, are called
'glorious fruits' and 'grand recollections.' It is a familiar
fact that of all his predecessors the one selected as his model
by Pius IX. is Pius V., who conquered at Lepanto, who was
first inquisitor, then Pope, and finally was canonised.

All who know what has been going on in Europe of late
years know that the time for smiling at rosaries is past. A
charm or a *chupattie* ceases to be a trifle when it becomes the
symbol connecting devotion with deeds of blood. At a time
when millions upon millions of children are in the hands of
those who, with gentle manners and profoundly conscientious
views, instil antipathies which time can scarcely extract,
charms become formidable when to such antipathies they are
the symbols of—as the *Civiltà* puts it—a pure conscience, a
sublime cause, and an immortal hope.

The significance of these demonstrations was greatest for
those who had watched the doctrines which were being ela-
borated by the Jesuits and diffused both through periodicals
and such scholastic books as that of Tarquini. The doctrine of
Boniface VIII., that the material sword was not in the hand
of the priest, but only at his beck, was being replaced by a
higher one. Boniface accused those of Manichean dualism
who did not confess that both swords were in his *power*. But
it proved that he had himself leaned too much towards
dualism, for he denied the material sword to the priest's own
hand. This doctrine would no longer do. Cardinal Tarquini,
who, it must not be forgotten, is set before us by Cardinal

[1] VII., iii., 43-50.

Manning as the modern example of teaching milder than that of Bellarmine and Suarez, goes beyond the theology of former times, and claims the *direct* right of the sword, even in war, for the *hand of the Pope and a Council*, though still denying it to inferior ecclesiastical authorities.

'I admit,' says Tarquini (p. 39), 'that the Church is a spiritual society as to its end; I deny that it is so as to its substance,—that is, as to the members composing it, since they are not mere spirits but men. I admit that it ought to use spiritual means,—that is, means *which are adapted to the attainment* of the spiritual end. I deny that it should use only means which are spiritual in themselves and in their nature. Every one who is not a simpleton knows that men (in whom soul is joined with body) are to be moved, corrected, and coerced; hence they cannot be led to an end, even a spiritual one, by purely spiritual means. But the matter, quality, and proportion of the means is to be determined by the requirements of the end.'

As to the words of our Lord, that His disciples shall not exercise lordship as the kings of the Gentiles do, he admits that they bind the Church to shun dominion *so far as that means a spirit of ambition whereby any one might subject others to himself for his own glory or advantage;* but he denies that they require her to shun dominion in so far as it means the office of ruling, and that of administering means contributing to the attainment of her end.

He labours to meet the objection against the use of force by the Church, drawn from her own doctrine that men are to be called to her bosom freely and without compulsion. He asserts that liberty here means freedom from *intrinsic necessity,* but not from *extrinsic necessity,* or coaction. This coaction or compulsion does not prevent either merit, or the attainment of the spiritual end; indeed, when applied by the Church, greatly promotes them. He admits that compulsion is not to be used towards infidels—that is, unbaptized persons—but denies that it is not to be used towards baptized persons.

As to the objection founded on 2 Tim. iv. 2-5, that 'the weapons of the Church are altogether confined to exhortations and tears,' ,he simply says, I deny it. Then he argues that the words of St. Paul in this place rather weaken than support those who oppose the use of force ; because the terms he employs are both *general and sharp: reprove, rebuke, be instant in season and out of season.* All means which necessity may call for are included. He admits that longsuffering and doctrine are to be employed, if necessity demands no harsher means ; but denies that they are to be employed exclusively. He demands that the character of the times in which these texts were written shall not be forgotten, namely, times in which the Church, being under the unfriendly government of the heathen, *was not able to put forth the fulness of her power.*

After arguing that the Fathers are not adverse to the use of force, he comes to the crucial point, advancing his own doctrine incidentally, while refuting the assertion that all the doctors deny the use of the SWORD to the Church. First, he says that, as to the authority of all the doctors, the assertion is false, for there are not wanting doctors who severely censure those who deny such power to *the Pontiff and a General Council.*

He then asserts that this direct power of the sword is not to be exercised merely by authority of the ecclesiastical law, or by inferior magistrates of the Church. But as to the Roman Pontiff and a General Council, *whose power cannot be restricted by any ecclesiastical law,* these points are to be weighed :—

(1) They indisputably have this power, at least *mediately ;* that is, in such wise that they have the right of demanding from a Catholic prince the use of the sword against delinquents if the necessity of the Church require it.

(2) But it cannot be proved by any arguments that this right (*jus gladii*) may not be *immediately* exercised by the supreme magistracy of the Church, if necessity call for it ; for the contrary indeed may be demonstrated from natural law,

since the Church is a Perfect Society; and no passage can be cited from positive divine law in which it is really prohibited, for Matthew xxvi. 52 is quite inapplicable, where Christ says to Peter, *then a private man*, 'Put up again thy sword into its place;' and 2 Cor. x. 4, where Paul, declaring the might of his own power, says, '*The weapons of our warfare are not carnal* (that is, are not fragile or futile), *but are mighty through God to the pulling down of strongholds.*' The argument drawn from the gentleness of the Church is equally inapplicable; as if the necessary administration of justice was opposed to the true virtue of gentleness. Even the one rather more solid argument from the example of the Church does not rise to the height of a proof, since we cannot determine whether her abstinence arose from a defect of power, and not rather from a defect of opportuneness, either because a greater evil might be apprehended *from the use* of the power, or because it was more expedient to employ the ministerial action of civil society.

This reasoning makes these points plain: (1) That no ecclesiastical law could restrain the Pope and Council; (2) That they might command any Catholic prince to take up the sword against delinquents; (8) That they might also draw the sword by their own immediate act, if necessity required; (4) That the moral necessity would arise whenever more benefit would accrue to the Church from the direct exercise of the power of the sword, than from the ministerial action of temporal powers; (5) That only the supreme magistracy of the Church could determine when this case had actually arisen.

And it is to be remembered that when Tarquini wrote, the 'supreme magistracy' might have been described as the Pope and a Council, or as the Pope acting with the consent of the Church. But the writing of divorcement afterwards given to the poor Church by her Bridegroom, as he is often called (*sposo*), in the words '*not by consent of the Church,*' leaves no doubt that all which he then could do with her consent he now can do without it.

The second of the above points is familiar. But the others, when put together, are very serious, and to some extent new, at least in form. They prepare a logical foundation for an œcumenical army,—not only an army of the Holy Office, but a regular œcumenical army. This foundation is now being firmly laid in the minds of the hundreds of thousands over the world who are being trained for the future service of the Vatican Church, or for the Crusade of St. Peter. The fact that the meaning of carnal weapons is coolly assumed to be fragile or futile ones, is not to be overlooked. It would naturally follow that the chassepots at Mentana, which were neither fragile nor futile, were not carnal weapons. Of course Tarquini would have said that though in their proper nature carnal, when serving a purely spiritual end they took on a spiritual character. But we cannot forget that the 'strongholds' which the weapons of Paul were mighty to pull down were 'imaginations,' and the captives they led bound were 'thoughts.' That is a sphere in which the proper weapon is not either shot or fetter, but the word and the works of men whom God makes wise to teach and holy to charm. There is one symbol which the Vatican never sees, that of the true and only Head of the Church, with no sword in His hand, much less two, but one sharp sword with two edges proceeding *out of His mouth.* That alone is the weapon that is not carnal but mighty through God.

We now begin to see the grounds cropping out on which Mr. Bryce's doctrine of two heads to the Catholic State, one civil and one spiritual, was condemned. The days of dualism and Manicheism in any form were numbered.

With their complaints that the Jesuits, both in the confessionals and in their text-books, corrupted Catholic morality, the Liberal Catholics mingled loud and bitter complaints that they sought to make the people superstitious and to keep them ignorant. It was often alleged that even their schools, or those under their virtual if not ostensible control, were themselves preserves of ignorance and superstition, keeping the scholars from an education, according to their capacity, for one 'suited to their position,' and at the same time preparing them to receive all kinds of fables and 'lying wonders,' —a term not infrequently quoted by Liberal Catholics. Those fables and wonders would open a field so large, and one lying on a level so low, that we have not cared even to glance at them. As found in local clerical papers, or books of what is called 'devotions,' they are so gross that a writer could hardly repeat them without incurring loss, not only in the respect of others, but in self-respect. Liberal Catholics, however, know that they are a real power in Jesuit hands, one of the powers in the future war against science, the press, and free government, and through these, against Protestantism. One specimen of the higher order we may give, from which some opinion may be formed of those vented in small places, by ignorant men, through low publications. .

We speak of the great *Civiltà*,[1] of the 'metropolis of the Christian world,' and of a deliverance of the Capitol itself. The plan of the Garibaldians, insists the *Civiltà*, in October 1867, was to seize the Capitol and to ring the great bell, at the sound of which all over Rome their hordes were to rise. But Anna Maria Taigi, who had died thirty years before, in the odour of sanctity, had seen prophetic visions of Rome wasted with fire and sword, and dreadful with heaps of unburied corpses, breeding dire pestilence. Some thought that 1849 might have been the fulfilment of the vision; others that it was the attempt of 1867. But by the special 'devotion' to this saintly woman, such dread event was to be averted. On the evening when all felt that the shock was coming, but no one saw whence or how, a priest of ninety years old, 'well known to all in Rome,' said to another, 'I feel assured that the venerable Anna Maria will defend the city; and her image must at once be carried to the Capitol, for that is the point they will aim at; the Capitol once saved, Rome belongs to the Pope.' The other priest objected that the hour was late and the streets unsafe. The old man insisted, reassured him, blessed him, and sent him away with the image, charging him to place it on the highest point. As the priest, bearing the image, reached the steps of the Capitol, a friend from a window, perceiving him, earnestly warned him to go home. Trembling, yet resolute, he pressed up the hill. All was silent as a desert. Having reached the utmost height under the bell-tower, he was fixing up the image, when he heard people move, and a door opened. A woman appeared. 'I came,' said he, 'solely for the purpose of setting up an image.' It would appear that it was a picture, for he had brought wafers with him to fasten it. Carlotta (for that was the woman's name) looked at the image, and cried, 'Why, that is the venerable Anna Maria Taigi; I also practise devotion to her.' The priest withdrew in silence and in haste. Meanwhile a priest from Bologna went in to visit the nonagenarian devotee of Anna Maria. 'Don Pedro,' cried the old man, 'the Venerable has taken possession of the Capitol in the name of the Pope, and she will defend it from the Garibaldians.' The attempt on the Capitol was almost immediately made and failed. Those who remember the tale of the Capitol when Brennus was the Garibaldi will be tempted to ask how great is the present elevation of faith above that of the days of the sacred geese.

CHAPTER XIII.

Great Ceremony of Executive Spectacle, called a Pro-Synodal Congregation, to forestall Attempts at Self-Organisation on the part of the Council—The Scene—The Allocution—Officers appointed by Royal Proclamation—Oath of Secrecy—Papers Distributed—How the Nine had foreseen and forestalled all Questions of Self-organisation—The Assembly made into a Conclave, not a General Council—Cecconi's Apology for the Rules.

THE event now to be described was called a Pro-Synodal Congregation. Being designed to give parliamentary effect to secret decisions of the Court, it was in reality a Ceremony of Executive Spectacle. Such a description seems obscure, but the official name is misleading. *Congregation* is the word used in Councils for deliberative sittings, in which measures are proposed and debated, in contrast to *Sessions*, which mean only grand public solemnities, where decrees already voted are formally adopted. Therefore the word Congregation would suggest deliberation and some sort of consultative participation, by the bishops, in the proceedings.

This prelude to the Council was not a vain show, but had been contrived by the best diplomatic and artistic skill of the Curia. After the Directing Congregation had spent nine months in elaborating rules of procedure to bind the bishops neck and foot, the Nine began to see that, should the Council meet before it was organised, it might fall into the temptation to organise itself. Some one skilled in parliamentary forms might move to elect officers, and to have, as in former times, open discussion, in order to hear questions of theology argued by the doctors, before they, the judges, began to frame their sentence. Some one might even suggest that they should agree upon their own rules of procedure. Now, all these points had been irrevocably settled beforehand against the episcopate by its superiors, and any attempt to discuss them might cause the greatest confusion. If some spirit, perhaps like Darboy, as is gravely said, 'excessively enamoured of liberty,' should once stir such questions, the records of Trent were there to show that it might cause trouble to settle them. Therefore the Nine were disquieted. Such possibilities must be forestalled.

Moreover, it had been resolved that, to take time by the forelock, the all-important Rules should be printed in advance, and should, before any possible self-action of the Council, be distributed during the grand public ceremonial of opening. Doubtless, when first adopted, this resolution seemed not only satisfactory, but far-seeing. It would be a direct assertion that in the presence of the Council, as in its absence, the Pope could and would make law by edict. It would place the bishops in the dilemma of either accepting as law to the Council what was merely an edict of the Pope, or of rebelling against a Bull actually issued. This would at first seem decisive. It was not till as late as the month of August that some one pair of eyes among the Nine caught sight of the fact that, the opening ceremony being legally a Session of the Council, some 'advanced spirit' might take advantage of that circumstance to assert that the Rules, being issued in a sitting of the Council, were an act of the Council, and therefore were liable to revision by it. That would never do. Therefore, at two sittings, on August 16th and 22nd, the former resolution was rescinded, and the ingenious expedient was devised of the Ceremony of Executive Spectacle now to be described.[1] The Rules could be issued as part of the ceremony, and thereby would every pretext for declaring them an act of the Council be forestalled. Of course Cecconi spends few words in narrating those vast transactions, yet every now and then the *naïveté* of his expressions, in the apology he presents for them, is amusing to those in whose ideas free deliberation and constitutional forms are not alarming, and to whom the idea of taking away from venerable legislators, by ceremonial legerdemain, prescriptive rights of their order necessary to give any

[1] *Cecconi,* p. 153.

reality to their deliberations is not only alarming but morally offensive.

The Sixtine Chapel, connected in the imagination of the Fathers with all the glories and sanctities of their Church, was specially fitted up for the event. From every region under heaven gathered prelates richly attired, each feeling the splendour of the scene, and consciously augmenting it. Their susceptibilities of spectacle were vividly awake. As boys, those susceptibilities had been trained and forced. As men, they had themselves trained and forced the same susceptibilities in others. Now, in old age, they came to have the art of government by spectacle practised upon themselves; practised by masters to whom their consciences, sympathies, and imaginations taught them to look up. Under the skilled touch of those masters were they now about to let drop, without a word, and for the most part unconsciously, privileges of their order, which had been guarded by their predecessors as carefully as they would themselves guard their episcopal rings. The place, the men, the scene, the coming displays, and the dawning future, big with events, were, for the moment, all in all to them. It was the historic eve of the day of days; and deep feeling fluttered under their silk and brocade and gold.

Before their eyes spread the wonderful painting of Michael Angelo, in which, according to M. Frond, he 'reproduced' the scene of the last judgment. It is a monument to the power of genius, even when driven to work on what the true æsthetic of the painter told him should be left to the imaging of the spirit, and should not be attempted by the pencil. There, again, stood the vacant throne, waiting for him who, when he first ascended it, had, as the reader will remember, these words solemnly impressed upon his ear, in the house and by the ministers of God:—" Know that thou art Father of princes and of kings, and art Governor of the world."[1]

---

[1] Professor Massi's *Life of Pius IX. Frond*, i., p. 16. Also *Vitelleschi.*

The Cardinal Priests and Cardinal Bishops were on the right of the throne, the Cardinal Deacons on the left. Near it stood Patriarchs, Primates, and Archbishops, in regular gradation, and after them in regular gradation came Bishops, Abbots, and Generals of Orders. Every brilliant figure in that throng was standing, except the Cardinals. Through a door, preceded by his household, was seen entering the form of him who holds the place of God upon earth. The Sacred College stood up, all clad in violet, with rochette, mantelleta, and mozzetta. Then all cast themselves down upon their knees.[1] The Pontiff, blessing his prostrate vassals, moved to the throne, seated himself, and, with beaming visage, looked paternally down on the rulers of docile millions,—rulers whose many tinted splendour was but the effluence of his own majesty.

Now, in his hale, ringing voice, the Pope read an allocution. It expressed much affection for his venerable brethren, and solicitude for the success of their approaching deliberations. To those who had come up full of confidence in the moderation of the Curia, all that they heard was reassuring. To those who had been troubled with fears of hazardous innovation, the bearing and words of the initiated had been soothing, and so was all that now fell from the throne. Still, the few who really studied would look in vain for light on the questions which had been agitated. Were they here for a 'free Council,' or only to receive ready-made resolutions, and vote upon them? Were they to treat religious matters, or to be spurred on to a crusade against the parliaments, press, and universities of the Old World and the New? Who were to be entitled to vote? What kind of votes were bishops to have? Would they have a right of initiative? Would their right to meet privately, to print, to hear theologians discuss, to elect

---

[1] This is what is stated in the descriptions; but the *Acta* do not seem entirely to sustain it (p. 26). *Cardinales surrexerunt, caeteri qui aderant genua submiserunt*, is language which seems to indicate that the Cardinals did not kneel.

their own officers, and to fix their Rules of Procedure, be conscientiously respected ?

Questions like these, touching the essence of free deliberation, would occupy the minds only of those who thought of something more than the pleasure of grand displays, and the privilege of sharing in the holiest and most fruitful solemnities of the Church. Those who had such questions in their minds did not know that from December to the middle of October the Nine had been engaged in answering them, and had already taken care that every seam through which any constitutional liberties might leak in should be tightly calked.[1] Nor did they know that they were to-day gathered together for the very purpose of having many of these questions laid so deep that they should never rise again. Had they known the whole plan, was there one of them man enough to defeat it ? Mighty against civil authority, were they not weak as water against a higher and more domineering priest ?

Even the few would hardly have time to realise the fact that the paternal and cordial allocution gave no light upon practical matters, when lo ! Cardinal Antonelli on the right of the throne, and Cardinal Grassellini on the left ! And, presently, Cardinal Clarelli, the Secretary of Briefs, comes forth and proclaims :—

'Our Most Holy Lord Pius IX., Pope, for the good ordering of things to be done in this Council, as more largely contained in the Letters Apostolic to be forthwith distributed, hath elected and named Presidents of the General Congregations, to preside over the same in his name and with his authority, the Most Reverend Lords Cardinals Charles de Reisach, Bishop of the Sabina, Antony de Luca, Joseph Andrew Bizzarri, Aloysius Bilio, and Hannibal Capalti ' (*Acta*, p. 30).

This was immediately followed by the proclamation of the name of Bishop Fessler as secretary, and the names of other high officials. Upon this announcement the Pope solemnly gave the pontifical benediction. Without the Council, and before the Council, he had bound on earth the question of

---

[1] *Cecconi*, p. 161.

presidents, of secretary, of officers, and of rules. But his first deed was not bound in heaven. Reisach, proclaimed by him as chief president of the Council, was never to behold it.

As the Fathers took their seats, the master of the ceremonies led in Prince Orsini in the insignia of Prince-in-Waiting. The temporal prince kissed the sacred foot, and then took his place on the steps of the throne.

Now a long line of dignitaries was presented, and going down on the ground, formed a crescent of beautiful kneeling figures before the sovereign. Two Cardinal Deacons brought out the volume of the Holy Gospels, and, standing close to the Pontiff, held it above his knees. Monsignor Jacobini then read out as follows :—

'We, elected by your Holiness officers of the General Vatican Council, promise and swear upon the Holy Gospels, faithfully to discharge the duties required of us respectively, and moreover not to divulge or disclose to any one outside of the bosom of the said Council any of the matters proposed for examination in the said Council, nor yet the discussions, nor the speeches of individuals, but on all these, as also upon other matters committed to us, to observe inviolable secrecy.'[1]

Thereupon, each one rising in turn, and advancing in front of the priest-king, laid his right hand upon the book, held by the two Princes of the Church, and then said :— 'I, N. N., promise, vow, and swear, according to the tenor of the words just read. So help me God and these God's Holy Gospels!' He then kissed the book and the sacred foot.[2]

About the middle of the long succession rose John Baptist de Dominicis Tosti, and stood to take the oath as one of the promoters of the Council. Suppose that a voice had at that moment cried.: 'Some two years hence, this De Dominicis-Tosti and Prince Chigi shall sit side by side with two ministers of the Reformed Faith, as joint presidents over a public discussion, in this city, on the question whether Peter ever visited Rome, between Catholic priests on the one side,

---

[1] *Acta,* p. 32. Also *Civiltá,* December 1869, p. 740. Cecconi, *Documenta,* lix.
[2] *Frond.*

and Evangelical ministers on the other.' What an anathema would have burst from the disgusted prelates ! No such shadow of an impossible shade dimmed the brilliancy of the scene.

While under the various charms of that scene, the beauty of the colours, the perfection of the postures, and the grace of the men, few would remark that the form of oath, binding, as it did, to strict secrecy on the very subjects discussed, and even on speeches, turned their forthcoming assembly from a General Council into a Roman conclave. A few indeed might see, but the overwhelming majority would not see, that several points which Councils had settled for themselves, even when they met under Emperors, were now being splendidly settled for them beforehand,—in their presence, indeed, but without their co-operation, and scarcely with their conscious- ness. How could they think of such commonplace affairs in a moment like that? What with the glorious garments of the Sacred College, the stars and ribbons of Prince Orsini, the beauty of the enthroned Priest-King, the crescent of kneel- ing dignitaries before him, and the touching symbol of the temporal prince kissing the priestly foot and reverently waiting at the priestly throne, there was enough to dazzle men less under the spell of robes. True, the temporal prince was here but a pale reminiscence of better days,—of those days which some of them had called to the mind of the people since the gathering of 1867; days when kings, ere they received the crown, lay prostrate before the altar, and swore on their knees to administer canon law; days when they had, more- over, to take both sword and sceptre from the hands of the bishop.[1] Still, this temporal prince served to assert rights which had never been renounced, and was a comforting token of brighter times after the Council.

No sooner was the swearing of the officers over, than the

---

[1] A picture of this scene, full both of regrets and latent desires, will be found drawn since the Council in Manning's *Four Great Evils*, p. 87.

Pope took his departure. Then came the master of the ceremonies, and distributed some papers to the Fathers.[1]

All this time, those who thought only of the spectacle, with
its splendid novelties and venerable antiquities, formed no
small portion of the prelates, including numbers of the best
and the worst, the confiding good and the self-seeking bad.
Both of these classes would also be much occupied with
another subject, the only one touching the part they should
themselves have to play in the Council, respecting which
they were in a position intelligently to prepare. On it their
information was complete,—as complete, indeed, as it was
defective on matters relating to divinity or the constitution
of the Church. This subject was Dress. The inventory
sacrorum paramentorum had, indeed, given them full instructions; so that in saying that the minds of some Fathers
would be occupied with the subject, we do not mean that
they would be distracted by doubts as to the proper number
of vestments, or as to the colour of any of them. That would
have been intolerable; and even the Nine would scarcely have
dared to trifle with bishops on that ground. But to have all
in order for the most effective appearance, was of sacred
importance, not only for the honour of their respective sees,
but also for the glory of the Church Universal, involved, to
a high degree, in the success of the forthcoming demonstration. To men whose minds were engaged on questions of this
sort, the papers distributed by the master of ceremonies would
not be exciting. They proved to be the Allocution just delivered, the Program of Ceremonies for the opening of the
Council, and another document, Letters Apostolic,—longer,
and seemingly duller, than the Program. But this, too, was
distributed by the master of ceremonies. At Courts where
government by spectacle is preferred to government by reason,
ceremonies enclose a wide area. We have already seen street-

---

[1] *Stimmen aus Maria Laach, Neue Folge*, Heft vi., pp. 154-155. *Civiltá*,
Serie VII., vol. viii., pp. 739-740. *Frond*, vol. vii., pp. 64-71.

lighting treated of among ceremonies. Those who looked would see that these letters which the Pope found it necessary to address to men who were present, related to the order to be observed in the Council. But that might only mean godly advice. It did, however, mean a good deal more. It fixed, without the Council, and before it, the points which had more to do with its proceedings than anything else, except the men of whom it was composed. It revoked the immemorial rights which made a council a legislature, and instead of constitutional legislation it established what Montalembert happily called 'consultative despotism.' This Bull, *Multiplices Inter*, has already been quoted thousands of times, and will be quoted thousands more. The program of ceremonies for the opening day, however, would, for the present, cast *Multiplices Inter* into the shade as much as a Roman Monsignore, in full pontificals, would cast into the shade our Minister of War appearing before Parliament (*Acta*, p. 33-46).

What was the right of proposition, or the right of definition, or the right of public discussion, or the right of printing, or the right of meeting, in comparison with the proper places, forms, and postures? Besides, seeing that the directions for the pageant extended over one hundred and forty-eight articles, it was not a light matter to master them all, and at the same time to do so was all-important for those to whom an imposing 'function' was the efflorescence of divine and human beauty.[1] Did not Article 136 direct that the sacred pallium was to be taken off the Holy Father by the Cardinal Deacon, and to be delivered over to the Sub-Deacon Apostolic? Did not Article 39 direct that the Sub-Deacon Apostolic, accompanied by two judges of the High Court of the Signet, should bear the slippers to the throne; and Article 40 direct that the Pontiff should put them on?[2] Did not Article 23 direct that the

---

[1] *Acta*, p. 228-242. The title is *Methodus Servanda in prima sessione.*

[2] *Signaturæ Votantes;* see *Frond*, iii., p. 10.

Pontiff should make another genuflexion before the Host, and having assumed the mitre, should enter into the Council Hall, and there having blessed the Fathers and having taken off the mitre, should go and pray at the altar ? Probably, for one bishop who, after retiring, looked first into the fateful Rules, ninety would look into the Program.

It was two days after the issue of these documents that Professor Friedrich arrived in Rome. He found the Archbishops of Munich and Bamberg and the Bishop of Augsburg with the Program in their hands, and also the Rules of Procedure. They were full of confidence that the Curia did not intend to propose anything dangerous. But Friedrich wanted to learn what were the subjects to be proposed, on which point the bishops knew nothing. The members of Commissions had all been bound by oath to conceal, even from their own diocesans, what was prepared for them to vote. It was to be presented to them with this alternative—Vote it, or become marked men !

On reaching the Palazzo Valentini, Friedrich found that all that was known by Cardinal Hohenlohe as to the subjects which he would have to vote upon amounted to this ;—a few days previously Cardinal de Angelis had asserted that nothing would be done beyond condemning the principles of 1789. This proves that the purple, at least of Cardinal Hohenlohe, was kept as far aloof from the secrets of the Nine as the black of Friedrich. Cardinal de Angelis, not being one of the Nine, probably did not know all, but from his age and position in the Curia it is scarcely conceivable that he was so innocent as he appeared to be to his too liberal brother. If he was so, he soon, by an able electioneering manœuvre, did service which lifted him to a chief seat. Quirinus says (p. 77) that the most distinguished theologian in Rome, Cardinal Guidi, was not only kept in perfect ignorance of all that was being prepared, but was never admitted to an audience with the Pope after he had expressed to him his own views. Another notability is said

by the same author to have been also out of the circle of the
trusted, and many writers share this view; this was Father
Beckx, the General of the Jesuits. Words ascribed to him by
Quirinus are these : ' To recover two fractions of the States of
the Church they are pricking on to a war against the world ;
but they will lose all.'

The first remark of Friedrich on the Program savours of
the Church historian as strongly as that of some bishops would
do of the master of ceremonies:—'The Council is called the first
Vatican Council ; that means that others are to follow.' This
observation has been repeated, but it is not justified by the
document as printed in the *Acta*. There we read ' the first
session of the Vatican Council,' not ' the first Vatican Council.'
He soon, however, had matter for remark which admits of no
question. He found that the decision of constitutional points
of vital importance was to be wrapped up in a gay gauze of
ceremonies. The very form to be given to the Decrees was
slipped in among the items of the pageant. The conciliar
formula used at Trent was replaced by that of Papal Bulls.
The collective hierarchy were not to be permitted to say,
It seemed good to the Holy Ghost and to us; nor to say,
This Holy Council ordains and decrees. The name of the
Pope alone was to appear as decreeing, and the only words
in the decree indicating the existence of any Council were
' The Holy Council approving.' Matters like this, affecting
not only the framework of the Church, but the seat of dogmatic authority, were settled without a note of preparation,
in a program of ceremonies, among directions about fald-
stools, incense, and the Pope's slippers. It was as if the
Lord Chamberlain, when the Queen was about to open a
new Parliament, should put out a program of precedence,
costumes, and ceremonies, foisting in a few clauses indicating that her Majesty would promulge a statute or two,
with the approbation of the assembled Lords and Commons.
It would be no trifle if he did so of his own motion, but

would become tremendously serious if it had been done with full cognisance of the monarch.[1]

No wonder that the keen-eyed Professor was driven from the Program to the Rules of Procedure. But the fact that the other was the document first read, even by him—a man in whom the decorative element is evidently too feeble for a useful priest, and the critical element too strong—indicates the direction which the studies of gentlemen like his archbishops and bishops would take; gentlemen who, knowing that they had been jealously kept in the dark respecting what they were to be called to vote upon as the faith of their Church for ever, were nevertheless satisfied, by a few bows and smiles, that it was to be something of no importance.

Friedrich was deeply moved by what he found in the Rules, coupled with what he considered the ignorance of the bishops.

'Every adept,' he cries, 'must see that virtually the form here used in propounding decrees contains Papal infallibility. It is the Pope, and he alone, that defines and decides. Infallibility is even now attributed to him, and not to the Council, and then, seeing that this formula is to be acted upon in the first session (or public ceremony), it is the Pope who formulates the decree without having taken even the advice of the Council, and without any discussion on its part. It is not so much as known what are to be the subjects of the Decrees which the Council will adopt; and yet Decrees containing definitions are announced for the 8th. What can this mean? Are we really to have Papal infallibility carried by acclamation, as the *Civiltà* suggested, or shall we only have a Decree, as they had at Trent, declaring the Council open, and regulating the mode of life of its members? Who can tell? For my own part I am uncommonly disquieted' (p. 10).

This disquietude of Friedrich represented the first shock of

---

[1] Theiner, speaking of the relation of the three Popes under whom the Council of Trent sat, to that Council, says: It is as clear as the sunlight that those Pontiffs were not Dictators but Approvers of the laws which the Fathers, in conjunction with the Legates, framed. In support of this he cites two letters, one from Paul III. and the other from Pius IV. They both faithfully promise to confirm whatever the Council adopts. The former says, Even though it may somewhat conflict with the decisions of former Councils, or with the privileges of the Holy See. When this was read in the Council, the Bishop of Fiesole cried out: 'Let it be without prejudice to the universal authority of this Council.' (*Acta Genuina*, vol. i., pp. xvi. and 154.)

collision against sunk fences, which had cost the Nine long labour. According to their faithful historian, the 'most arduous and thorny of their tasks was that of settling the procedure.'

Cecconi is perfectly satisfied that it would never have done to leave the Council to arrange its own form of procedure. One argument which weighs with him is, that it took nearly ten months for a few persons of almost one mind to complete the work.

Cecconi, curiously enough, quotes Jeremy Bentham, to show that the good done by deliberative bodies depends, first, upon the persons of whom they are composed; and, secondly, upon their methods of procedure. The Nine even deigned to discuss whether the Pope had a right to lay down rules beforehand. We need not say that his right was affirmed. Clear, however, as, on the Papal theory, that right was, the troublesome old times could not be silenced. Even the Archbishop of Florence, in comparing the prelates with the Pope, lets the awkward expression drop, that with him the bishops are true judges and legislators. For this slip we must blame history, not the historian. The latter, however, must have the credit of the assertion that this does not imply the right of settling the mode of discussion and the form of judgment. Here he makes the word 'settling' cover all the ground that we should cover by the expression 'having one word to say to it.' We presume that the secondary judges, in any case, do not settle the modes of procedure without their President. But it scarcely follows that he fixes it behind their backs, and compels them to follow it, without hearing a word from them. As to legislators, true legislators, the idea of their having forced upon them Rules of Procedure which take away the right to bring in a question and all its concomitant rights, and regulate the minutest points in a restrictive sense, is absurd. It was admitted by the Nine that, even in the fifth Lateran Council, the question was put to the Fathers, whether the Rules drawn up were acceptable. It was also feared that the bishops might be offended if the Pope settled the Rules without hearing their opinion. But, on the other side, there were three arguments: first, the danger of 'interminable' discussions; secondly, the danger of 'some spirit excessively enamoured of liberty, and of too advanced opinions;' and, thirdly, the history of former Councils (p. 148). So in June it was finally determined that the Council should not be permitted to have a word to say to its own rules and forms of procedure. And in August, as we have seen, the perfect plan of forestalling all attempts to say a word upon them was contrived.

One possible objection was brought under attention, by the history of previous Councils, namely, that there might be a danger of the Pope restraining the rightful liberty of the bishops. This idea, however, was dispersed by the light logic which passes at Court. 'It would be no less a folly than an insult to think that a pontifical law could aim at lessening the liberty of the Council' (p. 147). In this happy sentence the now mitred historian refines on the words of M. Veuillot, who was content to say that all would be free because the Pope would be free.

The consultations of the Nine must have been serious upon the critical point of denying to the Council the right of introducing proposals. The course finally decided upon called for boldness in the deed, combined with art in the drapery. It was first settled that the right of proposition *belonged* to the Pope alone. Then it was argued that if this right was *granted* to the bishops, 'it would turn the Council itself into a constitutional assembly,'—which was just what, with all their faults, the earlier Councils had been, and even that of Trent, in an inferior degree.

The serious question of excluding all members of the Church but those constituting the Council had to be faced. Cecconi cannot conceal that at Trent the entrance to the Council Hall, during the discussions of the Doctors, was free. Massarellus,

the indefatigable secretary of that Council, in his minute of
those present at the first session, gives more names of laymen
than of archbishops. The insertion of their names means more
than that they were in the building,—they had seats of honour.[1]
The number of the order of priests present at that first sitting,
far exceeded that of the bishops. True, they had no vote ; but
they had a most important office, that of discussing points of
doctrine, in the presence of the bishops, before the latter
· themselves began to do so. They were the Bar, the prelates
the Bench. Massarellus himself, secretary from the beginning,
was only a doctor, till the Council reached the days of Pius IV.,
who made him a bishop.[2]

All the dragooning of the middle ages had not taught men
that it was right for millions to sit outside in the dark, while
a few priests consulted, and determined how their creeds,
catechisms, ordination vows, marriage obligations, parental
rights, and national duties were to be altered. The vast
changes consummated at Trent had not yet done their work
in reducing the human mind to servility. The Bible had
not been shackled by a General Council. The press had not
been scientifically gagged. Authors and booksellers had not
felt the scourge of the Index. Schools and colleges had
not been shut up against discussion and free inquiry, in
any such degree as was then introduced. Consequently the
Western Catholic of that day, though in a sense Roman, was
by no means that passive creature of priestly authority into
which three centuries of the sway of the Tridentine Decrees,
administered by a monarch never checked by a public legislature, have moulded the modern layman.

At Trent the people were present to hear what was said. At
the Vatican their political position and religious belief were
both to be decided upon by decrees not reformable, like all

---

[1] 'Post prælatos sedent nobiles, si qui adsunt.'—*Massarellus, Acta Gen.*, i., 5.
[2] *Acta Genuina*, vol. i., 29, 30. Licet sub Paulo III., et Julio III., essem
tantum utr. jur. doct. et protonotarius apostolicus, sub Pio autem IV. eram
episcopus Telesinus.—*Acta Gen.*, i., p. 5.

that men do; but irreformable, as if God had made them. Yet the presence of the people was looked upon as 'the interference of persons from without,' and this, it was felt, would be 'a deplorable inconvenience,' notably aggravated by the temper of the times because of the enormous diffusion of the press. The journals could not be prevented from writing about the Council; but means were sought to keep the subjects under discussion from the knowledge of the 'democracy,' as Maret calls priests and people. They should learn the tenor of Decrees adopted only when they were ratified (*Cecconi*, p. 253). To this end, three points were resolved upon: first, the General Congregations (that is, the deliberative sittings) should be altogether private; secondly, the public Sessions (that is, the grand solemnities for adopting and promulgating Decrees already framed and voted) should be open only in the liturgical part, the legislative part being strictly close; thirdly, all the Fathers and officers should be bound to the deepest silence (p. 254).

We are far from saying that the bishops of the time before Trent would have accepted a Roman conclave like this, in lieu of a General Council of the Catholic Church; but if they had done so, the laity of that time, from Emperor to burgher, would not have suffered it. The laity then did not represent the offspring of ten generations successively confined in the Tridentine cribs. Their rights, though roughly defined, were readily asserted, and sturdily maintained.

In justification of this measure Cecconi says little. His first argument is, that the vulgar—and the vulgar are so many—do not respect a law the real or supposed defects of which are pointed out before it becomes law. Thus 'public discussion, going before the adoption of a law, is always a detriment to the principle of authority.' It is in those communities in which the practice of previous discussion is oldest and freest, that laws, even when unpopular, are kept with the least physical force to back them.

The second argument of Cecconi in favour of this secrecy is a quotation from an Italian writer to the effect that all associations have some part of their proceedings secret. The British government has many parts of its proceedings secret; but that does not prove that, when it is about to make laws, it should seal them up, till they are in the statute-book. Yet, if it had even done so, the law, once made, might be modified or indeed repealed the following year. But in the case in hand the law, once made, is incapable of either amendment or repeal. Moreover, a breach of the civil law carries, at the worst, only a temporal penalty. The next attempt to support the measure is by finding something in the history of Councils, and all the author can do, he does; that is, he says that the neglect of such precautions at Trent caused much inconvenience. Did the adoption of secrecy at the Vatican Council prevent inconvenience?[1]

The Directing Congregation, having now existed for nearly five years, had preordained all that was to come to pass in the Council. It had held fifty-nine formal meetings, very many of which were devoted to the Rules of Procedure. Beyond the purpled Nine, not a soul was ever admitted, save only Monsignor Giannelli, their secretary. Five of the Nine were the destined Presidents of the Council. So that, of the whole College of Cardinals, only four besides the Presidents were in the secrets of this body. Just at a few of the last meetings, Bishop Fessler, the secretary of the Council, was called in. It is not needful to say that the Directing Congregation was in constant official communication with the

---

[1] What Cecconi alludes to were complaints made at Trent, by the Legates, of breaches of prudence rather than of secrecy,—such complaints as might have been made in those days in any legislative assembly. They were made late in the proceedings, and were restricted to the one point, that persons, by sending away Drafts of Decrees still liable to all sorts of changes before their final adoption, had caused such to be published as if they were definitive Decrees of the Council; a sort of difficulty that can never be avoided by anything but the fullest publicity, and by the effects of it long acting upon the public mind.

Pontiff.[1] Cecconi's defence of the network of restrictions which
it was deemed well to cast over the heads of the bishops the
moment they entered the Hall, deserves serious study from
both statesmen and divines. We shall see in practice how,
step by step, the bishops found out that the net entangled all
their movements.

CHAPTER XIV.

The Eve of the Council—Rejoicings—Rome the Universal Fatherland—Veuillot's
Joy—Processions—Symbolic Sunbeams—The Joybells—The Vision of St.
Ambrose—The Disfranchisement of Kings.

THE *Civiltà* described how, in beholding prelates daily arrive,
the joy of Rome rose higher and higher; joy resembling
but surpassing that of the great events of 1854, 1862, and
1867. Not only prelates came, but champions of the sword,
the pen, and the tribune, ready to face the world in the cause
of the Pope-King. Count Henri de Riancey begs pardon of
Rome for indulging, at such a moment, in a word for France.
Yet his heart does not turn to France, except on account of
what she has done for the Pope.

'Let Rome, the fatherland of all fatherlands, permit to us this flash of
patriotism. It is France which has the honour of guarding the last
fragments of the pontifical dominions . . . She has loved righteousness;
and that is the reason why she is anointed with the oil of gladness above
her fellows' (*Frond*, vol. i., p. xix.).

Poor France! that love of righteousness, which had made
her slay so many Italians to keep up the temporal power,
was not to avert from her, 'in the year of the Council,' a
baptism other than that of the oil of gladness.

Ordinary Christians would not catch the reference in the
above quotation. To them, 'loving righteousness,' especially
when connected with the person of the Messiah, is not

---

[1] *Cecconi*, p. 268.

identified with, but in holy opposition to, the idea of setting Christian ministers in rank before secular princes, and in power above kings. But 'He loved righteousness and hated iniquity' stands upon the tomb of Hildebrand, who sought to establish the 'dominion of Christ,' the 'kingdom of God,' the 'reign of righteousness,' or as many similar expressions as you please, by subjecting all the kings of the earth to the Priest of God. Pius IX. is frequently spoken of as the founder of the lordship of the Pope over the whole earth in the future, as Hildebrand was the founder of his lordship over it in the past. Therefore the sweetness felt by a good Ultramontane in connecting the two together.

'I am bewildered with joy,' cried M. Veuillot. 'I try to depict that joy, to swim in life. There is an unspeakable gladness in men's souls. People feel an aurora. I picked up a number of journals, and was going to answer a lively article against myself, in the *Gazette de France;* but the author has no idea how all his eloquence falls short of a man who, in one and the same day, has seen Pius IX., Rome, and the Sun.'

Pius IX. had not admitted M. Veuillot to kiss the sacred foot for merely literary service. The devoted advocate laid at the feet he kissed three thousand pounds in money, collected, through his paper, for the expenses of the Council. M. Veuillot scolds M. Taine grandly, for having made some comparison between Rome and Paris,—Paris, stretching from the field of Pantin on one side, to the Follies Belleville on the other; and Rome, which has no limits but those of the world, and does not accept those;—Paris, which gives birth to M. Rochefort; and Rome, which directs the Nineteenth Œcumenical Council! Had M. Taine seen Rome yesterday, full of processions of all colours, and bishops of all countries, he would have said it was more lovely than Paris.

The processions of all colours were no fancy stroke. Nine days of solemn service in honour of the approaching anniversary of the Immaculate, and at the same time of the Council, gave an opportunity of showing to strangers all the confraternities of Rome. They marched to the various basilicas, especially to St. Peter's; the ostensible object being to worship the sacred relics which, with uncommon magnificence, were exposed to their veneration.

All visitors to Rome can set the costume before their eyes—a loose, long garment, covering the person to the foot, and a hood, shaped exactly like an extinguisher, and often drawn over the head and face, with a pair of holes for the eyes. When the dress is dark, the day thunderous, the scene the Coliseum, and the confraternity a group of twenty or thirty tall men marching with frequent and irregular turning of heads, the effect is one of the oddest to be witnessed anywhere.

One is told that it is penitence, or, perhaps more literally, penance; and the imagination seems challenged to picture what penitence is going on in there, where the masked man looks out on all the world, and no one can look in on him. At the time we now describe, all these bodies were set in motion. One troop in the blue of St. Joseph, another in the white of St. Catherine, yet another in the blue and white of St. Mary of Divine Help; then the brown of St. Felice, the violet of St. Bartholomew, the scarlet of the Trinity, the white and scarlet of Gregory, the scarlet and white of Jesus, the black of Death, and the red and purple of the precious Blood, and so on through almost every combination of colours. These, crossing the masses which thronged the narrow streets, and crossing one another in all directions, winding through quaint little piazzas of every shape, under the shadow of churches, of stern-looking convents, and of palaces with windows grated as if violence was at every door, amused the sight-seer and delighted the Catholic eye with the double solace of colours and of a show of spiritual life and physical force.

The clergy of all lands saw and were seen with wonder and delight. 'When therefore,' said Eusebius, speaking of Nicæa, 'the Emperor's order was brought into all the provinces, persons set out as if for some goal, and ran with all imaginable alacrity, for the hope of good things drew them, and the participation of peace, and lastly a new miracle, to wit, the sight of so great an Emperor.'[1] Dr. Friedrich does not express himself so prettily as Eusebius on the appearance of the assembled clergy. The Asiatic cries, 'And one city received them all, as it were some vast garland of priests, made up of a variety of beautiful flowers.' The Bavarian says, 'The clergy of every country have sent a strong contingent, from the proud monsignore to the dirtiest village priest.'

The importance of sunny weather for public events, great everywhere, is perhaps exaggerated in Rome. Pius IX. is believed to be peculiarly susceptible to sunbeams. Three of his most memorable days are, by his adorers, connected with a sunburst which shone for him especially. Professor Massi relates how, on the day of his 'taking possession,' the *apostolic cortége* followed the 'brilliant carriage' of the new Pope from the Via Sacra up the Cœlian Hill, the Cardinals being mounted on 'steeds richly adorned'—doubtless worthy to be compared with those Sicilian steeds which bore Gregory the Great, of whose stud Gregorovius soberly says, 'We scarcely doubt but that Pindar would have thought the apostolic horses worthy of an ode.'[2] The day was overcast—which omen had a damping effect—but just as the new Pope approached the Lateran, a glorious rainbow spanned the east, gladdening all with the certainty of a reign of peace. In like manner, Professor Massi tells of that proud April evening when the Pontiff, after a long exile, once more looked down upon the earth from his own Olympus. The clerical writers do not exactly call it heaven, but content themselves with speaking of the figure of the Pope so exalted, as 'standing between earth and heaven,' or as a spectacle which reminds

[1] *Life of Const.*, lib. iii., cap. 6.
[2] *Geschichte der Stadt.*, rom. ii., p. 60.

us of the Divinity (*Frond*, i., p. 16). The secularising of sacred terms, till we come down to 'apostolic cortéges' and 'apostolic horses,' and the materialising of spiritual terms, till 'the kingdom of Christ' sometimes means the temporal power, is a process which must go on until the heaven of the materialised imagination will be levelled to the height of the noblest dome, and to the beauties of the best decorator. The peerless piazza of St. Peter's was, on the day in question, filled with French uniforms. At the foot of the great staircase rose a platform covered with purple, and decked with flying banners. The heavens, all day covered with clouds, suddenly turned azure, and the setting sun poured his beams on the dome of Michael Angelo, on the cross of the Obelisk, and on the statues which adorn the Colonnade, just as Pius IX. 'raised his paternal hand to bless the arms which had avenged his throne.' The third day on which the sun shone expressly for Pius IX. has been already mentioned, that of the Immaculate Conception. In contrast with all this, no one who was in Rome at the Easter of 1860 can forget the impression made on both 'Catholics' and 'Liberals' by the fact that 'the weather had turned revolutionist;' that is, it rained so hard that the Pope could not assemble the people under the balcony, and give the benediction thence to the city and the world. Professor Massi does not mention that bad omen, but he does call 1860 the most fatal of years for Italy, because it was the year of Marsala, of the Volturno, and of Castelfidardo.

It was not only, as some say, the nuns, but also priests and *literateurs* who took it as both indispensable and certain that St. Peter's should be bathed in the brightest gold the skies could send on the day which was to unite three glories—the anniversary of the Immaculate, the opening of the General Council, and the probable acclamation of Pius IX. as infallible.

On the 7th of December, when the mid-day gun was fired from St. Angelo's, a peal of joybells rang out from more than four hundred churches. From the distant Cœlian came the deep note of the Lateran, floating over Coliseum and Capitol ; from the Esquiline came that of Santa Maria Maggiore, floating over the Quirinal. These two met the boom of St. Peter's swinging across the Tiber, and, blending with it, formed, in that sea of sound, a rolling base for the billows, on whose crests every variety of bell-note clashed and sparkled. Far beyond the gates, the lone and beautiful St. Paul's lifted up its voice, as if bidding the untilled plains to tell the unfrequented shore that there was joy in the cloister capital.

Hints from Jesuit pens lead us to see some of the Order standing on the Janiculum, by St. Pietro in Montorio, drinking in the view of the renowned panorama, while the impressions of years would be brought to a focus by the sensations of a moment. Every thrill would be taken either for a proof or a promise. Things done by the Order were being glorified, things to be done were being assured by the voice of many Churches. Before memory would rise the figures of Hildebrand, Dominic, Ignatius, illuminated by the imagination of the past. Before hope would rise the figure of the new Hildebrand, with his now unlimited sceptre, and new Loyolas and Dominics, illuminated by the imagination of the future. Other German Henrys would be seen standing in penance, other English Johns signing away their supremacy ; and surely if at Ingolstadt the Order had trained a Ferdinand II., another could now be trained, and the Virgin and St. Ignatius would not fail to raise up a more successful Tilly, and a more faithful Wallenstein. ' Be wise now therefore, O ye kings ; be instructed, ye judges of the earth,' would seem ringing with articulate speech from the tongue of every bell.

Close by St. Pietro in Montorio were the bases, already laid, of a column to commemorate the Council. Week after week, the digging for a foundation had discovered only sand, which clerical writers lamented, without noting it as symbolic. But fifty or sixty feet down the tufa was reached;

and the trophy was to tower above the city, commanding Vatican, Quirinal, and Capitol, and in sight of the Sabine and the Alban Hills, and of Mount Soracte. It was to be built of rare ancient African marble, found in recent excavations, close under the Aventine. The column was to be supported on blocks of marble numbering as many as there might be bishops at the Council. Thus were the treasures amassed by the Cæsars destined, said the *Civiltà* and its manifold echoes, to enrich the triumphs of the Church. Liberal Catholics told how the architect had purposely chosen his ground, and thereby had relieved the Church of a few thousands extra of her riches, by the enormous cost of the foundations.

The exuberant joy of M. Veuillot might be taken for French vivacity, but Italian and German Jesuits all 'feel an aurora.' The Order is about to be mistress of the Church, and the Church to be mistress of the world. So, very sweet to them was the silence after the Angelus, and the Jesuit calmly wrote down that the joy-peals had told the faithful throughout the world that in a few hours the greatest event of the age would open. Who now could fear for the throne of the Father of kings and princes, the Governor of the world? Every fighting fibre in the sons of Loyala would vibrate, as to a call from the sky. It was to this left bank that Evander pointed, indicating the unlooked-for Etruscan auxiliaries; when the heaven-sent hero heard, in this very air now pulsating with the voice of bells, the clang of the heaven-sent armour, swung and struck by his celestial mother. Like Æneas, the Society said: I am called for by Olympus! The hand of the Virgin and St. Michael had swung the bells.[1]

From another of the commanding points we may suppose eyes illuminated with different lights looking at the same moment on the landscape. There is scarcely a finer view of the Roman panorama than that from the tower of the Palazzo Caffarelli,

<hr>

[1] *Æneid*, VIII., 427.

the German embassy, on the Capitoline. Thence probably would Count Arnim and some of his countrymen survey the scene that day. They knew much more of the past than most Romans, and were not unaware of the grandiose future which was meant to be rung in by the chimes. They knew that the plans of that future provided for a fresh disruption of the Fatherland, as well as of that Italy which lay over yonder hills. At such a moment a German, familiar with Niebuhr, Bunsen, and Gregorovius, could not meditate upon that field, his imagination marching to the music of the bells, without seeing many a vision of the past flitting and eddying amid the mists of the future, and whirling the imagination round and round in utter defiance of order:—Numa, the first of the function-concocting Romans; Romulus, the first to whom they prayed after his death; Theodoric the mighty Goth, ignorant as either; Paul in bonds; Cæsar in his car and in his blood; Cecilia and her strains; Titus and Jerusalem; Cicero and Catiline; Sulla and all his blots; Genseric and the temple vessels; Benedict IX. and his vices; Anthony and Cleopatra; Regulus and his fortitude; Macbeth a penitential pilgrim; Otho III. dwelling and dreaming just over there on the Aventine; Charlemagne kneeling at St. Peter's tomb; Christina of Sweden; Belisarius sole hero of Byzantium in Italy; Galileo and Bellarmine in debate; Luther on the holy stair seeking pardon by penance, and finding mercy by faith; Hannibal on yonder Sabine heights; and there on Mount Mario, beyond the dome, the gibbets of Crescentius and the twelve Roman chiefs waving before the pilgrims on the April morn, telling them that the two cousins, flaxen-haired lads, Kaiser and Pope, were not to be trifled with,—all this, mingled with many a tumult and many a slaughter, with fabric of relics and parade of dead men's bones, with orgies in apostolic palace and pining in secular home, with ever and anon a confused rush across the scene of rioters and conquerors, of prætorians and inquisitors, and at intervals strangely rising up amid soiled figures in the frock, and ensanguined figures in the helm, a Christian form in pure linen, clean and white.

As the *Ave Maria* sounded in the sunset, the guns of St. Angelo saluted the happy eve. The Pope rode in state to the Church of the Twelve Apostles, and the crowd lined the entire way. The Jesuit writers heard enthusiastic cheers at every point. Some partial illuminations were attempted, but the weather was unfavourable. This, however, damped not the spirits of any one, for there was to be a glorious illumination on the morrow, when the rain was bound to cease. M. Veuillot, buoyant as were his spirits, admitted that, with all his love for Rome, he could not deny that it rains there in winter. But hope was exulting, enthusiasm unbounded. The preparation of ideas had, it was thought, done its work; the restoration of facts was now not far off. The *Civiltà* asks, Did ever Council meet under such a Pope, with his graces and his virtues, his rich experience, his burden of palms won in incessant victories over the enemies of Christ; the restorer of the hierarchy in two nations, the founder of many dioceses, the conqueror of the fallacies, hypocrisies, and fraudulence of the politicastres of our day, the glorifier of the Virgin, who 'sensibly' covers him with her mantle, and takes delight in twining roses with the thorns whereof the tiara that crowns him is altogether composed?[1] The words of a French layman equal those of the Italian Jesuit. It is again the Count Henri de Riancoy who cries, 'The Father of the Fathers, Sovereign Pontiff of the bishops, refuge of the bishops; he is the Universal Patriarch, the Prefect of the house of God, the Guardian of the vineyard of the Lord. He it is who confirms the faith of Christians; he is Abraham in his patriarchate, Melchisedek in order, Moses in authority, Samuel in jurisdiction, Peter in power, Christ in unction' (*Frond*, i., p. xxx.).

It was St. Ambrose's day. M. Veuillot, in imagination, saw the saint 'appear on this threshold on which the eyes of

---

[1] Serie VII., vol. ix., p. 21.

the human species are fixed, full of hope.' But M. Veuillot
seldom meets with a saint, dead or living, but a political end
soon appears. This was, he cries, a felicitous rencounter. What
made it so ? (1) When Ambrose was appointed prefect, he
was told to act like a bishop. Now, though just at present
people would feel affronted by having a prefect appointed to
act as a bishop, ' the time is coming when the nations will
demand this affront. Perhaps it is not far off.' (2) When
Ambrose had become bishop, he excommunicated the Emperor
Theodosius for the crime of inhumanity. His image in this act
is to M. Veuillot evidently the prototype of Pius IX. leaving
the kings out of the Council. But it is one thing to refuse
the Communion, which was open for the humblest believer, to
the greatest potentate alive, because his word has wantonly
handed his subjects over to death ; and it is another thing to
refuse to all believers in existence a place, even as hearers, in
the chamber where new laws binding them and their children
for ever are to be decreed. Constantine, before he was even
baptized, was not only present in a Council, but was convener
of it; and, indeed, its most influential speaker, if Eusebius is
trustworthy. The princes were left out, being the heads of
the people; but they were left out expressly on the ground
that *they now represented their people.* Had they claimed to
hold authority from God, not through the collective fathers of
their respective nations, but through the Pope, to be exercised, first, by 'observing and causing to be observed' Canon
Law, and, secondly, by personally submitting their measures
to the supreme judge, one prince would have been more welcome than a score of bishops. But the representative principle,
as is often shown by Court writers, destroys the very theory
of the ' kingdom of God among men.'

It is this evil of popular representation and deliberative
assemblies which galls M. Veuillot and all his school. King
or president does not matter so much, if either would only do
two things: first, reign 'by the grace of God,' in the Jesuit

sense; and, secondly, govern the realm as a 'part' of the 'dominion of Christ,' in the same sense. M. Veuillot goes over ground familiar to all readers of the clerical papers, about the first deliberative assembly being the one that built the Tower of Babel. Of course our modern parliaments build nothing else but Towers of Babel, rather they 'reject, break, dissolve,' although they 'try to build with the mud of the deluge in the midst of earthquakes.' But now, in contrast to all this, the 'supreme legislature' is about to assemble around the Vicar of Christ. These old men did not choose themselves. God chose them. They are the true representatives of humanity.

The scene at Milan, and that at St. Peter's, similar to the ardent Ultramontane, would strike us rather by contrast. On the former threshold we see a Christian pastor guarding the Lord's Table. On the latter, a king, and an aspirant after universal political supremacy, guarding the secret of his own counsels. Outside the Milan threshold we see one sinner in purple, while the common Christians are free to approach. Outside the Vatican are all members of Churches whom the king in purple and scarlet acknowledges as members of his own Church. The people are disfranchised with the princes at their head. No doubt they value their Church, but they do not value the place in its counsels which their forefathers would have defended with their might. Outside are also the whole of the priests. They, too, are disfranchised, with their doctors at their head. They are but of the democracy now. They are proclaimed not to belong to the Teaching Church. They are ostentatiously told that to the mere priesthood does not belong any claim to rule the Church. On the one hand, *pastor* is expounded to mean bishop, in opposition to the lower clergy; and, as if by a design, to form a humorous counterpart to this, *sheep* is expounded as meaning bishops in relation to the Pope, while priests and people are *lambs*. The priests had long been losing their franchise in the election of their bishops. More recently they had been losing their freehold in their parishes. When the Jesuits obtained possession of Pius IX., the parish priest had a life interest in his parish subject to good behaviour. But this formed too much of a tie to the nation. The parochial clergy had to be mobilized. So, gradually, they had been put into berths only by temporary appointment, and held the place *ad nutum*, at the nod of the bishop. They had been glad that the sword *in the hand* of the king should not be in his power, but at the nod of the priest. It was scarcely so pleasant that the parish, in the hand of the priest, should be at the nod of the bishop. The making of it so had already to a large extent been accomplished. It was now to be completed; but those tyrannous kings might attempt to check the move by what they would call protecting the lower clergy, what the Vatican would call destroying the liberty of the Church.

The whole spirit of the Jesuit press at this period indicated that the Modern State had so wearied out the Vatican that the only chance for kings to make their peace with it would lie in separating their cause from that of parliaments and constitutions. If they meant to be tolerated long after the Council, they must not only reign but govern—govern Catholic States under the Syllabus. A feeling also seems to transpire, but is not clearly uttered, that republics, of the South American type, are rather more tractable than kings. Hereditary monarchy and a constitution combined seem to be found hard either to bend or break. A President, of the American type, is almost as bad. One of the Ecuador type is commendable. But the form is apparently not the question. A ruler by divine right,—which among the baptized means one instituted by the Pope and corrected by him,— is the essence of the matter. 'THE POPE AND THE PEOPLE!' is the last exclamation of M. Veuillot, on the eve of the day when the nations were to come to judgment;—on the eve of the day when the salutary conspiracy recommended by the *Civiltà* with its first breath was to hold its crowning conclave, when the holy Crusade, heralded with the same breath, was to receive both its legal warrant and its world-wide impulse. Great way had been made, and a triumphal arch was to mark the completion of a stage of toil and the entrance upon a stage of transformation. 'THE POPE AND THE PEOPLE. I believe that these words are invisibly written on the door of this Vatican Council, which door forms the entrance to a *new world;* rather is it a triumphal arch erected on the rediscovered highway of the human race.'[1]

These popular forecasts anticipated the practical application of Tarquini's principles. The prospect, clear and even bright to eyes anointed with the eyesalve of privileges and profits wherewith Court favour blessed M. Veuillot, was nevertheless overcast to those of Liberal Catholics. The words of *Ce Qui se Passe au Concile* sum up what many said :—

'The problem of the relations between civil society and the religious society rises up obscure and menacing. Internally, the harmony of Church and State ; externally, the reconciliation of the independence necessary to the head of the Catholic Church, with the modern principle of the rights of nations : never did these problems raise questions more burning or more formidable ' (p. 3).

Modern principle of rights of nations! Even to Liberal Catholics the right of a nation to dispose of its own destiny was a modern principle! Because the right of the Pope to dispose of it was the ancient one! Such is their antiquity.

That triumphal arch and that rediscovered way of the human species which, to M. Veuillot, made the entrance to the Vatican Council sublime, invested it, to the eyes of Liberal Catholics, with clouds of doubtful omen. The triumph vaunted was real and even stupendous, but it was a triumph over the principles in the name of which Liberal Catholics had fought and won the battles of the Church. The rediscovered way was no other than the broad road of clerical dominion over spiritual and temporal things which, in the ages before

the Reformation, had led the Church down to a degree of corruption now denied by none ;—a broad road, which had since
then been swept and mended, but to which had in the meantime been added the countless sidepaths of Jesuit morals. If
all those sidepaths should by authority be opened for the
winding and the straying of human guile and passion, what
would the Catholic nations come to ? Every teacher would
become an adept in the art of asserting a good principle in
order, by qualifications, to rob it of all force; and every disciple
would become an adept in the corresponding art of self-govern-
ment; that is, in the art of evoking the praise of conscience
and of hushing its blame, according to a man's private judgment
of the lawfulness of the end he proposed to himself when he
employed evil means, and according to his judgment of the
lawfulness of the means he had employed when he accomplished an end that was obviously bad. Studious Liberal
Catholics were aware of the two sides of the Jesuit system
of morals, whereof Protestants generally were cognisant only
of one. These knew, indeed, that a lawful end renders the
means to it lawful; but Liberal Catholics knew that it was
also taught that an unlawful end did not infect with guilt
the means by which it had been reached, provided only that
in themselves those means consisted of acts not necessarily
unlawful. Thus on both sides—that of seeking a lawful
end by unlawful means, and that of employing lawful means
for an unlawful end—was the gate made wider, the road
broader, and the way more smooth for guile to creep or
passion to roll downward, but attended all along by the com-
forts of absolution, and sprinkled with holy water.[1]

And as to the new world to which the Council was to be an
entrance, Liberal Catholics had seen the Pope's special *college*

---

[1] See Gury, especially his *Casus Conscientiæ*. A small duodecimo *Doctrina
Moralis Jesuitarum* (Celle, 1874), gives copious extracts from Jesuit authors with
a German translation. For the English reader, Mr. Cartwright's work on the
Jesuits supplies a good outline.

of writers, in the *Civiltá*, dwell upon the act whereby Alexander VI. drew a line from pole to pole, and gave to Spain all regions that should be discovered to the west of it, and to Portugal all those that should be discovered to the east of it ; and contend that the Pope, in saying of those regions, I *give, concede*, and *assign* them to this king and to that, acted simply as the Vicar of Christ; nay, that by that act the autonomy of the Indians was not in the least offended ; that, indeed, the concession was a *sentence* of the competent authority, which resting upon right, moved for the ' supernal' good of religion ; that praise and not blame was due to the Pope for his sentence, and that, moreover, what in the jargon of infidel and of heretics was called the pretensions of Rome, was nothing else but the exercise of a clear and sublime right, resorted to by the Pope in seeking a solid protection, in new countries, for the autonomy of nations and of individuals, when otherwise, to the offence of religion, it might have been violated by barbarians.[1] But was this supreme power to dispose by sentence of the lot of nations, even though unknown, without in so doing offending in the least against their rights, to be exalted into eternal dogma ? If so, and if mankind would endure it, well might the door of the Council be regarded as the entrance to a new world.   But whether future ages will reckon it as the entrance to a new world or not, we are about to see that it was indeed the entrance to an arena on which was to be witnessed a process of revolution from above and a struggle of priest with priest, —a process as instructive, a struggle as curious, as any that our age has produced, among its many transformations of polity and redistributions of power.

[1] VI., i., 662-680.

APPENDIX A.

THE SYLLABUS WITH THE COUNTER PROPOSITIONS OF SCHRADER.

By reading the latter in the right-hand column the view which the Church asserts is at once obtained.

SYLLABUS OF THE PRINCIPAL ERRORS OF OUR TIME, WHICH ARE STIGMATISED IN THE CONSISTORIAL ALLOCUTIONS, ENCYCLICAL AND OTHER APOSTOLICAL LETTERS OF OUR MOST HOLY LORD, POPE PIUS IX.[1]

PROPOSITIONS OF FATHER SCHRADER, being in each case the logical *contrary* or *contradictory* of the propositions condemned ; and therefore, being those which the Church would assert as opposed to those denied. Schrader says, ' The *contradictory*, and not the *contrary*, is to be taken by the Catholic as the rule to guide his thoughts, words, and actions, as to the sense in which the several errors must be considered as being rejected, forbidden, and condemned according to the will and command of the Pope.' Schrader himself, however, sometimes gives what is clearly not the *contradictory* but the *contrary*.

SECT. I.—*Pantheism, Naturalism, and Rationalism Absolute.*

SECT. I.—*Pantheism, Naturalism, Absolute Rationalism.*

(*Note of Schrader.*—Absolute rationalism is that error which holds that revelation is impossible.)

1. There exists no Divine Power, Supreme Being, Wisdom and Provi-

1. There is one most high, all-wise, all-provident, and divine

[1] To give a translation from a Catholic source we use one issued at the office of the *Weekly Register.*

dence distinct from the universe, and God is none other than nature, and is therefore mutable. In effect, God is produced in man and in the world, and all things are God and have the very substance of God. God is, therefore, one and the same thing with the world, and thence mind is the same thing with matter, necessity with liberty, true with false, good with evil, justice with injustice.

Being, distinct from this universe of things; and God is not the same as nature, and therefore not subject to change. God does not actually come into existence in men and in the world. All is not God and has not the proper essence of God. God is not one and the same with the world, and hence mind is not the same as matter, necessity not the same as freedom, truth not the same as falsehood, good not the same as evil, nor righteousness the same as unrighteousness.

(*Remark of Schrader.*—But God is in man and in the world, because He is omnipresent.)

2. All action of God upon man and the world is to be denied.— (All. *Maxima quidem,* June 9th, 1862.)

2. All operation of God upon the world and upon man is not to be denied.

3. Human reason, without any regard to God, is the sole arbiter of truth and falsehood, of good and evil; it is its own law to itself, and suffices by its natural force to secure the welfare of men and of nations.

3. Human reason is not to be the arbiter of truth and falsehood, of good and evil, without any regard to God. It is not a law to itself; and it is not sufficient, by its native powers, to provide for the welfare of man and of nations.

4. All the truths of religion are derived from the innate strength of human reason, whence reason is the master rule by which man can and ought to arrive at the knowledge of all truths of every kind.

4. All the truths of religion do not flow from the natural force of human reason; therefore reason is not the highest rule by which men may arrive at the knowledge of truths of every kind.

5. Divine revelation is imperfect, and, therefore, subject to a continual and indefinite progress which corresponds with the progress of human reason.

5. Divine revelation is not imperfect, and therefore is not subject to a continual and unlimited progress which would respond to the progress of human reason.

6. Christian faith is in opposition to human reason, and divine revelation not only does not benefit, but even injures the perfection of man.

6. The Christian faith is not contradictory to human reason; and the divine revelation not only is no hindrance to human perfection, but is serviceable to it.

7. The prophecies and miracles told and narrated in the Sacred Scriptures are the fictions of poets, and the mysteries of the Christian faith are the result of philosophical investigations. In the books of the two Testaments there are contained mythical inventions, and Jesus Christ is Himself a mythical fiction.

7. The prophecies and miracles reported and related in Holy Scripture are no inventions of poets ; and the mysteries of faith are not the sum of philosophical research. In the books of the two Testaments there are no mythical inventions, and Jesus Christ Himself is not a mythical fiction.

SECT. II.—*Rationalism moderate.*

SECT. II.—*Moderate Rationalism.*

(*Note of Schrader.*—Moderate rationalism is the error of those who do not hold revelation to be impossible, but would have it subjected to reason.)

8. As human reason is placed on a level with religion, so theological systems must be treated in the same manner as philosophical ones.

8. As human reason may not be placed on a level with religion, theological studies are not to be treated exactly as philosophical ones.

9. All the dogmas of the Christian religion are, without exception, the object of natural science or philosophy ; and human reason, instructed solely by history, is able by its own natural strength and principles to arrive at the true knowledge of even the most abstruse dogmas, such dogmas being proposed as subject-matter for the reason.

9. All doctrines of the Christian religion are not, without distinction, subjects for natural science or for philosophy, and human reason cannot from its natural powers and principles arrive at the knowledge of all, even the most obscure, dogmas, if such dogmas be only proposed to reason as its object.

(*Note of Author of the present work.*—In this proposition Schrader omits one clause of the original— *Historice tantum exculta.* This is evidently a mere oversight. These words should come after 'human reason.')

10. As the philosopher is one thing and philosophy is another, so it is the right and duty of the philosopher to submit himself to the authority which he shall have recognised as true ; but philosophy neither can nor ought to submit to any authority.

10. Although the philosopher is one thing and philosophy another, the former has not only the right and the duty to subject himself to the authority which he recognises as true, but also philosophy itself can and must submit to authority.

11. The Church not only ought never to animadvert upon philo-

11. The Church must not only sometimes proceed against philo

sophy, but ought to tolerate the errors of philosophy, leaving to philosophy the care of their correction.

(*Remark of Author of the present work.*—'Animadvert' is the reproduction of the original word, not the English of it. The French renders it *sévir*, to act rigorously towards; the German, *forgehen gegen*, to proceed against; the Italian, *corregere*, to correct, making it synonymous with 'correct' in the last clause. Even the maddest theorist would hardly deny to the Church the right to 'animadvert upon philosophy' to her heart's content.)

12. The decrees of the Apostolic See and of the Roman Congregations fetter the free progress of science.

13. The method and principles by which the old scholastic doctors cultivated theology are no longer suitable to the demands of the age and the progress of science.

14. Philosophy must be treated of without any account being taken of supernatural revelation.—(Id., ibid.)

N.B.—To the rationalistic system belong in great part the errors of Antony Gunther, condemned in the letter to the Cardinal Arch-

sophy, but she must not tolerate the errors of philosophy itself, and must not leave it to correct itself.

(*Remark of Schrader.*—The Church has the right and the duty of proceeding against false philosophy. She must not tolerate the errors of this philosophy, but must expose them to it, and demand from it that it put itself into harmony with revealed truth.)

12. Decrees of the Apostolic See, and of the Roman Congregations, do not hinder the free progress of science.

(*Remark of Schrader.*—Because the Apostolic See is appointed by God Himself as the teacher and defender of the truth.)

13. The method and the principles according to which the old scholastic doctors pursued the study of theology completely correspond with the wants of our time and with the progress of science.

(*Remark of Schrader.*—They have been frequently quoted by the Church with the highest expressions of praise, and have been earnestly recommended as the strongest shield of faith, and as formidable armour against its enemies, and have been productive of great utility and splendour to science, and perfectly correspond with the wants of all time and the progress of science.)

14. Philosophy must not be pursued without regard to supernatural revelation.

N.B.—The errors of Antony Günther for the most part were connected with a system of rationalism, which errors were rejected in a brief to the Archbishop of Cologne, bishop of Cologne, *Eximiam tuam,* June 15th, 1847 ; and in that to the Bishop of Breslau, *Dolore haud mediocri,* April 30th, 1860.

Eximiam tuam, June 15th, 1847 ; and in the brief to the Bishop of Breslau, *Dolore haud mediocri,* April 30th, 1860.

SECT. III.—*Indifferentism—Toleration.*

SECT. III. —*Indifferentism and Latitudinarianism.*

(*Note of Author of the present work.*—The original word is not *toleration,* but, as Schrader gives it, *latitudinarianism.*)

(*Note of Schrader.* — Latitudinarianism is that error which although it does not declare all religions to be alike good, yet does not hold the Catholic Church to be the only one which brings salvation.)

15. Every man is free to embrace and profess the religion he shall believe true, guided by the light of reason.

15. Every man is not entitled to embrace and to profess that religion which he may hold for the true one, led by the light of reason.

(*Remark of Schrader.*—But he must embrace the revealed truth in the Catholic religion.)

16. Men may in any religion find the way of eternal salvation, and obtain eternal salvation.

16. Men cannot find the way of eternal salvation, and obtain eternal blessedness, in the practice of every kind of religion.

(*Remark of Schrader.*—For it is to be held as of faith that out of the Apostolic Romish Church no one can be saved.)

17. The eternal salvation may at least be hoped for of all those who are not at all in the true Church of Christ.

17. The eternal salvation of all those who do not live in any way in the true Church of Christ is not to be hoped for.

(*Remark of Schrader.*—But only are we to admit that they who suffer from ignorance of the true religion are not held guilty on that account before God if their ignorance be invincible.)

18. Protestantism is nothing more than another form of the same true Christian religion, in which it is possible to please God equally as in the Catholic Church.

18. Protestantism is not merely a different form of the same Christian faith ; and it is not given to be equally well pleasing to God as in the Catholic Church.

(*Remark of Schrader.*—But it is a falling away from the full revealed truth.)

Sect. IV.—*Socialism, Communism, Secret Societies, Biblical Societies, Clerico-Liberal Societies.*

Pests of this description are frequently rebuked in the severest terms in the Encyc. *Qui pluribus,* Nov. 9th, 1846 ; All. *Quibus quantisque,* April 20th, 1849 ; Encyc. *Noscitis et nobiscum,* Dec. 8th, 1849 ; All. *Singulari quadam,* Dec. 9th, 1854 ; Encyc. *Quanto conficiamur mærore,* Aug. 10th, 1863.

Sect. IV.—*Socialism, Communism, Secret Societies, Bible Societies, Liberal Clerical Associations.*

(*Note of Schrader.*—Liberal Catholic associations mean associations of Italian priests who are enthusiastic for a free Church in a free State. Such pests have often, and in the severest words, been condemned, as in the Epist. Encycl. *Qui pluribus,* Nov. 9th, 1846 ; in Alloc. *Quibus quantisque,* April 20th, 1849 ; in Epist. Encycl. *Noscitis et nobiscum,* Dec. 8th, 1849 ; in Alloc. *Singulari quadam,* Dec. 9th, 1854 ; in Epist. Encycl. *Quanto conficiamur mærore,* Aug. 10th, 1863.

Sect. V. — *Errors concerning the Church and her Rights.*

19. The Church is not a true and perfect and entirely free association : she does not enjoy peculiar and perpetual rights conferred upon her by her Divine Founder, but it appertains to the civil power to define what are the rights and limits within which the Church may exercise authority.

20. The ecclesiastical power must not exercise its authority without the toleration and assent of the civil government.

21. The Church has not the power of defining dogmatically that the religion of the Catholic Church is the only true religion.

22. The obligation which binds Catholic teachers and authors applies only to those things which are proposed for universal belief as dogmas of the faith by the infallible judgment of the Church.

23. The Roman Pontiffs and Œcumenical Councils have exceeded the limits of their power, have usurped the rights of princes, and have even

Sect. V.—*Errors respecting the Church and her Rights.*

19. The Church is a true and perfect society, entirely free, and possesses her proper and permanent rights granted to her by her divine Founder, and it does not belong to the State to define what are the rights of the Church, and what are the limits within which she can exercise them.

20. The Church may use her authority without the permission or consent of the State.

21. The Church has the power dogmatically to decide that the religion of the Catholic Church is the only true religion.

22. The obligation which completely binds Catholic teachers and authors must not be limited only to subjects which are propounded to all, to be believed as articles of faith by an infallible utterance of the Church.

23. The Pope of Rome and the General Councils have not exceeded the limits of their power. They have not usurped the rights of

committed errors in defining matters of faith and morals.

24. The Church has not the power of availing herself of force or of any direct or indirect temporal power.

25. In addition to the authority inherent in the Episcopate, further temporal power is granted to it by the civil authority either expressly or tacitly, which power is on that account also revocable by the civil authority whenever it pleases.

26. The Church has not the natural and legitimate right of acquisition and possession.

27. The ministers of the Church and the Roman Pontiff ought to be absolutely excluded from all charge and dominion over temporal affairs.

28. Bishops have not the right of promulgating even their apostolical letters without the sanction of the government.

(*Remark of Author of the present work.*—Apostolic Letters mean Papal not episcopal manifestoes ; therefore the expression 'their apostolic letters' is not clear, and is not in the Latin.

29. Dispensations granted by the Roman Pontiff must be considered null, unless they have been requested by the civil government.

30. The immunity of the Church and of ecclesiastical persons derives its origin from civil law.

31. Ecclesiastical jurisdiction for

princes ; and in defining doctrines of faith and morals they have not erred.

24. The Church has the power to use external force. She has also a direct and an indirect temporal power.

(*Remark of Schrader.*—Not minds merely are subject to the power of the Church.)

25. Beyond the power inherent in the Episcopate no other temporal power has been conceded to it by the State either expressly or tacitly, and therefore not any power which the government of the State can at its pleasure withdraw.

26. The Church has an innate and legitimate right of acquisition and possession.

27. The ordained servants of the Church and the Roman Pontiff are by no means to be excluded from all control and dominion over temporal affairs.

28. Bishops themselves may publish apostolical letters without permission of the government of the State.

29. Graces granted by the Pope are not to be regarded as invalid if they are not requested by the government of the State.

30. The immunity of the Church and of ecclesiastical persons has not its origin in civil law.

(*Remark of Schrader.*—But has its root in the proper rights of the Church granted her by God.)

31. Spiritual jurisdiction for tem-

the temporal causes, whether civil or criminal, of the clergy, ought by all means to be abolished even without the concurrence and against the protest of the Holy See.

poral causes of the clergy, both civil and criminal, is not, by any means, to be abolished, and not without consulting the Apostolic See or against its protest.

(*Remark of Schrader.* — For it is founded in the proper right of the Church, and can be handed over to the temporal tribunals only through the express consent of the Pope.)

32. The personal immunity exonerating the clergy from military service may be abolished without violation either of natural right or of equity. Its abolition is called for by civil progress, especially in a community constituted upon principles of liberal government.

(*Note of Author of the present work.* —Most English translations make this apply not to students for the priesthood, but only to the clergy. The word in the original is not *clerus,* but *clericus,* which certainly in Rome means not only a clergyman, but also one in training for the clerical office.)

32. The abolition of the exemption of the clergy and students for the priesthood from military service cannot take place without a violation of natural right and of justice ; and the progress of the State does not demand its abolition, especially in a State which is constituted with a free government.

(*Remark of Schrader.*—The abolition of the personal exemption of priests and students for the priesthood from military service violates not only natural right and justice, but also the rights of the Church. The progress of the State does not only not demand it, but is opposed to it ; and the more freely a society is constituted, so much the more must it respect the personal exemption of the clergy and the student for the priesthood from the military service.)

33. It does not appertain exclusively to ecclesiastical jurisdiction by any right proper and inherent, to direct the teaching of theological subjects.

34. The doctrine of those who compare the Sovereign Pontiff to a free sovereignty acting in the Universal Church is a doctrine which prevailed in the middle ages only.

33. It belongs exclusively to the power of ecclesiastical jurisdiction, and that of proper and innate right, to control theological studies.

34. The doctrine which compares the Roman Pontiff to a free prince employing his own power in the Church, is not a doctrine which prevailed only in the middle ages.

(*Remark of Schrader.*—But is one which corresponds with the constitution of the Church, and therefore must prevail in all times.)

35. There would be no obstacle to the sentence of a General Council or the act of all the universal peoples transferring the pontifical sove-

35. There are grounds which forbid that either through the decisions of a General Council or the act of all nations the pontificate should

reignty from the Bishop and city of Rome to some other bishopric and some other city.

be withdrawn from the Bishop of Rome, and handed over to another bishop or another city.

(*Remark of Schrader.* — Neither through the decision of a General Council, nor through the deed of all nations, can it be overthrown that the pontificate is given to the Bishop of Rome and to the city of Rome.)

36. The definition of a National Council does not admit of any subsequent discussion, and the civil power can settle an affair as decided by such National Council.

36. The decision of a National Council does admit of further discussion ; and the government of a State cannot submit any matter to this decision.

(*Remark of Schrader.*—The decision of a National Council requires in order to its validity the consent and confirmation of the Holy See ; and the government of the State cannot appeal to the decision of a National Council as the ultimate tribunal, but must appeal to that of the See of Rome.)

37. National Churches can be established after being withdrawn and separated from the authority of the Roman Pontiff.

37. No National Churches can be erected which are withdrawn from the authority of the Pope of Rome, and fully separated from him.

(*Remark of Schrader.* — National Churches which are withdrawn from the authority of the Pope of Rome, and fully separated from him, cannot be set up ; because that is no less than rending and breaking up the unity of the Catholic Church, and because the power and manner of this unity imperatively require that as the members are connected with the head, so all believers upon earth must be united with, and joined to, the Roman Pontiff, who is the vicegerent of Christ upon earth.)

38. Many Roman Pontiffs have, by their too arbitrary conduct, contributed to the division of the Church into Eastern and Western.

38. The excessive and arbitrary acts of the Roman Pontiffs have had no part in bringing about the division of the Church into Eastern and Western.

SECT. VI.—*Errors about Civil Society, considered both in itself and in its relation to the Church.*

SECT. VI.—*Errors relating to Civil Society, both in itself and in its relations with the Church.*

39. The State is the origin and

39. The State does not possess as

source of all rights, and possesses rights which are not circumscribed by any limits.

the origin and fountain of all rights an unbounded right.

(*Remark of Schrader*—The State is not the origin and fountain of all rights, and hence does not possess any unbounded right.)

40. The teaching of the Catholic Church is opposed to the well-being and interests of society.

40. The doctrine of the Catholic Church is not contrary to the welfare and advantage of human society.

(*Remark of Schrader.*—But even helpful to it.)

41. The civil government, even when exercised by an infidel sovereign, possesses an indirect and negative power over religious affairs. It therefore possesses not only the right called that of *exequatur*, but also that of the (so-called) *appellatio ab abusu.* ['*Appel comme d'abus.*']

41. The State has not a direct and positive nor an indirect and negative right in religious things, and still less when its power is wielded by an unbelieving prince. It has neither the right of *exequatur* nor the right of *appellatio* which is called *ab abusu.*

42. In the case of conflicting laws between the two powers, the civil law ought to prevail.

42. In case of conflict between the laws of the two powers, the temporal law does not prevail.

43. The lay power has the authority to rescind, declare, and render null solemn conventions or *concordats* relating to the use of rights appertaining to ecclesiastical immunity, without the consent of the Apostolic See, and even in spite of its protests.

43. The temporal authority has not the power to revoke solemn treaties commonly called concordats, which have been made with the Holy See in respect to the exercise of the rights of ecclesiastical immunity without its consent or against its opposition, nor the right to declare or make them void.

(*Note of Author of the present work.* —It is noteworthy that while in Rome the doctrine of concordats, as taught by Tarquini and in the pages of the *Civiltà*, was that they were not bipartite treaties, but laws issued by the Pontiff at the instance of the temporal prince, in Austria and Germany, Schrader and Bishop Martin (see his *Katechismus des Kirchenrecht*), in order to uphold concordats, taught that they were solemn treaties.

44. The civil authority may interfere in matters related to religion, morality, and spiritual government, whence it has control over the instructions for the guidance of con-

44. The authority of the State cannot interfere in matters of religion or morals, or of spiritual government. It cannot therefore judge of the admonitions which chief

sciences issued, conformably with their mission, by the pastors of the Church. Further, it possesses power to decree in the matter of administering the Divine Sacraments and as to the dispositions necessary for their reception.

45. The entire direction of public schools in which the youth of Christian States are educated, except (to a certain extent) in the case of episcopal seminaries, may and must appertain to the civil power, and belong to it so far that no other authority whatsoever shall be recognised as having any right to interfere in the discipline of the schools, the arrangement of the studies, the taking of degrees, or the choice and approval of the teachers.

pastors of the Church in pursuance of their office issue as a rule for the guidance of consciences. Also it cannot decide upon the administration of the Holy Sacraments nor the dispositions necessary to their reception of them.

45. The entire direction of public schools in which the youth of a Christian State are educated, excepting episcopal seminaries in some particulars, cannot and must not be given to the State, even so that no right of any other authority to interfere in the discipline of the school, in the arrangement of studies, in the conferring of degrees, or in the choice and approval of teachers can be recognised.

(*Remark of Schrader.*—The supreme direction of public schools in which the youth of a Christian State are educated *pertains to the Church.* It is her duty to watch over all public and private schools, so that in the entire school system, but especially in what relates to religion, teachers may be appointed and books may be employed which shall be free from every suspicion of error ; and that thus masters and mistresses of the most approved rectitude may be chosen for the schools of the children and youth in the earliest years. The Church would act against the commands of her Divine Founder, and would be unfaithful to her most important duty committed to her by God, to care for the salvation of the souls of all men, if she gave up or interrupted her wholesome ruling influence over the primary schools, and she would be compelled to warn all believers and to declare to them that schools out of which the authority of the Church is driven, are schools hostile to the Church, and cannot be attended with good conscience.)

46. Further, even in clerical seminaries, the mode of study to be adopted must be submitted to the civil authority.

46. The direction of studies in clerical seminaries is in no way in the hands of the State authority.

47. The best theory of civil society requires that popular schools open to the children of all classes, and, generally, all public institutes intended for the instruction in letters and philosophy and for conducting the education of the young, should be freed from all ecclesiastical authority, government, and interference, and should be completely subjected to the civil and political power in conformity with the will of rulers and the prevalent opinions of the age.

47. The best mode of regulating a State does not demand that the national schools, which are open to all classes of the community, and generally public institutions destined for the higher scientific instruction, and the education of youth, should be withdrawn from all ecclesiastical authority, and completely handed over to the direction of the temporal and political authority, and should be conducted according to the pleasure of the government and the standard of current opinion.

(*Remark of Schrader.*—Such a corrupting method of instruction separated from the Catholic faith and the influence of the Church already exists, and is of great disadvantage to individuals and society in respect to learned and scientific instruction, and to the education of youth in public schools and institutions destined for the higher classes of society. But still greater evils and disadvantages spring out of this method if it is introduced into the national schools; and all efforts and attempts to exclude the influence of the Church from national schools emanate from a spirit extremely hostile to the Church, as from all the efforts to extinguish the light of our most holy faith among the people.)

48. This system of instructing youth, which consists in separating it from the Catholic faith and from the power of the Church, and in teaching it exclusively the knowledge of natural things and the earthly ends of social life alone, may be perfectly approved by Catholics.

48. Catholic men cannot put up with a kind of education of youth which is entirely separated from the Catholic faith and the authority of the Church, and which keeps exclusively in view the knowledge of natural things and the ends of earthly social life as the great object.

(*Remark of Schrader.*—An instruction of youth which imparts only the knowledge of natural things, and keeps in view only the ends of earthly social life, cannot lead youths to necessary salvation, but must draw them away from it.)

49. The civil power is entitled to prevent ministers of religion and

49. The State authority is not allowed to hinder bishops and be-

the faithful from communicating freely and mutually with each other and with the Roman Pontiff.

50. The lay authority possesses as inherent in itself the right of presenting bishops, and may require of them that they take possession of their dioceses before having received canonical institution and the apostolical letters of the Holy See.

51. And, further, the lay government has the right of deposing bishops from their pastoral functions, and is not bound to obey the Poman Pontiff in those things which relate to bishops' sees and the institution of bishops.

52. The government has of itself the right to alter the age prescribed by the Church for the religious profession both of men and women ; and may enjoin upon all religious establishments to admit no person to take solemn vows without its permission.

53. The laws for the protection of religious establishments and securing their rights and duties ought to be abolished ; nay, more, the civil government may lend its assistance to all who desire to quit the religious life which they have undertaken, and to break their vows. The government may also extinguish religious orders, collegiate churches, and simple benefices, even those belonging to private patronage, and submit their goods and revenues to the administration and disposal of the civil power.

lievers from holding free communication with the See of Rome.

50. The temporal authority has not the right of itself to present bishops, and cannot demand of them that they shall enter upon the administration of their dioceses before they have received canonical institution and the apostolic letters from the Holy See.

51. The temporal government has not the right to withdraw from bishops the exercise of their pastoral office, and it is bound in whatever relates to the episcopate and the appointment of bishops to obey the Pope of Rome.

52. The government cannot of its own right alter the age prescribed by the Church for the taking of vows, whether by men or by women. Nor can it forbid religious orders to admit any one to the taking of vows without its permission.

53. Those laws may not be abolished which relate to the protection of religious orders, and to their rights and duties ; and the government of the State cannot grant support to all who forsake their chosen condition in any order, and wish to break their solemn vows. Also it cannot abolish houses belonging to the orders, the collegiate churches, or their endowments, even when they are subject to a right of patronage, and cannot hand over their property to the administration and discretion of the State.

(*Remark of Schrader.*—Those laws which relate to the protection of religious orders, to their rights and to their duties, must not be abolished, but every government must far rather grant protection to the religious orders. If the government of the State grants support to those who forsake their chosen condition in any order, and wish to break their solemn vows, it acts against the spirit and the will of the Church. If they do away with the houses of the orders, their collegiate churches, or private endowments, even though they are subject to rights of patronage, and if they hand over their property to the administration and discretion of the State, they thereby rob the Church of her legitimate property, and they fall under the greater excommunication, as also under the other censures and pains which have been established by the Apostolic Constitutions, the Holy Canons, and the Decrees of General Councils, in particular of the Council of Trent. Sec. 22, cap. ii., against the violators and desecrators, and against the usurpers of the rights of the Apostolic See.)

54. Kings and princes are not only exempt from the jurisdiction of the Church, but are superior to the Church in litigated questions of jurisdiction.

54. Kings and princes are neither excluded from the jurisdiction of the Church, nor do they stand higher than the Church in determining questions of jurisdiction.

(*Remark of Schrader.*—But as members of the Church they are subject to the decision of the pastors, and especially of the chief pastors. Princes should much rather remember that the kingly power has not been delivered to them only for the government of the world, but especially for the protection of the Church, and what is done by them for the welfare of the Church is done for their kingdom and for its peace.)

55. The Church ought to be separated from the State, and the State from the Church.

55. The Church is neither to be separated from the State, nor the State from the Church.

SECT. VII.—*Errors concerning Natural and Christian Ethics.*

SECT. VII. — *Errors relating to Natural and Christian Ethics.*

56. Moral laws do not stand in need of the divine sanction, and there is no necessity that human laws should be conformable to the law of nature and receive their sanction from God.

56. Moral laws need a divine sanction, and it is necessary that human laws should be brought into accord with natural right, and should receive their binding force from God.

57. Knowledge of philosophical things, and morals, and civil laws, may, and must be, independent of divine and ecclesiastical authority.

57. Philosophy and philosophical ethics, as well as civil laws, should not and must not deviate from divine revelation, and from the authority of the Church.

58. No other forces are to be recognised except those which reside in matter, and all moral teaching and moral excellence ought to be made to consist in the accumulation and increase of riches by every possible means, and in the enjoyment of pleasure.

58. Other powers are to be acknowledged besides those found in matter, and the discipline and comeliness of manners should not be placed in the accumulation and multiplication of riches of every kind, and in the enjoyment of pleasures.

(*Remark of Schrader.*—There are other powers to acknowledge, belonging to a higher mental order than those which are found in matter, and also morality and propriety is destroyed in the mere accumulation and multiplication of riches, and the indulgence of evil lusts according to the words of the Scripture—' If ye live after the flesh ye shall die, but if ye through the spirit do mortify the deeds of the body ye shall live.')

59. Right consists in the material fact. All human duties are vain words, and all human acts have the force of right.

59. Right does not consist in the material fact. The duties of men are no empty name, and all human facts have not the force of right.

60. Authority is nothing else but the result of numerical superiority and material force.

60. Authority is something more than numbers and the sum of material forces.

(*Remark of Schrader.* — Otherwise fools would form the highest authority, for it is said of them in the Scripture that their number is infinite.)

61. An unjust act being successful inflicts no injury upon the sanctity of right.

61. Unrighteousness, even when attended by good fortune, tarnishes the sacredness of right.

62. The principle of non-intervention ought to be proclaimed and adhered to.

62. The so-called principle of non-intervention is not to be proclaimed and not to be observed.

(*Remark of Schrader.*—For it is a fatal principle, and opposed to the spirit of love and order.)

63. It is allowable to refuse obedience to legitimate princes; nay more, to rise in insurrection against them.

63. Obedience must not be denied to legitimate princes, much less must they be rebelled against.

(*Remark of Schrader.*—For it is written, 'Be subject to every human creature for God's sake; whether to the king, who is the highest, or to his lieutenants as such, who are appointed by him;' and he who sets himself against the ruler with force, he resists the ordinance of God, and they that resist shall receive condemnation.)

64. The violation of a solemn oath, nay, any wicked and flagitious action repugnant to the eternal law, is not only not blamable, but quite lawful, and worthy of the highest praise when done for the love of one's country.

64. The breach of every oath and every godless and shameful action in contradiction to the eternal laws are not only worthy of condemnation but also are eternally to be reprobated, and are not praiseworthy even when they are done out of love to one's native country.

(*Remark of Schrader.*—But by such criminal and perverted reasonings all propriety, virtue, and righteousness are entirely destroyed, and the evil conduct of the thief and assassin is defended and recommended with unheard-of impudence.)

SECT. VIII.— *Errors concerning Christian Marriage.*

65. It cannot be by any means tolerated to maintain that Christ has raised marriage to the dignity of a sacrament.

SECT. VIII. — *Errors relating to Christian Marriage.*

65. It is not to be in any way denied that Christ has elevated marriage to the dignity of a sacrament.

(*Remark of Schrader.*—Many proofs can be brought forward that Christ did elevate marriage to the dignity of a sacrament.)

66. The sacrament of marriage is only an adjunct of the contract and separable from it, and the sacrament itself only consists in the nuptial benediction.

66. The sacrament of marriage is not something simply accessory to the contract, and to be separated from it, and the sacrament does not lie simply and only in the benediction of the marriage.

67. By the law of nature the marriage tie is not indissoluble, and in many cases divorce, properly so called, may be pronounced by the civil authority.

67. By natural law the marriage bond is indissoluble, and in no case can divorce in the proper sense be legally pronounced by the temporal authority.

(*Remark of Schrader.* — Christian marriage is truly and properly one of the seven sacraments of the evangelical law, instituted by Christ the Lord,

Therefore it belongs altogether to the ecclesiastical authority to decide upon anything which in any way regards marriage.)

68. The Church has not the power of laying down what are diriment impediments to marriage. The civil authority does possess such a power, and can abolish impediments that may exist to marriage.

68. The Church has the authority to set up impediments invalidating marriage, but this does not belong to the temporal power, neither does it belong to the latter to annul impediments already existing.

69. In the later ages, the Church, when she laid down certain impediments as diriment to marriage, did so not of her own authority, but by a right borrowed from the civil power.

69. The Church has not only in later centuries begun to set up impediments invalidating marriage, and she has done so out of her own rights, and not out of rights lent to her by the temporal authority.

70. The canons of the Council of Trent, which pronounce censure of anathema against those who deny the Church the right of laying down what are diriment impediments, either are not dogmatic, or must be understood as referring to such borrowed power.

70. The canons of the Council of Trent which pronounce an anathema upon those who dare to deny the right of the Church to set up impediments invalidating marriage are dogmatic in their nature, and are not to be understood as of a borrowed power.

71. The form of solemnising marriage prescribed by the said Council, under penalty of nullity, does not bind in cases where the civil law has appointed another form, and decrees that this new form shall effectuate a valid marriage.

71. The Tridentine form is binding under penalty of invalidity, even where the law of the State has prescribed another form and makes the validity of marriage dependent upon it.

(*Remark of Schrader.*—The State law is invalid.)

72. Boniface VIII. is the first who declared that the vow of chastity pronounced at Ordination annuls marriage.

72. Boniface VIII. has not been the first to declare that a vow of chastity taken in ordination renders marriage null.

73. A merely civil contract may among Christians constitute a true marriage, and it is false either that the marriage contract between Christians must always be a sacrament, or that the contract is null if the sacrament be excluded.

73. No true marriage can exist between Christians by force of a civil contract, and it is true that either the contract of marriage between Christians is always a sacrament, or that the contract is null if the sacrament has been excluded.

(*Remark of Schrader.*—And thus,

therefore, every connection entered upon between man and woman among Christians, by virtue of a civil law, and without the sacrament, is nothing else than a shameful and corrupt concubinage condemned by the Church. Therefore the marriage tie can never be separated from the sacrament.)

74. Matrimonial causes and espousals belong by their nature to civil jurisdiction.

N.B.—Two other errors may tend in this direction upon the abolition of the celibacy of priests and the preference due to the state of marriage over that of virginity. These have been refuted ; the first in the Encyclical *Qui pluribus,* Nov. 9th, 1846 ; the second in the Letters Apostolical *Multiplices inter,* June 10th, 1851.

74. Matrimonial causes and causes arising from betrothals, from their nature do not belong to the temporal jurisdiction.

SECT. IX. — *Errors regarding the Civil Power of the Sovereign.*

75. The children of the Christian and Catholic Church are not agreed upon the compatibility of the temporal with the spiritual power.

SECT. IX. — *Errors relating to the Temporal Principality of the Roman Pontiff.*

75. There is no contention among the sons of the Christian and Catholic Church in regard to the compatibility of the temporal dominion with the spiritual.

(*Remark of Schrader.* — Because they are persuaded of it.)

76. The abolition of the temporal power of which the Apostolic See is possessed would contribute in the greatest degree to the liberty and prosperity of the Church.

76. The abolition of the temporal dominion possessed by the Apostolic See would not at all contribute to the freedom and to the happiness of the Church.

(*Remark of Schrader.*—The happiness and the welfare of the Church will be much more compromised, if not annihilated, since it is through a special decree of Divine Providence that after the division of the Roman Empire into several kingdoms and various territories, the Roman Pontiff. to whom the government and care of the whole Church is entrusted by the Lord Christ, received the temporal power, certainly for this reason, that he might possess that entire freedom for the government of the Church, and the preservation of her unity which is demanded for the fulfilment of his high apostolic functions.)

N.B.—Besides these errors, explicitly noted, very many others are rebuked by the certain doctrine which all Catholics are bound most firmly to hold touching the temporal sovereignty of the Roman Pontiff. These doctrines are clearly stated in the Allocutions *Quantis quantumque*, April 20th, 1849, and ' *Si semper antea*, May 20th, 1850 ; Letters Apost. *Quam Cattolica Ecclesia*, March 26th, 1860 ; Allocutions *Novos*, Sept. 28th, 1860 ; *Jamdudum*, March 18th, 1861, and *Maxima quidem*, June 9th, 1862.

N.B. — Besides these expressly stated errors, many are implicitly rejected, through the statement and assertion of the doctrine which Catholics must hold with respect to the temporal dominion of the Pope of Rome. This doctrine is clearly set forth in the allocutions of April 20th, 1849 ; May 20th, 1850 ; in the Letters Apostolic of Sept. 28th, 1860 ; March 18th, 1861; and June 9th, 1862.

SECT. X.—*Errors having reference to Modern Liberalism.*

SECT. X. —*Errors relating to Modern Liberalism.*

77. In the present day it is no longer necessary that the Catholic religion shall be held as the only religion of the State, to the exclusion of all other modes of worship.

77. In our time, it is still essential that the Catholic religion should be held as the only State religion, to the exclusion of all other forms of religion.

(*Remarks of Schrader.*—The Pope also demands in those States in which only Catholics reside, the domination of the Catholic religion alone, to the exclusion of every other form of religion, and therefore has he in the Allocution of July 26th, 1856, reclaimed against the violation of the first article of the Spanish Concordat ; in which the exclusive dominion of the Catholic religion in Spain had been stipulated ; and he rejected the law by which freedom of worship had been introduced, and declared it for null and void.)

78. Whence it has been wisely provided by the law, in some countries called Catholic, that persons coming to reside therein shall enjoy the free exercise of their own worship.

78. Therefore it was not well that in certain Catholic lands immigrants should be guaranteed the free exercise of their religion.

79. Moreover it is false that the civil liberty of every mode of worship and the full power given to all of overtly and publicly manifesting their opinions and their ideas conduce more easily to corrupt the morals and minds of the people, and to the propagation of the pest of indifferentism.

79. It is true that freedom of worship granted by the States, and permission given to every one to publish all manner of opinions and views, leads easily to the corruption of manners and of sentiments among the nations, and to the diffusion of the bane of indifference.

(*Remark of Schrader.*—Through the unbridled freedom of thought, speech, and writing, morals are deeply sunken, says Pius IX. in his Encyclical of Nov. 9th, 1864. The holy religion has fallen into contempt, and the majesty of divine worship is despised; the authority of the Apostolic See attacked, and the authority of the Church contested and laden with shameful fetters. The rights of bishops are trampled under foot, the holiness of marriage is violated, every authority of government is shaken, and thus many other damages arise both to Church and State.)

80. The Roman Pontiff can and ought to reconcile himself to, and agree with, progress, liberalism, and modern civilisation.

80. The Roman Pontiff cannot be reconciled to modern civilisation and progress, or compromise with them.

(*Remark of Schrader.*—For those who defend the righteousness and the rights of our holy religion do rightfully demand that the unchangeable and immovable principles of eternal righteousness shall be observed entire and unimpaired, and that the power of our salutary and divine religion shall be upheld. The faithful shall be led in the sure way of salvation, and not upon the downward road of destruction. The Holy See is the highest support, protector, and pastor of the faithful. Therefore it cannot connect itself with liberalism, and with modern civilisation, without the most serious violation of conscience, and without the greatest universal scandal.)

APPENDIX B.

RELATION OF THE CHURCH TO THE BAPTIZED, AND ESPECIALLY TO HERETICS.

The following passages from the standard work of Phillips indicate the tenets of Rome on this subject, in the more moderate aspect of their recent phases. They are all found in the *second* volume of the *Kirchen-recht*, and we give the page with each separate citation :—

P. 435. 'By virtue of the supreme powers given to her, the Church has indeed a dominion over those who are without [not baptized]; but over these she does not give sentence in the same sense as over those who through the door of baptism have entered into the Church, and who through this sacrament have received the indelible token of membership in the kingdom of Christ. These latter have in baptism sworn the oath of allegiance; they have sworn *Fideltas* and *Homagium*, the oath of personal believing fidelity [*fidelitas*] and that of the vassal (*Lehnseid*), of true and active service with the talents which have been granted to them in fee (*Zu Lehen*).'

P. 436. 'No one is exempt from this obedience,—all are confided to the Church to be guided and brought up for heaven; for all, there-fore, without exception, is the Church an authority instituted by God. The possibility of attaining to his highest end, that of glorifying God, which man through disobedience had lost, Christ has given back to him again; but this end can be attained only in the way of obedience. Disobedience against the divine Word, the *rejecting or doubting even of a single one of the divine truths announced by the Church*, puts the individual human being again in the way of perdition, on which our first parents entered to their own ruin and that of their posterity, when they, instead of believing the simply and clearly announced Word, chose another exposition of the same, which was more agreeable to them.'

P. 438. 'Hence in particular must they grievously offend God who either directly put away from them the faith of the Church, or else accept it only in so far as it appears to them correct according to the selection [out of her tenets] which they have made; or, again, who so break the bond of the unity of the Church as to declare themselves loose from obedience to the lawful authority which in her has been set over them by God. Thus are we led to speak of the three ecclesiastical crimes—apostacy, heresy, and schism.'

P. 440. 'As to apostacy, which is the total rejection of the Christian faith, and the falling away into Judaism, or heathenism, or Islamism, it is here only to be remarked that in the view of the Church it is as the crime of insulting the majesty of God. The apostate must be compelled to return to the Church by force, and a milder judgment may be pronounced upon him only in the case of one who was compelled to deny his faith by the unbelievers.'

P. 441. 'In opposition to the entire rejection of the Christian faith, heresy implies the wilful selection of a number from out of the dogmas of the Church which are to be believed by men in all their fulness, and the restricting of faith to such selected doctrines as the man still adheres to; in general to this is added the acceptance of false articles of faith. In this wider sense, all those are called heretics who accept only particular doctrines of the Church; but we must distinguish between such. We must part off error from heresy. Any man may fall into error, with regard to one or another doctrine of the Church, against his own will, out of simplicity, or from want of instruction, or because he has received wrong instruction. Such an error of the understanding is called 'material heresy;' but proper heresy, which is called 'formal heresy,' has its seat in the will. The latter consists in this, that to error is added obstinacy of the will, which is disinclined to depart from it. If any one announces a doctrine and then learns that the Church teaches otherwise, thus discovering that he was in error, he does not fall into heresy if he only ceases to defend the doctrine which he has set forth, and submits himself to the teaching of the Church. On the other hand, one who does know that the Church teaches otherwise, and still affirms that something is an article of belief which is not so, or, contrariwise, that something is not an article of belief which is so, doing this in spite of the fact that the Church has delivered the truth upon the subject, he by so doing haughtily prefers his own judgment to that of the Church; and through this obstinacy, the characteristic mark of heresy, he becomes a heretic in the strict sense of the word.

'It is not necessary to heresy that the person shall, as a heresiarch, found a new sect, or that, by free choice, he shall go over to a sect condemned by the Church; but heresy is already present whenever any one in the bosom of the Catholic Church departs from only one single point of the faith, or understands one single passage of Holy Scripture otherwise than as the Church, with the assistance of the Holy

Ghost, expounds them. For so great is the importance of heresy that through want of faith even on one point, the proper foundation of faith itself is destroyed, so that he that makes himself guilty with regard to one dogma, becomes at the same time guilty as to every dogma of the Church. Thus not only is he who rejects one of the articles defined by the Church a heretic, but also he who after such a definition maintains that the point is still doubtful.'

P. 445. 'The Church prays for the return of her separated members, and she is entitled to proceed to compulsion by virtue of the jurisdiction over heretics as baptized persons which belongs to her ; but she uses, by prayer and by the instruction which is permitted to all, the only means by which she can now enter into communication with them, at least as relations at present stand.

'She may, indeed, tolerate the heathen, because they err through igno-rance ; she may tolerate the Jews as witnesses for the truth ; but she cannot tolerate heresy, because this shakes the foundation of the entire faith. The synagogue makes way for the Church as a dutiful handmaid, bringing her the Holy Scriptures. Heresy, however, lifts itself up as a mistress above the Church, discredits her utterly, sets itself to judge over her, and would condemn her out of Holy Scripture according to its self-chosen exposition, closing her mouth like that of Christ. It commences with the divine Word, but it treats that word like a lyre, from which every one, at pleasure, may draw whatever note will suit him.

'The Church pardons error, but she cannot subject herself to the obsti-nately erring will, but must destroy its dominion and its tyranny. She, as the teacher of the truth, cannot conclude a peace with such a will. She cannot lift it up to the throne beside her, she cannot share her dominion with it. Understood in its proper and true signification, heresy is a frightful crime. Do the heathen blaspheme God out of ignorance ? Heresy tears truth to pieces consciously. Did the Jews crucify Christ according to the flesh ? Heresy fastens the Church, His mystical body, to the cross. Therefore the Church cannot at all tolerate heresy, because the greatest danger of seduction is attached to it. The Christian can easily shun the heathen and the Jew, but not the Christian who by the baptismal vow is connected with him, but by heresy is separated from him.

'On these grounds is explained the complete intolerance which the Church, in all her laws, and especially in the *Bulla Cœna*, has manifested against heresy. Hence are explained the certainly hard-sounding expres-sions with which she speaks of heresy. Hence the punishments against heretics, the delivering up of the same to the temporal arm, and the calling upon temporal princes by law and by arms to come to her help in rooting out heresy. When the Church pronounces *excommunication* upon heretics, it is nothing more than a declaratory sentence of that which had already been announced by the heretics themselves ; for, all the more because these are Christians, must she separate them from herself, that they may not be accounted as of her, and that she may not appear a chargeable for their obstinacy.

'Hence it will be understood that the Church employs all means to keep her members from being infected with heretical teaching. She has therefore, with the apostle, forbidden *intercourse* with heretics ; yet she makes this apply, according to the Bull of Martin V., *Ad evitandos*, only to those who are personally, and by name, *excommunicated* on account of their obstinacy. To a like end the Church forbids to the faithful the reading of heretical writings, which still retain that character even when the author perhaps erred only out of ignorance, and has given his books to the fire. So according to the diversities of times and circumstances does she require from her members the assurance of fidelity in making the confession of faith, causing those who return into her bosom to abjure heresy, and prohibiting all to preach who have not thereto an express mission, and forbidding the laity to dispute as to the faith, except in cases in which especial exceptions are justified.'

P. 451. '*Schism*, in its proper meaning, consists in this, that the baptized person, while not doubting as to the faith, and while not intending to separate himself from it, declares himself free from the authority which God has set over him in the Church. In a looser sense of the word, schism may refer to one's own bishop, as well as to the Pope; properly, however, it requires separation from the centre of Church unity, from the Pope, to constitute a schism, although revolt against the proper bishop, recognised by the head of the Church, comprehends in itself separation from the entire Church. And how will the schismatic, separated from ecclesiastical unity, preserve himself in purity of doctrine? Does heresy lead to schism? So infallibly does schism lead to heresy, inasmuch as only through false doctrine can it be justified. Therefore does the Church regard schism as a crime just as great as heresy, and in general has dealt with it in the same manner.'

END OF VOL. I.